Words that Make a Difference

D1300914

Also by Robert Greenman:
The New York Times Captive Vocabulary
The Rap Book

Words that Make a Difference

FOR THOSE WHO WANT TO SPEAK
MORE EFFECTIVELY, OR WRITE
MORE COLORFULLY OR BE
BETTER PREPARED FOR THE SAT

SECOND EDITION

Robert Greenman

Farragut
Publishing
Company

2033 M Street, N.W.
Washington, D.C. 20036
(202) 872-4009

PRINTED IN THE UNITED STATES OF AMERICA

Second Printing 1989

Library of Congress Cataloging-in-Publication Data

Greenman, Robert.
  Words that make a difference.

    Rev. ed. of: Words in action.
    Bibliography: p.
    1. Vocabulary.   2. English language—Glossaries,
vocabularies, etc.   3. American newspapers—Language.
I. Greenman, Robert.   Words in action.   II. Title.
PE1449.G68   1988   428.1   88-24560
ISBN 0-918535-06-9 (pbk.)

Acknowledgments

For someone who has put together a book on words and how to use them, I am at a loss for those that will adequately convey my thanks to the people whose assistance, confidence and support enabled me to produce this book.

I am grateful to Marjorie Longley of *The New York Times* and to Leonard Schwartz, Patrick Filley and Susan Kane of Times Books, who made possible the creation of the first edition of this book, *Words in Action.*

Hundreds of reference works from the library of my friend Michael Simms served me constantly as I wrote this book, and I am grateful to Mike for parting with them for the better part of a year. For hard-to-get back copies of *The New York Times,* I wish to thank Charles Robinson, director of News and Information Services at *The Times.* Many thanks also to Jack Hines, Jodi Quigney, Debbie Sirico, Liz Costantini, Bea Meizlish, Barbara Elk and Susan Gogliormella Shay.

For this revised edition, I am indebted to Paul Dickson, who knows a good word book when he sees one, having written several good ones himself. Paul's encouragement and advice led me to Dan Rapoport at Farragut Publishing Company, and Dan's interest and ideas led to this bright new edition. Special thanks to them both.

I am especially happy for another opportunity to express my deep appreciation to my daughters, Lisa (who researched and typed up the pronunciations that accompany each word), Sara and Rachel, and to my wife, Carol, for their understanding, patience and support during the many months I was at work on the original manuscript, and for their continuing encouragement. I love them all very much.

Robert Greenman
Brooklyn, New York
August, 1988

To my father,
Bert Greenman

Preface
To The Second Edition

My goal in writing *Words in Action,* the title given to the first edition, was to create a book from which people who work with words or who want to increase their vocabularies, could learn new words in a new way. Instead of compiling lists of words and definitions to be memorized laboriously, followed by quizzes, or creating artificial sentences that used the words but had no inherent interest, I went to the pages of *The New York Times,* where I collected these 1,455 passages. Each features a language enriching word used in an engaging—and *real*—context. I was gratified by the book's reception by teachers, students, broadcasters, writers and word lovers.

This new edition represents an effort to do the job even better. The new title clarifies what the book is about. The new introduction explains more fully who can benefit from using the book. The new organization places the most important section up front. And now that it is in paperback, the book will be more accessible to students and word lovers of all ages. *Words That Make a Difference* is a book to carry with you in a book bag or a briefcase, to use in the classroom or to browse through on the sofa. It offers something for everyone, from junior high school students to veteran public speakers.

R.G.

Contents

Introduction
to the Second Edition

This book features 1,455 special words, along with their definitions, pronunciations, and real life examples of how they have been used. They are special words because they can make a difference in how you speak, write and even think. When you use them, people will tend to remember what you've said or written because your language was exact, colorful and vivid.

The words, and the settings in which they were used, were taken from one newspaper, *The New York Times,* over a period of ten months. Each appears in an amusing anecdote, a sparkling quote, or simply a graceful piece of writing. Each passage is succinct and self-contained, providing enough of a context for someone unfamiliar with a word to understand how it is used.

Knowing and employing these words will help give you a broad, rich vocabulary. True, we can easily go through life with a limited vocabulary. Nobody needs such words as *perfunctory* or *obfuscate* to lead a happy, interesting or fulfilled life. But the fewer words we use, the more we limit our ideas, not only as we express them to others but as we conceive them ourselves. If you expand your vocabulary, you will expand your ability to think.

In that respect, every word we know makes a difference. For every word *is* an idea. *Love. Adore. Cherish.* Although closely related, each conveys a different idea, and when we know the differences between those three words we use each one as the occasion requires. They are not interchangeable. Each one means something specific.

You will recognize the advantage of an expanded vocabulary the instant you use a "new" word to express a thought and realize no other word could have served you as well.

The words featured in this book will make a difference because they will help you to speak, write and think precisely. You will profit from them if you are a professional communicator, such as a teacher, writer or broadcaster, if you are a student, or if you are simply someone who wants to express yourself more effectively and imaginatively. When you use the words in this book, people will tend to remember what you've said and written. There's a big difference between *faking* and *malingering*, between *pick out* and *cull*, between *obvious* and *manifest*, and even between *fine* and *hunky dory*.

How to Use This Book

For anyone who plans on using *Words That Make a Difference* to enhance their vocabulary, my advice is: don't study it; relax and have fun with it.

If you are a student with the Scholastic Aptitude Test (SAT) or other verbal aptitude test in your future, you'll find about 1,400 words here that have shown up or are likely to show up on it. (Almost 40 percent of the "vocabulary" words in the verbal section of the May, 1988 SAT are in *Words That Make a Difference*.) Plop yourself down in a comfortable spot and browse through the book. Check off the words you know. Underline with a felt-tip pen the featured words that are new to you and say them aloud. Take in the meaning of the passage. Consider these examples little stories (which most of them are) and you'll find the new words taking hold. You'll find yourself absorbing new words effortlessly.

Besides serving as an educational aid for students, this book is an especially useful resource for communicators and teachers. Writers, speakers and broadcasters should be able to glean hundreds of new words from this book that will add color, vitality and humor to their work. In addition, they will find the book a cornucopia of usable anecdotes, quotations and one-liners.

English and social studies teachers, from elementary school through college, will find this book a rich classroom resource: The passages are models of good writing, and many of them are natural springboards for class discussions and writing assignments.

Here in abundance are words that teachers will recognize from the literature and textbooks read by their students. Their appearance here, in settings more topical and immediate, will make the words' usefulness here and now apparent to students. One such word is *ignominy*, which appears many times in *The Scarlet Letter* and is presented here in a powerful modern context. Four words featured in this book appear in the very first pages of *Gulliver's Travels* (dexterity, diminutive, prudent and prodigious), while three other words here (Brobdingnagian, Lilliputian, and Yahoo) were coined by Swift for people and places in his great satire and are now part of the English language.

For social studies teachers, *Words That Make a Difference* is a bonanza of textbook words and terms used in fresh, contemporary contexts—*adventurism, anarchy, de jure, embargo, fifth column, sweatshop* and *theocracy,* to mention only a few.

In most cases, the definitions accompanying a featured word apply only to the word as it is used in the passage beneath it. The definition for *vehicle,* for example, says nothing about its being a device for carrying people, because that is not the sense in which *vehicle* is used in the passage. In cases where two or more examples illustrate different uses of the same word, I've preceded each usage with a separate definition (see *vacuum*). In other cases, a single definition sufficed for the way the same word was used in different passages (see *pirate*). An annotated bibliography of the most frequently consulted reference works used in preparing the definitions and language notes in *Words That Make a Difference* appears at the end of the book. Sources used only once or twice are cited at the specific points where they have made their contribution.

With more than 100 of the passages, I have provided supplementary language notes containing word histories, linguistic sidelights, background material on news items, quotations from literature using the featured word, and some of my own comments.

Following the main section of *Words That Make a Difference* are several short chapters that I hope will make the book even more useful to you. They will give you many insights into the dynamics of the English language and show you how to speak and write correctly, effectively and confidently.

A word is dead
When it is said,
Some say.
I say it just
Begins to live
That day.
  —Emily Dickinson

1,455
WORDS THAT
MAKE
A DIFFERENCE

Pronunciation Key

The pronunciations in this section are presented in a form called respelling, adopted from the *N.B.C. Handbook of Pronunciation* (Thomas Y. Crowell, Publishers: 1964), the bible of radio and television announcers. If some of the pronunciations sound a bit strange or stilted when you say them aloud, that's because they are not supposed to be spoken as independent units but as they would sound in conversational speech. Try them that way and they will sound natural.

Most pronunciations will be obvious at first glance. The following key will be helpful, however, in distinguishing the way all the vowel sounds, and several consonant sounds, are respelled. Stressed syllables are printed in upper-case letters.

h*at*	(hat)	b*oi*l	(boil)
art	(ahrt)	h*our*	(OW er)
b*ear*	(bair)	sh*ow*	(shoh)
f*all*	(fawl)	p*ut*	(poot)
d*ate*	(dayt)	r*oot*	(roo:t)
end	(end)	r*ouge*	(roo:zh)
h*eat*	(heet)	*th*in	(thin)
s*erver*	(SER ver)	*th*en	(th:en)
*ph*one	(fohn)	*above*	(uh BUHV)
w*it*	(wit)	fa*ce*	(fays)
tr*y*	(trigh)	fa*ze*	(fayz)

If a pronunciation differs from the one you've been using or hearing, check your dictionary. For the purposes of this book, I have provided only one pronunciation per word, but it's quite possible that the pronunciation you're familiar with is equally "correct." I placed quotation marks around that last word because dictionaries do not attempt to dictate correctness in pronunciation, but to indicate the way, or *ways*, words are pronounced by educated speakers. For that reason, dictionaries provide alternate "correct" pronunciations for thousands of words.

For example, the pronunciation for *usurp* is given as *yoo ZERP*. However, *you SERP* is just as commonly heard among educated speakers, and will be found in the dictionary as well. *Vacuum* is another example. In its sense as *an empty space* it is as acceptable to pronounce it *VA kyoom* as it is *VA kyoo uhm*.

Readers may question why pronunciations for words like *altruism* (*AL troo i zuhm*) and *innuendo* (*in yoo EN doh*) do not include colons after the *oo's*, since they would seem to be sounded as in *root* and not in *foot*. The reason is that in relaxed, normal speech, the second syllable vowel sounds in those words do, indeed, come out shorter and less stressed than they do when we say the words as independent units. For that reason, the unstressed *ee* sound, as in *anarchy* and *caveat*, is respelled as *i* (*A ner ki, KA vi at*).

aberrant   *a BAI ruhnt*
(deviating from the normal or the typical)

In one of his last articles, "The Social Stress Syndrome," Dr. Kardiner commented on what he termed the violence, fanatacism and aberrant sexual behavior common in contemporary society—qualities that he considered symptoms of decline. He contended that such antisocial behavior, when it affects more than 10 or 15 percent of a society, weakens the pillars that support it.

abhor   *uhb HAWR*
(to detest)

HIROSHIMA, Japan, Feb. 25—Pope John Paul II today made a strong appeal for peace at the place where the first atomic bomb was detonated on Aug. 6, 1945. "To remember Hiroshima is to abhor nuclear war," he declared. "To remember Hiroshima is to commit oneself to peace."

abjure   *uhb JOOR*
(to renounce or repudiate)

He abjures drinking and smoking, avoids parties and rarely entertains visitors. "To me, it's a big deal when the mail comes," he says.

Abjure means to renounce, repudiate or put aside: *She has abjured the company of men. Adjure* means to command or direct: *The judge adjured the witnesses not to talk to reporters until the trial was over.*

---

abomination   *uh bahm uh NAY shun*
(anything hateful and disgusting)

The deterioration of tea began when bags were substituted for leaf tea. Then came powdered instant tea, a still worse progression, and finally the abomination of ready-to-drink tea from cans or dispensers.

aboriginal   *a buh RI juh nuhl*
(native; indigenous)

Some 6,000 years ago, aboriginal Americans found their way to the great meadow on Nevada's 11,949-foot Mount Jefferson, hunters from the parched lowlands in pursuit of game. They established a permanent camp, with pit houses and hunting blinds of stone, to which they and their descendants returned many a summer over the centuries.

Aborigines: Persons of little worth found cumbering the soil of a newly discovered country. They soon cease to cumber; they fertilize.

Ambrose Bierce, "The Devil's Dictionary," 1911.

---

abort   *uh BAWRT*
(to cut short)

The two Americans who aborted their around-the-world balloon voyage over northern India said today that a futile search for air currents had led them to end the trip.

abortive   *uh BAWR tiv*
(failing to accomplish an intended objective; fruitless)

Barry Rosen is not likely to forget the moment, months after the event, when he found out about the abortive helicopter attempt to rescue the American hostages in Iran. "It was," he said the other day, "the most depressing moment of the captivity."

abrasive   *uh BRAY siv*
(causing irritation; rubbing people the wrong way)

On his part, Mike Wallace agreed that Mr. Buckley was indeed inimitable, but differed on the precise nature of his charm. "Bill's such a gentle person," he said. "I think he would find it quite hard to be abrasive and insistent the way I am, but he has a style and it's a style that clearly works.

abrogate   *A bruh gayt*
(to abolish or annul by authority)

Nuclear specialists note that no signer of the treaty banning the spread of weapons has ever abrogated safeguards. Most of the nations that appear to be developing weapons have refused to sign.

abstain   *ab STAYN*
(to refrain from something by one's own choice)

A woodchuck, he discovered, cannot be trained with behavior modification techniques to abstain from raiding the author's garden.

The American Indian name for the woodchuck was *otchek* or *otchig*. White traders Anglicized the name, which had nothing to do with wood or chucking, through the process known to linguists as folk etymology, a change in spelling or pronunciation to make words look or sound more similar to familiar words, with little regard to similarity in meaning or derivation.

---

abstemious   *ab STEE mi uhs*
(in its strict sense, moderate or sparing in eating or drinking: the word is used here in a broader sense)

After Ronald Reagan became the nation's 40th President yesterday, Mrs. Reagan prepared to appear at the inaugural balls in a hand-beaded gown designed by James Galanos. Its cost is estimated by industry experts to approach five figures, and the overall price of Mrs. Reagan's inaugural wardrobe is said to be around $25,000. Limousines, white tie and $10,000 ball gowns are in; shoe leather, abstemiousness and thrift that sacrifices haute couture are out, it seems, as Nancy Reagan sweeps from fete to fete in a glistening full-length Maximilian mink.

abstinence   *AB stuh nuhns*
(voluntary restraint from food, drink or other pleasures; self-denial)

To protect her voice, she now leads an abstinent life, having completely given up smoking and drinking.

abstract   *AB strakt*
(without physical form)

A concert is an event in which the sounds made, though abstract and evanescent, can and should evoke a real and palpable response, not unlike a religious experience.

abstraction   *ab STRAK shuhn*
(an idea separated from its physical reality)

Proposals for reviving Manhattan's West Side along the Hudson River have been around so long they have become abstractions, even as they continue to be weapons and levers in political tradeoffs.

abyss   *uh BIS*
(a bottomless pit; often a reference to Hell, chaos, or the end of the world)

If there ever was a playwright who knew exactly what he wanted to do and then did it, it is Sophocles in "Oedipus the King." This tragedy is relentless as it plunges both its hero and the audience into the abyss of a dark and horrible truth. There's no fooling around, no waste. Each character provides the hero with another key to his real identity, his involuntary crimes. Piece by piece, the entire picture comes together with a tidal force that is quick and deadly enough to shake the world.

a cappella   *ah kuh PE luh*
(without instrumental accompaniment: Italian, in the manner of the chapel)

Revolutionary Tea, a five-member a cappella ensemble, will perform early American music in period costumes in a free concert at 1 P.M. at the Citicorp Market Atrium.

accede   *ak SEED*
(to give in; agree to)

That was when the American hostages overheard a radio message on the Turkish Airlines DC-9 relaying the terrorists' threat to kill all the Americans if the Turkish Government did not accede to their demands.

accolade   *A kuh layd*
(anything done or given as a sign of great respect, approval, appreciation, etc.)

"It's the greatest honor I could ever receive," Tony Bennett said Monday night, and who could argue? After all, Mr. Bennett's Lifetime Achievement Award came from the National Academy of Popular Music, an association of songwriters, and whose accolades could a singer cherish more? As another award winner, Lionel Hampton, put it, "If they didn't make it, we couldn't play it, and if we couldn't play it, we'd have no gigs."

accost   *uh KAWST*
(to approach and speak to before being greeted, especially in an intrusive way)

Conrad Valanos, owner of the Monocle restaurant on Capitol Hill, once accosted a young woman who was rushing to greet former Senator Jacob K. Javits. "Why don't you wait until he finishes his lunch?" Mr. Valanos admonished sternly, realizing only later that the woman was the Senator's favorite niece. "Boy," he later recalled, "was I embarrassed."

accouterments   *uh KOO: ter muhnts*
(personal outfit; clothes; dress)

In the medieval Catholic Church the umbrella became a symbol of authority, and umbrellas are still among the Pope's accouterments.

acerbic   *uh SER bik*
(sharp, bitter or harsh in temper, words, etc.)

Le Monde, Le Matin and the satirical paper Le Canard Enchaîné have been strongly anti-Giscard and pro-Mitterand. In the case of Le Canard, which is unfailingly acerbic, support for Mitterand was expressed by not writing about him.

acolyte   *A kuh light*
(an attendant or follower: originally, one who assists a priest in the celebration of Mass)

Dressed in a sheet, he plays a holy man seeking acolytes at a shopping mall in New Jersey. "Let's face it," he says with a pseudo-swami accent that could curdle yogurt, "we're all unhappy."

acrid   *AK rid*
(sharp, bitter, stinging or irritating to the taste or smell)

Mexico City has been inundated by acrid smoke carrying twice as many poisonous substances as a human being can safely withstand, environmental officials said yesterday.

acrimonious   *a kruh MOH ni uhs*
(bitter or caustic in temper, manner or speech)

LOUISVILLE, Ky., June 13—The United States Conference of Mayors opened its annual convention here today in an acrimonious atmosphere, its once cohesive and influential membership sharply divided over whether to support President Reagan's economic program.

acronym   *A kruh nim*
(a word formed from the first—or first few—letters of a series of words. To be considered an acronym, the letters must be spoken as a word.)

Mr. Weinberger, in a recent order, told the Navy to reactivate its Extremely Low Frequency project near Clam Lake, Wis., while a study of strategic communications was being completed. The project, which is intended to improve communications with submarines on patrol, is better known by its acronym, ELF.

Familiar Acronyms

AWOL	Nabisco
CARE	NOW
CAT scan	OPEC
CETA	radar
CORE	SALT
Fiat (car)	scuba
GEICO	snafu
HUD	UNICEF
laser	VISTA
M*A*S*H	ZIP code

---

adamant   *A duh muhnt*
(*unyielding: Greek,* adamas, *a hard stone or supposedly unbreakable substance*)

King Hussein has adamantly refused repeated requests by the Palestine Liberation Organization to allow the guerrillas to reestablish military bases on Jordanian soil.

addled   *A duhld*
(*muddled; confused*)

I agree with Louis Alexander (letter Aug. 21) that Governor Carey's brains must be addled to declare milk the state beverage, but I can't go along with Mr. Alexander's suggested replacement. The Manhattan? That poor cousin of the martini? Really, Mr. Alexander, does anyone drink Manhattans anymore?

ad hoc   *ad HAHK*
(*for a special case only; without general application: Latin, toward this*)

It takes only a drop of the proverbial hat for solo musicians to join forces in a concert of chamber music these days. When the chemistry is right, no matter how ad hoc the instrumental combination might seem, the musical results can be stimulating for all concerned if the performers are evenly matched and temperamentally in tune.

ad hominem   *ad HAH mi nem*
(appealing to one's prejudices rather than to reason, as by attacking one's opponent rather than debating the issue: Latin, to the man)

A theory is offered and the students evaluate it for fallacies, circular reasoning and ad hominem arguments.

adjunct   *A juhngkt*
(a person connected with another as a helper or subordinate; associate)

The 70-year-old Mr. Woodcock, a former president of the United Automobile Workers, will become adjunct professor of political science at the University of Michigan at Ann Arbor.

(a thing added to something else, but secondary and not essential)

Dance has long been offered as an adjunct to university physical-education, music and theater courses. Now these are being expanded into full-scale departments offering programs that lead to bachelor's or master's degrees in art, science, education or fine arts. In many cases, the facilities of the academic programs far surpass those of private studios.

admonish   *ad MAH nish*
(to caution or warn; inform or remind, by way of a warning)

Henry David Thoreau once admonished his audience to "read not the Times, read the Eternities." We take comfort in the fact that he wasn't referring to this newspaper, which had not yet been founded.

adulation   *a juh LAY shun*
(excessive praise)

At the height of her tragically brief career, cellist Jaqueline du Pré inspired her audiences to frenzied adulation. She strode onto the stage, a golden, strapping creature, though daintily attired, but when she wrapped herself around her cello, she drew sounds so charged with emotion and sensuality that her listeners were transfixed.

adulterate   *uh DUHL ter ayt*
(to make inferior, impure, not genuine, etc., by adding a harmful, less valuable or prohibited substance)

Part of a shipment of boneless beef destined for the United States was adulterated with kangaroo meat, the Australian Government said today.

advent   *AD vent*
*(arrival: in its religious sense, Advent is the period including the four
Sundays just before Christmas)*

Since the advent of credit cards, more catalogue-shoppers are calling in
their orders rather than mailing them.

adventurism   *ad VEN cher i zuhm*
*(actions or tactics, especially in politics or international relations, that
are regarded as recklessly daring and involving the risk of serious consequences)*

Today, Oleg A. Troyanovsky, the Soviet delegate, repeatedly pictured
Washington as the source and inspiration of Israel's attack. Mr. Troyanovsky insisted that Israel "would not have dared to challenge the entire
international community unless it were convinced of the understanding
and virtual encouragement for its adventuristic and expansionist policies
from Washington."

aegis   *EE jis*
*(sponsorship; auspices: originally, the aegis was the shield of Zeus; it was
also carried by his daughter, Athena. It symbolizes divine protection.)*

Many of those in the arts will take to the streets today at 3 P.M. for a Rally
to Save the Arts, one of several in the nation. Not exactly in the streets
but in the Lincoln Center Plaza, under the aegis of the American Coalition to Support the Arts, which embraces arts organizations, unions,
artists and people who are concerned about the arts.

affable   *A fuh buhl*
(pleasant and easy to approach and talk to; friendly; gentle and kindly)

In conversation after his Philadelphia Beethoven rehearsal, Mr. Tenn-
stedt, speaking in German, emerged as an affable, almost childlike man,
full of a nervous, eager earnestness and a sometimes undisguised pleasure in his own success ("I have received four prizes for my Mahler recordings," he announced out of the blue).

affluent   *A floo uhnt*
(wealthy; prosperous; rich)

"I'll tell you what's important in fashion today. Clothes for the corporate
wife, the businesswoman. Especially because these are poor times, people
must look affluent. But the clothes must be understandable. You see all

those silly Parisian clothes in the paper, but you don't see them anywhere else." [Halston]

aggravate *A gruh vayt*
(to make worse; make more burdensome, troublesome, etc.)

If the Pope has to curtail his public appearances and his travels as a result of the assassination attempt on May 13, it may further aggravate the financial problems of the church, Vatican sources today said. Contributions from Catholics had been stimulated by the spectacle of a dynamic, vigorous Pope visiting Catholic areas, they said.

akimbo *uh KIM boh*
(with hands on hips and elbows bent outward: Old Norse, kengboggin, *bow-bent)*

In "Lion of the Desert" we see Mussolini at the height of his power. This is Mussolini as the world knew him—vain, arrogant, ambitious. There is the outthrust chin, the arms akimbo, the abrupt gestures, the strut.

akin *uh KIN*
(similar; related to)

Dr. Samuel Gridley Howe established in Boston in 1832 the Massachusetts Asylum for the Blind—now the Perkins Institute—to provide blind children with an education akin to what public schools were offering.

alacrity *uh LAK ruh ti*
(eager willingness or readiness, often manifested by quick, lively action)

There are many ways to catch crabs, but I never progressed much beyond the long-handled net routine. In late summer and fall I visit the ocean end of a salt pond, where, in many places, the sandy bottom shelves slowly away. Crabs will be foraging for food in the shallows and if one moves with alacrity one will often, in a few hours' scampering, fill a 12-quart bucket.

albatross *AL buh traws*
(an obvious handicap, burden, or heavy cross to bear: Coleridge's Ancient Mariner sinned by killing an albatross, and had to wear it around his neck in penance)

Alexander's Inc., the New York-based department store chain that has been plagued by earnings declines and, more recently, losses, moved yesterday to rid itself of what it considered an albatross. The company announced that it would sell its Margo's La Mode chain of fashion apparel specialty stores, which it acquired two years ago, to the Elder-Beerman Stores Corporation.

albeit   *awl BEE it*
(although; even though)

Even though the scope of the home-office deduction has been drastically limited by Congress and the Internal Revenue Service over the years, it nonetheless remains one of the most cherished—albeit difficult to claim —deductions available to taxpayers.

al fresco   *al FRE skoh*
(in the open air; outdoors: Italian, in the cool)

We live in a brownstone in Brooklyn Heights with a pleasant garden, and it was there, through the summer heat, that most of the social activity went on. At the end of the work day friends prepared dinners at home and brought them over or shopped for gazpacho or lasagna or tortellini salads—and exquisite desserts—for al fresco feasts.

Al fresco is an 18th-century Italian loan word. Other "Words That Make a Difference" 18th-century Italian borrowings are *cognoscenti, crescendo* and *sotto voce.*

allay   *uh LAY*
(to put fears, etc., to rest; quiet; calm; lessen, relieve or alleviate pain, grief, etc.)

In the hope of someday allaying the social and physical handicaps of albinos, scientists at the University of Minnesota are unraveling the intricacies of pigment formation, looking for an understanding that may help them correct the genetic flaws that cause the disorder.

alleviate   *uh LEE vi ayt*
(to relieve, reduce or decrease)

Beachgoers who are stung by jellyfish can alleviate the pain by mixing a paste of meat tenderizer and cool water and spreading it over the sting.

allusion   *uh LOO: zhuhn*
(an indirect, but pointed or meaningful, reference)

A woman asked about improving "the quality of life for people who use Sydenham Hospital," the recently closed medical facility in Harlem. She never mentioned blacks directly. But the allusion was not lost on the Mayor.

(in music, art, etc., some aspect of a work that reveals a debt to, or indicates the influence of, others in the field)

In many respects, "Attila" is the first "pure" Verdi opera, a score that finally consolidates his own unique musical voice and contains few if any direct allusions to the more classically restrained styles of Rossini, Bellini and Donizetti.

aloof   *uh LOO:F*
(reserved and cool)

He plays with clarity, intelligence and immense authority. Yet he is a cool pianist. Proportion to him is more important than color. He refuses to make a play for the audience, and he performs miracles of virtuosity in a detached, aloof manner.

altruism   *AL troo i zuhm*
(unselfish concern for the welfare of others; selflessness)

Some species of ants studied, for example, have been found to be compassionate toward their nestmates, showing altruistic tendencies that include dying in defense of their fellow workers.

amalgam   *uh MAL guhm*
(a combination or mixture of diverse elements; blend)

The National Right to Life Committee, an amalgam of anti-abortion lobbying groups in the 50 states, said that it would mobilize its members to "prevail upon senators to oppose this nomination." The committee said that Judge O'Connor was "pro-abortion" as a member of the Arizona State Legislature.

ambidextrous   *am buh DEK struhs*
(able to use either hand with ease)

Roughly two-thirds of humans are right-handed, according to a current estimate, while the rest are either left-handed or ambidextrous to varying degrees. But why humans should have this preference for one side over the other is a mystery. One clue, known for years, is that most newborn infants tend to lie with their heads turned to their right sides.

ambience   *AM bi uhns*
(atmosphere; environment; milieu: also spelled ambiance)

For ambience and fine food try the Hotel du Village on Route 32 north of New Hope at Phillips Mill Road. It is a country inn with fireplaces on both ends of the dining room and warm-weather dining on the terrace.

ambiguous   *am BI gyoo uhs*
(not clear; indefinite; uncertain; vague; having two or more possible meanings)

Mr. Koch himself is often ambiguous about how great his powers truly are. It would seem to depend on circumstances. For example, he took credit this week for the 110,000 new jobs generated in the city in the last four years. "I would say I helped by creating the climate" that lured businesses to New York, he said. But when asked if he thought there would be similar job growth in the next four years, Mr. Koch declined to make predictions. "I don't believe government can do very much on a local level to enhance prosperity," he said.

ambivalence   *am BI vuh luhns*
(conflicting feelings toward a person or thing)

And there was an ambivalence about bees in the Scriptures. The Bible points out that while the bee's honey is a sweet nectar, its sting is a painful thorn.

ameliorate   *uh MEE lyuh rayt*
(to make or become better; improve)

Mr. Mitterrand outlined a five-point program aimed at ameliorating the economic deprivation of the third world. "France is convinced," he said, "that it is only in the framework of a global development strategy that action in favor of the least advanced countries will have any real significance."

amenable   *uh MEE nuh buhl*
(able to be influenced or controlled; responsive)

What problems are you having with your marriage or children? Might these be amenable to therapy? If so, get help, the sooner the better, from a marriage or family counselor, psychotherapist or sex therapist. Similarly, get help if you are very depressed and unable to pull yourself out of it.

amenity   *uh ME nuh ti*
(an attractive or desirable feature, as of a place or climate; anything that adds to one's comfort; a convenience)

Cafeterias became a much more important employee amenity when companies moved to the suburbs and to isolated campus settings in which the workers were "captive."

amicable   *A mi kuh buhl*
(friendly in feeling; showing good will; peaceable)

She spent 444 days as a hostage with other Americans in Teheran, and now Elizabeth Ann Swift is going to get a year in a more amicable setting. She has been selected as one of 20 fellows at Harvard's Center for International Affairs.

amok   *uh MUHK*
(in a violent rage or frenzy; in a blind, heedless manner)

An 80-year-old white woman, who cowered in her house while the skinheads ran amok outside, throwing missiles through her windows and those of her neighbors, said this morning: "They were running up and down asking where the Indians lived. It was not nice at all."

Skinheads, so called because they have close-cropped hair, are white British youths who have been involved in racist violence in London and other cities, especially against Indian and Pakistani immigrants. They have provided many recruits for the white-supremacist National Front organization.

---

anachronism   *uh NA kruh ni zuhm*
(anything that is or seems to be out of its proper time in history: Greek, ana, against + chronos, time)

In person, Senator Helms is a courtly man, no less a contradiction than any other politician. He can dwell with sincerity on the plight of an elderly neighbor newly widowed, a man who needed the Senator's companionship in grief. Then again, he can utter a startling anachronism when he describes his floor fight over busing: "On the floor we fight hard; we're both free, white and 21, as we say in North Carolina."

anarchy   *A ner ki*
(the complete absence of government; political disorder and violence; lawlessness)

Beirut is settling into a permanent state of anarchic war. The victims are not the defenders of various causes in their tailored fatigue uniforms, who are hunkered down in heavily sandbagged shelters, but the old woman buying eggs, the auto repairman, the young couple on the beach and the children growing up with nothing else.

In 1976, Mr. Grossman was told he had multiple sclerosis. A year later, the progressive disease confined him to a wheelchair. Today, the 53-year-old writer lives alone in a sunny apartment, no longer able to control the anarchy of his body but very much in control of a mind that is often wickedly funny.

anathema   *uh NA thuh muh*
(a thing or person greatly detested; any strong curse)

"Genetic determinism is anathema to Americans, who want to believe everyone is born equal, with an equal chance for a happy life," Dr. Berscheid remarked in an interview here. "It's simply not so. The most important factors governing success in life are genetically determined: appearance, intelligence, sex and height."

Though Horace is the play's sanest and gentlest white man, and though he is ill besides, he is here seen plunging wildly up and down wine-dark staircases while roaring anathemas at his untrustworthy wife.

ancillary   *AN si le ri*
(subordinate; helping; auxiliary: Latin, ancilla, *maid servant)*

Quite apart from the ancillary social activities, the wedding will cost a great deal of money. One estimate, published today in The Times of London, put the cost at more than $1 million, part of which will be borne by the Queen and part by various governmental departments.

anecdote   *A nik doht*
(a short, entertaining account of some happening, usually personal or biographical)

One Beckett anecdote that I have heard in several variations strikes at the quintessence of the man as a master of uproarious pessimism. On a bright sunny day he was walking through a London park with an old friend, Mr. Beckett exuding a feeling of joyfulness. His friend said, "On a day like this it's good to be alive." Mr. Beckett answered, "I wouldn't go *that* far."

angst   *ahngst*
(a gloomy, often neurotic feeling of generalized anxiety and depression)

If Mother's Day arrives Sunday before you have a chance to buy just the right gift, there's no cause for angst. Potential presents will line Park Avenue South from 16th to 32d Streets from 11 A.M. to dusk.

annotated   *A nuh tay tid*
(containing critical or explanatory notes, as in a literary work)

Nearly a third of the book is devoted to a concise and surprisingly comprehensive sexual encyclopedia (it even includes words like frottage and defloration), an annotated list for further reading and resources for help in sexually related areas.

antecedents   *an tuh SEE duhnts*
(one's ancestors, ancestry or past life)

Mr. Paton, who has no Afrikaner antecedents and still speaks with a suggestion of his father's Scottish burr, observed in his autobiography in an arresting sentence that "the birth and rise of Afrikaner nationalism is one of the most powerful subthemes of my life story."

antediluvian   *an ti di LOO: vi uhn*
(very old, old fashioned or primitive; colloquially used for anything hopelessly outdated: Latin, ante, *before* + diluvium, *flood—a reference to the Biblical Flood)*

When Blanda was throwing passes and place-kicking for the Oakland Raiders in 1975, he was celebrated as a geriatric wonder, a graying 48 in a game that counts a man of 38 as an antediluvian relic.

anterior   *an TI ri er*
(at or toward the front; forward: opposed to posterior)

The prairie sphinx moth has four anterior wings of mottled shades of gray and brown, and its underwings are a pale yellow outlined in black. Lepidopterists (scientists who specialize in the study of moths and butterflies) prize the moth for its beauty and rarity and sometimes refer to it as the "holy grail" of the insect world.

According to medieval legend, the Holy Grail is the cup or platter used by Jesus at the Last Supper, and by Joseph of Arimathea to collect drops of Jesus' blood at the Crucifixion: the quest for the Grail, which disappeared, is treated in Malory's "Morte d'Arthur," Wagner's "Parsifal" and Tennyson's "Idylls of the King."

---

anthropomorphic   *AN thruh puh MAWR fik*
(acting like, or appearing to be, human in form or characteristics)

It is hard to imagine most of the electronic games existing before George Lucas's "Star Wars" in 1977. The exception is Midway's Pac-Man, a relatively gentle game with a sense of humor in which a round, anthropomorphic ball with an enormous appetite gobbles up shining gold beads and an occasional piece of fruit while four fuzzy monsters try to gobble him up.

anthropomorphize   *AN thruh puh MAWR fighz*
(to think of, or treat, a nonhuman object as though it were human)

And, as everybody in an automated office knows, people end up anthropomorphizing the computer. There is talk of "putting the computer to bed," of "feeding" it programs. There are computer terminals named Chuck, Muffy and John Travolta now processing insurance claims.

anticlimactic   *AN ti kligh MAK tik*
(dropping suddenly from the dignified or important in thought or expression to the commonplace or trivial)

"The Shining" and "Heaven's Gate" were not finished in time to be tested with an audience. "The Shining" was released with a banal and anticlimactic hospital scene which destroyed the tension at the end of the movie. Three days later, after Stanley Kubrick had had a chance to see audience reaction to his movie, he cut out the scene.

antipodes   *an TI puh deez*
(two opposite or contrary things; any two places directly opposite each other on the earth: originally, the people on the other side of the earth)

King Carl XVI Gustaf of Sweden, whose popularity has increased visibly since his marriage to a young German woman and the birth of their two children, is probably the antipodal figure among European monarchs in relation to Juan Carlos's direct political role. He maintains that his political functions have been reduced more completely than any other monarch's in Europe.

antiseptic   *an ti SEP tik*
(preventing infection by inhibiting the actions of microorganisms: figuratively, lacking warmth or vitality; coldly impersonal; barren)

Dr. Halsted was the first to put rubber gloves on members of the surgical team in the operating room. His superior results were attributed to his extraordinary antiseptic techniques as well as his meticulous handling of human tissues and control of bleeding during surgery. These were details to which few other surgeons paid attention and were crucial in improving surgical results.

Last summer, "Pirates" vacated the Uris to make room for "My Fair Lady"—only to land in Broadway's *second* most antiseptic house, the Minskoff.

antithesis   *an TI thuh sis*
(*the exact opposite*)

For Mr. Begin, the Holocaust is the great metaphor. It is the ultimate argument, the final measurement of contemporary events. And here he taps a strong current of admiration in Israel for the proud unyielding model of self-sufficiency and self-defense, the angry antithesis of the stereotyped Jew who allegedly went calmly into the gas chamber thinking he was going to take a shower. In his own way, Mr. Begin was among those who fought back. And he is still fighting back, propelled by the instinct of resistance, the strain of defiance. There is a little bit of him in every Israeli.

apercu   *ah pair SOO*
(*a quick impression or insight: French*)

"Firing Line," its producer Warren Steibel argues, has never tried to condescend to its viewers, but rather has proceeded on the principle that "if Bill thinks something is interesting, the audience will think so too." The formula has apparently worked. The program won an Emmy Award in 1969, and its host, through frequently controversial for his acerbic apercus, has earned the respect of conservatives and liberals alike.

aphorism   *A fuh ri zuhm*
(*a short, pointed sentence expressing a wise or clever observation or a general truth; maxim; adage*)

. . . Miss Colwin has a flair for aphorism. "Fulfillment," she writes in "The Lone Pilgrim," "leaves an empty space where your old self used to be." Of two lovers married to other people, she observes: "They would never have love's greatest luxury: time. They would never own anything in common or travel together." "A love affair is like a shot arrow," a character says. "It gives life an intense direction, if only for an instant."

aphrodisiac *a fruh DI zhee ak*
(a drug or other substance believed to arouse or increase sexual desire: derived from Aphrodite, *the Greek goddess of love, beauty and sexual rapture)*

Loggers who encounter rhinoceroses may be tempted to kill them for their horns, which are still highly valued among the Chinese as an aphrodisiac. A rhinoceros horn slightly less than a foot long and weighing less than a pound can bring more than $9,000. The horn powder can sell for as much as $680 an ounce.

aplomb *uh PLAHM*
(self-confidence; poise; assurance)

Buckingham Palace has assigned two guards to Lady Diana, who is said to have impressed the royal family with her aplomb in handling the corps of reporters, photographers and television camera crews during her five-month courtship.

apolitical *ay puh LI ti kuhl*
(not concerned or connected with political matters)

While Mrs. Gouletas-Carey said in a recent interview with The New York Times that she was not interested in politics—"I'm very apolitical," she said—she has made substantial political contributions since 1976, according to public documents. In 1979 and 1980, for example, she donated $17,500 at the national level, Federal campaign records show, and she has served on Senator Kennedy's finance committee.

apostle *uh PAH suhl*
(an early advocate or leader of a new principle or movement, especially one aimed at reform)

Also at 8 P.M. on Sunday, WNEW-TV, Channel 5, has its own musical offering in the form of "The Beach Boys 20th Anniversary Special." Yes, the tuneful apostles of youthful innocence and good times have been around for 20 years, selling enough records to put them in the superstar class of the Beatles and Elvis Presley.

append *uh PEND*
(to attach or affix; add as a supplement or appendix)

The Islamic Republicans appear to be losing an important base of support among the traditionalist merchants of the bazaar—the original bankrollers of the revolution—who in the past have been thought of as quite religious. Most append "haj" to their names, indicating that they have made the religious pilgrimage to Mecca.

Because the word "charisma" has been carelessly appended to every politician with a good smile and every rock star capable of unnerving adolescents, one hesitates to use it when describing Karol Wojtyla. Until, that is, one reads again the dictionary definition: "An extraordinary power of healing . . . a personal magic."

aquifer   *A kwuh fuhr*
(an underground layer of porous rock, sand, etc., containing water, into which wells can be sunk)

Santa Fe, which sits on a 7,000-foot-high plateau at the southern base of the Rocky Mountains, is, like much of the West, dependent on the annual snowfall to the north to recharge the underground aquifers on which the area has so far depended for its water supply.

arbiter   *AHR bi ter*
(a person fully authorized or qualified to judge or decide)

SAN FRANCISCO, May 12—Herb Caen, the columnist for the San Francisco Chronicle who probably comes as close as anyone to being an arbiter of taste in this city, was more or less speechless after visiting the new $7 million Maxwell's Plum restaurant, which officially opened here last night. "The place puts me in mind of W.C. Fields' definition of sex," Mr. Caen wrote, quoting the late comedian: "I don't know if it's good and I don't know if it's bad. All I know is that there's nothing quite like it."

arbitrary   *AHR buh trai ri*
(not fixed by rules but left to one's judgment or choice; discretionary)

Short, bowl-like cuts on older women are still common, perhaps because they remember the days of the Cultural Revolution when Red Guards carried scissors and arbitrarily snipped off locks they deemed too long or fancy.

archetype   *AHR kuh tighp*
(a perfect example of a type or group)

Stefan Gierasch brings conviction to the role of the malevolent sergeant named Bloody Five, and Kevin O'Connor and James Greene have an archetypal authenticity as earthy soldiers. Grizzled and bedraggled, they look like sad sacks from a timeless army.

"The Sad Sack" was a popular comic strip drawn by George Baker for armed service publications during World War II. *Sad sack* was Army slang for a confused, disheveled, maladjusted and unhappy soldier. He was a well-meaning bungler who consistently got himself into trouble. In the 1930's the word had been used by students to describe an introverted, socially unacceptable person—the same type they might today call a nerd.

archipelago   *ahr kuh PE luh goh*
(a group or chain of many islands: Greek, archi, *chief* + pelagos, *sea)*

Hundreds of Marshall Islanders sued the United States today for injuries and damages that they said were caused by 12 years of atomic testing in the United States-administered archipelago in the western Pacific.

ardent   *AHR duhnt*
(intensely enthusiastic or devoted)

Blossom Dearie is a jazz singer, pianist and songwriter whose style and choice of material have captured an ardent following in New York.

arduous   *AHR joo uhs*
(difficult to do; laborious; onerous; full of hardships)

The Mount Evans Hill Climb is an arduous 28-mile bicycle race that ends on the highest paved road in the United States—14,264 feet above sea level.

arguably   *AHR gyoo uh bli*
(as can be supported by argument)

In a country [Russia] where the reverence for poets, singers and writers often gives them authority rivaling that of officials of the state, Mr. Vysotsky was arguably the most popular of his time. It was a popularity that few Westerners, even those living in Moscow, could fully appreciate, perhaps in part because his ballads rarely dealt explicitly with politics, because the street language he used with such effect is almost untranslatable and because the life he sang about is so alien to the West.

ascribe   *uh SKRIGHB*
(to attribute to a specified cause, source or origin)

Gen. Aharon Yariv, who is head of the Center of Strategic Studies, said in a recent discussion that the Israeli high command ascribed importance to the forward stationing of Syrian guns and missiles. Such deployment, he said, gives Syria the option of bringing much of northern Israel under fire.

assiduous   *uh SI joo uhs*
(done with constant and careful attention)

Instead of celebrating May Day, many local union chapters are mobilizing to commemorate May 3, the 190th anniversary of the Polish Constitution, the first written Constitution in Europe. The date has been assiduously ignored by the Communist governments until now.

assuage   *uh SWAYJ*
(to make less severe or burdensome; ease)

But is it a valid premise or simply a rationalization used to assuage guilt? Can working mothers truly compensate for the 40 to 60 hours a week they are absent from the home by compressing shared occasions with their children into smaller slices of time?

astronomical   *a struh NAH mi kuhl*
(extremely large, as the numbers or quantities used in astronomy)

Each year the Kenyans burn 27 million tons of wood and 25 million gallons of imported kerosine for heating and cooking. At present consumption levels, there will be no wood left by 1995 and the country's petroleum needs will then be astronomical.

astute   *uh STOO:T*
(keen in judgment; clever; shrewd)

The abolition of retail price controls on wine last year has meant a bonanza for consumers. Many stores have been selling popular brands at cost—sometimes even below cost—and astute buyers have been filling their cellars with wines that will never be priced lower.

athwart   *uh THWAWRT*
(across; from one side to the other of)

They blocked the bridge before dawn with about 15 cars, pickup trucks and campers parked athwart both lanes. A sign at the front of the bridge read: "Crow Reservation Closed to Fishing Today, Tomorrow and Forever." Some fishermen got around the bridge by taking other, unblocked roads.

atrophy   *A truh fi*
(*to waste away*)

The idea that the electric guitar was a magical lance and that guitarists were rock-and-roll heroes, began to get out of hand during the late 60's. Guitar solos, which had originally been short breaks in songs, grew long and bloated. The songs atrophied until they were flimsy excuses for endless displays of guitar prowess.

attenuate   *uh TE nyoo ayt*
(*to weaken; dilute*)

The 1980–81 Broadway season reached its official conclusion last night with the opening of "It Had to Be You," the last show to arrive in time to qualify for this year's Tony awards. I'm afraid the season didn't end with a bang or even a whimper—just an attenuated yawn.

atypical   *ay TI pi kuhl*
(*not typical; not characteristic*)

Reel life bearing no arithmetically calculable resemblance to real life, Miss Stanwyck is noted for her generosity and modesty. "She's atypical of actresses," says her close friend, Shirley Eder, the columnist. "She has pride in her work, but I don't think she realizes her worth as an actress or as a person. She thinks she's average; she thinks it's an imposition to ask her friends to come help honor her."

au courant   *oh koo RAHNT*
(*up-to-date; well-informed; with-it: French*)

On 68th Street just east of Columbus Avenue and a short walk from Lincoln Center, Simon's was the setting of a farewell party for Walter Cronkite. From that time on, it has been on the must list of the au courant.

au pair   *oh pair*
(*a young person, usually foreign, who does housework, tutoring, etc., for a family in exchange for room and board: French, as an equal*)

After a few months she became homesick for England and returned to work [there] as an au pair for an American couple and take a course in cooking, the accepted preparation for upper-class English girls raised primarily for marriage.

aura   *AW ruh*
(an atmosphere or quality that seems to arise from and surround a person or thing)

Husky and agile, gentle and competitive, Valenzuela gives off an aura of immense natural ability and superior athletic intelligence, a sense that he is always doing the right thing. He exhibits no flaws, no insecurities; the people in his own dugout sit and gape at his advanced state.

auspicious   *aw SPI shuhs*
(of good omen; boding well for the future)

In the last decade or so, before his auspicious directing debut with "Rachel, Rachel" in 1968, Mr. Newman has turned increasingly toward directing: His most recent project was the widely praised television version of "The Shadow Box," which starred his wife.

autocrat   *AW tuh krat*
(a ruler with absolute power; dictator; anyone having unlimited power over others)

Admitting the Shah to the United States seemed honorable to those who saw a fallen friend needing a place to die, dishonorable to those who saw an autocrat plotting to regain his throne.

autocratic   *aw tuh KRA tik*
(ruling with absolute power, as a dictator; having unlimited power over others)

The teamsters' union, chartered in 1899, is an autocratic organization with intense centralized power. It has been marked for decades by secrecy, nepotism, lucrative amenities for union executives and violence.

autonomy   *aw TAH nuh mi*
(independence)

Why are engaged couples so apprehensive? The list seems endless: Getting married means giving up a degree of freedom and autonomy, leaving yourself open to hurt and abandonment, having to reveal the truth about everything, from idiosyncracies to the bank balance you said you had but don't.

avant-garde   *ah vahnt GAHRD*
(the leaders in new or unconventional movements, especially in the arts: French)

For the premiere of her "One World Percussion," the avant-garde composer will enlist some 50 costumed players, 5 conductors and a formidable array of instruments: garbage-can lids, gongs, cymbals, drums, steel plumbing, ship bells, foghorns, police whistles and conch shells, for instance. "I like to bang on things," explains the 28-year-old musician, who has a masters degree in composition from the State University at Stony Brook.

avocation   *a vuh KAY shuhn*
(something done in addition to one's vocation or regular work, and usually for pleasure; hobby)

For the past eight years, Mr. Singer, a 55-year-old newspaper route driver, has been giving tours of Brooklyn in his spare time, an avocation that "I stumbled into while delivering newspapers."

avuncular   *uh VUHNG kyuh luhr*
(of, pertaining to, or resembling an uncle, especially a benevolent uncle)

Having worked for so many years in the shadow of Mr. Cronkite, Mr. Chancellor seems eager to take over Mr. Cronkite's longstanding—though unofficial—role as Dean of Avuncularity, the anchor's anchor.

Anchorman arose in the 1950's to describe the newscaster who coordinates a television or radio program. *Anchor* is now commonly used not only because of its brevity, but because it eliminates any reference to gender. The British equivalent of anchor is *presenter.*

---

awash   *uh WAHSH*
(flooded)

Outside, the handsome buildings along Park Avenue were awash with light in the splendid spring sun.

axiomatic   *ak si uh MA tik*
(universally accepted as true)

It has become axiomatic that local newscasts celebrate lurid and titillating subjects during the ratings "sweep" periods, but increasingly that preoccupation is spilling into the rest of the year as well.

babel   *BA buhl*
(a confusion of voices, languages or sounds; tumult)

Urumqi seems more like a Central Asian bazaar than a city of the People's Republic. The resemblance is especially close at the animated "free market," a babel of Turkic tongues at the intersection in front of the Red Hill Department store.

bailiwick   *BAY luh wik*
(one's particular area of authority)

Most of the umpires at the United States Open were reluctant to comment on the McEnroe situation. But Robert Rockwell, chairman of the umpires' committee, indicated that his group was satisfied with the punishment. "Judging when or how to fine players is not in our bailiwick," Rockwell said. "You can just hope the punishment will discourage him from making the same mistakes in the future."

Umpire should really be *numpire.* The original French term for a third party who settles disputes was a *noumpere (not equal),* but the term was Anglicized as *an umpire.* Similarly, from the faulty separation of articles and nouns we have *an adder,* from *a nadder; a newt* from *an ewt; an apron* from *a napron;* and *a nickname,* from *an eke name* (an "also" name).

---

balk   *bawk*
(to hesitate or recoil)

With food, as with clothing, the extremes set the direction of fashion, and even if those extremes are not adopted completely at the popular level, they change the way we see and taste. Although the average woman at first may balk at the idea of a drastically raised hemline and vow not to shorten anything, if the style takes hold with fashion arbiters, longer skirts and dresses begin to look dowdy.

balky   *BAW ki*
(stubbornly resisting)

Voyager 2's balky camera platform failed to respond correctly to commands today as engineers struggled in vain to diagnose and perhaps fix the spacecraft's problem.

ballast   *BA luhst*
(anything heavy carried in a ship, aircraft or vehicle to give stability or in a balloon or airship to help control altitude)

At the end of the last century, excavations at Bubastis and other Egyptian sites produced so many mummified cats that they were shipped out by the boatload, either as ballast or to be spread on fields as fertilizer.

banal   *buh NAL*
(dull; trite; commonplace)

As for Miss Walters, she still combines sharp, edgy questions with banal meanderings. This time around she was asking her guests what kind of tree or flower they would prefer to be.

"Messidor," which opens today at the Lincoln Plaza Theater, is a very beautiful, arid and difficult-to-sit-through movie in which Mr. Tanner, as he has done before, makes further use of Switzerland—small, clean, uptight and land-locked—as the ultimate metaphor for the banality of contemporary existence.

bandy   *BAN di*
(to pass gossip, rumors, etc., about freely and carelessly)

If you are edgy about your name being bandied about or are tired of getting junk mail . . . write to the Direct Mail/Marketing Association, 6 East 43d Street, New York, N.Y. 10017 (689-4977) and request its free "mail preference form." When the association receives the completed form, it will be circulated to 180 list brokers, mail-order houses and computer mail operations. Within seven months, the amount of mail should diminish.

bane   *bayn*
(the cause of distress, death or ruin)

Pets are the bane of a decorator's life. What the decorator has put together—the perfect home—the imperfect pet can tear asunder. There are cats that dig up wood floors, and dogs that shred Naugahyde sofas and rugs.

banter   *BAN ter*
(to tease or joke in a playful, good-natured way)

After the hearing Mr. Haig seemed jovial as he bantered with reporters. He said articles in the press about the decline in his power reminded him of the telegram sent by Mark Twain after the writer saw his obituary in print: "The reports of my death are greatly exaggerated." When he was asked if that meant he did not intend to resign, he replied, "Well, somebody said I looked 'Bushed' this morning, but I'm not sure."

barb   *bahrb*
(a cutting or biting remark)

As the Secretary of State rose to speak, several demonstrators in the Hilton Hotel ballroom balcony threw down leaflets and shouted: "You're a war criminal!" and "U.S.A., stop the war in El Salvador!" Mr. Haig stood unruffled at the microphone and traded barbs with his hecklers. He called them "people who espouse social justice and can't cope with a reasoned logical exposition." As the demonstrators were led away by guards, Mr. Haig said, "It's a shame."

barbarism   *BAHR buh ri zuhm*
(brutal behavior; savagery)

WIESBADEN, West Germany, Thursday, Jan. 22—A visibly shaken Jimmy Carter said after an emotional meeting with the freed hostages last night that they had been subjected to "acts of barbarism that can never be condoned."

barfly   *BAHR fligh*
(a person who spends much time drinking in barrooms)

Mr. Austin, who is a capable director as well as actor, seems to be making a career out of playing crude barflies, lowlife characters that one prefers to encounter on stage rather than in blind alleys.

barometer   *buh RAH muh ter*
(anything that reflects or indicates change)

Mr. Reagan's humor, Dr. Giordano said, "made him more natural and easier to approach as a patient." The doctors also used it as a barometer to judge his recuperation. Dr. Aaron said that "we could tell when he wasn't feeling well because he wouldn't talk much. When he felt good, he talked and joked incessantly."

baroque   *buh ROHK*
(fantastically overdecorated; gaudily ornate)

There are endless recipes for salmon, and many early ones, perhaps to dress up this poor man's fish, are baroque. Salmon was served garnished with crawfish, quenelles of truffled forcemeat, truffles "fashioned like olives," tiny goujons of sole and small fried smelts. Escoffier, who gives a litany of such dishes in his cookbook, said he liked the fish best served plain.

The term *baroque* is applied to the fantastic and over-decorative in art. The baroque style dominated 17th- and 18th-century art, sculpture and architecture. The "Oxford English Dictionary" has *baroque* derived from *barroco,* the Portuguese word for a rough or imperfect pearl, but adds, "of uncertain origin." The "American Heritage Dictionary," alone among all the dictionaries consulted, provides this derivation of *baroque,* and no other: "from Italian *barocco,* after the founder of the style, Federigo Barocci (1528–1612). Barocci, a painter, was an influential figure in 17th-century European art."

---

bastion   *BAS chuhn*
(a well-fortified or defended position: often used figuratively)

Traditional English sweets, with their reliance on dried fruits, nuts and egg custards, are particularly warming and satisfying in winter. In Britain, the last bastions of these desserts are the dining rooms of grand hotels. And in London, two in particular specialize in English desserts: Claridge's, with its beloved bread-and-butter pudding, and the Dorchester.

bathos   *BAY thahs*
(false pathos; sentimentality)

"On the Stroll" is about an elderly bag lady, a 16-year-old runaway girl and the young pimp who "turns her out" as a prostitute. If Miss Shulman had not been so skillful, the subject might easily have turned to bathos, or a documentary earnestness.

bawdy   *BAW di*
(humorously coarse or indecent; vulgar; lewd)

At the age of 41, Tina Turner is well on her way to becoming the Mae West of rock music. Making her first New York appearance in five years at the Ritz last Thursday, Miss Turner presented the same bawdy female caricature that has endeared her to rock audiences ever since she toured with the Rolling Stones 12 years ago.

bear-baiting   *BAIR bay ting*
(an old form of diversion in which dogs were made to torment a chained bear)

Secretary of State Alexander M. Haig Jr. announced in Peking last week that the United States would for the first time offer to sell "lethal weapons" to China. Mr. Vance said this decision "was neither sound nor well-timed." "It was a very bad mistake," he said. "It was needlessly provocative and smacked of bear-baiting rather than well-thought-out policy."

bedeck   *bi DEK*
(to cover with decorations; adorn)

WARSAW, Tuesday, Aug. 4—A demonstration against food shortages turned into a confrontation between the Polish authorities and the Solidarity union yesterday when the police halted a column of buses and trucks bedecked with flags and placards.

bedevil   *bi DE vuhl*
(to plague or frustrate)

In Burma, one of the world's more isolated places, I saw a woman wearing a T-shirt that posed that once-bedeviling question: "Who shot J.R.?" The question was answered on a T-shirt in Bali: "I shot J.R."

beguile   *bi GIGHL*
(to charm in a fascinating way)

Although origins of recipes are generally difficult to pin down, credit for the invention of Irish coffee usually goes to Shannon Airport in Ireland's County Clare. Its entry into this country in 1952 resulted from the efforts of Stanton Delaplane, a columnist with the San Francisco Chronicle, who was beguiled by the drink at the airport bar and gave the recipe for it to a bartender at the Buena Vista Cafe on Hyde Street, near Fisherman's Wharf.

behemoth   *bi HEE muhth*
*(any animal or thing that is huge or very powerful: originally used in
the Bible—Job XL—to describe a huge animal, possibly a hippopota-
mus)*

The popular notion of the dinosaur pictures a ponderous, lumbering
behemoth whose great hulk and weight and deliberate movements kept
it from roaming far from its birthplace.

There will be scheduled stops at Newfoundland's largest wooden church
as well as at the St. George cliffs at the peninsula's tip overlooking Iceberg
Alley—through which frozen behemoths drift down from the Arctic.

belie   *bi LIGH*
(to give a false idea of; misrepresent)

Forty years ago Miss Asbury would have been called a chorus girl. Nowadays that title is rarely used. Most find it a demeaning expression that
belies their competence as dancers and their status as working women.

Recent studies belie the widespread belief that the stress of retirement
often precipitates serious illness and death. And there are unquestionably
many happily retired people who are doing just what they want, within
the constraints of physical abilities, fixed incomes and rampant inflation.

belittle   *bi LI tuhl*
*(to make seem less important; speak slightingly of; depreciate: coined by
Thomas Jefferson about 1780)*

The shingled houses of East Hampton and its neighboring villages sit
calmly by the sea. They do not attempt to belittle the ocean or to upstage
it as do the palaces of Newport, glorious confections designed with deliberate indifference to the landscape they sit beside.

belle époque   *bel ay PAHK*
*(the era of elegance and gaiety that characterized fashionable Parisian
life in the period preceding World War I: French)*

In the legendary belle époque that preceded World War I, Rodin was
universally looked upon as an artistic colossus—at once the heir and
equal of the great masters of the past and a giant among the artists of the
modern age.

bellicose   *BE luh kohs*
(of a hostile nature; eager to fight or quarrel)

"Since the change of leadership in the White House, candidly bellicose calls and statements have resounded from Washington, especially designed, as it were, to poison the atmosphere of relations between our two countries," [Brezhnev] said. "We would like to hope, however, that those who shape United States policy will ultimately manage to see things in a more realistic light."

bellwether   *BEL we th:er*
(a leader, especially of imitative followers)

In San Francisco, which has long been a bellwether for the illicit drug culture, as has New York, heroin use has remained stable, while the trend of mixing drugs has increased significantly, according to Dr. George R. Gay, director of the emergency medical and "rock medicine" section of the Haight-Ashbury Free Medical Clinics.

The original, and still used, meaning of *bellwether* is a male sheep, usually castrated, that carries a bell around its neck and acts as a leader of the flock.

bemoan   *bi MOHN*
(to deplore or lament)

Mr. Vysotsky's ballads, spoofing or bemoaning the harsh realities of Soviet life, captured the hearts of Russians of all ages and from all walks of life. His funeral in Moscow last July developed into a demonstration by tens of thousands of fans.

benchmark   *BENCH mahrk*
(a standard or point of reference in measuring or judging quality, value, etc.: from a surveyor's mark made on a permanent landmark of known position and altitude used as a reference point in determining other altitudes)

Scattered about the country, teased by a scrap of information here, a scrap there, the hostages spent the middle months of 1980 trying to cope with the reality of a life without benchmarks, of a tedious imprisonment that showed no signs of ending, and of all-too-frequent reminders of their precarious and hazardous situation.

benign   *bi NIGHN*
(good-natured; kindly)

Everyone likes the human way in which the white whales rise on their tails to honk at visitors, and the benign, blissful smiles that stretch over their fleshy faces.

(not malignant, i.e. cancerous)

Ted Petersen, the offensive tackle, is out while recovering from surgery to remove a benign tumor on the hip. Is this to be last year all over again, another season with injuries striking all parts of the team?

(doing little or no harm)

The sea nettle and the moon jellyfish are often seen in the Northeast. The moon, by far the most common in the area, is especially benign; its toxin usually results in no more than a pinprick sensation. The sea nettle can deliver a painful sting that leaves a red welt; however, the irritation is usually gone in a few hours.

berate   *bi RAYT*
(to scold or rebuke severely)

Mr. Saroyan's third play, "Love's Old Sweet Song" in 1940, failed in the view of most critics and at the box office. He insisted it was "one of the best plays in the American theater," and berated audience and critics alike.

bereft   *bi REFT*
(left at a loss; desolate)

"Ultimately the West Side will be bereft of a wholesale meat market," said Benjamin Young, a spokesman for the Meat Purveyors Association. "It's just a matter of time before it will be driven out, because this property has greater value for other purposes."

besot   *bi SAHT*
(to stupify or confuse, as with alcoholic drink)

Hard as it may be to believe for those brainwashed by our youth-besotted society, which regards people from about the age of 45 onward as hopelessly over the hill, let me say emphatically that, while we are tottering toward our precipitate end, we are having lots of fun along the way.

best   *best*
(to win out over; defeat or outdo)

By willing his own death, Bobby Sands has earned a place on Ireland's long roll of martyrs and bested an implacable British Prime Minister. It is a bitter and joyless victory, but it was predictable.

To best and *to worst* mean exactly the same thing.

---

bestial   *BES chul*
(brutal or savage)

No, the United States does not have the wisdom or the power to right all the wrongs of the world. But the experience of Hitler surely taught us the danger of pretending that bestial governments can safely be ignored while they operate only at home.

bibelot   *BI bloh*
(a small object whose value lies in its beauty or rarity; trinket: French)

On Bleeker Street near Abingdon Square, Scott Hamilton and his partner, Ed Hyre, continue to offer such wares as 19th-century French faux-bamboo furniture and assorted bibelots at their antiques shop, much as they have for 15 years.

bibliomania   *bi bli uh MAY ni uh*
(a craze for collecting books)

Edward Robb Ellis lives contentedly with his bibliomania in the space people normally allow for their bookshelves. The rest of his Chelsea apartment is given over to his books—more than 8,000 of them lining shelves, resting on chairs, tables and sofas, stacked waist-high all over the living room, dominating the kitchen, the hallway and the bedroom, forming aisles between rooms.

bibliophile   *BI bli uh fighl*
(a person who loves or admires books; a collector of books)

WILMETTE, Ill., May 31—From Maine and Arizona and points between, ready with shopping carts and guided by maps, on the lookout for first edition classics and pulp tear-jerkers, 25,000 bibliophiles descended last week on the Brandeis Used Book Sale, billed as the largest in the world. The first customer arrived at 2:30 A.M. last Saturday, 15½ hours before the gate opened on 300,000 used books spread under two circus tents in a shopping center's parking lot.

bier   *bir*
(a platform or portable framework on which a coffin or corpse is placed)

By evening, thousands waited solemnly under a steady drizzle to file into the audience hall, past the bier holding the closed simple metal coffin inscribed only with Cardinal Wyszynski's name and age. His red hat was placed on top, and nearby hung a copy of the Black Madonna, Poland's sacred relic.

billet   *BI lit*
(to quarter soldiers, especially in nonmilitary buildings)

Fresh from the Angola bush, South Africa's white hunters are all but displaying the mounted heads of Soviet military advisers killed in last week's invasion. "Undeniable evidence" of a Soviet military presence in Angola, says South Africa's Defense Minister. So what else is new? Everyone knows that a thousand Russians and East Germans, plus some 20,000 Cubans, have long been billeted in Angola. The trick is not to find new evidence that Communist troops are there, but to get them out.

biopsy   *BIGH ahp si*
(the removal of bits of living tissue, fluids, etc., from the body for diagnostic examination)

The spokesman, James Battaglio, said a biopsy taken Thursday from the six-term Connecticut Democrat showed a pancreatic tumor to be malignant.

blanch   *blanch*
(to turn pale)

Many Parisian purists blanch at the thought of eating Provence's food in which olive oil replaces butter, just as Yankees express contempt for the grits and "greasy" fare of our own South.

In its broadest sense, *Yankee* means *American*. In its strictest modern sense, it means *New Englander*. *Yankee* is from the Dutch *Jan Kees* (John Cheese), and was first a disparaging nickname for any Hollander, then for Dutch pirates. During the 1700's it was used by Dutch New Yorkers to describe the English settlers of Connecticut, whose commercial practices they found morally questionable. Eventually, New Englanders adopted it themselves and even converted it into a complimentary adjective (Yankee ingenuity, Yankee craftsmanship). During the Civil War, it was a Southern term of contempt for Northerners (some Southerners still maintain the tradition), but since World War I it has come into worldwide use as a synonym for an American.

---

bland   *bland*
(tasteless; insipid; dull)

I have also found that the initial reaction to some no-salt dishes is that they are boringly bland at first bite. But with the second and third bites I find that the depth of flavor increases severalfold.

blandishment   *BLAN dish ment*
(a flattering or ingratiating act or remark meant to persuade, usually used in the plural)

To the Editor: What does it profit a man if he gains a 25 percent tax cut but loses his job, his Social Security and his children's educational benefits? I think many in Congress who listen to the Reagan blandishments will find themselves among the unemployed when the full consequences of the Reagan plan have wreaked havoc with the economy.
PAUL K. STEWART, Portland, Me.

blasé   *blah ZAY*
(having a casual and unexcited attitude toward something because of habitual or excessive exposure to, or experience with, it: French)

Even blasé Bloomingdale's was thrown into a flutter recently when Carmen Romano de López Portillo, wife of the President of Mexico, bought $1,600 in Madeleine Mono products, including the tester display.

blatant   *BLAY tuhnt*
(glaringly conspicuous or obtrusive)

If an entire party has not finished a course, it is blatantly rude to remove plates from those who have finished, thereby rushing slower eaters.

blemish   *BLE mish*
(a flaw, defect or shortcoming)

The battle pits the afternoon Times with its cool, professional approach and detached reporting, against the morning Trentonian, a lively tabloid that rarely points out this aging industrial city's blemishes and cheers it with photographs of children having birthday parties and the vacation snapshots of anyone who sends them in.

blitz   *blits*
(a sudden, overwhelming attack)

Some years back, the dinner parties of the Western world were blitzed by fondue pots.

Blitz is a short form of the German *blitzkrieg* (lightning war), a term used to describe World War II military tactics, originated by the Germans, involving high-speed, coordinated attacks of tanks and planes. Donner and Blitzen (Thunder and Lightning) were two of Santa's reindeer.

---

bloc   *blahk*
(a combination of legislators—not all of the same party—political parties or countries functioning together to achieve common objectives)

WARSAW, July 15—For the first time in the Soviet bloc, a Communist party has decided to elect its entire leadership by secret ballot with a choice of contenders.

bluenose   *BLOO: nohs*
(a puritanical person, especially one who tries to impose his or her moral views on others)

To some people, of course, any portrayal of a kid in a birthday suit is obscene, but fortunately the Constitution does not allow bluenoses to impose their standards on society. A good deal of decent but explicit material should remain available, including valid sex education materials.

bluff   *bluhf*
(a high, steep, broad-faced bank or cliff)

Coastguardsmen who stand watch at the station here, high on a bluff near Northport, say that nonfatal accidents—capsizings, groundings and collisions—have increased in what F. Scott Fitzgerald called "the most domesticated body of salt water in the Western Hemisphere, the great wet barnyard of Long Island Sound."

(having a rough and frank but affable manner)

Especially in the last few years, Prince Charles has emerged with a personality quite his own—his father's bluff heartiness, tempered by his mother's kindness and obvious devotion to duty.

blunt   *bluhnt*
(to make dull or insensitive)

The problem with drinking isn't so much "alcoholism." The problem is death and destruction—of lives, property, relationships. Warped personalities and blunted perceptions may be annoying, but that is inconsequential when weighed against the protection of life—yet there is a parking lot next to every cocktail lounge.

blurb   *blerb*
(a publisher's note on the dust jacket of a book, describing the book's contents and usually of a laudatory nature)

"Important" books were those books they forced you to read in high school because they were good for you, the ones that felt 20,000 pages long. When I open a book and read a jacket blurb that says it is an "important" book, I drop it as gingerly as a pit viper.

bode   *bohd*
(to be an omen of; presage)

Her face colored lightly by makeup, but with deep circles under her eyes, she [Jean Harris] arrived at the courthouse this evening after two days of absence—depressed, her friends said, by the drawn-out deliberation of the jury, a delay she correctly guessed did not bode well for her.

bogus   *BOH guhs*
(not genuine; spurious; counterfeit; fake)

Mr. Wallenberg printed thousands of bogus Swedish passports and slipped them to Jews awaiting shipment to Nazi extermination camps.

boldface   *BOHLD fays*
*(a type with a heavy, dark face, **like this**)*

Hundreds of New Jersey physicians may be violating a rule of the State Board of Medical Examiners that says doctors may not put their names in boldface in the Yellow Pages.

bolster   *BOHL ster*
(to support, strengthen or reinforce)

Along with astronauts and Olympic gold medal winners, few things bolster the pride of the ordinary Russian like the Bolshoi Ballet. Throughout the world, the company is synonymous with dance.

bombast   *BAHM bast*
(talk or writing that sounds grand or important but has little meaning; pompous language)

In the process of guiding the N.A.A.C.P., Mr. Wilkins traveled more than half of each year, visiting branches of the organization and giving lectures in which he espoused civil rights causes. His sparse gray hair and gray mustache and his slim figure clad in conservative suits were familiar to millions of Americans who saw him on television as he argued, literally and eloquently but without bombast, for the emancipation of his people.

bona fide   *BOH nuh FIGHD*
(authentic; genuine)

Each year there are fewer bona fide outdoor eating places in New York because owners put roofs over their gardens so they can realize profits from the space regardless of the weather.

bonhomie   *bah nuh MEE*
(easy good humor; amiability: French, bon, *good* + homme, *man)*

The President [Valéry Giscard d'Estaing, of France] has been attempting to put increasing doses of feeling into his campaign tours. Sometimes it is in the form of bonhomie. In the southwest he downed a glass of Armagnac, but that part of the press that, not being adulatory, is vindictive, printed a picture of him screwing up his face afterward. In Corsica he brushed aside a glass of water at a meeting and called for wine, over which, the same press noted, he choked.

bonkers   *BAHNG kers*
(crazy: a slang word)

I don't know what this actor is up to in "Macbeth," and I doubt that he does, either. In the early scenes, he is so shifty-eyed and bonkers that one expects him to be arrested for suspicion of murder before he actually commits one.

boorish   *BOOR ish*
(rude or ill-mannered)

This is not to suggest that boorishness on the courts is an American monopoly. John McEnroe and Jimmy Connors can be as coarse as goats, and they are Americans, but Ilie Nastase has scaled peaks of vulgarity in his time, and he is a Rumanian.

bottom out   *BAHT om owt*
(to level off at a low point)

The economic decline that began in January 1980 bottomed out just seven months later, making it the shortest recession on record, according to the National Bureau of Economic Research.

bourgeois   *boor ZHWAH*
(middle-class: French)

There was a sense, of course, in which Pissarro was quite literally an outsider among the French painters of his time. He was born into a bourgeois Jewish family in the Virgin Islands, then a Danish possession to which his father had emigrated from Bordeaux in 1824. And although he spent five years (1842–47) at boarding school in a suburb of Paris, Pissarro did not settle in France until the age of 25.

(middle-class in beliefs, attitudes and practices; in Marxist doctrine, that which, being middle-class, is antithetical to the proletariat or laboring class)

They closed all the flower shops in China in 1966 and ordered people who kept goldfish to dump them into sewers and rivers. These and other tiny items of beauty were deemed bourgeois, so they became targets when Mao Zedong opened his Great Proletarian Cultural Revolution against, among other things, the "four olds"—old ideas, culture, habits and customs.

> Pinyin is a system for transliterating Chinese into Roman characters which The New York Times and other publications have adopted to replace the Wade system, devised in the mid-1800's by Sir Thomas Wade, a British diplomat and Chinese scholar. The Pinyin system was introduced in China in 1958 as a teaching aid, and has been adopted in the United Nations. The Times still retains some well-known names such as Canton and Peking, but now prints Mao Tse-tung as Mao Zedong and Chou En-lai as Zhou Enlai, thereby more closely approximating the way those names sound in Chinese.

----

bowels   *BOW uhls*
(the interior or inner part)

They needed 350 cockroaches for "A Stranger Is Watching," a picture being partly shot in the bowels of Grand Central Terminal, so they called an exterminator. He provided the bugs at a dollar each.

bracing   *BRAY sing*
(invigorating; stimulating; refreshing)

There is a good deal to be said for the bracingly direct and unmannered approach to the piano that Nancy Boston cultivated at her debut recital in the Abraham Goodman house on Wednesday night.

brash *brash*
(offensively bold; pushing; impudent)

At her peak, Billie Jean King performed a great service to any female athlete. By her brash aggressiveness, she made it more acceptable for women to push themselves, to release anger with themselves for a bad play, to want openly to beat their opponents, to question the officials or even the financial structure of their sport. She gave most women a sense of leadership and pride during vital years of the women's movement.

bravura *bruh VYOO ruh*
(brilliant technique or style in performance)

"Leave 'Em Laughing," on CBS-TV tonight at 8, is that old-fashioned theatrical commodity: a vehicle for a star. The chief product is a bravura performance surrounded by a good deal of capable but not distracting support. In this instance, the star is Mickey Rooney and, despite some uneven moments, he delivers the emotional goods.

bray *bray*
(the loud, harsh cry of a donkey, or a sound like this)

In the Sinai Desert, a crew filming a difficult sequence for the television series nervously eyed a grazing donkey that luckily waited until the shot was done before emitting an ear-splitting bray.

Kai Winding, the Danish-born trombonist who made his first major impression in jazz as the lustiest of Stan Kenton's braying trombonists in the late 40's and later teamed with J.J. Johnson in the trombone duo known as Jay and Kai, is making his first club appearance in New York in almost a decade this week at Sweet Basil.

brazen *BRAY zin*
(showing no shame; bold; impudent)

Half the Israelis evidently admire the brazen quality that foreign statesmen resent in Menachem Begin. "He doesn't turn the other cheek," an admirer said.

breach   *breech*
(to break through)

Screaming protesters had breached the great wrought-iron main gates and were pouring over the walls. Some waved clubs and sticks. Huge posters of the Ayatollah Ruhollah Khomeini bobbed on poles as the crowd went wild.

The Vermont Supreme Court has been asked to breach the practice of secrecy in juvenile court by letting the public attend the trial of a teenager accused of torturing and killing a 12-year-old girl.

brio   *BREE oh*
(vivacity; zest: Italian)

The slow and sad middle movement was sustained wonderfully well, and the finale, "Theme Russe," went off with tremendous brio.

Brobdingnagian   *brahb ding NA gi uhn*
(gigantic: from Brobdingnag, a land in Swift's "Gulliver's Travels"
inhabited by giants about 60 feet tall)

Approaching, for example, his [Chuck Close's] most recent large-scale acrylic work, "Mark," completed in 1979, the viewer is taken aback by the scale of the eyeglasses, as big as two tennis racquets; the stubble beard with hair follicles the size of ant holes; the freckle on the nose as large as a quarter. On such Brobdingnagian terms, the image is both a face and a startling abstraction of one.

brunt   *bruhnt*
(the heaviest or hardest part)

Mrs. Kudukis has become head of Clevelanders for 100,000 Families, a new organization that will, she said yesterday, "take to task anyone who makes a negative remark about Cleveland." "No person or city should be continually the brunt of a joke," said Mrs. Kudukis.

brusque   *bruhsk*
(rough and abrupt in manner and speech; curt)

Decades of success never entirely mellowed Mr. Shumlin, a Colorado rancher's son with a booming voice, who could be as brusque as a drill sergeant.

bubeleh   *BOO buh luh*
(a Yiddish term of endearment, used commonly for "darling," "dear child," "honey," etc.)

Like the rest of the new Children's Zoo, the appeal seems universal. A pair of hulking teen-aged boys talked earnestly to a goat on a recent members' preview day, while four women bent over a nearby ducklings' enclosure, crying, "Hello, bubeleh," to a mass of peeping yellow fuzz.

Bubeleh is an affectionate diminutive of grandmother, literally "little grandmother." In "The Joys of Yiddish," Leo Rosten says, "Jewish mothers call both female and male babies *bubeleh.* This carries the expectation that the child in the crib will one day be a grandparent. It also honors the memory of the mother's mother: in calling a baby "little grandmother," a mother is addressing the child in the way the child will in time address *its* grandmother—and its child."

----

bubkes   *BUHB kis*
(something trivial, worthless, insultingly disproportionate to expectations: in Russian the word's literal meaning is beans, but as a Yiddish word it is used only as below)

As is common in many industries, Hollywood often bestows titles in lieu of raises. "There are vice presidents in this industry who make $800 a week and vice presidents who make $800,000 a year," says Charles Powell, who went from "senior vice president worldwide advertising, publicity and promotion" at Universal to chairman of his own marketing firm. "There are 22-year-old vice presidents who aren't earning bubkes. But the title is the new negotiating ploy, the major perk."

bucolic   *byoo: KAH lik*
(relating to country life; rustic)

EAST FISHKILL, N.Y.—The picture-postcard rolling hills and valleys along the Hudson River near here are no longer just bucolic backdrops for travelers between New York City and the upstate resorts and cities—they now make up the fastest-growing area in New York State.

buff   *buhf*
(a devotee or enthusiast; fan)

Civil War buffs find much of interest in Chattanooga, which was the scene of some of the fiercest fighting of the conflict.

buffaloed   *BUH fuh lohd*
(intimidated: a slang word)

No one who has spent so many years in public life is likely to be buffaloed by any reporter's news conference question.

buffoonery   *buh FOO: nuh ri*
(clowning around)

The carefree buffoonery of the 27 clowns, three of them women, who perform acts and entr'actes in the Ringling Bros. and Barnum & Bailey Circus unit playing Madison Square Garden through May 31, is a series of infinitely varied capers.

bumper   *BUHM per*
(unusually large or abundant)

HILLSDALE, Okla.—With another bumper crop of winter wheat nearing maturity, farmers in this highly productive region are anxiously listening to the market news and watching for reports of grain prospects in the Soviet Union.

burgeon   *BER juhn*
(to grow or develop rapidly; expand)

Astronomers say Arizona's observatories are being jeopardized by the state's burgeoning population, as man-made lights glow steadily brighter and make the stars harder to see.

burgher   *BER ger*
(a solid citizen: originally a middle-class inhabitant of a European town, but used today in English usually in a humorous or facetious way)

After lunch, the Hall of Famers were driven a few blocks to Doubleday Field, named after Abner Doubleday, who either invented the game of baseball here in 1839 or never visited here or never played baseball, depending on whom you read. The burghers of Cooperstown prefer the first version, which gives them the chance to sell a lot of hot dogs, homemade pies and sun visors two days every August.

burnout   *BERN owt*
(a loss of drive, motivation, incentive, etc., resulting from the stresses or demands of a particular job that have taken an emotional or spiritual toll on a person)

When I looked into the eyes of a friend of mine, a burned-out social worker, I couldn't get an accurate reading on whether she had just lost her Title XX funding or forgotten to defrost something for dinner. All zones of pain and disappointment are equally pressing during burnout. The judgment blurs.

bush league *boosh leeg*
(*second-rate: in its original sense, bush league describes a second-rate or small minor league*)

It has always seemed obvious to me that the millions who settle for the bush-league trash on television do so only because they are unaware of the truly top-notch junk available in other forms.

buttress *BUH tris*
(*to support or reinforce; bolster*)

Prime Minister Menachem Begin, accompanied by senior military officers, made a visit to northern Israel today to buttress morale as Palestinian guerrillas across the border in Lebanon continued their rocket fire for the eighth day.

buzz word *buhz wurd*
(*a word or phrase used by some in-group, having little or imprecise meaning but sounding impressive to outsiders*)

Under cover of the buzz words "conservatism" and "budget-cutting," President Reagan is pushing ahead with natural-resource policies that are radical, inflationary, economically unsound and environmentally degrading.

Byzantine *BI zin teen*
(*resembling the government or politics of the Byzantine empire in structure, spirit, etc.: specifically, characterized by complexity, deviousness and intrigue*)

President Duvalier is supported by a Byzantine network of old families who shop in New York City, educate their children in United States universities, and vacation in Europe. Though constituting less than 5 percent of the population they own 90 percent of the wealth. They inherited the corrupt power structures, benefit greatly from them, and remain alert to scotch threats to stability.

To scotch means to put an end to; stifle; stamp out. Shakespeare used the word in "Macbeth" to mean wounded. When Macbeth's henchmen kill Banquo but fail to kill his son, Fleance, who might one day pose a danger to his throne, Macbeth says,

> "We have scotch'd the snake, not killed it:
> She'll close and be herself, whilst our poor malice
> Remains in danger of her former tooth."

―――――――

cache   *kash*
(anything stored or hidden, especially in large numbers)

Recently, the antiques shop called the Place Off Second Avenue came upon a cache of 1940's tin pails in a toy store that was going out of business and bought up the entire stock.

cacophony   *kuh KAH fuh ni*
(harsh, jarring sound; dissonance)

Amid a cacophony of blasts, beeps and whines, two of Commissioner Bruce C. Ratner's inspectors then taped shut the coin slots of more than 50 games, such as Battlezones, Asteroids, Defenders, while several dozen late-morning customers, all but oblivious to the invasion, burrowed deeper into the galactic violence in front of them.

cadence   *KAY duhns*
(a rhythmic flow of sound)

There was laughter in the poet's weathered eyes. How did it feel to receive a foundation award of $60,000 a year for the next five years simply to go on living the life he loves? "Walll," drawled Robert Penn Warren in a voice soft and husky with the cadences of his Kentucky boyhood, "how do you feel about just stumbling on a piece of money on the pavement and it's yours?"

cadge   *kaj*
(to beg or get by begging; sponge)

Marjorie Gross, for example, travels to and from all of her around-Manhattan gigs on her secondhand bicycle because she cannot afford taxicabs, and she carries her minuscule wardrobe with her in shopping bags and plastic luggage as she cadges places to stay from sister—and brother—performers.

cajole   *kuh JOHL*
(to coax; influence or persuade by soothing words)

It was Roy Wilkins's painstakingly orchestrated legal strategy that ultimately persuaded the Supreme Court in 1954 to outlaw school segregation. And he was a leader in the civil rights coalition that cajoled and pressed and persevered until Congress finally banned discrimination in the great civil rights enactments of the 1960's.

candid   *KAN did*
(very honest or frank in what one says or writes)

The money from Paris arrives monthly, and officials readily concede that without it the Government could not pay its 23,000 civil servants. Two-thirds of the national budget is used to pay salaries. French aid officials here are candid about the reasons for Paris's generosity. "We do not want a revolution here," said a French aid official. "If the Central African Republic had a revolution, it could bring in its train the destabilization of surrounding countries."

candor   *KAN der*
(sharp honesty or frankness in expressing oneself)

"A Prince of Wales has to do what he can by influence, not power," he once explained with characteristic candor. "There isn't any power. There can be influence. The influence is in direct ratio to the respect people have for you."

cannibalize   *KA nu buh lighz*
(to strip old or worn equipment or parts for use in other units to help keep them in service)

Losses to Iraqi fighters and poor maintenance have sharply reduced Iranian air strength. Of 202 F-4 Phantoms available when the war began in September only about 50 are now operable. The air force has begun cannibalizing wrecked F-4's and hopes to have a force of about 100 ready to support the offensive.

canny   *KA ni*
(careful and shrewd in one's actions and dealings; clever and cautious)

They called Carl Vinson the Swamp Fox, a tribute to his canny flair for running the Pentagon from his seat in the United States House of Representatives. Admirals quaked and generals quavered when the tall Georgian called them before the House Armed Services Committee, which he ruled like a potentate for 14 of his 50 years in the House before retiring from Congress at the age of 81.

canon   *KA nuhn*
(a body of rules, principles, criteria, etc.)

"Another block not often included in tours is West 81st Street, also between Columbus and Amsterdam," Mr. Zito said. "These houses were built in the age of individuality. This is where design really takes off, defying all architectural canons. There is such an exuberance here. They used every kind of device: cherubs, lyres, every kind of ornament you can imagine."

cantankerous   *kan TANG ker uhs*
(bad-tempered; quarrelsome; perverse)

Barring the unlikeliest of mathematical surprises—the French electoral system is a complex and highly cantankerous piece of machinery—the Socialists will control the National Assembly without needing to seek allies.

canvass   *KAN vuhs*
(to conduct a survey on a given subject; poll)

If you were to canvass any group of serious cooks and ask the name of the one basic ingredient best suited to no-salt cookery, you would doubtless receive more answers than the components of a Macedonian salad. I would answer without pause: mushrooms.

capricious   *kuh PRI shuhs*
(tending to change abruptly and without apparent reason; erratic; flighty)

Farmers are at the mercy of nature's capriciousness: it can kill off a year of tender nurturing in a single day; it can cause the buds of one orchard to freeze and drop off while not bothering the trees on a hill a few miles away.

career   *kuh RIR*
(to move at full speed; rush wildly)

The car injured 27 pedestrians when it careered into the crowd while the driver and two passengers were trying to elude a pursuing police car.

caricature   *KAR uh kuh choor*
(an imitation that is so distorted or inferior as to seem ludicrous)

"I did research," the dark-haired, dark-eyed actress said the other day. "An actor friend and I drove around to places where hookers hang out, and I watched them. I saw the way they approached the cars, the business-like way they handled themselves. I also talked to a hooker I knew in Boston. My goal was to make Gloria a real person and not a caricature of a hooker."

Among several purported origins of *hooker,* a prostitute, is that when Joseph Hooker, a Civil War general, ruled Washington, D.C.'s red-light district off-limits to his men, they retaliated by nicknaming the women there "hookers." Another theory has hookers named for the Hook of Holland, where the clientele were sailors from the ships that traded between there and British ports. But *hooker* may have originated in New York City before the Civil War, when a number of brothels flourished at Corlear's Hook. Marian Touba, currently a research librarian at the New York Historical Society, located Corlear's Hook on an old map, placing it just south of where the Williamsburgh Bridge now stands, and on a piece of land that jutted into the East River but which no longer exists.

carnage   *KAHR nij*
(bloody and extensive slaughter; bloodshed)

The impact of today's shelling, coupled with yesterday's carnage at both Moslem and Christian beaches in which 8 persons were killed and about 60 were wounded, was to once again turn sections of this city into ghostly places. Shuttered shops sit behind heaps of sandbags, and streets are devoid of people or traffic.

carriage   *KA rij*
(the manner of carrying the head and body; posture; bearing)

When they first met in late 1979, he was the prince in "Swan Lake." She remembers his regal carriage and his dark, curly hair.

cartel   *kahr TEL*
(an association of industrialists, business firms, etc., for establishing a national or international monopoly by price fixing, ownership of controlling stock, etc.)

When the Organization of Petroleum Exporting Countries meets in Geneva next week, the cartel will face its toughest challenge since it began dictating oil prices eight years ago.

cashier   *ka SHIR*
(to dismiss, especially in dishonor, from a position of command, trust, etc.)

Robert D'Aubisson, a cashiered army major, came out of hiding last week hinting broadly that a coup was in the offing in El Salvador and asserting that the Reagan administration "would not be bothered" by it.

castigate   *KA stuh gayt*
(to punish or rebuke severely, especially by harsh public criticism)

At his first press conference, President Reagan castigated Soviet leaders as "immoral," ready to stop at nothing, including lying and cheating, to advance their goal of world domination.

cataclysm   *KA tuh kli zuhm*
(a great upheaval that causes sudden and violent changes, as an earthquake, war, etc.)

The Mount St. Helens volcano, called Loowit, or Lady of Fire, by the Indians of the Pacific Northwest, erupted with cataclysmic force on the sunny Sunday morning of May 18, 1980. The explosion, which tore 1,300 feet off the 9,607-foot peak, was calculated by geologists to have released the equivalent of 500 times the energy that was unleashed by the atomic bomb dropped on Hiroshima.

catalyst   *KA tuh list*
(a person or thing acting as the stimulus in bringing about or hastening a result)

Perhaps the most dramatic example of how Presidential attention influenced a book, and of how a book influenced public policy, occurred with Michael Harrington's "The Other America: Poverty in the United States" (Macmillan), which is generally credited with being the catalyst of the Kennedy-Johnson "war on poverty."

catcall   *KAT kawl*
(a shrill noise or whistle expressing derision or disapproval, as of a speaker, actor, etc.)

Mrs. Thatcher's speech, like most of her recent statements on the economy, was greeted with catcalls by the opposition.

catechism   *KA tuh ki zuhm*
(a handbook of questions and answers for teaching the principles of a religion)

In catechism lessons, nuns used to ask, "Why did God make the world?" and the answer was "For His glory." Samuel Johnson might be said to have made the first great English dictionary in the same way.

A few selections from Samuel Johnson's (1709–1784) "Dictionary of the English Language" (published 1749):

Net. Anything reticulated or decussated at equal distances, with interstices between the intersections.
Oats. A grain, which in England is generally given to horses, but in Scotland supports the people.
Patron. Commonly a wretch who supports with insolence, and is paid with flattery.

-----

categorically   *ka tuh GAW ri kli*
(without qualifications or conditions; absolutely; completely)

To the Editor: I want to go on record as being categorically opposed to Governor Carey's recommendation that 24-hour sales of beer, wine and liquor be allowed in the State of New York. Alcoholism is the greatest addictive problem in the United States, and the interrelationship between alcohol and mayhem on our highways is well known.

caterwaul   *KA ter wawl*
(to make a shrill, howling sound like that of a cat in heat; screech; wail)

Prince sings exclusively in a falsetto, which he pushes at times to an eerie caterwauling intensity.

cathartic   *kuh THAHR tik*
(providing relief of emotional tensions through a real or vicarious experience that allows one's pent-up feelings to flow freely or be purged)

Mr. Simon's first wife, Joan, died of cancer in 1973. Later that year he married the actress Marsha Mason. ("I'm a person who must be married," he says.) Out of that second marriage, and presumably out of a feeling of guilt for having entered it, Mr. Simon wrote "Chapter Two." " 'Chapter Two' shows you how I'm always using my life in my work," he said.

"It was extremely painful writing it. It's my favorite play for many reasons. It was cathartic for me."

In its literary sense, *catharsis* had its origin in Aristotle's "Poetics," where it referred to the purging of the audience's emotions of pity and fear aroused by the actions of the tragic hero. It has never been established with certainty just what Aristotle meant when he wrote, "Tragedy through pity and fear effects a purgation of such emotions," but the concept remains basic to the idea of what a tragic play ought to effect among audiences.

---

caucus   *KAW kuhs*
(a private meeting of a committee to decide on policy, pick candidates, etc., especially prior to a general, open meeting)

Ignoring a review that should have warned us off, we exposed ourselves to a tasteless film called "The History of the World, Part I." I was proud of my children when a family caucus produced a 4-0 vote to walk out.

caustic   *KAW stik*
(cutting or sarcastic in utterance; biting)

McEnroe's feud with British reporters throughout this tournament was evident in an angry postmatch news conference today. After a series of caustic exchanges, triggered by a question about whether he had split with his girlfriend, Stacy Margolin, a tennis player, McEnroe walked out of the press room.

cavalier   *ka vuh LIR*
(casual or indifferent toward matters of some importance)

As recently as their previous album, "Emotional Rescue," the Rolling Stones were still striking adolescent poses, playing bad boys. Their lyrics were especially cavalier in their treatment of women, who were often depicted as sex objects or, at best, playthings to be discarded at a moment's whim.

caveat   *KA vi at*
(a warning)

Want an oil company credit card? A few caveats are in order. Make sure you answer all questions on the application. Be careful about estimates of how much gas you expect to use. Take pains to see that your previous credit performance is up to par. And be accurate—a tough computer is watching and scoring you.

cavort   *kuh VAWRT*
(to romp about happily; frolic)

Remarkable-looking animals will cavort at the Bronx Zoo on Saturday and Sunday, and some of them may resemble your children.

cede   *seed*
(to give up one's rights to; yield; grant)

Congress is the special preserve of print reporters, and television cedes them the field while it concentrates on the President and the Cabinet.

celerity   *suh LE ruh ti*
(swiftness in acting or moving; speed)

Perhaps the most admirable aspect of "The Laundry Hour" is the celerity of the actors. During each blackout, one or both of them quickly change costume—from clerical black to Las Vegas glitter. Despite these frequent switches in attire and the talk about samsara, "The Laundry Hour" remains singleminded—60 minutes spinning on one cycle.

Samsara is the Hindu and Buddhist concept of the eternal cycle of birth, suffering, death and rebirth.

---

celibacy   *SE luh buh si*
(the state of being unmarried, especially that of a person under a vow not to marry and to practice complete sexual abstinence)

Father Wagner, in his letter, questioned the meaning of celibacy, and the tone of his letter was considered by the Church leaders to question the vow. "I suggest that for many priests," his letter said, "the lack of physical intimacy, which is supposed to assure their availability to loving service, is in fact an exhausting, debilitating privation which makes them less healthy, less creative and less giving."

cenotaph   *SE nuh taf*
(a monument or empty tomb honoring a dead person whose body is somewhere else)

The 60-year-old Pope spoke before the memorial cenotaph in Hiroshima's Peace Park, close to the epicenter of the blast from a bomb dropped by a United States B-29 in the final days of World War II.

censure   *SEN sher*
(a condemning as wrong; strong disapproval; a judgment or resolution condemning a person for misconduct: specifically, an official expression of disapproval passed by a legislature)

A Criminal Court judge who let a woman charged with murder stay at his home for the night has been censured by the State Commission on Judicial Conduct for "extraordinarily poor judgment and a serious misunderstanding of the role of a judge in our legal system."

centrist   *SEN trist*
(one taking a position in the political center)

Mr. Timerman started La Opinión in 1972 with a group of leftist writers, but moved the paper to a more centrist position as it encouraged the coup that overthrew President Isabel Martinez de Perón in 1976.

cerebral   *suh REE bruhl*
(intellectual)

Mr. Sahl is a cerebral humorist who enjoys working along the cracks of contradiction in society and in jabbing its institutional faces. He has recently completed his autobiography, "Heartland," and is writing a screenplay for Sidney Lumet, the director.

cessation   *se SAY shuhn*
(a ceasing, or stopping, either forever or for some time)

WASHINGTON, July 9—A Presidential commission recommended today that the states endorse the concept that human life ends when the brain stops functioning. It urged all 50 states to adopt a simple uniform law defining death as the "irreversible cessation of all functions of the entire brain, including the brain stem."

chanteuse   *shahn TOO:Z*
(a woman singer, especially of popular ballads: French)

The incomparable—Hildegarde! That introduction has been as much a trademark as her long white gloves and dainty handkerchief. And the chanteuse, who has been in show business for "54½ years" by her reckoning, will appear, gloved fingers dancing on the piano keys, at Marty's in a two-week engagement starting tonight.

chaos   *KAY ahs*
(extreme confusion or disorder)

My overwhelming observation is that history is neither the product of design nor of conspiracy but is rather the reflection of continuing chaos. Seen from the outside, decisions may often seem clear and consciously formulated; interrelations between governments may seem to be the products of deliberately crafted, even if often conflicting, policies. [Zbigniew Brzezinski]

charade   shuh RAYD
(a pretense that continues even though both sides in a controversy or
relationship see its transparent falseness: after charades, a game in which
words or phrases to be guessed are acted out in pantomime)

When angry baseball players and club owners broke off their latest meeting, Mr. Moffett said he would not call them back together until he heard "something positive" from both sides. "It's kind of futile and sort of stupid," Mr. Moffett commented, "just to be going through a charade of getting together on a regular basis when there's no movement as far as the parties are concerned."

charisma   kuh RIZ muh
(a strong personal appeal or magnetism)

And Mr. Vidnovic, who made his mark in the recent revivals of "Brigadoon" and "Oklahoma!" is more than simply professional. He is every inch a star. With his flashing eyes, commanding baritone and bursting physical exuberance, he exudes more charisma than any Broadway leading man in years.

charismatic   ka riz MA tik
(the designation of various religious groups or movements that stress
divine inspiration, manifested by speaking in tongues, healing by the
laying on of hands, etc.)

Many sat barefoot on the floor and held Bibles. For the first half hour, they sang Jesus songs, raising their hands in the air in the charismatic invoking of the Holy Spirit, and many spoke in tongues.

charlatan   SHAHR luh tuhn
(a person who pretends to have expert knowledge or skill; fake)

In Egypt the Mayor met with President Anwar el-Sadat, whom he had met as early as 1975 when Mr. Koch was a Congressman. At that time, the Mayor was uncertain whether the Egyptian leader was a "charlatan or a great statesman." "I have concluded," Mr. Koch says, "that he is in fact one of the world's great statesmen adored by his subjects."

chasm   *KA zuhm*
(a wide divergence of feelings, sentiments, interests, etc.; rift)

A poll taken by WNBC and The Associated Press as people emerged from voting places showed chasms between white and black attitudes. Asked if "Mayor Koch really cares about people like me," 68 percent of the blacks said no, while 54 percent of the whites said yes.

chauvinism   *SHOH vi ni zuhm*
(fanatical patriotism; jingoism; unreasoning devotion to one's race, sex, etc., with contempt for other races, the opposite sex, etc.)

Food chauvinism is among the most virulent of all prejudices, and perhaps the most dogmatic of all food chauvinists are clam chowder devotees. In New England, where the American version of clam chowder originated, the three warring factions (clear broth, cream broth and Rhode Island-style pale tomato broth) have planted their respective flags over the territory, and woe to anyone who challenges them.

Nicolas Chauvin was a soldier in Napoleon's army who, even after the final defeat at Waterloo, retained such enthusiasm for Napoleon, and so often sang out his praises, that he made a ridiculous figure of himself. Characters based on Chauvin were written into several French plays of the time, and that helped to spread his name as a synonym for excessive patriotism. *Chauvinism* is one of the many thousands of eponyms in our language, words which have sprung from the name of a person, place or thing. Some others are: aphrodisiac, hector, mentor, pander, dunce, babel, mecca, maudlin, chimera, guy, lynch, boycott, quisling, quixotic, tantalize, macadamize, vandal, assassin, malapropism, bowdlerize, panic, stentorian, sandwich, shrapnel, derrick, guillotine, silhouette, dahlia, wisteria, ohm, volt, ampere, watt, champagne, cognac, sherry, cashmere, mesmerize, bedlam, damask, cynical, serendipity.

---

cheek by jowl   *cheek bigh jowl*
(close together; side by side)

Cheek by jowl were tabletop flea markets, health-care information desks, a live honeybee display, block association stands, a Shetland pony ride and the Knights of Columbus booth.

cheeky   *CHEE ki*
(saucy; impudent; insolent)

Mr. Geary has distinguished himself from the plastic stereotype of soap opera males with his cheekiness, sense of humor and "mod" wardrobe. True to his claim in a Saturday press conference that "Luke Spencer is a very specific facet" of his own personality, Mr. Geary growled, wise-cracked, hammed it up, kissed his admirers and generally displayed Luke's usually winning disregard for social convention.

chef d'oeuvre   *she DER vruh*
(a masterpiece: French)

"S.O.B.," Blake Edwards's hilarious chef d'oeuvre of bile, slapstick, ill will and hurt feelings, is set in a paranoid's vision of a Hollywood populated entirely by people double- and triple-crossing each other.

chichi   *SHEE shee*
(very smart or sophisticated: usually used in a somewhat derogatory sense, suggesting affectation, showiness, effeteness, etc.: French)

"Neil Simon writes exactly the way I talk," Mr. Matthau notes. "That is, the more serious the situation, the funnier he gets. His humor is ironic, sardonic, sweetly sarcastic, just like mine. I know the chichi critics say that Simon is shallow, but that's because they feel something has to be incomprehensible to be profound."

chide   *chighd*
(to scold; now, usually, to reprove mildly)

Jody Powell, spokesman for Jimmy Carter, chided the Reagan Administration yesterday for what he called a "basically false" report that Mr. Carter had applied for the privilege of shopping at low-cost post exchanges on military bases.

chivvy   *CHI vi*
(to nag; manipulate)

The late Jean Monnet, who imagined and chivvied into existence what is now known as the European Community, was insistent about institutions. Their creation is the one way people can apply the lessons of experience and escape the raw repetition of collective follies, he felt. In another fashion, the late President de Gaulle also stressed institutions as the key to coherent society.

chockablock   *CHAHK uh blahk*
(crowded or jammed)

When news programs produced no profits, audience ratings didn't matter. Now, the primary goal for a local newscast is generally no different than it is for a prime-time series: achieving the largest possible audience. And the method is often the same too: aim for the lowest common denominator. "Live at Five," for example, is chockablock with five-minute celebrity interviews.

chronicle   *KRAH ni kuhl*
(to tell or write the history of; record; recount)

The film, which is none too frank about Elvis's problems, nonetheless closely chronicles his decline. The polite, bashful fellow who beams with pride when Ed Sullivan pronounces him "a real decent fine boy" becomes flashy, bloated and crude. The Elvis whose face is so fresh and unguarded, whose expression reveals so much when the press asks him about his sweetheart or his mama, becomes a glassy-eyed wreck.

chuck   *chuhk*
(to discard; get rid of; quit: a slang word)

The academy's graduates include two former highway patrolmen, a former United Press International photographer, a former film and drama critic and an actor, as well as art historians, plumbers and teachers who decided to chuck it all to become chefs.

chutzpah   *KHOOTS pah*
(the *ch* is gutteral, as in the German *Ach!*)
(gall, brazen nerve, effrontery, incredible "guts"; presumption-plus-arrogance such as no other word, and no other language, can do justice to—definition by Leo Rosten, in "The Joys of Yiddish": *a Hebrew word, via Yiddish)*

"Anybody who has got the chutzpah and the gall," Mr. Berger said, "to try and convince us that, in an election year, saying that we don't need a fare increase is not political, has got to be taking us all for fools." Deputy Mayor Robert F. Wagner Jr. objected to Mr. Berger's remarks by shouting, "That's a cheap shot."

Cinderella   *sin duh RE luh*
(a person or thing whose merit, value, beauty, etc., is for a time unrecognized)

If the oboe ever manages to rival the flute as a popular solo instrument, Heinz Holliger will probably be regarded as the musician who started it all. The 41-year-old Swiss oboist, in New York for a recital at the Metropolitan Museum of Art tomorrow night at 8, has been acclaimed all over the world for his virtuosity and compelling musicianship on this Cinderella of instruments.

cinéma vérité *si nay MAH vay ri TAY*

(a type of documentary film or film making that attempts to capture the sense of documentary realism by spontaneous interviews, the use of a hand-held camera and a minimum of editing of the footage: French)

"Best Boy," a documentary by Ira Wohl, was first shown at the 1979 New York Film Festival and then shown again in New York a year later. It is about Philly, a 52-year-old retarded man, and his elderly parents, and whereas the most common criticism of cinéma vérité is that it exploits, distorts and ridicules, there was general agreement among film critics that "Best Boy" was done with the best of intentions. They said it was moving, intelligent and full of love.

circuitous *ser KYOO: i tuhs*

(taking a roundabout, lengthy course)

The livery car turned west across Allen Street's two-way traffic and rushed into Rivington Street, with the police car in pursuit. A circuitous chase went south on the next street, Eldridge, then east on Delancey, and back north on Allen, amid light Sunday traffic.

circumscribe *SER kuhm skrighb*

(limit; confine; restrict)

To eyes uninitiated into the subtleties of traditional Buddhist dance and music, the dance was fairly circumscribed ritual movement and gesture built on slow pivoting turns, hops and wreathing of hands and arms, performed at a stately, gracious pace to the deep roar of long horns, low-voiced drums, trumpets, cymbals and muted chants.

circumvent *ser kuhm VENT*

(to overcome by artful maneuvering; prevent from happening by craft or ingenuity)

More than 20 years ago Mr. Kavanagh made headlines when he painstakingly hand-printed a work called "The John Quinn Letters." The letters of Mr. Quinn, deceased, who was a distinguished patron of the arts, were available only to scholars at the special-manuscripts room of the New York Public Library, provided they were read but not copied or quoted from directly. Mr. Kavanagh circumvented these caveats by memorizing parts of the letters, dashing repeatedly out to Bryant Park, jotting those parts down and eventually printing his book. A court brouhaha ensued, ending when Mr. Kavanagh destroyed most of his printing.

civility   *suh VI luh ti*
(politeness; courtesy; decency in behavior toward)

To the Editor: In his March 30 reply to my March 16 letter, Carlos Fuentes, while breaking no new ground, sets a dubious standard for civility by saying that perhaps I was "ill" the day I read his March 5 Op-Ed article.

clandestine   *klan DE stin*
(kept secret or hidden, especially for some illicit purpose; done without the knowledge of those who would regulate or punish such actions)

Mr. Mercer said there are no open slave markets [in Mauritania] but that men, woman and children are bought and sold clandestinely, traded from one master to another. He did not know the going price for a slave but said a young woman had been sold to a suitor by her owner, an Islamic judge, for 2,000 British pounds, the equivalent of $1,870. The biggest trade is in children, the report said.

claque   *klak*
(a group of admiring or fawning followers; also, a group of people paid to go to a performance and applaud)

Miss Scotto is hailed by some as the successor to Maria Callas (as in a nonmusical sense, Jacqueline Kennedy Onassis was) but is damned by others as "Renata Screecho." Miss Scotto has a fiercely loyal claque who will follow her to hell, but she also has a group of growling standees who profoundly distrust her talent. One claque wildly applauds the least laudable of her performances while the anti-claque claque comes ready to hiss and boo at her slightest off-key note. She is the Al Haig of the Metropolitan.

class action   *KLAS AK shun*
(a legal action brought by one or more persons on behalf of themselves and a much larger group, all of whom have the same grounds for action)

Now local white fishermen and the Klan have been accused in a lawsuit of conspiring to threaten and intimidate the Vietnamese into leaving. The case pits two longtime courtroom enemies against each other—the Klan and the Klanwatch organization, an arm of the Southern Poverty Law Center in Birmingham, Ala., that filed the class action lawsuit on behalf of the Vietnamese fishermen.

classicist   *KLA si sist*
*(one whose attitudes or principles adhere to the traditional or standard
methods and pursuits of a field, rather than to the acceptance of new or
experimental directions)*

Classicists believe that botanical research should be confined to the sys-
tematic exploration and analysis of the plant world. More and more
botanists, however, have come to believe that they are failing in their
obligations to society if they do not apply their knowledge to solving
global problems such as hunger and energy shortages.

cleave   *kleev*
(to adhere; cling to; be faithful to)

There is only one tax cut that cleaves closest to fairness, makes sense and
deserves instant support. Each year, let the Government say to one tax-
payer in 10: This year, you don't have to pay any Federal income tax.

(to split; separate; divide)

Six warships of the North Atlantic alliance, their gliding silhouettes cleav-
ing the choppy bay waters and the early morning mists, sailed into New
York Harbor yesterday to signal the start of the city's 1981 Harbor Festival over the Fourth of July weekend.

Cleave has the paradoxical quality of having two meanings that
are the opposite of each other.

---

cliffhanger   *KLIF hang er*
*(an early type of movie serial, each episode ending with a suspenseful
climax—such as the hero hanging from a cliff—that induced the viewer
to return to see the next part: now often used figuratively, as when
describing a meeting that is recessed just before a crucial vote)*

One man swears that his mother hypnotized him into eating. "She'd make
up cliffhangers, really thrilling adventures. If I didn't eat, she wouldn't
tell me the ending. And sometimes she got so carried away, she'd keep
piling more food on my plate and I'd keep right on eating just so the story
could continue."

clique   *kleek*
(a small, exclusive circle of people)

Mr. Sadat will make his speech in a new development town called May
Fifteen. The town's name commemorates May 15, 1971, when Mr. Sadat

quashed a clique that was attempting to oust him from office. The episode is referred to as "the corrective revolution."

cloying *KLOI ing*
(having an excess of a quality, as sweetness, richness or sentimentality, to the point of arousing distaste or disgust)

Like so many restaurants with an expressionist chef who free associates, [it] falls down on main courses, primarily because intricate and complicated flavorings and food combinations that can be diverting in appetizer-size portions become cloying in larger amounts.

coalesce *koh uh LES*
(to unite or merge into a single body, group or mass)

In the beginning, circa 1975, "Saturday Night Live" offered a kind of outrageous sassiness that served as a refreshing antidote to the normal blandness of television entertainment. In a year or two, the program had reached its peak, coalescing in a superb ensemble that included Chevy Chase, Gilda Radner, John Belushi and Dan Aykroyd.

coalition *koh uh LI shuhn*
(a temporary alliance for some specific purpose)

A coalition of six local unions is scheduled to meet this morning with negotiators for The News and The Times to discuss the wage pattern set by the deliverers. The coalition includes mailers, photoengravers, paper handlers, electricians and two machinist locals.

cocksure *kahk shoor*
(sure or self-confident in a stubborn or overbearing way)

Teamster leaders have long rejected complaints against the union. From Daniel J. Tobin, who guided the union almost 50 years, through Mr. Fitzsimmons, they have been tough-minded and cocksure. "Problems have a way of solving themselves," Mr. Hoffa was quoted as telling Ralph C. James and Estelle D. James for their 1965 book, "Hoffa and the Teamsters." "If you stall long enough, the troubles, or troublemakers, will disappear." He also said: "I don't trust anybody; everybody has his price."

coffer *KAW fer*
(a treasury; funds: a coffer is a chest or strongbox in which money or valuables are kept)

Alaska's coffers were so bulging with oil and other mineral royalties, that the state announced a treasury giveaway in April 1980. The Legislature voted to end the income tax for most residents, refund all income taxes paid in 1979 and 1980 and distribute a cash dividend every year to each resident 18 years or older.

Doublets, like *coffer* and *coffin*, are two or more words derived from the same original word but reaching English through different routes and currently used with different meanings. *Dish* (from Old English) and *disk* (from Latin) stem from the Latin *discus*. Other doublets: frail/fragile; gentle/genteel; amicable/amiable; major/mayor; particle/parcel; potion/poison; secure/sure; balsam/balm; adamant/diamond; scandal/slander; whole/hale; no/nay; from/fro; shirt/skirt; liquor/liquid; guarantee/warrantee; channel/canal; shatter/scatter.

---

cognoscenti   *koh nyoh SHEN ti*
(people with special knowledge in a field, especially the arts; expert: often used with a flavor of irony)

It used to be that only the cognoscenti knew about the New York City Ballet-affiliated School of American Ballet's annual spring workshop performances, which will take place tomorrow night and Monday afternoon and evening at the Juilliard Theater at Lincoln Center.

cohabitation   *koh ha bi TAY shuhn*
(living together as husband and wife, especially when not legally married)

The highest state courts in Maine, South Dakota and Oklahoma recently have held that if a divorced person who receives alimony from a former spouse begins to live with a new lover without remarrying, the cohabitation does not entitle the former spouse to stop paying alimony.

colloquy   *KAH luh kwi*
(a conversation, especially a formal discussion; conference)

LOS ANGELES—Last Sunday morning, as millions of people were leisurely celebrating Easter, 60 men and women from several continents met in a hotel conference room for an intense three-hour colloquy entitled "The Behavior of Large Corporations."

collusion   *kuh LOO: zhuhn*
(a secret agreement for a fraudulent or illegal purpose; conspiracy)

Rabbi William Berkowitz, president of the Jewish National Fund, said the P.L.O. was operating out of southern Lebanon with the collusion of Syria and with increasing supplies of Soviet-bloc and Libyan weapons.

combative   *kuhm BA tiv*
(ready or eager to fight; pugnacious)

A good way to get rid of a resting bee, without panic, Mr. Auditore says, is to blow on him. "They're susceptible to wind and more often than not if you blow on them they'll fly away. I would go so far as to say that they are friends," he says. "They're very docile. You never find two bees fighting over a blossom, for example. They *never* fight. They're not combative. And always remember, if there weren't any bees, nothing in the city would be green."

comely   *KUHM li*
(pleasant to look at; attractive; fair)

Several times since he started punching people for pay in 1972, Bobby Chacon lost his enthusiasm for the Sweet Science. For anyone watching on television Saturday while Cornelius Boza-Edwards took fungo practice on Bobby's comely head, it was not difficult to understand why. There are many pleasanter ways to earn a living, including being shot out of a cannon at county fairs.

commemorative   *kuh ME muh ruh tiv*
(a postage stamp bearing a design and inscription honoring a person, place or thing, or depicting a notable aspect of a country's culture, wildlife, history, etc.)

The 300th anniversary of the birth of the composer Georg Philipp Telemann is this Saturday, and it has been marked by West Germany with a 60-pfennig commemorative with a contemporary portrait of him over a background of the music of one of his cantatas.

commensurate   *kuh MEN shoo rit*
(proportionate)

The treasure to be found on the sunken British warship Edinburgh probably far exceeds that recently retrieved from the liner Andrea Doria, and the risks are commensurate.

commiserate   *kuh MI zuh rayt*
(to sympathize)

I caught the obituary of a dear friend last week. She and I had been counselors in the same children's camp during our college summers. We'd kept in tenuous touch for 50 years, sharing secrets and strategies, following each other's marriages, divorces, remarriages, rejoicing over each other's professional achievements and commiserating at the setbacks. But I hadn't seen her for years.

commodious   *kuh MOH di uhs*
(*spacious; roomy*)

The bus in which the members of my group were traveling could penetrate the thick stone city walls easily enough through commodious archways. But the store-lined boulevards were often jammed solidly with bicyclists. The bus driver could inch forward only by intimidating them with his horn.

compatriot   *kuhm PAY tri uht*
(*a person of the same country*)

One of the more consistent and perplexing prejudices encountered in traveling around the world is the feeling of superiority northerners of almost any country have for their southern compatriots; if, in fact, they even consider them as such. ("It is really another country down there," one often hears them say.)

compendium   *kuhm PEN di uhm*
(*a brief compilation derived from a total field of knowledge*)

Across town, the Museum of Broadcasting at 1 East 53d Street has dipped into its collection of television programs to put together "Satire in the Air," a compendium of television programs from 1961 to now. It includes "That Was The Week That Was," "Saturday Night Live" and "Laugh-In," as well as programs with Jack Benny and the Smothers Brothers.

complacency   *kuhm PLAY suhn si*
(*quiet satisfaction; contentment; self-satisfaction; smugness*)

Riis's pictures of life at the bottom of society—in this case, lived out in the hovels of the Lower East Side—are now firmly established among the classics of photojournalism. They remain very powerful—pictures that disturb our complacency and remain fixed in the mind, with their details of filth and squalor. There is nothing about them that makes their images of suffering picturesque. They were intended to upset us, and they still do.

Jacob Riis (1849–1914) was born in Denmark and emigrated to New York in 1870. As a police reporter he became familiar with the city's slums; and through books, articles and photographs he campaigned to improve tenement conditions, urged the institution of child-labor laws, and exposed the exploitation of the poor. His best known book is "How the Other Half Lives" (1890).

complement *KAHM pluh ment*
(something that completes, makes up a whole or brings to perfection)

The two men respect each other, and they speak of how they complement each other—Mr. Perella with his intuitive approach to closing deals and Mr. Wasserstein with his strategic thinking.

complicity *kuhm PLI suh ti*
(partnership in wrongdoing)

A Frankfurt court today sentenced William Backhus, a 45-year-old American private detective, to four years in jail for complicity in procuring a chemical for the manufacture of LSD from a Hamburg company.

composure *kuhm POH zher*
(calmness of mind or manner; self-possession)

Mrs. Harris reacted with the composure that has become her hallmark during the often-agonizing testimony about the shooting death of Dr. Herman Tarnower, the author and physician who for most of 14 years had been her companion and lover: chin up, eyes clear, blinking slightly.

conceit *kuhn SEET*
(a small, imaginatively designed item)

Candied violets are used in ꞏꞏy home to decorate custard desserts, such as an English custard, white and yellow ice creams, yellow puddings and so on. They are, as I have stated often, my favorite conceit where dessert garnishes are concerned.

concomitant *kahn KAH muh tuhnt*
(accompanying; attendant)

Your eyes are small, red and runny; your nose is large, red and runny; and your sneezes rock the room. "Nobody ever died of hay fever," your friends say. A lot they know. Thanks to a spring drought, however, and a concomitant drop in the production of ragweed, this year promises to be less of a misery than any since the mid-60's.

concrete   *kahn KREET*
(specific, not general or abstract)

GDANSK, Poland, Sept. 6—Solidarity leaders said today that the union must expand its role and come up with a concrete program to lead Poland out of its economic crisis.

concurrence   *kuhn KER uhns*
(a happening together in time or place)

The 52 Americans were freed only minutes after Ronald Reagan was sworn in as the 40th President of the United States. The concurrence in timing held millions of Americans at their radios and television sets, following the pageantry of Inauguration Day and the news of the hostages' release.

condescending   *kahn duh SEN ding*
(disguising one's disdain by obvious indulgence or patience)

Pleasant, amusing, a good performance: these are the sorts of expressions evoked by "Voices in the Garden," Dirk Bogarde's second novel. They are not necessarily condescending, for how many novels can you call pleasant or amusing?

condominium   *kahn duh MI ni uhm*
(a joint rule by two or more states)

Until Vanuatu gained independence last July, Paris and London ruled the archipelago, formerly the New Hebrides, whose romantic beauty was celebrated by James A. Michener in his "Tales of the South Pacific." The Anglo-French condominium set up two of everything on the island: school systems, police forces, courts, languages, currencies and more.

A condominium, in its popularly known American sense, is an apartment house held by joint ownership: Each apartment is bought and owned individually as if it were a house. The land the building is on is usually held by a corporation.

---

confidante   *KAHN fuh dahnt*
(a close, trusted friend, to whom one confides intimate matters or secrets)

LISBON, May 22 (Reuters)—Maria Caetano Freire, the lifelong companion, secretary and housekeeper of the former dictator Antonio de Oliveira Salazar, died here today. Her exact age was unknown, but she was believed to be in her 80's. Known throughout Portugal as "Dona Maria," she guarded access to Mr. Salazar, keeping him abreast of popular gossip and acting as a confidante to the bachelor Prime Minister.

configuration   *kuhn fi gyuh RAY shuhn*
(*arrangement of parts*)

Architects who specialize in children's rooms stress simple, floor-oriented spaces that are flexible enough to provide for changing configurations as children's ages change and to accommodate children's own creativity in arranging their environments.

conflagration   *kahn fluh GRAY shuhn*
(*a big, destructive fire: as used here, a war*)

"The Middle East, as one prominent American observed last week, provides combustible matter for international conflagration akin to the Balkans prior to World War I, a circumstance made all the more dangerous today by the possibility that nuclear weapons could be employed in a future conflict." [Jeane J. Kirkpatrick]

confluence   *KAHN floo: uhns*
(*a flowing together of two or more streams*)

The Robbers Roost Ranch, five miles from town, is the classic Western ranch. It has 26,000 acres, almost twice as many as the island of Manhattan. The ranch buildings, some of the cabins 60 years old, are at the confluence of the two rivers that run through its dry land, Rock Creek and the Medicine Bow.

conglomerate   *kuhn GLAH muh rit*
(*a large corporation formed by the merger of a number of companies in unrelated, widely diversified industries*)

Working out of paper-strewn offices here on busy Burbank Boulevard, Steve Allen is a virtual one-man media conglomerate. His versatility qualifies him as a personal hedge against the uneven nature of the sundry entertainment businesses. If a television series is out of favor with the Nielsen ratings, there's always songwriting. If the book business is sluggish, there's always the nightclub act.

conjurer   *KAHN jer er*
(a magician)

The 52-year-old Mr. Schindler put himself through Brooklyn College with magic and now makes a living with it at conventions, bar mitzvahs, theaters, industrial shows and the other stopping places of practicing conjurers.

consecrate   *KAHN suh KRAYT*
(to make or declare sacred for religious use)

Current Catholic theology teaches that only ordained celibate men may consecrate the bread and wine that symbolize the body and blood of Christ.

consort   *KAHN sawrt*
(an ensemble of musicians or musical instruments)

The ear-tickling sounds of shawms, recorders, krummhorns, dulcians, racketts, cornettos, sackbuts, lutes and viols in consort can be festive enough to suit almost any occasion.

consternation   *kahn ster NAY shuhn*
(great fear or shock that makes one feel helpless or bewildered)

Twice a day the twin towers of New York's World Trade Center rise and fall about 14 inches. They also tilt about two inches, first to the west and then to the east. Such behavior by the city's tallest structures might cause consternation were it not for the fact that all of New York responds in the same way to the passage of earth tides, the terrestrial counterpart of ocean tides, as do all land masses, to a greater or lesser degree.

constraint   *kuhn STRAYNT*
(restriction; confinement)

Like senior officers of all services, the admiral says he is worried by a Soviet buildup at Vietnam's Cam Ranh Bay. The stationing of strong forces there, he said, would enable the Soviet Pacific Fleet to escape its geographical constraints. To reach the open Pacific from the naval base at Vladivostok, Soviet surface ships and submarines have to pass through two straights.

It was Magellan, in 1520, who gave it its name—the Pacific Ocean —because he found its weather and waters pacific (peaceful;

calm; tranquil) after his stormy voyage through what is now the
Straits of Magellan.

---

consummate   *KAHN suh mayt*
(to bring to completion; accomplish)

The merger, if consummated, would create one of the world's strongest
financial services organizations, rivaling in services, though not in size,
even Merrill Lynch & Company.

Mating occurs only once in the life of the female blue crab, just after her
final molt, and the affair must be consummated in a short period of time.

kuhn SOO: mit
(supreme; very skillful; highly expert)

Mr. Sinatra can phrase a conversational song or a standard pop ballad like
nobody in the business. Those teasing hesitations, those dramatic asides
that only rarely lapse into melodrama, those gruff percussive attacks—
they add up to a consummate stylist.

contention   *kuhn TEN shuhn*
(a statement or point that one argues for as true or valid)

Despite Iraq's contention that the nuclear reactor that was destroyed by
Israel was purely for research, American specialists remain baffled as to
its real purpose, noting that its reported power rating of 40 megawatts
is not typical of research installations.

contentious   *kuhn TEN shuhs*
(involving or characterized by dispute; controversial)

Within the Church of England, which still forbids the remarriage of
divorced people, a meeting of the general synod next month is expected
to be dominated by a contentious proposal that the ban be eased. The
theological debate was heightened recently by the disclosure that an
Anglican bishop in Derbyshire, a 62-year-old widower, had himself married a divorcée.

contiguous   *kuhn TI gyoo uhs*
(in physical contact; touching along all or most of one side)

The Washakie, named after a Shoshone chief, is the first among 220
wilderness preserves in the 48 contiguous states where oil and gas de-

velopment may be allowed under a little-known provision of the 1964 act that allows oil, gas and mineral activity in the areas until Dec. 31, 1983.

contraband   *KAHN truh band*
(*smuggled*)

NEWARK (UPI)—Correction officers at the Essex County Jail Annex, acting on a tip from a prison informant, confiscated an arsenal of contraband weapons intended for use in an uprising, officials said. Warden Donald Schmidt said that the weapons—knives, scissors, pipes, wooden clubs, rock slings and blackjacks—were to be used in an attack on Monday.

contrapuntal   *kahn truh PUHN tuhl*
(*relating to* counterpoint: *the art of adding a related but independent melody or melodies to a basic melody, in accordance with the fixed rules of harmony, to make a harmonic whole*)

No one knows precisely what instrument or instruments Bach had in mind for his Art of Fugue, a monument of contrapuntal composition he left unfinished at his death. It can be performed on harpsichord and organ and by ensembles of various kinds and, in any case, must always be given in a practical arrangement devised by someone other than the composer. Chances are that this would not have bothered Bach at all.

contrition   *kuhn TRI shuhn*
(*a feeling of remorse for sins or wrongdoing*)

Mehmet Ali Agca, the 23-year-old Turkish militant accused of attempting to murder Pope John Paul II last week, gave no sign of contrition today as his police interrogation ended and he was moved to a civil prison. "I am sorry for the two foreign tourists but not for the Pope," he shouted in English to reporters while two policemen armed with submachine guns hustled him across the courtyard of the Rome police headquarters to an armored van.

conversant   *kuhn VER suhnt*
(*familiar or acquainted with, especially as a result of study or experience; well versed in*)

Even someone thoroughly conversant with Shakespeare's language will fail to catch every word in performance unless he has recently re-read the work.

copacetic   *koh puh SE tik*
*(fine; excellent: the word has been attributed to the entertainer Bill
"Bojangles" Robinson (1878–1949), but whether he coined the word,
or just popularized it, is uncertain)*

James Lopez, the Marine Guard, described the Christmas services as "a
dog and pony show," and he expressed bitterness about the visit by
clergymen the following Easter, too. He was shocked, he said, to learn
that the clerics were "saying conditions were nice and everything was
copacetic and we were having such a good time in Camp Teheran. We
couldn't believe that they were actually buying that garbage the Iranians
were putting out."

copious   *KOH pi uhs*
(plentiful; abundant)

He was able to reconstruct conversations with people long dead because
he had kept copious notes. Mr. Hoving said, "I'm a compulsive writer,
and I habitually keep a daily journal in which I note even the shade of a
person's complexion when I speak with them."

cornerstone   *KAWR ner stohn*
(the basic, essential or most important part; foundation)

Historically the British have passionately protected their privacy, the
cornerstone of their manners and morals. When the idea of a census was
first raised here in 1753 it provoked heated debate. William Thornton,
a Member of Parliament, charged that it was "totally subversive of the last
remains of English liberty."

corniche   *KAWR nish*
(a roadway that winds along a cliff or steep slope: French, cornice*)*

There were still scores of strollers and picnickers along the corniche
overlooking the Mediterranean, as is usual on Sundays, but they shied
away from the usually crowded corner near the American Embassy.

cornucopia   *kawr nuh KOH pi uh*
(an overflowing fullness; abundance)

The six-day fair—this year's is the 136th—ends Sunday. It is open 10
A.M. to midnight and offers a cornucopia of events, agricultural and
otherwise, on a 140-acre site.

In Greek myth, the cornucopia (literally, horn of plenty) was a horn of the goat that suckled Zeus: it would become full of whatever its owner wanted. More commonly, the cornucopia is the horn represented in painting and sculpture overflowing with fruit, flowers and grain.

corpulent   KAWR pyuh luhnt
(*stout; obese; fat*)

For years, this weight-obsessed nation has considered fatness and slimness matters of willpower. The corpulent are blamed—by others or by guilty conscience—for a disgusting inability to turn down dessert. And the verdict is surely just in some cases. But more and more evidence suggests that many fat people may be in the grip of biochemical forces that are indeed hard to control.

corpus   KAWR puhs
(*a complete or comprehensive collection*)

Hundreds of symphonies in a dizzying variety of styles have been written since 1911, but the one corpus of work that seems to be entering the standard repertory is the set of 15 written by Dmitri Shostakovich.

corroborate   kuh RAH buh rayt
(*to confirm; bolster; support*)

Mr. Begin gave no details on his accusation that Soviet advisers were going into Lebanon, except to say that they usually traveled with large Syrian units. Today, Israeli military officials were unable or unwilling to offer any corroborating evidence of the Prime Minister's charge.

cosset   KAH sit
(*to treat like a pet; pamper*)

As the producer who persuaded Elizabeth Taylor to make her Broadway debut in "The Little Foxes," Zev Bufman knows how to cosset, pamper and otherwise please his star. He is said to have spent more than $20,000 to redecorate Miss Taylor's dressing room in her favorite color, lavender, and, on opening night last Thursday, to have given her a small, perfect diamond.

coterie   KOH tuh ri
(*a close group of people who share a common interest*)

For almost 30 years El Charro on Charles Street in Greenwich Village has had a loyal coterie that has come to rely on certain dishes.

coterminous   *koh TER muh nuhs*
(having a common boundary; contiguous: same as "conterminous")

There will be no total eclipse next year, and none visible from the coterminous United States until the next century.

countervail   *kown ter VAYL*
(to counteract; be successful or useful against)

The church has become the principal countervailing power in Brazil to the governing military because of its involvement in social issues, but it has not drawn the same support from the Brazilian public in matters of social morality. Divorce and civil weddings have come to Brazil despite the church's opposition, and about six million Brazilian women, 90 percent of them Catholic, are believed to be using birth-control pills.

coup   *koo:*
(a sudden, successful move or action; brilliant stroke)

It was a dinner for a few "chums," said Pat Buckley, but to the social world that follows such things with a microscopic and sometimes jaundiced eye, it was a coup. For the guest of honor was the First Lady, and the party Monday night at the Buckley maisonette just off Park Avenue was the first such event that Nancy Reagan had attended in New York since the Inauguration.

courtly   *KAWRT li*
(suitable for a king's court; dignified; polite; elegant)

The Wimbledon championships are under way, that courtly gathering of knights and ladies, the beauty and chivalry of the All England Lawn Tennis and Croquet Club with its strawberries and cream, its white gloves and flowery hats, meticulously manicured lawns and impeccable manners. It is also the stage on which a spoiled brat like John McEnroe can demonstrate how ugly an ugly American can get.

couture   *koo TOO:R*
(women's clothes in new or specially designed fashions)

Designers in the United States no longer flock to couture shows to copy line for line what Paris designers are doing. They have developed their own confidence to the point where they feel they know better what their customers want to wear.

covet   *KUH vit*
(to want ardently, especially something that another person has; long for with envy)

One of the largest private butterfly collections in the Western Hemisphere, one that had been coveted by several American museums, has been donated to the University of Florida in Gainesville, university officials have announced.

crass   *kras*
(grossly stupid, dull or obtuse)

[Malcolm Forbes's] chums all arrived with packages, because although the host would never be crass enough to ask for gifts, he did put a postscript on his invitations that read, "Since it's a surprise party, don't tell me what you're bringing."

creature comforts   *KREE chir KUM ferts*
(anything providing bodily comfort, as food, clothing or shelter)

"Americans were spoiled by the muscle cars," Mr. Bishop said, referring to the powerful American cars produced during the 1960's. "Those cars had huge road performances, as well as air-conditioning and all the other creature comforts you could want."

"A very strong smell of brandy and water forewarned the visitor that Mr. Squeers had been seeking in creature comforts a temporary forgetfulness of his unpleasant situation."
Charles Dickens, "Nicholas Nickleby."

---

crescendo   *kruh SHEN doh*
(a gradual increase in loudness or intensity)

As the London social season races toward the crescendo of The Wedding, it has acquired in this special year a glamour not seen in decades. Parties range from the Earl of Effingham's decorous little back garden cocktail party this week for members of the House of Lords to Prince Andrew's birthday bash for 500 at Windsor Castle last Friday.

crestfallen   *KREST faw luhn*
(dejected, dispirited or depressed)

An American woman who is a resident of Peking and who enrolled her 5-year-old son in the Peking No. 1 kindergarten this fall was crestfallen when she was told that her child was the only one in his class who misbehaved.

criterion   *krigh TI ri uhn*
(a standard, rule or test by which something can be judged)

The criterion for insanity in criminal trials here is the standard formulated by the American Law Institute. It states that "a person is not responsible for criminal conduct if at the time of such conduct, as a result of mental disease or defect, he lacks substantial capacity to appreciate the wrongfulness of his conduct or to conform his conduct to the requirements of the law."

cross-over   *KRAWS OH ver*
(in music, to cross over in style, as from jazz to rock; or in appeal, as from a jazz to a rock audience)

The Commodores, the pop-soul sextet, who will be singing tonight, tomorrow and Sunday night at 8 at the Radio City Music Hall, are probably today's most successful black cross-over group, having scored hits in all three major categories—pop, rhythm and blues, and country.

cul-de-sac   *kuhl duh SAK*
(a dead-end street; blind alley)

SADDLE RIVER, N.J., June 11—Mr. and Mrs. Richard M. Nixon plan to buy for $1 million a modern home on a quiet cul-de-sac near a peach orchard in this small, wealthy community in northern Bergen County, an aide to the former President said today.

"When I write I get so wrapped up in another world that I sometimes forget appointments and people's names. When I reached a cul-de-sac in my writing I'd finally try to pay attention to other things." [Toni Morrison]

cull   *kuhl*
(to select and gather)

More than 110 distinguished collections of American, Asian and European antiques culled from 16 states and overseas will be on display.

cult   *kuhlt*

(a group of people sharing an esoteric interest or an obsessive devotion or veneration for a person, principle or ideal)

According to current Nielson figures, 42 percent of "General Hospital" viewers are under 25. And this count does not include the thousands of college students forming a cult that rivals the collegiate following of "Star Trek" a decade or so ago.

cum   *koom*

(with: used chiefly in hyphenated compounds with the general meaning "combined with" or "plus")

Five months ago, Havana Village, a Cuban restaurant-cum-bar, moved from University Place to 68 Fifth Avenue, at 13th Street, where its spare but attractive Hispanic formality contrasts with the easygoing Sun Belt style of the Lone Star Cafe just across the border on the other side of the avenue.

cynosure   *SIGH nuh shoor*
(any person or thing that is a center of attention or interest)

On the night of Oct. 2, 1979, as Pope John Paul II was paraded in triumph from the right-field bullpen at Yankee Stadium, elevated in clear sight of 80,000 people, the latest of two dozen threats on his life that day was being received by the largest security operation in New York history. The moment was harrowing. Shimmering in white, moving ever so slowly, reaching out for the crowds, the Pope was as much a target as a cynosure.

Cynosure is from the Greek *kynosoura*, dog's tail, and was the old name for Polaris, the North Star, and its constellation, now called Ursa Minor. Because the North Star was essential to navigation, and was carefully observed, its name passed into use as meaning anything that is the center of attention.

---

dacha   *DAH shuh*
(in Russia, a country house or cottage used as a summer home)

Under the Soviet system, the dacha is not simply a bourgeois indulgence; for all except the highest officials, it is a plot of land that the *dachnik* is obligated to cultivate. And so the first wave of *dachniki* fanned out on the suburban trains, lines of city slickers in clean high boots carrying crates of seedlings purchased at the farmers' markets, to work manure into their plots and plant their salads, cucumbers and berries, and to dream of lazier days to come.

The Russian suffix *-nik* means "one who does or is connected with something." It has been used many times since 1957, when Sputnik's successful launch introduced the Space Age, as an American slang suffix, beginning with *beatnik* in the late 1950's, and going on to denote the devotees of various fads, ideas and life styles. A refusenik is a Soviet citizen, especially a Jew, whose application for emigration is rejected.

---

dais   *DAY is*
(a platform raised above the floor at one end of a hall or room, as for a throne, seats of honor, a speaker's stand, etc.)

Burgess Meredith squinted under the glare of the television lights, looked out from the dais across the shimmering pool surrounded by 224 wine enthusiasts crammed into the Four Seasons restaurant and declared: "I'm not here because I'm in the trade. I'm here because I buy more wine than anybody else. So I deserve to be here!"

dalliance   *DA li uhns*
(amorous play; flirting)

Eva Perón came to Buenos Aires from the provinces at the age of 14, an aspiring actress who through her wits and dalliances rose to become mistress and then wife of the populist strongman Juan Domingo Perón.

daunting *DAWN ting*
(making one afraid or discouraged; intimidating; disheartening)

I would say that in most kitchens, professional or otherwise, pastry making is and has been over the centuries the most daunting aspect of cooking. Many a home cook who may be a master of casseroles or a perfectionist when it comes to pastas and pâtés cringes inwardly at the thought of blending flour, fat and liquid to produce a crust for pie.

deadlock *DED lahk*
(a standstill resulting from the action of equal and opposed forces, as when both sides in a strike refuse to budge, or when the members of a jury cannot agree on a verdict; stalemate)

A Federal jury declared yesterday for the second time that it was deadlocked in the mail-fraud and extortion trial of Joseph M. Margiotta, the Nassau County Republican chairman, and that "further deliberation is pointless."

dearth *derth*
(a scarcity or lack)

Mr. Simpson said the Transit Authority had been forced to hire people lacking stated minimum qualifications because of a dearth of qualified applicants.

debacle *day BAH kuhl*
(an overwhelming defeat or rout)

In his one try for elective office, his race for Governor on the Republican ticket in 1934, he [Robert Moses] was defeated by 800,000 votes, the largest margin in New York State history. After the debacle, his administrative power continued unabated, but he never again considered running for office.

debilitating *di BIL uh tay ting*
(making one weak or very tired by sapping one's energy or health)

Having labored mightily to get there, is [Blair Brown] happy as a movie star? Yes and no. "I find the movies I've done to be debilitating. I end up physically weaker. I can't deal too well with the stress. Whereas on stage, I usually end up stronger. I've been working, my voice is strong, my body's strong."

debonair   *de buh NAIR*
(suave; nonchalant)

Before his arrival in Liverpool, Colm knows so little about everything from sex to urban life that he makes John Merrick of "The Elephant Man" look as debonair as Fred Astaire.

debunk   *di BUNGK*
(to expose the false or exaggerated claims of)

Though the notion of a "male menopause" comparable to the hormonal changes that women experience has been soundly debunked, there is considerable evidence that many—if not most—men undergo an unsettled and often life-disrupting period sometime between the ages of 35 and 50.

Bunk, as a synonym for nonsense, had its origin around 1820, when Congressman Felix Walker made a long, tedious and irrelevant speech to Congress, the only purpose of which was to impress the voters back home in Buncombe County, North Carolina. He later explained that he had felt bound to "make a speech for Buncombe." *Buncombe* or *bunkum* (and since 1900 the shortened form, *bunk*) soon became a synonym for empty political claptrap.

---

deciduous   *di SI joo uhs*
(shedding leaves annually: opposed to evergreen)

Plants are living air-conditioners: they evaporate water, cool and can make direct, refreshing breezes. An average full-size deciduous tree such as Norway maple can dissipate as much heat as five 10,000-B.T.U. air-conditioners as long as the temperature is not excessively high. It may also screen 90 percent of the sun's rays and make the shaded area beneath it as much as 20 degrees cooler than the surroundings.

decimate   *DE suh mayt*
(to destroy or kill a large part of: literally, to kill a tenth part of, though rarely used in this sense today)

A wave of bombings, suicide grenade attacks and shootings from speeding motorcycles have succeeded in decimating the top ranks of the clerical leadership. But Ayatollah Khomeini has said there are plenty of Moslems ready to take their places.

decipher   *di SIGH fer*
(to translate a coded message; make out the meaning of ancient inscriptions, illegible writing, etc.)

Gary Betz, a United States Attorney, said that what Mr. Helmich supplied Soviet officials could have been enough for them to make a code machine of their own and decipher American intelligence messages in the Vietnam War.

The Reagan Administration is struggling to decipher an apparent and annoying contradiction: Why, if Mr. Reagan has done so much for business, isn't its applause rolling in? Why, if Wall Street supported his tax cuts, budget cuts and restrictive monetary policies, is The Street now so critical of the Reagan program and driving down the values of stocks and bonds?

decorum   *duh CAW ruhm*
(conformity to social conventions)

Japan is a nation enormously attached to formality, decorum and to a politeness that verges on the exquisite. There is a way to do things and a way not to. Anyone who steps out of line is likely to get into trouble. "The nail that sticks out shall be hammered down," a proverb says.

decry   *di CRIGH*
(to speak out against strongly and openly; denounce)

Reggae developed in the slum areas of Kingston and other Jamaican cities and towns, and the island's poor have always been its core audience. Its lyrics decry racism and economic oppression, and its rhythms are derived from Afro-Jamaican folk sources.

deface   *di FAYS*
(to spoil the appearance of; disfigure; mar)

A team from the National Geographic Society reported last month that magnificent Maya drawings they found in a remote Guatemalan cave had been defaced by thieves trying to saw them off.

deferential   *de fuh REN shuhl*
(yielding in opinion, judgment, wishes, etc.; showing courteous regard or respect)

Mr. Carter said he would write the entire manuscript. "But my contract calls for Bantam to give me an editor of my choice, and I hope it's a tough one, not too deferential to me because I'm a former President," he said.

defile   *di FIGHL*
(a narrow valley or mountain pass)

SION, Switzerland, April 30 (Reuters)—At least three mountaineers were killed by an avalanche on 14,154-foot Grand Combin peak early today, the police said. A team of 30 rescue workers using helicopters and dogs searched the area for three other climbers believed to have belonged to the same group, which was crossing a narrow defile near the Italian border when the snowslide struck.

definitive   *di FI nuh tiv*
(complete and authoritative on a certain subject, said of certain scholarly works)

When it was rumored some years ago that my much admired colleague Waverly Root was engaged in compiling a definitive encyclopedia of food, there were loud huzzahs from my end of the table. Mr. Root is the American-born expatriate now living in France who wrote the definitive English-language book on French gastronomy, "The Food of France" (Knopf, 1958).

defoliant   *di FOH li uhnt*
(a chemical spray that strips growing plants of their leaves)

Mr. Hopkins, a combat veteran, complained that he suffered deafness and other effects from exposure to Agent Orange in Vietnam, a jungle defoliant suspected of causing cancer.

defoliate   *di FOH li ayt*
(to strip of leaves)

Gypsy-moth caterpillars did a record amount of damage in the Northeast in 1981, eating the leaves off trees covering at least nine million acres from Maine to Maryland, according to estimates by forestry experts. That was twice the area defoliated last year, they say.

deft   *deft*
(skillful in a quick, sure and easy way; dexterous)

The victory was especially sweet since the Prince, who distinguished himself with some long, well-placed passes, deft backhands and a goal, had been warned before the match that the New Zealand brand of polo was much rougher than the English variety he is used to.

defunct   *di FUNGKT*
(no longer living or existing; dead or extinct)

Woodchucks hibernate in winter, although not too deeply, and they sometimes pop out of their dens during warm spells. This tendency probably helped create the now nearly defunct custom in certain areas of this nation to attribute weather-forecasting abilities to the creatures.

Woodchuck is among the more than 100 American words borrowed from the Algonquian Indian languages, most during the 17th and 18th centuries. Among the survivors, and the dates of their first recorded use, are:

caribou, 1610	porgy, 1775
caucus, 1745	powwow, 1624
chipmunk, 1841	quahog, 1799
hickory, 1634	raccoon, 1608
hominy, 1629	skunk, 1634
mackinaw, 1827	squash, 1643
moccasin, 1612	squaw, 1634
moose, 1613	terrapin, 1672
opossum, 1610	toboggan, 1829
papoose, 1634	tomahawk, 1612
pecan, 1778	totem, 1609
persimmon, 1612	wampum, 1647
Podunk, 1666	wigwam, 1628
pone, 1612	woodchuck, 1674

---

dégagé   *day gah ZHAY*
(free and easy or unconstrained in manner, attitude, etc.: French)

In the day clothes, hemlines run from knee to calf lengths, though skirts can be artfully draped or full. Mr. Blass has a tendency to tie a knot at the hem of overblouses, tunics and skirts to contribute to the dégagé spirit.

deify   *DEE uh figh*
(to make a god of; glorify, exalt or adore in an extreme way; idolize)

"Eno is God," says the graffiti spray painted on the walls of Greenwich Village and SoHo. Why Brian Eno? In the past, rock musicians were considered worthy of deification only if they were powerfully sensual singers like Elvis Presley or virtuoso instrumentalists like the guitarist

Eric Clapton. But Brian Eno sings only occasionally and self-consciously, and he is not a virtuoso on any instrument.

deign   *dayn*
(to think it not beneath one's dignity; condescend)

The private automobile in Texas is as food, clothing and shelter: it is a virtual necessity. Regular bus riders are either poor people or eccentrics. He who might deign to prefer public transportation over the car as a matter of principle is held to be as morally suspect as he is politically dangerous.

déjà vu   *DAY zhah voo:*
(the illusion that one has previously had an experience that is actually new to one: French, already seen)

" 'Send in the Clowns' was two years old when I first heard it," Miss Collins recalls, "and Sinatra had already recorded it. But as soon as I heard it, I knew it belonged to me. I have that feeling of déjà vu sometimes about a song. It's almost as though I knew it from another life."

de jure   *dee JOO ri*
(by legal establishment: as opposed to de facto, meaning in actual fact, though not by legal establishment)

Congressional opponents of busing for desegregation last week moved to make de jure a policy that is already de facto. By an overwhelming 265 to 122, the House of Representatives voted to prohibit the Justice Department from pursuing school desegregation cases that could result in busing.

delusion   *di LOO: zhuhn*
(a false belief or opinion)

Expressing their concern for what they called "poverty of the spirit," the bishops said: "It would be a serious delusion, especially in our more affluent societies, to imagine that poverty is confined to the lack of material resources."

demagogue   *DE muh gahg*
(a person who tries to stir up the people by appeals to emotion, prejudice, etc., in order to win them over quickly and so gain power)

Then, in his strongest rebuke of Congress since he took office, Mr. Reagan extended his nationally televised news conference beyond the customary half hour to attack House Speaker Thomas P. O'Neill Jr. Mr. Reagan labeled as "sheer demagoguery" the Democratic leader's charge that the President and his advisers did not understand working people.

demean   *di MEEN*
(to lower in status or character; degrade)

To the Editor: I trust The New York Times will nip in the bud any practice to refer to our new President as "Ronnie" or "Ron." Mr. Carter's downfall started with "Jimmy." Familiarity breeds contempt, of the President of the United States as well as of any other head of state. Let us not demean the office of the President by referring to Mr. Reagan as "Ronnie" or "Ron," no matter what his wife may call him in private.
WALTER T. OAKLEY.

The proverb, "Familiarity breeds contempt" appears in English as early as the mid-16th century and farther back in Aesop (6th century B.C.) and Thomas Aquinas (1225–1274), who wrote "Nimia familiaritas parit contemptum." Its original meaning is not that the better you get to know people the less you like them, but that one grows unappreciative of what is too easily had, or that one grows careless when familiarity with something leads to overconfidence. Winston Churchill took his turn with the proverb when he said, "Without a certain amount of familiarity, you will never breed anything."

---

demeaning   *di MEEN ing*
(degrading)

PEKING, April 4 (AP)—A Chinese messenger who delivered telegrams felt his job was demeaning, so he hid or destroyed 348 telegrams in December, including 56 money orders totalling the equivalent of $667,000.

demise   *di MIGHZ*
(death)

Many fish begin to lose their sweet essence immediately after death. Brook trout are at their very best when they go into the pan within minutes of their demise.

demure   *di MYOOR*
(modest; reserved)

In the months during the engagement, Lady Diana made a visible transition from girl to woman. She shed her demure style of dress that she has loved since childhood, and emerged in a frankly sexy black gown.

denigrate   DE nuh grayt
(to disparage the character or reputation of; defame)

Their products are denigrated by connoisseurs, who wince at the sight of screw caps and such redundant names as "chablis blanc," but no one gainsays the Gallos' extraordinary success.

depressant   di PRE suhnt
(an agent that lessens functional activity)

Taken black, iced coffee is a perfect appetite depressant, and so is a pleasant help to dieters. Iced tea, on the other hand, seems to induce hunger.

derelict   DE ruh likt
(neglectful of duty; remiss; negligent)

"All of a sudden the child was gone," Mr. Rebhann said. "The guard ran into the room, saw the crib empty and immediately informed the police." Mr. Rebhann said the guard had been suspended for five days, but that an investigation had shown he was not derelict in his duty and that he would return to work Monday.

(deserted by the owner; abandoned; forsaken)

Arlene Hoffman, an executive with Intermarco Advertising in Manhattan, and her partner, Ray Gaulke, bought a derelict Colonial house in the Lakeville section of Salisbury, Conn. They decided to restore it as authentically as possible.

deride   di RIGHD
(to ridicule)

No Soviet publication had reported the date of the Russian Orthodox Easter, which varies from year to year like the Greek Orthodox Easter, also being celebrated today, and the Western Easter, celebrated last week. No official body had authorized observance of a holiday that the Soviet Union's atheistic textbooks deride as a tool for the "spiritual hoaxing of workers."

de rigueur *duh ree GER*
(required by etiquette; according to good form; fashionable: French, in strictness)

Keeping a gun for self-defense is still a private, even furtive matter; it is not yet de rigueur to exchange home-gun stories at dinner parties.

desecrate *DE suh krayt*
(to abuse the sacredness of; subject to sacrilege; profane)

Teen-age vandals broke through the heavy metal doors of a Queens mausoleum yesterday afternoon, smashed open a coffin and desecrated the corpse inside, according to a spokesman for John Santucci, Queens District Attorney.

desolate *DE suh lit*
(uninhabited; deserted)

Here, among the greasewood, black lava buttes and abandoned silver mines of southwestern Idaho, southeastern Oregon and northeastern Nevada, the country is so desolate and so remote that, as recently as the early 1900's, maps described portions of it as unexplored.

despise *di SPIGHZ*
(to look down on with contempt and scorn)

"All Night Long," a comedy starring Gene Hackman and Barbra Streisand, has joined the select group of movies that audiences actively despise. "For most pictures, we'll have a full house, and maybe one person will ask for his money back," a Bruin [Theater] usher says. "For this movie, there will hardly be anyone in the theater, and five or six of them will ask."

destabilize *di STAY buh lighz*
(to upset the stability or equilibrium of, as of a country by promoting unrest, discontent, economic insecurity, etc.; unbalance)

In the toughest language yet used by a Politburo member, Marshal Ustinov, who is 74 years old, accused the West, and particularly the United States, of carrying out subversive activities in Poland to destabilize the country, discredit the Communist system and weaken the Warsaw Pact, the Soviet bloc's military alliance.

desuetude   *DE swi too:d*
(the condition of not being used anymore; disuse)

She has been thrown away by her husband and by the world. Poking in trash cans with the shaft of a broken umbrella, she tries to reverse the tide of desuetude, to salvage things and put them back into their places.

detachment   *di TACH ment*
(the state of being disinterested or impartial)

Having gone through 444 days of captivity in Iran, Kathryn Koob was able to look with some detachment upon an incident at a college in Iowa in which a speech she was giving was interrupted by shouting Iranian students. "I almost felt at home, if you will," Miss Koob said, "because Iranians love political discussions, particularly Iranian men. When they discuss something, they become very active and it was a very typical Iranian political discussion."

détente   *day TAHNT*
(a relaxation of tension in political and international affairs, in recent years with particular reference to the improvement of relations between the U.S. and the U.S.S.R. through nuclear treaties, trade agreements and other forms of cooperation)

The Soviet Union said today in a Moscow radio commentary that the Reagan Administration had mounted an assault against détente and added that American "military hysteria" was encouraging a return to the cold war.

detractor   *di TRAK ter*
(one who disparages the worth or reputation of something)

Social scientists have long encountered difficulty proving their work worthwhile enough to warrant Government support. Detractors have included both political conservatives who say the Government has no business poking into peoples' personal and sexual lives, and natural scientists who have cast doubt on the scientific quality of much social research.

detrimental   *de truh MEN tuhl*
(harmful; damaging)

No one is quite certain why the Cubs have been so bad so long. Ron Santo, the onetime third baseman for the Cubs, said that playing in

Wrigley Field was detrimental. "It is the only park in the major leagues without lights," he said. "And playing in the sun day after day wears you out over the long haul."

detritus   *di TRIGH tuhs*
(an accumulation of debris)

He made a printing press from oddments and scraps, the detritus of secondhand shops and the lucky find on the street.

deus ex machina   *DEE uhs eks MA ki nuh*
(anyone who unexpectedly intervenes to change the course of events)

Ayatollah Ruhollah Khomeini, the constitutional deus ex machina of Iran's Islamic republic, descended last week into the midst of his country's cutthroat politics, but even he could not impose an instant truce.

Deus ex machina is a Latin phrase meaning god from a machine. In ancient Greek and Roman plays, a deity was sometimes brought in by stage machinery to intervene in the action and resolve problems. It was lowered into the stage action, and then raised out of it, by a hoist.

---

devastate   *DE vuh stayt*
(to lay waste; ravage; destroy)

A devastating freeze in the vineyards of upstate New York threatens to wipe out most of the grape crop of 1981, and a severe cutback in wine production is in prospect.

devotee   *de vuh TEE*
(one ardently attached or devoted to anything; enthusiast; fan)

Few devotees of fine wines would disagree that the chardonnay grape produces the greatest dry white table wines made in North America.

dexterity   *dek STER uh ti*
(skill in using one's hands, mind or body; adroitness)

Whether in the unadorned but orderly Chinatown dining room or in the somewhat more gracious uptown outpost, the one dish not to be missed is the marvelous duck—available on no more than 20 minutes' notice and carved at the table by a chef who wields a scalpel-sharp cleaver with a dexterity that Dr. Christiaan Barnard might envy.

diametrically   *digh uh ME trik li*
(completely; absolutely; utterly)

Louella Hatch, who rents an apartment in the Bronx, and Louise Henry, who owns apartments in Brooklyn, have diametrically opposite views on most aspects of rent stabilization. But in one thing they agree: Each feels it has been administered unfairly.

diaspora   *digh AS puh ruh*
(the Jewish communities outside Israel: more generally, any scattering of people with a common origin, background, beliefs, etc.)

Within the Jewish world itself, both in Israel and in the diaspora, opinion is more divided over the continuing occupation of the West Bank than over any other issue since the state was created.

dichotomy   *digh KAHT uh mi*
(division into two parts, groups or classes, especially when these are sharply distinguished or opposed)

A democracy as large as the American, dominated by the mass media, tends to be particularly vulnerable to simple-minded generalizations and, more particularly, simple-minded dichotomies of the either-or character. [Zbigniew Brzezinski]

dilettante   *DI luh tahnt*
(a person who follows an art or science only for amusement and in a superficial way; dabbler)

"Let me say we did not sweat and bleed to get the economic package passed only to abandon it when the going gets a little tough," Mr. Reagan said in a speech here to the National Federation of Republican Women. "We will not practice dilettante economics," he added, pledging that he would not change his plan to reduce spending, cut income taxes and trim the Federal budget at the same time.

diminutive   *duh MIN yuh tiv*
(a word or name formed from another by the addition of a suffix expressing smallness in size and, sometimes, endearment or condescension)

BUENOS AIRES, May 16—She is a legend, the subject of television shows and Broadway musicals, known the world over by her diminutive, Evita. And here, in the country that both bore her and reflects her, she is not dead. Eva Perón lives. She lives in memories so powerful that the former country girl who rose to be a willful ruler continues to tug at the nation, still dividing those who adore her and despise her.

dint   *dint*
(force; exertion: now chiefly in "by dint of")

As the Associated Press reporter at City Hall until he retired last December after 47 years in the business, Schroeder was not often read by people in this city. But by dint of knowledge and personality, he guided colleagues through the many mazes of government. Inevitably, his perceptions—and they were perceptions, not biases—were those absorbed by newspaper readers and television viewers.

diocese   *DIGH uh sees*
(the district under a bishop's jurisdiction)

The Pittsburgh diocese, which has negotiated four successive contracts with its teachers, is a leader among Catholic school systems in collective bargaining.

dire   *dighr*
(dreadful; terrible)

If it does nothing else, "Richard's Things" illustrates what dire trouble an actress can land in when she works with a director with no understanding of her talents. Liv Ullmann, who can be so very sensitive and authentic, is this time called on to play a preposterous soap-opera queen.

disabuse   *dis uh BYOO:Z*
(to rid of false ideas; undeceive)

Both in private conversations and at a news conference, Mr. Haig's principal aim appeared to be to disabuse Spaniards of the impression, widespread here since the attempted military coup on Feb. 23, that the Reagan Administration was lukewarm in its support of Spanish democracy.

disarming   *dis AHRM ing*
(removing or allaying suspicions, fears or hostility)

Of all the Cabinet members seeking to sell President Reagan's budget reductions, T.H. Bell is perhaps the most disarming. He listens patiently to complaints. He never gets angry. And he leaves his critics smiling, though not converted.

disarray   *dis uh RAY*
(*an untidy condition; disorder; confusion*)

In the confusion following the revolution, the Iranian caviar business was said to be in disarray, with a flourishing black market, unhygienic products and risky delivery. Christian Petrossian, the exclusive importer of Russian caviar in Europe, said his company stopped buying Iranian caviar.

disavow   *dis uh VOW*
(*to deny having any connection with; disclaim; renounce*)

Miss Keough has been something of a rebel among the families of the former hostages because she developed an affection for Iranians in a three-month visit to Iran while her father was the head of the American school there. It was a feeling she refused to disavow, even after her father had become a prisoner of Islamic militants.

discerning   *di SER ning*
(*having or showing good judgment or understanding*)

Stores such as Macy's, Dean & Deluca, Bloomingdale's and Zabar's are competing so hard for the attention of the discerning olive oil user that they dispatch buyers to Europe to scout the small groves for the finest oils.

disclaimer   *dis CLAY mer*
(*a disavowal, as of pretensions, claims or opinions*)

According to a careful opening disclaimer, the four young men who star in "Beatlemania" are "not the former members of the musical group known as the Beatles." This laughable announcement is made for legal reasons, not esthetic ones, because anyone fond of the real Beatles will immediately spot the fraudulence of the enterprise.

discomfiture   *dis CUHM fi choor*
(*uneasiness; frustration; confusion*)

Last weekend, at an oceanside retreat in the Crimea, top Soviet officials again confronted the Polish problem. By all indications the officials decided, as before, that in spite of all their discomfiture over developments in Warsaw they will continue to work for their ends by political rather than military means.

disenchantment   *dis in CHANT muhnt*
(*a loss of belief in an illusion; disillusionment*)

Mr. Cronkite is exceptional primarily in light of the awesome power and responsibility that prolonged national television exposure has thrust upon him. His disenchantment with the Vietnam War was instrumental in shifting public opinion to the side of the peace movement. Lyndon Johnson is reported to have concluded, "If we've lost Walter, we've lost the country."

disgruntled   *dis GRUHN tuhld*
(grumblingly or peevishly discontented; displeased and sulky)

Disgruntled that the riding paths at the Presidential retreat in Camp David, Md. had been paved, he has ordered aides to check out riding trails in Rock Creek Park in the capital.

disingenuous   *dis in GEN yoo uhs*
(insincere)

"Beatlemania" was a horror on the stage, and it's even more of a horror at close range, where the seams really show. This isn't a loving impersonation, or even an honest one. It's cheap, disingenuous and loathsome.

dismember   *dis MEM ber*
(to cut or tear off arms or legs)

In film as in other media, violence has long since become commonplace, with people dismembered, impaled, incinerated, blown up, machine-gunned or otherwise annihilated with numbing regularity.

disparate   *DI spuh rit*
(essentially not alike; widely different)

The Sudan is Africa's largest and probably most culturally disparate nation, with 18 million people scattered over nearly a million square miles. It has more than 1,000 languages and tribal dialects.

dispensation   *di spuhn SAY shuhn*
(in the Roman Catholic Church, an exemption or release from the provisions of a specific church law)

Evangline Gouletas-Carey said last night that she would ask a Roman Catholic marriage tribunal to nullify her first three marriages so that Governor Carey could seek dispensation from the church for his recent marriage.

dispiriting   *di SPIR uh ting*
(lowering the spirits of; making sad, discouraged or apathetic)

Although Winfield's good nature has not been tested by a personal slump, he has not sulked after Yankee losses. After a dispiriting defeat in Oakland, he was one of only a few New York players who signed autographs on the way to the bus.

disport   *di SPAWRT*
(to indulge in amusement; play; frolic)

While much of the city disported itself yesterday in a sunny start to the holiday weekend, several hundred professional magicians spent an afternoon without illusion at an East Side auditorium talking with one another about the secrets of the conjuring art.

From *disport* we get *sport*, through the linguistic process known as apheresis, the dropping of an unaccented syllable or vowel at the beginning of a word. That process gave us: *though* from *although*; *squire* from *esquire*; *fender* from *defender*; *cute* from *acute*. " 'Scuse me" and "Morning!" (for "Good morning!") are examples of the same process.

---

disrepair   *dis ri PAIR*
(needing repairs; dilapidation)

At Mr. Claypool's automobile repair shop here in rural Will County near Chicago, there are Corvairs in various states of disrepair scattered all over the lot and two ramshackle sheds full of Corvair parts.

dissident   *DI suh duhnt*
(one who disagrees or dissents, as from an established church, political system or school of thought)

A former dissident priest of the Episcopal church who vigorously opposed that church's decision to allow female priests has been ordained by Terence Cardinal Cook for service in the Roman Catholic Archdiocese of New York.

dissipate   *DI suh payt*
(to vanish by dispersion; disappear)

A senior Chinese Government official said today that the worst of the Yangtze River flooding was over as flood crests dissipated upon reaching the industrial city of Wuhan.

dissonance   *DI suh nuhns*
(*a lack of harmony; discord*)

Though most couples spend a lot of time talking to each other, many lack the skills needed to get their messages across effectively, to express their feelings or resolve conflicts without hurting each other or provoking anger and dissonance.

distended   *di STEN did*
(*swollen*)

Scrawny dogs scampered through the dirt. A few cows stood in the background. Hundreds of crying, filthy, half-naked children with distended bellies and women waiting to be evicted sat on heaps of clothes and other possessions in rope bags.

dithering   *DI th:uh ring*
(*nervous excitement or confusion*)

In India, which dominates this region whatever it does, the people affirmed their claim to the title of the most populous democracy in 1977, when they voted out Prime Minister Indira Gandhi's authoritarian regime. But in the dithering of the disparate government that succeeded hers, democracy degenerated into just politics, and she was returned to office last year.

ditty   *DI ti*
(*a short, simple song*)

"We don't want to fight,/ But, by Jingo, if we do,/ We've got the ships, we've got the men,/ We've got the money, too." Ships, men and money have been considered the essential ingredients of military preparedness since long before that music hall ditty became popular at a moment of tension between the British and Russians in the 1870's.

From the British music hall ditty referred to in the passage, arose the term *jingoism,* meaning aggressive or warmongering patriotism, the equivalent of the French *chauvinisme.* The song was popular during the Russo-Turkish War (1877–1878), when Prime Minister Benjamin Disraeli ordered the British fleet to Constantinople, where it prevented a Russian takeover. The lines that follow those in the passage are: "We've fought the Bear before,/ and while we're Britons true,/ The Russians shall not have Constantinople." "By Jingo!" is a euphemism for "By Jesus!"

---

diva   *DEE vuh*
(a leading woman singer, especially in grand opera: Latin, goddess)

Miss Mills made her name playing Dorothy in the Broadway production of "The Wiz." But since then she has grown from an adolescent wonder into a pop-soul diva peddling adult eroticism in steamy numbers like "Two Hearts" and "Feel the Fire."

dive   *dighv*
(a cheap, disreputable, low-class establishment, especially a bar, gambling place, dance-hall or the like: a slang word)

Some spoke with nostalgia of the poolrooms of the past. "They were all dives," said Jake LaMotta, the former middleweight champion known as the Bronx Bull, who was a spectator at the tournament. "The only home you had was the poolroom. What else you had to do in the Bronx? After we came back from work, we always went there," the 60-year-old Bull recalled of his youth. "By 'work' I mean stealing. Not that we stole anything, just stuff beginning with A—a truck, a car, a bike."

divest   *duh VEST*
(to strip)

Like all crustacea, crabs must, in order to grow, periodically divest themselves of their bony exterior skeletons, which have no growth cells. This molting takes place from 21 to 23 times for the male and 18 to 20 for the females.

The Swarthmore College board of managers divested itself of nearly $2.4 million in stock from corporations that deal with South Africa, saying American concerns should be "responsible agents for progressive social change in South Africa." The board voted to divest itself of stock in Citicorp and the Newmont Mining Corporation, both of New York, and the Timken Company of Canton, Ohio.

docile   *DAH suhl*
(easily managed or handled; tame)

Albino animals also tend to be docile and are preferred subjects in laboratory research.

doctrinaire   *dahk tri NAIR*
(adhering to a doctrine or theory in an unyielding, dogmatic way)

Though he was often identified with doctrinaire positions on foreign policy as a candidate, Ronald Reagan as President has assembled a largely nonideological team of managers and career Government officials to direct foreign and defense policy in his administration. Drawn from large corporations, blue-chip law firms, universities, the military and the upper ranks of the Federal bureaucracy, the newly appointed policymakers, with some notable exceptions, appear to represent the mainstream of the Republican Party.

docudrama *DAHK yoo drah muh*
(a television dramatization based on facts, often presented in the style of a documentary to impart a sense of authenticity)

For three hours this evening, beginning at 8 o'clock, CBS-TV is offering "The Bunker," a dramatization of the final days of Hitler and his Third Reich. . . . [John Gay, the scriptwriter] explains: "I can't guarantee that what you are about to see is historical truth. I do believe the stories present a kind of psychological truth," referring to the accounts of survivors. We are, once again, in the murky twilight world of the "docudrama." The dangers remain undiminished.

dolce far niente *DAWL che fahr NYEN te*
(pleasant idleness or inactivity: Italian, sweet doing nothing)

Mayor Koch is to be congratulated for discovering double parking. It reportedly took a lady at a dinner party to tell him what many already know—that the intended thoroughfares of midtown Manhattan are in fact just elegant parking lots. Those who have learned the New York version of dolce far niente can sit in a taxi watching the passing parade, studying the cab's scabrous interior, listening to the meter tick. The city has not exactly come to a halt, but it's barely moving, at an average of 4.4 miles an hour.

doldrums *DAHL druhms*
(sluggishness or complete inactivity; stagnation)

Although seasonality is becoming less important in selling wedding gear, the peak season remains January through March, with an eye to summer weddings. The people doing the alterations are busiest from April to July. And by all accounts December is the doldrums for the bridal industry. Nobody shops for wedding gowns at Christmas.

doleful *DOHL fuhl*
(full of sorrow or sadness; mournful; melancholy)

Yesterday was the 77th birthday of Vladimir Horowitz. "I'm an old man and I don't know if I can play any more," he dolefully said, looking out at an interviewer from the corner of his eyes. He wandered over to the piano. "But perhaps." The Horowitz hands began to play pearly Scarlatti, crashing Liszt, songful Rachmaninoff, the coda of Chopin's F minor Ballade. "Maybe," he admitted, "the reflexes are not so bad, after all."

In music, a coda is a passage at the end of a movement or composition that brings it to a formal close. The word is Italian for *tail.*

---

dollop   DAH luhp
(*a lump or blob of some substance; a measure or amount*)

Imagination and invention have infinitely extended the list of possible cold soups. Fruit, vegetables, seafood and chicken, in delectably pale pastel tones and crowned with a dollop of whipped cream or sour cream, are the rule.

The traditional Democratic approach, represented by Mr. O'Neill, calls for "targeted" tax cuts, giving special attention—an extra dollop of tax relief—to those with low or middle incomes.

dormant   DAWR muhnt
(*in a state of suspended animation; live, but not actively growing; torpid*)

Each winter blue crabs lie just under the mud in a dormant stage, and in some areas regulations permit harvesting them with a dredge towed behind a boat.

(*quiet; still; inactive*)

The Peronists, long dormant, are restless again and Mrs. Perón, the widow of Juan Domingo Perón, the Argentine strongman, has become their rallying cry and symbol. They have refused to engage in the Government's formal "dialogue" with civilian leaders over the country's future until she is set free.

double entendre   DOO: bluh ahn TAHN druh
(*a term with two meanings, especially when one of them has a risqué or indecorous connotation: French, double meaning*)

When rock-and-roll enjoyed its initial surge of popularity in the mid-50's, many fundamentalist Christians recoiled in horror. To them, rock's "savage rhythms," and the thinly concealed double entendre of many rock-and-roll lyrics, made it "the Devil's music."

double take   *DUH buhl TAYK*
(a delayed reaction to some remark, situation, etc., in which there is at first unthinking acceptance and then startled surprise or a second glance as the real meaning or actual situation suddenly becomes clear)

When the tough narcotics detective named Gus Levy first appears on the screen in Sydney Lumet's "Prince of the City," some unsuspecting members of the audience are likely to do double takes. Is it? Could it be? Yes, it is Jerry Orbach, the song-and-dance man, star of the current "42d Street" and other Broadway musicals.

doughty   *DOW ti*
(valiant; brave: now used humorously with a somewhat archaic flavor)

Rising toward 5 in the morning, when the desert stars are just starting to pale, the doughtier visitors make their way back up to the hermitage to watch the dawn.

dour   *doo: r*
(sullen; gloomy; forbidding)

Former Mayor Beame was too dour, which is why he became former. Now we have Mayor Koch, who learned the Beame lesson well and seems to have done a good job of jesting us away from gloom.

dowager   *DOW uh jer*
(an elderly woman of wealth and dignity)

In the old days, Opening Night of New York's Metropolitan Opera was a grand occasion when dowagers could show off their jewels, singers could sing out their hearts and opera lovers could thrill to the return to the state of America's claim to world-class culture.

A Wilshire Boulevard landmark, the hat-shaped building of the Brown Derby restaurant, is being torn down to make way for an office building. But across the street, another landmark is still in business, the dowager Ambassador Hotel, where movie stars of the 1930's and 40's celebrated in the Coconut Grove, and where Senator Robert F. Kennedy was gunned down by an assassin in 1968.

doxy   *DAHK si*
(a woman of low morals, specifically a prostitute or mistress: obsolete
British slang)

The playwright's third character is Janet, a doxy from Illinois who arrives
at the cafe one night on her way to seek stardom in Hollywood, but ends
up staying as a waitress.

doyen   *daw YEN*
(the senior member, or dean, of a group)

Alphonse Cimber, the Haitian-born drummer who was considered the
doyen of traditional musicians of African ancestry in the United States,
died Monday of respiratory ailments in Mount Sinai Hospital. He was 83
years old and lived in Harlem.

draconian   *dray KOH ni uhn*
(extremely severe or cruel)

In 1784, Benjamin Franklin, then the American Ambassador to France,
calculated that because Parisians liked to stay up late and sleep morn-
ings, they burned 64,050,000 needless candles each summer, at a cost
of $19 million. His proposal was draconian: "In the mornings, as soon
as the sun rises, let all the bells in every church be set ringing. If that is
not sufficient, let cannons be fired in every street to wake the sluggards
effectively."

———

Draco, a 7th-century B.C. Athenian statesman, drew up a code of
laws in 621 B.C., nearly every violation of which was punishable
by death, even petty theft and laziness. Hence, his name has
become synonymous with harsh and merciless laws. Draco was
the first to put Greek laws into writing, but those he chose to
codify were, for the most part, the ones that benefited the rich
and powerful.

———

dry   *drigh*
(humorously intended, but said matter-of-factly)

Sipping orange juice, the Prince of Wales stood studying a modernistic
bronze sculpture titled "Icarus" at the National Air and Space Museum.
Finally, he turned away from the oddly misshapen work of art. "I'd love
to have seen it," he remarked drily, "before it melted."

ducal   *DOO: kuhl*
(in the fashion of a duke; condescending; imperious)

Interviewed on television, Mr. Chirac displayed the ducal manner to-ward journalists that, to one degree or another, all the candidates use. He repeatedly informed his principal questioner when it was time to change the subject, and at one point, sensing resistance, scolded him for impoliteness.

dumbfounded   *duhm FOWN did*
(made speechless through shock, amazement or astonishment)

"Harvey's mother explained that the only bed available was Harvey's and he was in it. The young lady agreed to sleep with Harvey and got in bed with him. When Harvey, who was about 14 years old, awoke and saw this voluptuous blonde next to him, he was dumbfounded. The blonde opened one eye and said: 'Don't worry, young man, I won't hurt you.' "

dun   *duhn*
(to ask a debtor insistently or repeatedly for payment)

Many of the former students who are being dunned by the Federal Gov-ernment for unpaid student loans in southern Ohio are making the same plea that brought them to the student loan officer in the first place—they don't have the money.

dynasty   *DIGH nuh sti*
(a succession of rulers who are from the same family; the period during which a certain family reigns)

In 221 B.C. Qin unified China, built the Great Wall, burned the books valued by Confucius and declared himself China's first sovereign em-peror. He asserted that his dynasty would rule for 10,000 years, but it turned out to be the shortest dynasty in the history of China. He ruled for only 14 years but in that time he accomplished sweeping changes that made his dynasty a turning point in history.

earmark   *EER mahrk*
(to set aside or reserve for a special purpose or recipient)

Secretary of Transportation Drew Lewis said yesterday that if Mayor Koch and Governor Carey submitted a joint request, he would approve a plan to trade in funds earmarked for the Westway project for use on mass transit.

ebullient   *i BUH lyuhnt*
(overflowing with enthusiasm or high spirits; exuberant)

The versatile talents of Leonard Bernstein were omnipresent during the Lincoln Center Chamber Music Society's final Haydn-Stravinsky concert, held in Alice Tully Hall on Sunday night. His ebullient musical presence as both conductor and pianist gave the occasion a distinctly buoyant character—as Stravinsky himself reportedly remarked after hearing his "Rite of Spring" conducted by Mr. Bernstein: "Wow!"

ecclesiastical   *i klee zi A sti kuhl*
(relating to the church or the clergy)

The religions of the world are represented in music on records that cover every kind of ecclesiastical composition from Gregorian chants to gospel, masses from Bach to Bernstein, passion plays from medieval times to "Jesus Christ Superstar."

echelon   *E shuh lahn*
(a level of command, authority or rank)

Adri, the sportswear designer who has always had her special following, has catapulted into the top echelon of fashion makers.

eclectic *i KLEK tik*
(composed of material or ideas gathered from a variety of sources)

Live artillery shells, a dead sea turtle half the size of a Volkswagen Beetle, a drowned giraffe, antique crockery, pocketbooks, chemical sludge, raw sewage and about 5,000 cords of driftwood a year—the waters of New York Harbor yield a strange and eclectic bounty.

A cord is 128 cubic feet of wood cut for fuel, and usually arranged in a pile 8 feet long, 4 feet wide and 4 feet high.

eclipse *i KLIPS*
(to overshadow or make dim by comparison)

The brief remarks of a mother whose daughter had been murdered eclipsed speeches by politicians and officials at a City Hall ceremony yesterday marking the opening of National Victim Rights Week. "It is not just the pain of losing a loved one," Diana Montenegro said. "I buried my daughter, but I cannot bury my anger and my pain. Time and again we see short-term sentences given to the criminals while we, the victims, serve lifetime sentences of fear, grief and violation."

effervesce *e fer VES*
(to be lively and high-spirited)

Columbus Avenue continues to effervesce, and the young, from the East Side and elsewhere, are drawn in ever-increasing numbers to its galleries, its secondhand clothing boutiques, its bars and restaurants these warm evenings.

efficacy *E fi kuh si*
(power to produce effects or intended results; effectiveness)

Dr. Peter J. Hauri, director of the sleep disorders center at Dartmouth Medical School, says that while most sleeping pills "are initially effective, most lose efficacy when used chronically."

effigy *E fuh ji*
(a crudely made statue or portrait of a despised person that is displayed or carried in a demonstration and later burned or hanged as a public expression of indignation, ridicule or contempt)

At a tense moment in one of the last budget-cutting sessions at the White House, President Reagan and his aides were discussing a domestic program. "Go ahead and cut it," the President commanded. Then he added with a chuckle, "They're going to hang me in effigy anyway, and it doesn't matter how high."

effusive   e FYOO: siv
(expressing excessive emotion in an unrestrained manner; overly demonstrative; overflowing)

Fashion designers are ecstatic about Mrs. Reagan's emphasis on clothes and effusive in their descriptions of her personal style. "She represents what I would call a thoroughbred American look: elegant, affluent, a well-bred, chic American look," said Adolfo, one of Mrs. Reagan's favorite designers. "She has very feminine taste, but not cute, not frumpy. If she has a blouse with a little ruffle, it's elegant, it's not overbearing."

egalitarian   i gal uh TAIR i uhn
(treating or considering all classes of people as equals)

An organization called Parents for Public Schools, with a membership of 1,000 whites, was formed 18 months ago. Its president is a businessman, Walter Smiley, who has two children in public elementary schools, and who says: "I'm not a liberal. I don't think I'm anything unusual. I'm not egalitarian in the sense that you can take my money and give it to somebody else, but I'm egalitarian about the first grade. I think they're all alike at that age, and they all deserve the same chance."

egregious   i GREE juhs
(outstanding for undesirable qualities; remarkably bad; flagrant)

Fifteen or twenty years ago—at some point right after "Perry Mason" and "Gunsmoke" were sent to the elephant's graveyard—I observed that if it was on prime time it was probably such egregious trash that it was not worth tuning in, and quit cold turkey.

Cold turkey, in the sense most often used today, refers to the sudden and complete withdrawal of drugs from an addict during an attempted cure, or a similar withdrawal of anything one is addicted to, such as cigarettes, alcohol or gambling. Other senses in which the expression is used are *to talk cold turkey* (be frank or blunt about something), and *to do something cold turkey* (without rehearsal or preparation).

---

elect   i LEKT
(persons belonging to a specially privileged group)

Watching various reviewers trying to avoid saying anything unkind about Kurt Vonnegut's new book, "Palm Sunday," one realizes that, contrary to public opinion, a literary reputation is the hardest thing in the world to lose. Once among the elect, a novelist is as difficult to impeach as a President. Again and again, he is given the benefit of the doubt, and since literary criticism is such a doubtful business, this is all the margin he needs.

elephantine   *el uh FAN teen*
(*huge; ponderous; clumsy*)

Rhododendrons grow rapidly, and the longer they grow without discipline, the larger they get. Sometimes these evergreen shrubs become elephantine and block light from the front windows of a house or dwarf everything else in the garden.

elicit   *i LI sit*
(*to draw forth; evoke*)

Some of the hunger strikers have elicited pledges from their families not to order food or medical treatment in their behalf after they lose consciousness in the final stages as death nears.

elusive   *i LOO: siv*
(*difficult to find or locate*)

Officials of the World Wildlife Fund, which has fought to preserve the giant panda in the mountains of China and the humpbacked whale in the seas off Hawaii, visited the lost colony of the rare and elusive prairie sphinx moth today at a secret site on the high plains of northeastern Colorado.

emancipated   *i MAN suh pay tid*
(*released legally from control and supervision*)

Now 17, Mr. Brown is legally emancipated from his parents. His mother, who has a drinking problem, lives in a small town in upstate New York, Mr. Brown said, and his father works in Saudi Arabia for an oil company.

embargo   *im BAHR goh*
(*a prohibition of trade in a particular commodity*)

The Carter Administration made a point of going beyond the requirements of the United Nations embargo on arms sales to South Africa, ruling out the sale of equipment of any description to the armed forces or the police.

embellish *im BE lish*
(to beautify through ornamentation or adornment)

Instrumental music of the late Renaissance tends to be fairly simple and straightforward compared with the more complex vocal forms of the period, and its primary purpose was to entertain or add embellishment to ceremonial events.

emblematic *em bluh MA tik*
(representing something else; serving as an emblem; symbolic)

In front of a red backdrop on a brightly lit stage, everything is emblematic: a small red flag represents a chariot, two chairs become a bed chamber.

embodiment *im BAH di muhnt*
(a concrete expression of some idea or quality; personification)

Distance is what fuels a fantasy. Too little, and the object loses mystery; too much, and it loses visibility. For centuries, the British royal family has correctly gauged the point at which man and myth marry. As human beings they are, like all of us, dispensable; as embodiments of history, they have been invaluable.

emeritus *i MAI ruh tuhs*
(retired from active service, usually for age, but retaining one's rank or title)

Harrison R. Steeves, professor emeritus of English at Columbia College, where for many years he had been chairman of the English department, died Saturday at his home in Kingston, R.I. He was 100 years old.

emigrate *E muh grayt*
(to leave one country or region to settle in another)

The Soviet Union announced today that it had lifted the citizenship of Vladimir Voinovich, a 49-year-old satirical writer who emigrated to West Germany in December after years of conflict with Soviet authorities.

émigré *E muh gray*
(an emigrant, especially one forced to flee a native land for political reasons)

The Israelis contend that the refusal of many Soviet Jews to settle in Israel jeopardizes the emigration of others, and Israel has therefore decided to put pressure on émigrés by not helping them go elsewhere unless they have close family ties in other countries.

emotive   *i MOH tiv*
(*directed toward the emotions*)

Most of us have absorbed the long and tenacious tradition that laying down one's life is a "far far better thing," that death gives a cause a sacred and validating stamp. The hunger strikers in Ireland are heirs to this tradition, and they and their directors are exploiting its emotive and ratifying power.

emulate   *EM yoo layt*
(*to try to equal or excel; imitate with effort to equal or surpass*)

"Why is Houston falling apart?" trumpets the magazine Texas Monthly. Lynn Ashby, a columnist for the Houston Post, writes, "This city is going down the tube and no one is stopping it." The economic journal Texas Business concluded flatly last month that Houston "doesn't provide an example for other growing Texas cities to emulate—but rather an example of what to avoid."

Down the tube began its slangy existence in the late 1960's as a term meaning "to lose," "to be finished" or to "go down the drain." In surfing slang, a tube is the hollow space within the curl of a breaking wave. A ride in the tube is thrilling; a spill in it quite jolting, a "wipe out," in surfers' language. In "On Language" (1980) William Safire points to the use of "I tubed it" as surfing lingo for "I flunked it" and suggests that the surfing phrase merged in concept with the old "down the drain" to give us "down the tube."

---

enclave   *EN klayv*
(*a distinctly bounded area enclosed within a larger area*)

Mr. Kaplan is one of millions of elderly people in Florida and one of about 15,000 residing in the Century Village retirement community, one of the scores of Florida's sprawling, sunwashed enclaves designed for living out the golden years.

endangered species   *en DAYN jerd SPEE sheez*
(*in its original sense, a plant or animal species in danger of becoming extinct, but figuratively applied to anything in danger of dying out, disappearing or being wiped out*)

If skirts become an endangered species, blame Giorgio Armani. A year ago he decided short pants were the wave of the future and banished relics like the skirt from his runway.

endemic   *en DE mik*
(constantly present in a particular country or locality)

Burglaries are so endemic and the Police Department so depleted from fiscal retrenchment (down from 31,100 officers in 1974 to 22,600 now) that most of the break-ins are not even investigated.

endow   *in DOW*
(to provide with some talent, quality, etc.)

A visitor to my vegetable garden might wonder why two-thirds of it is given over to Hubbard squash, butternut squash, potatoes and tomatoes. I grow those particular squashes because nature endows them with a protective rind that keeps them good in a cool, walled-off part of the cellar most of the winter.

endowment   *in DOW muhnt*
(a bequest or gift that provides an income for an institution or person)

The Richard Rodgers Production Award was set up in 1978 with a $1 million endowment from the composer to bring the work of promising new composers and librettists to the New York stage. The award, which comes from income generated by the endowment, is turned over to the theater producing the winning musical.

engulf   *in GUHLF*
(to swallow up; overwhelm)

Twenty casts later a salmon of about two pounds engulfed my fly and danced upon the dark water.

enhance   *in HANS*
(to raise to a higher degree)

Early in his presidency, Mr. Sadat enhanced his popularity by eliminating many of the police-state controls that Nasser had relied on to keep himself in power in the years after the officers' revolt that brought down the monarchy in 1952.

enigma   *i NIG muh*
(a perplexing, baffling or seemingly inexplicable matter)

In some ways, Mr. Agca remains as much an enigma as when bystanders grabbed him moments after two bullets struck the Pope. The suspect's precise motives, beyond a distaste for authority and a desire to shock, are not clear. It is not known how he paid for his extensive travels, although there are hints that the money may have come from drug sales or from robberies.

enigmatic   *e nig MA tik*
(perplexing; baffling)

SUNSPOT, N.M.—Astronomers have found that the sun is ringing like a bell, reverberating in a manner that enables scientists at this solar-research community near Alamogordo to explore for the first time the interior of that enigmatic star.

Is there a music of the spheres? Yes, according to Pythagoras, the 6th century B.C. Greek philosopher and mathematician. From his knowledge that the pitch of notes depends on the speed of vibrations, and that the planets rotate at different speeds, he concluded that each planet must make its own sound. And, he reasoned, since all things in nature are harmoniously made, the sounds made by the rotating planets must harmonize.

---

en masse   *ahn mas*
(in a group; as a whole; all together: French, in mass)

Orion, which was formed in February 1978 by the management of United Artists after they resigned from the company en masse, has had some box-office failures and three hits—"10," "Caddyshack" and "Excalibur" —during its 41 months.

enmity   *EN muh ti*
(the bitter attitude or feelings of an enemy or of mutual enemies; a strong, settled feeling of hatred, whether displayed or concealed)

The enmity between the Croatians and the Yugoslav Government is longstanding. It dates to 1918, when the Austro-Hungarian Empire was broken up and Croatia became part of Yugoslavia.

ennoble   *i NOH buhl*
(to give a noble quality to; dignify)

Philosophers have sometimes suggested that pain is ennobling to the human spirit. However, it is safe to say that most of those who share this view in the abstract would seek relief in the face of actual pain.

ensconced   en SKAHNST
(placed or settled comfortably, snugly or securely)

Trevor Howard and Celia Johnson. Rarely have two names been so inextricably linked by a single production, in this case a film. "Brief Encounter" was made in 1945 and its Noel Coward story of bittersweet love in a suburban English railway station has ensconced itself in the "Casablanca" category of movie classics.

entice   in TIGHS
(to attract by offering hope of reward or pleasure; tempt)

LITTLE ROCK, Ark., Sept. 12—This city's boosters have just made a film designed to entice industry here. Entitled "One in a Million," it is a handsomely mounted 17 and a half minutes of fresh-faced Southerners at work and at play in central Arkansas.

entomologist   en tuh MAH luh jist
(a zoologist who specializes in the study of insects)

Though it may seem like a sick joke to those whose vacations are now being ruined by the persistent and painful bites of black flies, Edward Cupp, an entomologist at Cornell University, spent five years and about $150,000 figuring out how to mass-breed the pesky creatures in his laboratory.

entrepreneur   ahn truh pruh NOOR
(a person who organizes and manages a business undertaking, assuming the risk for the sake of the profit)

Ted Turner, the Atlanta entrepreneur who last year launched the Cable News Network, a 24-hour news service for cable systems, is planning a second news network aimed at competing with a similar service announced last week by Westinghouse and ABC.

environs   in VIGH ruhnz
(the districts surrounding a town or city; suburbs or outskirts; surrounding area; vicinity)

Everyone agrees that loss of the commuter trains would be a heavy blow to Philadelphia and its environs. The trains run on 13 lines fanning out like veins in a maple leaf to the north and northwest, with two extending like a split stem to the south and southwest.

envisage   *en VI zij*
(to conceive of as a future possibility; imagine)

DAMASCUS, Syria, June 16 (Reuters)—A proposal for building a chain of nuclear power plants across the Arab world was put forward here today at a conference of Arab countries also attended by representatives of the International Atomic Energy Agency. The plan, evidently drawn up before the Israeli air strike against Iraq's Osirak reactor, envisages the construction and joint operation of about 20 nuclear power stations in Morocco, Iraq, Tunisia and Saudi Arabia to help insure fuel supplies for the 21st century.

ephemeral   *uh FE muh ruhl*
(short-lived; transitory)

Visiting a remote lake for a few days is something like glimpsing the face of a lovely woman in a crowd: the encounter, albeit ephemeral, quickens the heart with wonder and delight.

epicenter   *EP i sen ter*
(a focal or central point: usually, a geological term, meaning the point on the earth's surface directly above the focus of an earthquake from which the shock waves radiate)

For the French, who have made Cannes the epicenter of the film world for two weeks every year, there is new competition from the American Film Market in Los Angeles, a similar film festival.

epicure   *E pi kyoor*
(a person who enjoys and has a discriminating taste for fine foods and drinks)

There is also, for the first time since 1975, a hunting season for American brant on the East Coast. These small geese—an epicure's delight if the birds have been eating the right fare—nest farther north than do the Canada, snow or blue geese.

The Greek philosopher Epicurus (341?–247 B.C.) taught that the goal of women and men should be a life of quiet pleasure, governed by self-discipline, morality and cultural development. One of the meanings of *epicure* that has come down to us—someone devoted to luxury and sensual pleasure—is, therefore, a gross distortion of what Epicurus taught.

---

epigram   *E puh gram*
(a short poem with a witty or satirical point, or any terse, witty, pointed statement)

OAKLAND, Calif., Jan. 26—The story is told that Gertrude Stein, who spent her girlhood in Oakland, once said that the problem with Oakland was, "When you get there, there isn't any THERE there." Like most such acid-etched epigrams, the assessment is more clever than true.

epilogue   *E puh lahg*
(a closing section added to a novel, play, etc., providing further comment, interpretation or information)

In a strange epilogue to the suicide last December of the novelist Romain Gary, a relative of Mr. Gary's, Paul Pavlowitch, says in a new book that Mr. Gary was the author of a 1975 Goncourt Prize-winning novel attributed to a writer named Emile Ajar.

epithet   *E puh thet*
(an abusive or contemptuous word or phrase used to describe a person)

Of all the scornful epithets hurled at Government regulators in recent years, none was more telling than "national nanny." Don't drink saccharin, you'll probably get cancer. Don't eat candy bars in school, you need your vitamins. Be careful of sugared cereal, it may cause cavities. Nanny knows best.

epitome   *i PI tuh mi*
(a person or thing that is representative or typical of the characteristics or general quality of a whole class)

For the epitome of Greek entertainment, try a night at a bouzoukia, one of the spacious clubs lining the seafront, where patrons listen to popular singers and reach a frenzy of post-midnight merriment that culminates in dancing on the tables, smashing plates at the feet of singers and dancers and showering each other with flower petals.

equivocal   *i KWI vuh kuhl*
(that can have more than one interpretation; uncertain; undecided)

Many doctors use many drugs for uses that are not approved by the Food and Drug Administration. Many times those uses are being investigated and are later approved. However, in many other cases, scientific proof of efficacy is equivocal or lacking.

eradicate   *i RA di kayt*
(to wipe out completely; get rid of; destroy)

The incidence of measles in New York City in the first three months of the year plummeted by 94 percent over the same period last year, causing officials to predict that they would meet their goal of eradicating the disease in the city by October 1982.

ergonomics   *er guh NAH miks*
(the study of the problems of people in adjusting to their environment, especially the science that seeks to adapt work or working conditions to suit the worker)

Ergonomic chairs, which have proliferated in Germany in the last few years, are meant to conform and adjust to the sitter's body on the job. They have pneumatic and hydraulic mechanisms, operated by levers or buttons, that adjust the backs and seats to varying heights and angles; their signature is usually a five-pronged base and a molded back.

erratic   *i RA tik*
(having no fixed course; irregular)

Until menopause is complete, it is unsafe to discontinue contraception, since you may continue to ovulate erratically for a while even if your periods seem to have stopped.

ersatz   *ER zahts*
(a substitute, especially an inferior imitation; artificial)

Many of the restaurants on Monterey Bay are seeking to convince customers that squid, when flattened, tenderized, breaded and sautéed, tastes very much like abalone. To purists the ersatz abalone is not like the real thing, having a more "fishy" flavor.

escalate   *E skuh layt*
(to grow or increase rapidly, often to the point of becoming unmanageable, as prices or wages)

Quilts, which have been in revival since the early 1960's, have escalated in price at an astounding rate in recent years. Last November an appliquéd and trapunto cotton quilt awash with flowers, stitched probably in Pennsylvania around 1850, sold at Sotheby Parke Bernet's York Avenue galleries for $7,750, the auction record for a quilt—five times the price paid for such bedcoverings a decade ago.

eschew   *es CHOO:*
(to keep away from something harmful or disliked; shun; avoid)

Behind the modesty of a temperament that eschewed self-assertion and elaborate display, there was a protean talent we have only begun to appreciate. That is one reason—the main reason—why it requires a retrospective on the scale of the current exhibition for the full weight of Pissarro's achievement to make itself felt.

esoteric   *e suh TE rik*
(understood by or meant for only the select few who have special knowledge or interest)

The language gap is not too serious if one orders from the standard menu, but it results in considerable frustration for those who want to try more esoteric specialties offered only on the Japanese menu.

espalier   *e SPAL yer*
(a lattice or trellis on which trees and shrubs are trained to grow flat)

Katherine is an exceptionally fine crabapple, producing two-inch, soft-pink blossoms that are reminiscent of roses late in May. It also espaliers well.

espouse   *i SPOWZ*
(to embrace, support or advocate a cause, idea, etc.)

The Moral Majority is a Christian fundamentalist political movement founded in 1979 by a television evangelist, the Rev. Jerry Falwell. It espouses conservative views on a wide range of social, religious and political issues and has lobbied against the proposed equal rights amendment, abortion and civil rights for homosexuals.

ethereal   *i THI ri uhl*
(delicate; heavenly; celestial)

"Dreamtime" is a splendid, ethereally beautiful record, with Mr. Verlaine's dreamlike imagery, wonderfully tender songs about sex and whimsical tales of imaginary characters like "Mr. Blur" set off by guitar solos that are soaring, melodious and executed with remarkable technical aplomb.

ethnic stew   *ETH nik STOO:*
(a mixture of ethnic groups living within a particular boundary: it implies the harmonious coexistence of groups that maintain their separate identities, and is replacing the term "melting pot," which suggests assimilation or a loss of separate identities)

In the ethnic stew of New York, the Eskimo flavor has been lacking. Now the Eskimo, represented by art rather than in person, has a center in town, the Alaska Shop, a gallery at 31 East 74th Street that sells and exhibits objects made in northern Canada and Alaska.

ethnocentrism   *eth noh SEN tri zuhm*
(the emotional attitude that one's own ethnic group, nation or culture is superior to all others)

This ethnocentric Western belief, that the lives of non-Westerners are less important than those of Westerners and that ultimately Westerners are superior people, has always been misguided and has absolutely no place in today's crowded, interdependent world.

eulogy   *YOO: luh ji*
(a formal speech praising a person who has recently died)

At a funeral service yesterday attended by 500 people, including notables from the literary and theatrical worlds, Paddy Chayefsky, who died Saturday at the age of 58, was eulogized as a family man and friend, and as a writer who used his pen with passion to expose the injustices of ordinary life.

euphemism   *YOO: fuh mi zuhm*
(a mild or inoffensive word substituted for one that is more direct or blunt)

One of the things that persuaded Mr. Matthau to do the film was his respect for the play. "When you left the theater after seeing 'First Monday,' you felt good because you hadn't been taken. That play isn't escapist entertainment. 'Escapist entertainment,' by the way, is a euphemism for junk."

euphoria   *yoo FAW ri uh*
(a feeling of well-being or high spirits)

Like marijuana, cocaine is not widely regarded as a dangerous drug. Nevertheless, figures show that cocaine figured in 350 emergency-room deaths in 1979. A stimulant of the central nervous system, cocaine produces an initial sense of euphoria and self-confidence.

South Africa's leaders were euphoric when Mr. Reagan appeared to reverse America's Africa policy in a television interview with Walter Cronkite. He described South Africa as a friendly country "that has stood behind us in every war we fought." He stressed the West's strategic stake in South African minerals, and praised Pretoria for its "sincere and honest efforts" to remove apartheid.

Apartheid (uh PAHRT hight: Afrikaans, *apartness*) is the South African policy of strict racial segregation and discrimination against blacks, Asians and others of nonwhite or mixed parentage. The apartheid system involves separate transport, schools, and residential areas, travel restrictions and the prohibition of intermarriage. The policy was adopted officially in 1948 by South Africa's Afrikaner Nationalist Party, and led to the country's break with the British Commonwealth in 1961. The official name for apartheid in South Africa is "Separate Development."

---

evanescent   *e vuh NE suhnt*
(*tending to fade from sight; transitory; short-lived; ephemeral*)

Xenon is a $2 million discothèque. It regards itself as one of the ultimate discos. According to its spokesman, Xenon has not built its reputation on keeping people out. Of course, it has admitted its share of the truly famous and its quota of evanescent celebrities. But the eternally anonymous have been there, too.

exacerbate   *ig ZA ser bayt*
(*to aggravate; intensify*)

White House officials now openly admit that the President's budget problems are exacerbated by two things: the President's refusal to increase taxes or defer the recently approved tax cut, and his refusal to trim military spending by more than the recently announced $2 billion next year.

excise   *ik SIGHZ*
(*to remove by cutting out*)

The new version of "Trade Wind" consists of the original opening chapter as well as several other chapters that were excised in the earlier version.

excoriate   *ik SKAW ri ayt*
(to denounce harshly; skin verbally: originally, to strip off or remove the skin from)

It's a great yet quite serious sport in the Sun Belt these days to excoriate everything in, from or vaguely pertaining to New York City.

exculpate   *EK skuhl payt*
(to clear from a charge of guilt or fault; free from blame)

Color prints and slides start to fade from the moment the materials are processed, and in order to alert users to this photographic fact of life, film manufacturers have been printing an exculpatory statement on their packages for years explaining this possibility.

exegesis   *ek suh JEE sis*
(an explanation, critical analysis or interpretation of a word, work of art, literary passage, etc., especially of the Bible)

Mr. Johnson recalled how Mr. Barr had persuaded the Modern's collections committee to buy a triptych of Marilyn Monroe, painted by James Gill. "He was intensely interested in the Monroe mythology, the symbolism," Mr. Johnson said. "He harked back to Aphrodite and even the White Goddess. By the time he finished his exegesis, there wasn't a dry eye in the house."

A triptych (TRIP tik: Greek, three folds) is a set of three panels with pictures, designs or carvings, often hinged so that the two side panels may be folded over the central one. Triptychs are usually religious in nature and often used as altarpieces.

---

exemplar   *ig ZEM plahr*
(a model worthy of imitation)

Bob Marley, who had become the world's best-known reggae artist before his death this year, was more than a leading pop songwriter and musical innovator; in Jamaica, he was looked up to as a spiritual and moral exemplar.

exhort   *ig ZAWRT*
(to urge, advise or caution earnestly)

Stanley Kaplan paces, hands on hips, exhorting in Knute Rockne fashion. "Words! Words! Words!" he exclaims to a class of 20 high school-age students. "Very important!" Mr. Kaplan runs a special school, one of a growing number of its kind that cater to a particular desire: improving scores on the Scholastic Aptitude Test.

exhume   ig ZYOO:M
(to dig out of the earth; disinter; bring to light; revive or restore after a period of neglect or forgetting)

Twenty-five bodies have been exhumed in Los Angeles and Riverside Counties so far in an investigation into the mysterious deaths of more than 50 patients in five southern California hospitals.

Jose Quintero's unwarranted exhumation of Eugene O'Neill's 1924 "Welded" at the Horace Mann Theater at Columbia University succeeds in proving that this is one of O'Neill's most dreadful plays.

exodus   EK suh duhs
(a going out; a departure of a large number of people)

Shortly after noon, a tremendous exodus takes place during Ramadan in downtown Cairo as people leave for home. By 3 in the afternoon, a street like Kasr el-Nil is as deserted as an old American mining town that went bust. The shops are closed, the restaurants are shuttered, everyone is gone except for clusters of men praying in corners of buildings and sidewalks where they have laid down straw prayer mats.

Ramadan (ra muh DAHN) is the Moslem month during which the faithful fast from sunrise to sunset. It is traditionally the month when Allah sent down the Koran to earth.

---

exonerate   ig ZAH nuh rayt
(to clear, as of a charge; free from blame; exculpate)

TAMPA, Fla., March 4 (AP)—A state board today unanimously exonerated Capt. John Lerro, the pilot of a freighter that toppled part of the Sunshine Skyway Bridge in a storm last May, sending 35 persons plunging to their deaths in Tampa Bay.

expansionism   ik SPAN shuhn i zuhm
(the policy of expanding a nation's territory or its sphere of influence, often at the expense of other nations)

Answering repeated Greek charges of "Turkey's expansionist aims," the Defense Minister declared, "Since the establishment of the republic, no war has been engaged by Turkey." He said Turkey had no desire to acquire land outside its own territory but would not "give one inch to anybody."

expeditious   *ek spuh DI shuhs*
(efficient and speedy; prompt)

The sea robin, the various puffers or blowfish, the horned pout or the catfish all present a problem to those preparing them for the table: they have to be skinned, deheaded and gutted in the most expeditious manner possible.

expiate   *EK spi ayt*
(to make amends for; atone for)

Mr. Speer (the name is pronounced shpair) was the only Nazi leader at the Nuremberg war-crimes trials in 1945–46 to admit his guilt. There were those who thought he spent the rest of his life trying to expiate the horrors of the concentration camps and slave factories, and others who found his memoirs self-serving, showing the pure technician unmoved by human misery.

expletive   *EK spluh tiv*
(an exclamation or oath, especially one that is profane or obscene)

McEnroe, the left-hander from Douglaston, Queens, who is seeded second, left England last summer as a hero after having battled Borg in a memorable five-set final. Today he smashed two racquets, lost two points on penalties, called the umpire, Edward James, an "incompetent fool" and then uttered a four-letter expletive during a final confrontation with Fred Hoyles, the referee.

explicit   *ik SPLI sit*
(clearly stated and leaving nothing implied; distinctly expressed; definite)

Both you and John Updike are longtime New York writers. What is the difference between John Cheever and John Updike? "Well, I'm 20 years older than John. I'll be 67 on May 27. Updike writes far more explicitly about sex, for one thing. Explicit sexual scenes don't particularly interest me. Everybody knows what's going on. I can't think, in the whole history of literature, of an explicit sex scene that was memorable, can you?"

expound   *ik SPOWND*
(to set forth or explain in detail)

The Secretary seemed to go out of his way to woo the Western governors, most of whom are Democrats. Wearing a cowboy hat and an open-neck plaid shirt, he expounded on his own Western roots—he grew up on a ranch in Wyoming—and the West's natural beauty. And he paid enthusiastic compliments to the Governors, each of whom he addressed by their first name.

expunge   *ik SPUHNJ*
(*to erase or remove completely*)

Now, Alla and Stakhan sing only for friends in their Moscow apartment. They have been banned from Soviet stages, their foreign tours canceled, their records removed from the store shelves, their videotapes erased, their voices no longer heard on the radio. An encyclopedia on the arts was held up so that an entry about them could be expunged. The reason is that two years ago they applied to emigrate to Israel.

extant   *EK stuhnt*
(*still existing; not lost or destroyed*)

The elaborately carved ivory cross, still tentatively attributed to Master Hugo, a lay artist working at the English monastery of Bury St. Edmunds, is considered one of the finest works of medieval art extant.

extemporize   *ik STEM puh righz*
(*to speak without preparation; improvise*)

One could make the case for a meeting to "clear the air," except that the 74-year-old Mr. Brezhnev is in such poor health that he is said to be unable to extemporize and to talk only from prepared statements.

extol   *ik STOHL*
(*to praise highly; laud*)

In the 1960's, when gasoline was cheap and high-performance cars ruled the roads, songs were written about Pontiacs. In fact, a tune by Ronnie and the Daytonas extolling the engine of the Pontiac GTO rose as high as No. 4 on the pop music charts in 1964.

extradite   *EK struh dight*
(*to turn over an alleged criminal, fugitive, etc., to the jurisdiction of another country, state, etc.*)

Although his extradition was immediately demanded by the Iranian Government, Mr. Bani-Sadr, 48 years old, will be permitted to stay in France so long as he refrains from political activity.

extrapolate   *ik STRA puh layt*
(to arrive at conclusions or results by hypothesizing from known facts or observations)

In estimating the total loss of Federal aid to New York in 1981–82, Mr. Carey said he was extrapolating from figures provided by Gov. James R. Thompson of Illinois. Mr. Carey said Mr. Thompson's rough estimate of a $500 million loss on his state's $11 billion budget "would bring us up to maybe $700 million in New York on a $16 billion budget."

extraterrestrial   *ek struh tuh RE stri uhl*
(originating, located or occurring outside the earth or its atmosphere)

EDWARDS AIR FORCE BASE, Calif., April 14—The space shuttle Columbia rocketed out of orbit and glided to a safe landing on the desert here today to conclude the successful first demonstration of a bold new approach to extraterrestrial travel, the re-usable winged spaceship.

extricate   *EK stri kayt*
(to set free; disentangle)

At breakfast, the beautifully bright and fresh grapefruit is so badly cut that fork and knife are needed to extricate the fruit.

exude   *ig ZOO:D*
(to send out gradually in drops through pores or small openings; ooze out)

This butterfly lays its eggs in the flowers of thyme. The caterpillars feed there for a period, but are then picked up by ants that are attracted by the sweet fluid that the caterpillars exude. They are carried back to the ant's nest, where they complete their development, feeding on the young ant brood while the ants, in turn, feed on the caterpillar secretion.

In addition to skill and steadiness, Winfield, at age 29, exudes a childlike joy in playing and in his own celebrity. He has a contagious, gap-toothed smile, like Magic Johnson's, that television cameramen have learned to zoom in on after he reaches base on a hit or makes an especially satisfying catch.

exultant   *ig ZUHL tuhnt*
(triumphant; jubilant)

The voice-over announcer growls "we are driven" as a sleek Datsun car whips down a twisting highway in a recent television commercial. An exultant Toyota owner leaps skyward as a chorus trills "Oh, what a feeling!" A throaty singer implores viewers to take "just one look" at Mazda's offerings.

fabrication   *fa bri KAY shuhn*
(*a falsehood*)

The Washington Post said today that an article it printed about the life of an 8-year-old heroin addict in the slums of Washington, for which the author won a Pulitzer Prize this week, was a fabrication.

facade   *fuh SAHD*
(*the front of a building*)

The Bonaventure, whose mirrored, futuristic 35-story facade is often shown in television programs shot in Los Angeles, may be losing guests because its lowest rooms are on the 10th floor, above an atrium and shopping area, Mr. Hawes said.

(*a superficial appearance or illusion of something*)

There was no Joe Louis behind any facade. He was the same slow-spoken, considerate person in a close social group as he was to the vast crowds that surged in on him to clutch his every word when he was at the apogee of the boxing world.

facetious   *fuh SEE shuhs*
(*not meant to be taken seriously or literally*)

On a wall of the National Cattlemen's Association office in Denver hangs a bumper sticker urging: SUPPORT BEEF—RUN OVER A CHICKEN! Facetious, of course, but the slogan reflects a new disquiet among America's cattle ranchers and cattle feeders as they struggle to survive in one of the most expensive and risky of farm industries.

factionalism   *FAK shuhn uh li zuhm*
(*partisan conflict within an organization or a government*)

CAIRO, Sept. 5—President Anwar el-Sadat, denouncing religious factionalism, deposed the nation's Coptic Pope tonight and said he would dissolve Islamic groups that threaten national unity.

fallible   *FA luh buhl*
(liable to err or make a mistake)

The quality of orchestral playing, both soloistic and ensemble, that Sir Georg Solti drew from the Chicagoans last night at Carnegie Hall was so consistently high that an air of unreality settled over the entire evening. The listener could virtually forget that mundane, fallible instruments and musicians were mediating between him and the music; direct contact of a rare sort was made possible.

fastidious   *fa STI di uhs*
(careful in all details; exacting; meticulous)

Parisians, fastidious in many things, do not hesitate to toss their used yellow Metro tickets on the station platforms and corridors.

Paris's subway system is the Metro. So is Moscow's. London's is the Underground. In London, pedestrian passageways under crowded intersections are called subways.

---

fatalist   *FAY tuh list*
(one who accepts every event as inevitable)

For three hours the 10 National Guardsmen stationed in the town were pinned inside their barracks by rifle fire as the rebels shot up houses and looted stores. An 11-year-old boy was killed and eight townspeople were wounded. From inside the barracks the soldiers' desperate call for help went unanswered. "We have become used to it," José Osnel Colato, a 25-year-old soldier, said later. "We are all going to die sometime." His was the fatalistic attitude of the Salvadoran peasant, in and out of uniform, for as the world debates the fate of El Salvador it is in small communities such as San Agustin that the brunt of the war is being felt.

faux pas   *foh PAH*
(a social blunder; error in etiquette; tactless act or remark: French, false step)

She also faces a lifetime of ribbon cuttings, ship christenings, tedious official dinners, worthy causes and tree plantings. The constant glare of publicity will reveal the smallest faux pas in her comportment and dress.

By her vows she has chosen one of the world's most transparent goldfish bowls, that of the adored British royal family.

fawn *fawn*
(to show favor or attention by servile, flattering or obsequious behavior)

From the start, the "21" strategy has been to make good customers part of its extended family. Regulars are greeted by name at the door, seated at their usual table and fawned over by their customary waiter.

faze *fayz*
(to disturb; disconcert)

Though Reagan is alarmed by the size and number of U.S. Government agencies, he doesn't seem fazed in any way by the size or power of, say, General Electric.

feckless *FEK luhs*
(weak; ineffective)

Although he was dismissed by many as a somewhat feckless interim leader when he became President after the death of Gamal Abdel Nasser, Mr. Sadat gradually showed that he had staying power, political skill and an ability that transformed him into a world statesman when he paid his historic visit to Jerusalem in the search for peace.

feign *fayn*
(pretend)

In response to another question, critics' allegations that he is warlike, the President, feigning amazement, cracked, "I've been here more than six weeks now and haven't fired a shot."

feisty *FIGH sti*
(spiritedly ill-tempered and aggressive; full of fight)

For 444 days, television viewers came to know "Mary," the feisty young student militant in Teheran. The interpreter and spokesman for the group holding the 52 hostages, she became a news-media personality, a link between the militants and journalists. We saw her steadily, right from the beginning of the crisis, when she would trot out daily to deliver hostile attacks on the United States, to her final interviews with the hostages, conducted a day before their release.

felicitous   *fuh LI suh tuhs*
(aptly chosen; suitable; appropriate)

The all-male cast has been felicitously chosen, and what might have passed as stereotypes in a less-sensitive production become fully-fleshed human beings.

ferret   *FE rit*
(to search out and bring to light: ferrets are small, weasel-like animals which people train to enter the burrows of rats and rabbits and drive them to the surface)

A dismaying case of repression surfaced a decade ago at the Church-owned Brigham Young University when the administration recruited students for a "spy ring" intended to ferret out faculty radicals.

fester   *FE ster*
(to become infected; rot; degenerate)

BEIRUT, Lebanon, May 11—This once rich little country, ripped apart by a half dozen years of violence, again stands at the brink of war. Its seemingly ceaseless internal troubles, worsened by international meddling, have festered and become an international crisis with Israel and Syria rattling fighter planes and missiles at each other in possibly the most dangerous situation in the Middle East since the 1973 Arab-Israeli war.

festoon   *fe STOO:N*
(to adorn by suspending strings of flowers, ribbon, fabric, etc., between two points)

In Mr. Buatta's English sitting room, the walls are glazed dark red and the windows majestically festooned with an elaborate curtain. "The special lining is essential," he explained, "but most clients wouldn't pay extra for it." The chintz—a gorgeously rich Chinoiserie pattern with birds, flowers and pagodas—is also used for some of the upholstery. "I'm in my Chinese period," he said.

CAPE TOWN—Festooning his remarks with quotations from a British antislavery crusader and Abraham Lincoln, the South African official who by law has vast powers to regulate the lives of the black majority unveiled a package of legislation late last year that, he said, marked the beginning of an irreversible process of betterment for blacks who have managed to establish themselves in urban areas.

Chintz is a printed and glazed cotton fabric, usually of bright colors and with flower designs or other patterns. Because of the cheap and sleazy quality of some chintz fabrics, *chintzy* came to mean *cheap, stingy, petty* or *gaudy*. Chinoiserie is an ornate style of decoration for furniture, textiles, ceramics, etc., based on Chinese motifs.

fiasco   *fi A skoh*
(a complete failure, especially an ambitious project that ends as a ridiculous failure)

Mr. Silverman's impatience for success at NBC led him to rush series on the air—and then off again at the first hint of ratings failure. The biggest fiasco was "Supertrain." Put on the air six months before its producers felt it was ready, and then extravagantly promoted, the show was a failure. It cost NBC $5 million and Mr. Silverman a lot of credibility.

fifth column   *FIFTH KAH luhm*
(a group of people who aid the enemy from within their own country)

The Teheran radio denounced the demonstrators as fifth columnists bent on creating tension despite warnings on radio and television last night that the rally was banned. The leftists, the radio said, had sought to turn the attention of the people away from the war with Iraq, "thus trying to help their American masters and the fifth column of the enemy."

The expression *fifth column* was first used by General Emilio Mola, a rebel leader during the Spanish Civil War. Closing in on Madrid in November, 1936, he boasted to journalists that the four columns he commanded would be aided by a fifth column of sympathizers within the city who would rise when the time was right. However, Madrid did not fall for another two and a half years.

figuratively   *FI gyoo ruh tiv li*
(in a manner of speaking; not literally)

Ending a long dispute in which multimillion-dollar lawsuits were filed against one another, the Bee Gees singing group and their longtime manager, Robert Stigwood, have figuratively kissed and made up.

fillip   *FI lip*
(an extra something that stimulates, livens up or adds interest)

The presence of Prince Charles will add a fillip to an evening-long celebration of the Royal Ballet's 50th anniversary at Lincoln Center, an event no self-respecting Anglophile would dream of missing.

finesse   fi NES
(to avoid by adroit maneuvering; get around)

Bertrand Russell was quite certain that his telegrams to Nikita Khrushchev at the time of the Cuban missile crisis managed to finesse World War III.

fingerling   FING ger ling
(a small fish about the length of a finger, or a young fish up to the end of the first year)

A profitable catfish business first requires heavy clay soil to form a stable pond, a cheap supply of clean water, flat land and a warm climate. In Mississippi, which averages 240 days a year of weather no cooler than 65 degrees, six-inch fingerlings put in the ponds in March will usually be ready to harvest in November at 1¼ pounds, the size the processors prefer.

firebrand   FIGH er brand
(a person who stirs up others to revolt or strike)

A calm and reasoning man, Mr. Wilkins did not avoid the limelight, and Presidents and governors sought his counsel on racial matters. But Mr. Wilkins did avoid both words and deeds that would seem to cast him in the role of a firebrand.

fishmonger   FISH mahng ger
(a dealer in fish)

Fish bargains can be found in fishmongers along Ninth Avenue between 38th and 42d Streets, where whole large bluefish big enough to serve four to eight people are selling for 99 cents a pound. They are good wrapped in foil and baked with slices of lime or lemon, garlic, and dill or parsley.

fix   FIKS
(any self-administered indulgence that brings on euphoria, thrills or intense pleasure with each repetition: originally the term for a single narcotics injection that brought on a sudden "rush" of intense pleasure)

"When I was in my late teens and early 20's, I used to get my 'fix' from high-diving and breaking aviation records," Col. Frank Kurtz said yesterday. "Nowadays, the greatest fix for me is seeing my daughter, Swoosie Kurtz, giving people in the audience a wonderful time when she performs onstage in 'Fifth of July.' "

flaccid *FLAK sid*
(*soft and limp; flabby*)

The concluding Brahms Symphony No. 3 was less happily done. Mr. Mehta had the orchestra playing truly; some of the lyrical moments were ravishing. But Brahms is not really about ravishment. His music prospers with more firmness. Mr. Mehta's Brahms Third was a flaccid affair.

flagrant *FLAY gruhnt*
(*outrageously glaring, noticeable or evident*)

Until recent years, banks refused to count working wives' salaries, alimony or child support in establishing credit, and there were many other instances of flagrant sex discrimination in lending.

flagship *(FLAG ship)*
(*originally, the ship that carries the commander of a fleet and displays his flag, or the finest, largest and newest ship of a steamship line; now, also, a store, radio or television station or other business that is the leading or most conspicuous part of a chain*)

Two years after it disappeared from Fifth Avenue, Bonwit Teller's is coming home again to the corner of 57th Street and Fifth. The move is a key part of the strategy by the Allied Stores Corporation to strengthen Bonwit's image as a fashion innovator and restore the flagship of the chain to a prestigious location.

flak *flak*
(*strong, clamorous criticism: a slang word*)

"Pressure?" Winfield repeated later after his two-hour workout, talking generally about what he might encounter in his first year as a Yankee. "I really don't know what to expect here. If I'm in good shape, I'll play good baseball and contribute to the team. I don't know how I'll be received here. I don't know what kind of static and flak Reggie had to take."

Flak is a World War II German acronym for anti-aircraft gun: *fl(ieger)a(bwehr)k(anone)*. The word was used by all nations in the war for the bursting shells fired from such artillery, whose fragments could pierce nearby aircraft. In peacetime, the word has come to describe noisy criticism resulting from one's actions.

---

flamboyant   *flam BOI uhnt*
(*showy; extravagant*)

In 1942, at a New York boxing writers dinner, former Mayor James J. Walker made a presentation to Louis and, in his flamboyant, sentimental style, said, "Joe Louis, you laid a rose on Abraham Lincoln's grave."

flotsam and jetsam   *FLAHT suhm and JET suhm*
(*the wreckage of a ship or its cargo found floating on the sea or washed ashore: specifically, flotsam is goods found floating on the sea, and jetsam is cargo thrown overboard to lighten a ship in danger*)

In addition to the Columbia, there are 1,156 other spacecraft orbiting the earth, as well as 3,419 pieces of debris, including spent rocket bodies, nuts, bolts—the flotsam and jetsam of space shots conducted not just by the United States and the Soviet Union, but by everybody else, too.

flounder   *FLOWN der*
(*to struggle awkwardly or clumsily in order to move, as in deep snow or mud*)

An Israeli bulk carrier ship with 35 crewmen aboard sank today in heavy seas 96 miles southeast of Bermuda, leaving three crewmen dead and others floundering in rough seas while they awaited rescue, the Coast Guard said.

(*to proceed clumsily or helplessly in confusion*)

Weighed down by excess capacity and imperiled by growing demand for energy sources other than oil, the world oil tanker industry is floundering in the wake of the current oversupply of oil.

fluke   *floo:k*
(*a result, especially a successful one, brought about by accident; stroke of luck: a slang word*)

Mr. Moriarty's entry into the fireworks business at age 15 was a fluke. When the government began auctioning off the belongings of interned Japanese-Americans during World War II in Washington State, Mr. Moriarty bid $15 for what he thought was a handful of fireworks. To his surprise, however, the $15 purchased an entire truckload.

flummox   *FLUH muhks*
(to bewilder; confuse; perplex: a slang word)

Sony is about to introduce its Walkman II, which is hardly bigger than the cassette itself and fits into a shirt pocket with room to spare. To hear orchestral sonorities richly flowing at full concert level from such a diminutive device never fails to flummox first-time listeners.

flux   *fluhks*
(continuous change)

New York often seems a city in perpetual flux, with change the only constant. One morning, with a small belch of explosives and a puff of plaster dust, the building around the corner is reduced from a sum to its parts. The next day, the grocery down the street becomes a gourmet shop. Once thriving businesses are abandoned. Abandoned buildings are transformed into cooperative lofts.

foible   *FOI buhl*
(a minor weakness or failing of character)

According to its producers, the difference between "Another Life" and major network soap operas is that the new serial will have an underlying religious theme and present positive answers to moral perplexities. Otherwise, viewers can look forward to the usual array of human foibles and miseries.

foment   *foh MENT*
(to stir up; instigate; incite)

MADRID, May 8—With tensions running high after the assassinations of seven military men and Civil Guards in less than a week, Prime Minister Leopoldo Calvo Sotelo tonight accused unidentified foreign states of fomenting terrorism in Spain.

forage   *FAW rij*
(to search for food; feed)

Alligators live within and near New Orleans "in fairly large numbers," 30,000 to 40,000, Mr. Ensminger said. Real estate developers have built houses along canals in the city's eastern wetlands, a rich foraging spot for alligators.

foray   *FAW ray*
(a raid in search of plunder)

Henry Kaplan, a New York dealer, whose shop, Sideshow, at 184 Ninth Avenue, benefits from his forays through flea markets, says that he has noticed that Art Deco trivia is "on its way out."

(a venture or initial attempt in some field)

Jane Fonda is making a foray into network television—as a producer. ABC-TV has ordered four one-hour episodes of "Nine to Five," a comedy based on the hit movie of the same title. Miss Fonda, who starred in the film with Lily Tomlin and Dolly Parton, will be executive producer of the series along with Bruce Gilbert.

forebear   *FAWR bair*
(an ancestor)

Diana, a former kindergarten teacher whose forebears include the first Duke of Marlborough, is now formally styled Diana, Princess of Wales—not Princess Diana, because only someone born a princess may use that style. But one day, all being well, she will be Queen Diana as the wife of King Charles III.

———

To forbear is to avoid or shun: "Remember your diet and forbear the dessert." However, *forbear* is also a variant and acceptable spelling for *forebear,* an ancestor.

———

forensic   *fuh REN zik*
(the application of medical knowledge to questions of law affecting life or property, including ascertaining the cause of death—used in connection with court testimony by a medical professional; also called medical jurisprudence)

The teeth of a man accused of murdering a prison guard match bite wounds found on the guard's body and on the body of a Schenectady woman the same man was accused of murdering, a forensic dentist testified.

formidable   *FAWR mi duh buhl*
(difficult to surmount or undertake)

Obviously, the production problems surrounding "Khovanshchina" are formidable, not the least of which is the fact that Mussorgsky died before orchestrating the opera. What exists is the piano-vocal score with the Fifth Act only sketched in.

forte *fawrt*
(*something in which a person excels; strong point*)

TOKYO, May 7—Prime Minister Zenko Suzuki of Japan, who arrived in Washington yesterday to meet with President Reagan, is a short, thickset man whose surprising forte as a Japanese leader is to be frank.

forthrightly *FAWRTH right li*
(*directly; frankly*)

A musical about Charlie Chaplin, called, forthrightly, "Charlie Chaplin," will open on Broadway next April.

The gate of the tall green bullpen fence in right field in Shea Stadium swung open, and Mike Marshall appeared. Marshall, the Mets' 38-year-old relief pitcher, took one skipping step, like a boy on a lark, and then trotted forthrightly across the outfield to the mound, like a man on a mission.

fractious *FRAK shuhs*
(*hard to manage; unruly; rebellious*)

In signing the treaty with Israel, Mr. Sadat alienated most of the fractious Arab world, which broke relations with Egypt.

Francophile *FRAYNG kuh fighl*
(*a person who admires or is extremely fond of France, its people, customs, etc.*)

Comparisons between California wines and French wines inevitably invite howls of protest, often from Francophiles who object to the suggestion that California producers may be capable of making a superior product. No matter how scientific the tasting nor how sophisticated the tasters, a finding that a California wine has vanquished a renowned French wine in a blind competition is always challenged.

frenetic *fruh NE tik*
(*frantic; frenzied*)

Pudgy's style is to "work a room." The frenetic comedian, whose other name is Beverly Cardella, stalks the tables of a nightclub, insulting guests in a style somewhat reminiscent of Don Rickles but with less reliance on name calling or criticism of people's appearances.

frigate   *FRI git*
(a U.S. warship larger than a destroyer and smaller than a light cruiser: originally, a fast, medium-sized sailing warship of the 18th and early 19th centuries, having a lofty ship rig and heavily armed on one or two decks)

A United States Navy frigate rescued 43 Vietnamese refugees who had been drifting for 10 days in the South China Sea with no food and water, a Navy spokesman said today.

fritter   *FRI ter*
(to waste bit by bit on petty things, usually used with "away")

Barrymore, his great "Hamlet" behind him, would eventually bring about his own destruction by frittering away his talent and psyche in Hollywood.

frugal   *FROO: guhl*
(not wasteful; thrifty; economical)

As a bride, a long time ago, I poured over the newspaper advertisements on Thursday and spent most of Friday driving from market to market buying the specials. My husband thought that was so wonderful that he told his mother how frugal I was. It certainly beat staying home and cleaning house.

fruition   *froo: I shuhn*
(a coming to fulfillment)

Construction of the mall, to be known as Broadway Plaza, would bring to fruition an idea that has been discussed since the early 1970's as a way to revitalize a shabby area.

frumpy   *FRUHM pi*
(dull, plain and unfashionably dressed, said of girls or women)

Looking doughy and frumpy, wearing a perpetual hit-me expression, Miss Ullmann is cast as a widow who does little but sulk and tremble.

fudge   *fuhj*
(to refuse to commit oneself or give a direct answer; hedge)

What do you call a jazz ensemble that consists of 8 to 10 musicians and combines the loose agility of a small combo with the density and fire-power of a big band? Jazz musicians and critics have never been sure, and they have usually fudged the issue by referring to such groups as octets, nonets, or tentets, or, more informally, as "little big bands."

fulcrum   *FUHL kruhm*
(a means of exerting influence, pressure, etc.)

Proponents of the project, including the Koch administration, argue that the new Portman Hotel would serve as a fulcrum for revitalizing the deteriorating Times Square area.

fulminate   *FUHL muh nayt*
(to issue a thunderous verbal attack or denunciation)

While the fallout from Israel's raid on Iraq's Osirak nuclear reactor was still around us, Flora Lewis, in an almost unprecedented attack on a candidate in a foreign election by a Times correspondent (column June 22), fulminates against Menachem Begin, describing him as a "man whose vision is limited to denouncing the past" and who favors "blasting the world with words and bombs."

furbelows   *FER buh lohz*
(showy, useless trimming or ornamentation)

Dressed in a lavender gown with amazing furbelows and a frumpy bonnet, Mr. Ohno has made himself up like a glittering old hag.

furor   *FYOOR or*
(uproar; fury; rage)

During the post-publication furor over "Lolita," Nabokov himself, who died in 1977, dismissed charges of pornography as "foolish" and called his book "just a story, a fairy tale, as all stories are." He patiently informed another interviewer, "My knowledge of nymphets is purely scholarly, I assure you. In fact, I don't much care for little girls."

A nymphet is a sexually precocious young adolescent or preadolescent girl. In "Lolita" (1955), Vladimir Nabokov applied the term to his 12-year-old title character.

---

furtive   *FER tiv*
(done in a stealthy manner to avoid observation; surreptitious)

Certainly we all have habits we should be ashamed of, and I think it is salutary to confess them. Me, I lick the inside lids of cans after I open them. At my age! I do this furtively. No one has ever caught me at it.

fusion   *FYOO: zhuhn*
(a blend of jazz and rock or other popular musical styles)

A few of fusion music's pioneers, the members of the group Weather Report, for example, have continued to make challenging music out of rock, Latin and ethnic rhythms, electronics, and elements of the jazz tradition.

gadfly   *GAD fligh*
(a person who repeatedly and persistently annoys others with schemes, ideas, demands, requests, etc.)

Mr. Radoff, a 43-year-old social studies teacher at the Bronx High School of Science, loves to play gadfly to the Koch administration on what he considers its "brownout" policy of "neglect and abandonment" of trees.

gaffe   *gaf*
(a social blunder; faux pas; saying the wrong thing: French, blunder)

In foreign commercial dealings, Representative Simon lists these embarrassing gaffes: A major American fountain pen manufacturer inadvertently suggested in Latin American advertisements that its product would prevent unwanted pregnancies; "Body by Fisher" in Flemish came out "Corpse by Fisher"; the first Chinese version of "Come alive with Pepsi" promised that "Pepsi brings your ancestors back from the grave"; Chevrolet's Nova told potential Latin American customers that the car "doesn't go"—"no va."

gall   *gawl*
(rude boldness; impudence; audacity)

To the Editor: I certainly hope that in one of his first strikes against inflation President Reagan tears up Nancy's credit cards and that he does not let her again shame the less-fashionable of us by having the insensitive gall to wear a dress that costs as much as a sports car and treat herself to a new wardrobe that is worth more than the sum of my paychecks for two and a half years. We're having hot dogs for dinner. Again.

(to irritate, annoy, vex)

"All we want is to print the truth," said Witold Slezak, head of the printers' union in Warsaw. "We feel that we have a moral responsibility for the information that we provide to society through our work." This position has led, inevitably, to a clash with the censors, whose heavy red-pencil markings on page proofs have long galled the printers, who were in a position to read the information that was denied to the rest of Poland.

galvanize   *GAL vuh nighz*
(to stimulate as if by electric shock)

Subway safety is always a galvanizing issue, a point underscored by a statistic Miss Bellamy released the other day. It suggested that a person who rides the subway at night on a daily basis stands a 1-in-40 chance of becoming a felony victim over the course of a year. The daytime odds are 1 in 200.

gambit   *GAM bit*
(a maneuver or action intended to gain an advantage)

For their most recent release, "Sandinista!" they produced a three-record set, hoping that CBS Records would accept it as the equivalent of three albums, thus fulfilling the band's contract with the label. The gambit failed; the Clash still owe CBS two more albums.

gambol   *GAM buhl*
(to jump and skip about in play; frolic)

In the Northeast, most of those who visit the seashore in summer are there to sail, to gambol in the waves or to lie like slowly ripening squashes in the sun, while, through much of July and August, the surf caster languishes.

gamely   *GAYM li*
(in a plucky or courageous manner)

"I'm here, I have been all the intervening years," says William Saroyan's entry in "Who's Who in America." Yesterday the 72-year-old author was reported hanging in gamely following a stroke that felled him Monday at his home in Fresno, Calif.

gamine   *GA min*
(a girl with a roguish, saucy charm: French, a child having an attractive impertinence supposedly characteristic of street urchins: originally, a neglected child left to roam the streets)

She has none of the nymphetlike sex appeal of Jodie Foster or Brooke
Shields; Kristy McNichol is the girl next door, the female cousin to Huck
Finn. Yet she's something more than an engaging gamine.

gamut   *GA muht*
(the entire range or extent)

As the latest in a long line of distinguished "Peter and the Wolf" narra-
tors, a group that has run the gamut from Eleanor Roosevelt to David
Bowie, Mr. Koch was not to be outdone, and he gave his all to the job.

gargantuan   *gahr GAN choo uhn*
(of immense size; huge; colossal)

The showiest pieces for the gargantuan, fully developed symphony orchestra come from the late 19th century and the early years of our own
century.

Gargantua, a giant of medieval legend, was adopted by François
Rabelais (1494?–1553) in his epic satire "Gargantua and Panta-
gruel." His most famous attribute was his colossal appetite:
17,913 cows supplied him with milk in his infancy, and in one of
his exploits he swallowed five pilgrims in a salad. *Gargantuan* is
usually found in reference to someone's appetite. Indeed, the
original character got his name from *garganta,* the Spanish word
for gullet.

---

garish   *GAI rish*
(gaudy; showy)

Some of the best dyed furs around are in the collection by Anne Klein
& Company for Michael Forrest. Colors—wine, navy, olive green, mustard—are not garish and very wearable.

garner   *GAHR ner*
(to collect or gather)

At another bait site, Dr. Lynch pointed to a group of ants that seemed
to fear a piece of food they had garnered might be stolen by other species.
To prevent this, they had camouflaged the bit of tuna by covering it with
forest debris so it would not be recognized by their competitors.

gastronomic   *ga struh NAH mik*
(of the art or science of good eating)

"Pudding" is a vague term in English gastronomic history, originally applied to sausages and later to desserts wrapped in cloth and boiled. Today, "pudding" can mean desserts in general, or it can mean that category of baked, steamed or boiled gastronomic finale that has ended meals in England since the Middle Ages.

gatekeeper   GAYT keeper
(the editor on a newspaper staff responsible for deciding which news gets into the paper)

Coverage of third-world social and economic news should be expanded in Western journalism. The most responsible media already practice it. But a thousand other editorial gatekeepers should do far more.

gauche   gohsh
(lacking social grace; crude; awkward; tactless: French, left [hand])

Mrs. Scherrer, a cool blonde and one of Paris's most elegant hostesses, will as usual be breaking the rules with a buffet where everything can be eaten with fork only and even with one's fingers, considered gauche in French society, where even sandwiches are eaten with a knife and fork.

gazebo   guh ZEE boh
(a roofed but open-sided pavilion from which one can gaze at the surrounding scenery)

The setting is a breeze-swept, seaside gazebo that belongs to a dilapidated tourist guesthouse in Tobago.

gel   jel
(to become a solidified whole)

When asked how he judged talent, Mr. Meiklejohn replied: "It's a seventh sense, I suppose. You acquire the knack over a period of years. Star potential consists of a combination of personality, type, appearance, voice and manners. If they gel, you may have something."

Gel is an example of a back formation, a word actually formed from, but looking as if it were the base of, another word. In this case, the noun, *gelatin*, came first, and the verb, *gel*, was derived from it. Similarly, while *burglar* may seem as though it means one who burgles, with *burgle* being the earlier word, the opposite is true: *burgle* has been used since the 19th century, *burglar* since the 16th. Other examples of back formations are *beg* from *beggar*, *opine* from *opinion*, *enthuse* from *enthusiasm*, *edit* from *editor*, *peddle* from *peddler, orate* from *orator, reminisce* from *reminiscence, gloom* from *gloomy, upholster* from *upholsterer* and *peeve* from *peevish.*

---

gemütlichkeit   *guh MOOT li kight*
(having a feeling of warmth and congeniality; coziness; hominess: German)

Describe an interior as glowing with gemütlichkeit and you summon up images of velvet, lace, painted furniture and antique porcelain stoves. At Vienna '79 warmth and snugness are achieved in a suave, gray modern interior that suggests a smart supper club, Northern European style.

genealogist   *jee ni A luh jist*
(a specialist in the field of tracing family histories)

A genealogist is on hand to explain that Lady Diana's famous family tree includes everyone from Winston Churchill and Bertrand Russell to Humphrey Bogart and Lillian Gish. The branches have obviously been stretched.

genesis   *JE nuh sis*
(origin; beginning)

Country clubs, it is easy to forget, had their genesis in the decades after the Civil War, when America discovered organized sport, and a new generation of young men—those with the money and time to be sporting —took to the country to play.

genteel   *jen TEEL*
(belonging or suited to polite society)

Although their cool three-part harmonies evoke a genteel placidity that is very different in spirit from the emotion-charged gospel-oriented style of most contemporary black groups, the Mills Brothers are regarded as the founders of modern-day black harmony singing.

geriatrics   *je ri A triks*
(the study of the physical process and problems of aging)

Well past retirement age, Mr. Strunck and Mr. Bayer stay on year after year as their contracts are renewed. And each year, according to their superiors, they defy all the geriatric rules by coming through with steadily higher sales and profits in one of the most keenly competitive areas in retailing.

ghoulish   *goo: lish*
(deriving pleasure from loathsome acts or things)

Just what did the voters of Northern Ireland mean by electing an imprisoned nationalist guerrilla to the British Parliament? To some, the victory of Robert Sands constitutes an endorsement of the Irish Republican Army and its bloody ways. Some bitter-enders may even hope, ghoulishly, that Mr. Sands will persist to the death in his 53-day prison hunger strike. But his death would be a tragedy serving no worthy purpose, and to view his election as a mandate for violence is a shallow distortion.

gift horse   *gift hawrs*
(full expression, "Don't look a gift horse in the mouth": accept gifts graciously, without inquiring about their value—from the practice of judging a horse's age by its teeth)

Peering into the mouth of a gift horse, Georgetown University last week returned a $600,000 gift, plus $41,721 interest to the Government of Libya, saying it did not want "its name associated" with a country that advocates terrorism.

gingerly   *JIN jer li*
(cautiously, carefully or warily: it has nothing to do with ginger; its derivation is not precisely known, but it is thought to have originated more than 400 years ago from a French word, gensour, *meaning delicate or dainty)*

Though Mr. Kelly, 69 years old, claims he no longer dances, he gingerly executed several steps to the audience's delight.

gizmo   *GIZ moh*
(gadget; contraption: a slang word)

Is the transistorized ubiquity of music perhaps too much of a good thing? The question invites different answers, depending on one's philosophy and foibles. But something is surely to be said for a gizmo that puts the Philharmonic—or Linda Ronstadt—in your pocket.

glib   *glib*
(easy, smooth and fluent in speech or writing, though often at the expense of sincerity, precision and depth of thought)

Mr. Reagan is right, supremely right, to keep harping on economic strength. Without it, America cannot promote its interests abroad or further develop its own society. But the President's glib inaugural slogan, that the Federal Government itself is the main obstacle to economic revival, denies reality and his obligation to lead.

glower *GLOW er*
(to stare with sullen anger; scowl)

Gossage has long been recognized as the most intimidating late-inning reliever in baseball, with a blazing fastball and a glowering expression that menaces opposing batters. "Hitters always have that fear that one pitch might get away from him and they'll wind up D.O.A. with a tag on their toe," said Rudy May.

glut *gluht*
(a supply that is greater than demand)

A new glut in world oil supplies may be developing, officials of Western governments and international oil companies say, and by summer more oil may be available to consumers than they require.

glutton *GLUHT uhn*
(a person who greedily eats too much; a person with a remarkably great desire or capacity for something)

The revolution eats its children, goes the saying, and the greater the upheaval the greater the gluttony. Iran now, like the Soviets three generations ago and France in the 18th century, is descending into a dictatorship of blood and horror.

———————

The glutton is the European variety of the North American wolverine, a stocky, carnivorous mammal about 3 feet long and 14 inches high. Both varieties are ferocious, have huge appetites, and have been known to attack animals many times their size. Hence, the name wolverine (little wolf) in North America and glutton (great devourer) in Europe.

———————

gnomic *NOH mik*
(wise and pithy; saying a great deal in a minimum of space)

The seven symphonies of Sibelius show us a composer working out his own destiny, nowhere more uncompromisingly than in his terse, gnomic and expressively severe Fourth Symphony.

grass-roots *gras roo: tz*
(originating among the common people or ordinary citizens)

WASHINGTON, Feb. 6—About 500 of President Reagan's political supporters met here today in private sessions to plan a grass-roots campaign to put public pressure on Congress to approve Mr. Reagan's economic program.

gratuitous   *gruh TOO: uh tuhs*
(without cause or justification; uncalled for; unwarranted)

A spokesman for SmithKline also said that the president of the company, Henry Wendt, wrote to the three networks last month to express concern about the level of "gratuitous violence and sex on prime-time shows." SmithKline advertises such products as Contac and Dietac.

gravitate   *GRA vuh tayt*
(to be attracted or tend to move toward)

Episcopalians tend to gravitate toward professions and the business world, and a significant amount of Episcopal money can be found in the nation's finest museums and universities. But the percentage of Episcopalians actually involved in producing art or pursuing purely intellectual matters does not appear to be anywhere nearly as great as the percentage in business and the professions.

gregarious   *gri GAI ri uhs*
(fond of the company of others; sociable)

Milanov was gregarious. She liked to talk to colleagues on stage during a performance. Here is George London getting ready to pour his soul out in the Nile scene. Just as he starts, Zinka whispers, "How's the baby, George?"

grimace   *gri MAYS*
(a twisting or distortion of the face, as in expressing pain, contempt, disgust, etc.)

We had dined well, no doubt about that, and on some extraordinary combinations of flavors. There had been, for example, a marriage of baked lobsters with a savory, silken, vanilla-flavored sauce. Lobsters? Vanilla? It would seem to be one of the least compatible flavor liaisons conceivable. If the reflexive reaction to such a dish was a grimace, it was quickly dispelled. The combination not only worked, it was a triumph of taste over logic.

grouse   *grows*
(*to complain; grumble*)

A lot of people who are busy growing old right now are just going to have to stop it. I lunched the other day with a fellow who spent the hour grousing about how retirement was going to drive him into poverty. It was hard to sympathize with him. "You wouldn't have to retire if you hadn't gone ahead and gotten old," I was tempted to tell him, but didn't.

grudgingly   *GRUH jing li*
(*with reluctance or unwillingness*)

LONDON, April 26—The centuries-old English belief that a man's home is his castle was cited here again this month as Britons grudgingly completed their 1981 census forms. "As a nation we don't like it," conceded a spokesman for the Office of Population Censuses and Surveys. "It's simply part of the British character to be suspicious of personal questions."

guffaw   *guh FAW*
(*a loud, coarse burst of laughter*)

While reading H. L. Mencken, he recalled, he once broke the library calm with loud laughter. It was a Saroyan hallmark: he was frequently ejected from class for guffawing, was removed under guard from a San Francisco courtroom and, to his puzzlement, was shushed by an usher at a performance of James Thurber's "The Male Animal."

guile   *gighl*
(*slyness and cunning in dealing with others; craftiness*)

The footage of Elvis's early press conferences makes it even more abundantly clear why his fans fell in love with him. In those days, Elvis was so guileless that his every thought registered clearly on his face. When he met with the press, he was trusting and sweet. He grew to be more oddly comfortable with all of these inquisitive strangers, in fact, than he may have been in private. In any case, it must have been easy for his fans to imagine that Elvis was someone they really knew.

guise   *gighz*
(*outward appearance; semblance*)

Miss Pascoe, an adult actress, with her hair in pigtails and her socks drooping, effectively conceals herself within the guise of an adolescent.

gung-ho   *gung hoh*

(enthusiastic, cooperative, enterprising, etc., in an unrestrained, often naive way)

Remembering his rookie year with the Lions, he said: "I was really gung-ho for the team. But a vet took me aside one day and said, 'One day you'll learn. This is a business. A cold business. If you're of no use to them, you're gone.' "

Gung-ho was the motto of Lt. Col. Evans F. Carlson's Marine Raiders in World War II. Impressed by the zeal of the Chinese Industrial Cooperatives Society, which he had witnessed in China, Carlson adopted the Chinese name of the group as an example to his men of the spirit and dedication of the Chinese Communists during the war. *Gung-ho* is a shortening, with some linguistic liberties, of the Society's name, which means "Work together."

---

habeas corpus   *HAY bi uhs KAWR puhs*
(in law, a writ, or order, requiring that a detained person be brought before a court at a stated time and place to decide the legality of that person's detention or imprisonment. The right of habeas corpus safeguards one against illegal detention or imprisonment: Latin, that you have the body)

With the exception of The Buenos Aires Herald, a small but influential English-language paper, all Argentine papers have steered away from reporting on disappearances and allegations of torture, usually consigning occasional small articles on habeas corpus suits to the back pages.

habitué   *huh BI choo ay*
(a person who frequents a particular place: French)

A swing through the museums and galleries just outside New York City can hold a number of happy surprises for even the most sophisticated habitué of the salons of SoHo and upper Madison Avenue, and a day or a weekend in the country may be just the tonic for the late-summer doldrums.

hackneyed   *HAK need*
(made trite and commonplace by overuse)

This hackneyed melodrama sets its tone in the first few minutes with talk about home and families being "the heart of this heartland" and about people having a "heavy heart." The heaviest thing about "Heartland" is the burden of the actors and of the audience.

haggard   *HA gerd*
(having a gaunt, wasted or exhausted appearance, as from prolonged suffering, anxiety, etc.; worn)

Mr. Carter, looking haggard and worn after spending two largely sleepless nights trying to resolve the hostage crisis as the final chapter of his Presidency, flew from Washington after the inaugural ceremony to Plains, Ga., his home town.

haggle *HA guhl*
(to argue about terms, price, etc.; bargain; wrangle)

Despite the heat, the business of Cairo continues. At the Khan el Khalil, the city's huge maze of stalls and shops that stretches for about two miles, Egyptians in long robes haggle over copper and brass items with tourists in shorts.

halcyon *HAL si uhn*
(calm; peaceful; happy; idyllic: halcyon days are those which are looked back on with nostalgia)

In its halcyon days, The Star was to Washington what The Herald Tribune was to New York: a model of crisp writing, graphic elegance and reasoned Republicanism.

In Greek myth, Halcyone was the daughter of Aeolus, the keeper of the winds. When her husband Ceyx drowned in a shipwreck, the grieving Halcyone threw herself off a cliff into the sea. But as she fell, the gods changed her and Ceyx into kingfishers. Legend has it that kingfishers nest upon the open ocean's waters, which Aeolus calms during their breeding season.

---

hallmark *HAWL mahrk*
(a mark or symbol of genuineness or high quality)

Strawberries and raspberries are familiar favorites, but how many Americans know the taste of blackberries, gooseberries and red or black currants? These berries are the hallmarks of a summer in England. There, they are made into unusual ice creams, jellies and pies, or stewed and served with crème fraîche.

hammerlock *HA muhr lahk*
(a wrestling hold in which one arm of the opponent is twisted upward behind his back)

The Mayor held forth on his theory that the lost tribes of Israel settled a long time ago in Ireland and that therefore he was Irish. The crowd loved it, and Mr. Koch's procession up the avenue was greeted with cheers. Mr. Koch, a politician in the envious position of facing re-election without serious competition to date, walked the avenue with his thumbs up, relishing the early acknowledgment of his hammerlock on City Hall.

hanker   *HANG ker*
(to crave, long or yearn)

Compared with other nationalities such as South Americans, who have a hankering for orange drinks, "the American consumer is in love with the cola taste," said Lawrence Adelman, first vice president of Dean Witter Reynolds.

haphazard   *hap HA zerd*
(casual, unplanned; random)

Still, supervision is so haphazard around the country that fighters not fully recovered from concussions are allowed to box again only a few days later, of course after a physical examination that would approve a corpse. In many cases, to get around the unenforceable rules, they merely have to change their names.

harbinger   *HAHR bin jer*
(a person or thing that comes before to announce or give an indication of what follows; herald)

The teaching shortages here are apparently the harbinger of what the National Center for Educational Statistics predicts will be a favorable job market for teachers by the late 1980's.

hardscrabble   *HAHRD skra buhl*
(providing meagerly in return for much effort: scrabble means to scratch or paw as though looking for something; struggle)

The Agca family lives a hardscrabble life, as it always has, in the Boztepe, or Gray Hill, area of Malatya, a slum where most of the houses, like theirs, are made of mud bricks and roofed with tile.

haughty   *HAW ti*
(having or showing great pride in oneself and disdain or scorn for others; proud; arrogant)

In its first year, Ammirati & Puris Inc. took a rather haughty approach for a fledgling advertising agency with no clients whatsoever: It turned down business representing $3 million in billings.

haunt　　*hawnt*
(*a place often visited*)

"Downtown is dead without the Indians this summer," said Buddy Spitz, manager of the downtown Theatrical Restaurant, a haunt of visiting ballplayers that has been hurt by the strike.

haute couture　　*oht koo TOOR*
(*the leading designers and creators of new fashions in clothing for women, or their creations; high fashion: French, high sewing*)

When she took over La Côte Basque, Mrs. Spalter stuck to the Soule traditions and standards, and proved to be a highly competent restaurant operator. She was charming, beautifully dressed and demanding. She wore haute couture dresses at dinner, and refused tables to women who wore pants suits. She explained in an interview that some pants suits had "chic" and others did not, and that she did not want to discriminate between women.

haute cuisine　　*oht kwi ZEEN*
(*the preparation of fine food by highly skilled chefs, or the food so prepared: French, high cooking*)

Also on the menu is an item called friande, the ultimate marriage of haute cuisine and fast food: a hot dog in puff pastry.

hawk　　*hawk*
(*to advertise or peddle goods in the street by shouting*)

Since there is no worldwide patent on Rubik's Cube, it is not surprising to find copies (Wonderful Puzzler, Magic Cube) from Taiwan and Hong Kong replacing "designer" T-shirts as the hottest-selling item on the streets. They are also being hawked on the sands of Coney Island, where, according to one entrepreneur, they are outselling cold beer and inflatable green frogs imprinted with "Kiss Me"; but they are not outselling the hot knishes.

heady　　*HED i*
(*tending to affect the senses; intoxicating*)

Ancient astronomy was a rich and heady mix of myth, religion, mathematics, art and astrology, and all ancient peoples were transfixed by it.

hector *HEK ter*
(*to browbeat; bully*)

Foreign leaders of all kinds are tired of Prime Minister Begin: of his hectoring, his self-pity, his pedantry, his demagogy, his crude abuse of anyone who disagrees with him.

Hector, a brave and noble warrior, was the eldest son of Priam, the King of Troy. He was killed in single-handed combat by Achilles, who lashed his body to his chariot and dragged it in triumph round the walls of Troy, in revenge for Hector's slaying of Patroclus, Achilles' dearest friend. Hector, himself, was known only for his noble qualities, but after a late-17th century London street gang called the Hectors was portrayed in several popular dramas of the time, the word was applied to others who bullied and browbeat.

---

hegemony *hi JE muh ni*
(*leadership or dominance, especially of one nation over another: used today almost exclusively by China and Russia when accusing each other of expansionist aims*)

Tass asserted that the decision to lift restrictions against selling weapons to China was a "provocative decision of the White House to supply Chinese hegemonists with offensive weapons which they could use against neighboring countries and peoples."

hegira *hi JIGH ruh*
(*a journey made for the sake of safety or as an escape; flight: Arabian, to leave, from the forced journey of Mohammed from Mecca to Medina in 622 A.D. from which the Moslem era dates*)

In the Northeast, the angler who is unable to spend the time or money for a winter hegira south tries to throttle the lust for angling until March. To overindulge in daydreams of breaking surf or purling mountain streams for months on end is like waiting too long in a crowded bar for one's sweetheart to arrive.

heinous *HAY nuhs*
(*outrageously evil or wicked; abominable*)

On the theory that evil sells, the Pearl Brewing Company of San Antonio began last October to market J.R. Ewing's Private Stock, a beer named for the heinous star of the television show "Dallas." "People today buy an image, not a beer," a brewery official said. He added: "This beer will do well as long as the television show does well."

helter-skelter   *HEL ter SKEL ter*
(in haste and confusion; in a disorderly, hurried manner)

The island's sandy soil makes the wells especially vulnerable to pollutants that could seep through the ground. "We can't afford to have this kind of dumping helter-skelter all over Long Island," said Sen. Marino, a Republican from Lattingtown.

Helter-skelter is an example of reduplication, the process of forming a word by repeating the same two sounds *(beep-beep, goody-goody, yuk-yuk)* or by changing a letter in the second half of the unit *(boogie-woogie, hocus-pocus, flim-flam, palsy-walsy)*. Many reduplications are examples of onomatopoeia, the imitation of a sound *(bow-wow, quack-quack, boing-boing, choo-choo)*. Others seem to have been created to emphasize a point *(buddy-buddy, nasty-wasty, okey-dokey)*. In many cases, both halves are meaningless alone *(itsy-bitsy, fuddy-duddy, mumbo-jumbo, roly-poly)*, and even together cannot be traced to any known origin, as in the case of *helter-skelter* and *hanky-panky*, although such pairs convey some sort of sound-impression of what they mean.

---

herculean   *her KYOO: li uhn*
(requiring the strength of a Hercules; calling for great strength, size or courage)

"Ready!" shouted the judge, raising his arms to the sky. And the eight thick men in shorts on either side of the long rope thumped down their hiking boots for a foothold and the earth shuddered. "Take the rope!" called the judge. The rope straightened as the 16 heavy hands gripped it. "Toll!" Groans, herculean in depth, rent the air. Muscles strained and bodies swayed in unison. The coach for each team ran up and down the line beside his squad, shouting, urging, hopping, crawling, pleading with his mates to pull with all their heart.

heresy   *HE ruh si*
(any opinion opposed to official or established views or doctrines: originally, a religious belief opposed to the orthodox doctrines of a church or the rejection of a belief that is a part of church dogma)

Seven members of the Baha'i faith, which Iran's Moslem Shiites consider heretical, were also executed on charges of spying for Israel.

* * *

Last month the members of the New York Drama Critics Circle committed what could be taken for an act of theatrical heresy; they elected not to give an award to a "best new musical" of the 1980–81 season.

hermetic   *her ME tik*
(completely sealed, especially sealed against the escape or entry of air; sealed off from outside influence or interference: from Hermes Trismegistus, the Greek name for the Egyptian god Thoth, among whose supposed inventions was a magic seal to make vessels airtight)

Born in Sighet, a small town in the Carpathian mountains of Rumania, Mr. Wiesel grew up in a Hasidic community, studying the Talmud and the mysteries of the cabbala. It was a hermetic life devoted to study and prayer, a life devoted to God.

heterogeneous   *he tuh ruh JEE ni uhs*
(composed of unlike or unrelated parts; varied; widely different: the opposite of homogeneous, meaning similar, identical or uniform)

One of the better-kept secrets of recent art-book publishing has been the appearance of "Marcel Duchamp, Notes" in a bilingual French and English edition. The book consists of a heterogeneous quantity of lately discovered handwritten notes, every last one of which is reproduced in facsimile original size, in as noble a production as any artist could desire.

hiatus   *high AY tuhs*
(a break or interruption in the continuity of something; gap)

Now, after a hiatus of 28 years, the author of "Cry, the Beloved Country" is waiting with all the anxiety and hopes of a literary unknown for the publication of his first novel since "Too Late the Phalarope."

highflown   *HIGH flohn*
(high-sounding but meaningless; bombastic)

Thomas De Quincey, in a highflown piece of rhetoric about Joan of Arc, declared that he could not find a Mozart or a Michelangelo among the female sex. But "Sister Woman . . ." he wrote, "I acknowledge that you can do one thing as well as the best of us men—You can die grandly. . . ." The sight of a woman on the scaffold, he continued, eclipsed Luxor, or the Himalayas, or St. Peters on Easter Day in grandeur.

hinterland   *HIN ter land*
(an area far from big cities and towns; backcountry: German, back land)

In the Soviet Union, as in the United States, some of the best home brewed alcohol comes from the hinterlands of Georgia, where rural residents are as proud of their moonshine as they are of having sent one of their homegrown sons to Moscow to lead the nation.

Hinterland originated with German colonial expansion in the 19th century. Although it may now be used to describe any out-of-the-way area, it then referred to the area lying behind an occupied coastal district, which the occupier claimed belonged to it by right of its possessing the coast, even if the inland region was as yet unexplored or unoccupied.

---

hitherto   *HITH: er too:*
(*until this time*)

A Soviet reader would have had no inkling that the congress was preparing to elect a new party leadership by secret ballot, a development hitherto unthinkable in the Soviet bloc.

homage   *HAH mij*
(*something done to show respect, reverence or honor*)

The liquor will flow, the steaks will sizzle, the neckties are already out of the box. Father's Day, that early summer homage to the gods of retailing, has by and large caught up with Mother's Day, despite the latter's long headstart. (Mother's Day was authorized by law in 1914, a status Father's Day only acquired in 1971.) "Nearly $3 billion in total retail sales are expected from this Father's Day, virtually the same amount as for Mother's Day," said Ted Kaufman, executive director of both the Father's Day and Mother's Day Councils, which are nonprofit groups whose members include such top corporate names as Sears, Roebuck & Company and J.C. Penney.

homily   *HAH muh li*
(*a sermon, especially one about something in the Bible*)

ILOILO, The Philippines, Feb. 20—In the region of these islands where the contrast between those who labor in the fields and those who live in luxury is the starkest, Pope John Paul II delivered an impassioned homily today on the unjust division of the world's riches.

honorarium   *ah nuh RAI ri uhm*
(*a payment in recognition of professional services for which custom or propriety forbids a price to be set, as for certain speaking engagements, services as contest judges and adviserships*)

Members of Congress now can accept honorariums equal to 15 percent of their annual salaries, or about $9,100 a year. However, the Senate temporarily raised the ceiling for senators to $25,000. The ceiling, which was due to expire Jan. 1, 1983, would be eliminated altogether in the new measure.

hoodwink   *HOOD wingk*

(to deceive or trick: from the act of blinding someone by pulling a hood down over their eyes)

"The public is being hoodwinked," the Bishop charged. "We are told that fighting inflation is the primary goal of government, and yet the most inflationary spending—defense—is massively building. We are told of a safety net, but that net is spread well below the waters of poverty. Our people will drown in that safety net."

hook   *hook*

(an arresting or catchy section of a song that "grabs" the listener or gives the song a more singular identity)

Mr. Hadley's cavernous, Bowie-esque singing contributes to the melodrama. But the real impact comes from the hook-filled songs and the richness of their textures.

hoopla   *HOO:P lah*

(showy publicity; ballyhoo)

Amid tributes, telegrams, yet another award and a healthy dose of pomp and hoopla, Walter Cronkite yesterday closed out his 18-year career as anchor of "The CBS Evening News."

horse trading   *HAWRS tray ding*

(bargaining marked by shrewd calculation by both sides)

The reasons for budget decisions are seldom committed to paper. Final figures often reflect complex horse trading among the White House, the budget office and the agencies.

hubris   *HYOO: bris*

(excessive pride or self-confidence that brings down the wrath of the gods for such insolence)

The fabricated story that won a Pulitzer Prize has made newspaper people think about their business as nothing else has for years—and not just on the paper that printed it, The Washington Post. There is a sharpened concern about the responsibility of reporters and editors: the standards we impose on ourselves. But the episode points to a deeper problem, and I wonder how many in the press will face it. That is the danger of hubris, the overweening pride that leads to a fall. In our case, it is a constitutional hubris, a belief that the First Amendment gives journalism an exalted status. It is in particular a belief that the Constitution gives us a right to use anonymous sources without being called to account.

———

Hubris is the insolence or self-pride in Greek tragic heroes that leads them to ignore warnings from the gods. In Greek tragedies it is this lack of wisdom that proves the "tragic flaw" leading to the hero's fall. At the end of Sophocles' "Antigone," after Creon has rejected the prophet Tiresias's warnings and suffered the death of Antigone, whom he ordered executed, and the self-destruction of his wife and son, the leader of the chorus says: "Wisdom is the supreme part of happiness; and reverence toward the gods must be inviolate. Great words of prideful men are ever punished with great blows and, in old age, teach the chastened to be wise."

———

humanities   *hyoo MA nuh teez*
(the branches of learning concerned with human thought and relations
—as distinguished from the social and natural sciences—especially literature, philosophy, history, languages, art, theology and music)

"Our students get an excellent education not just in dance but in the humanities as a whole," said Carolyn Brown, dean of the dance program at the State University College at Purchase. "The more you know, the more you are able to give."

hunker   *HUNG ker*
(to settle down on one's haunches; squat or crouch: here used figuratively)

The center of the fabulous Reagan ranch is the big house where Nancy and the boss live. That's it over there, sort of hunkered down in the shelter of those big gray buildings with the big old trees all around it.

hunky-dory   *HUHNG ki DAW ri*
(all right; fine: a slang word)

"Unleash greed and everything will be hunky-dory," was Mr. Stone's brief analysis of the Reagan economic theory.

husband   *HUHZ buhnd*
(*to manage economically; conserve*)

Liberal party leaders last night selected City Councilwoman Mary T. Codd of Staten Island as their candidate for mayor. Although she is a Democrat, Mrs. Codd will not challenge Mayor Koch in the Democratic primary. She plans to husband limited financial resources for the general election campaign.

hybrid   *HIGH brid*
(*the offspring of two distinct types or species*)

Although there are only 25 basic species, mints have a tendency to hybridize in the wild, and all sorts of variants can be found. There may be as many as 600 named varieties.

(*anything of mixed parentage, unlike parts, etc.*)

The development of the shuttle, a hybrid spacecraft-airplane, has cost almost $10 billion since the project was initiated in January 1972.

hype   *highp*
(*exaggerated, inflated or sensationalized promotion or publicity: a slang word*)

As the number of potential college applicants grows smaller, the typical high school "college night" is becoming an exercise in hype. On one such occasion, we heard one student say of the parade of admissions officers, "They're acting like a bunch of used-car salesmen."

hyperbole   *high PER buh li*
(*exaggeration for effect, not meant to be taken literally, as in "He's as strong as an ox," or "I'll love you till the end of time"*)

"At the time," Mr. Slatkin said, "considering the President was in the audience, I indulged in some hyperbolic praise of the Mozart symphony, even calling it a 'minimasterpiece.' It is not that terrific, of course, but considering that it was written by Mozart when he was only 9 years old, I would call it amazing and a very pleasant piece of music, but not a great one."

hyphenate   *HIGH fuh nayt*
(*a title, name or designation whose parts are connected by a hyphen, such as Irish-American, actor-director or poet-politician*)

Tossing a tennis ball up and down in one hand, Michael Davis says, "It's not what you do, but how you do it." Mr. Davis is joking, but he is also clearly a man of style. He is an inspired juggler-comic—a distinguished hyphenate once worn by W.C. Fields.

iatrogenesis   *i a truh JE nuh sis*
*(the creation in patients of illnesses and disorders as a result of medical
treatment)*

If one looks at what is truly happening in medicine today, one sees that
there is a general outcry at its iatrogenesis, its wastefulness, its mystifica-
tion and its inhumanity. Nurses have always been aware of these defects.
And it has been the nursing profession that has done most of the innovative work in a reconception of the concept of caretaker.

_____

Iatrogenic diseases are those resulting from medical treatment,
usually when prescribed medication causes unforeseen side
effects. Thus, diethylstilbestrol (DES), a drug prescribed in the
1950's to prevent miscarriages, has been shown to cause a form
of cervical cancer in women whose mothers used it while they
were pregnant with them; the drug Rauwolfia, used to treat
high blood pressure, may produce iatrogenic depression; and
thalidomide, a sedative, produced serious deformities among
babies born to women who had taken the drug during pregnancy.

_____

icon   *IGH kahn*
*(in the Orthodox Eastern Church, an image or picture of Jesus, Mary,
a saint, etc., venerated as sacred; any revered object)*

For people who are not aficianados of Indian music, Ravi Shankar must
seem like some faded icon from the 1960's, inextricably mixed in the
mind with love beads, flower children and lazy clouds of incense and
marijuana. As it happens, Mr. Shankar, who just turned 61, is very much
active and alert, as his schedule in the next few weeks indicates.

ideology   *igh di AH luh ji*
*(the body of ideas reflecting the social needs and aspirations of an
individual, group, class or culture)*

"He is a psychopath with no defined ideology," the Istanbul security chief said today of Mehmet Ali Agca, the 23-year-old Turk who is under arrest in Rome on charges of shooting Pope John Paul II.

idiom   *I di uhm*
(*a characteristic style, as in art or music*)

Mr. Darnell's most impressive accomplishment is his blending of a wide variety of contemporary musical idioms: his songs for "Fresh Fruit in Foreign Places" combine reggae rhythms, the funk style of James Brown and a melodic sensibility that recalls the show tunes of bygone days. But these elements blend so smoothly that one tends not to notice how disparate they are.

idiosyncracy   *i di uh SING kruh si*
(*a peculiarity, habit or mannerism of an individual*)

Great singers are an amazing species. Fairly early in life they discover that their lungs and throats can do certain things better than anybody else in the world. As such they are irreplaceable, and Lord! how they know it. They grow up, most of them, vain, spoiled, pampered, rich, accustomed to having things their own way. They have idiosyncracies that would simply not be tolerated in a normal society. Olive Fremstad, she of the sumptuous voice and equally sumptuous figure, insisted on being paid in cash before every performance. No cash, no Fremstad.

idyllic   *igh DI lik*
(*having a natural charm and picturesqueness; simple, pleasant and peaceful*)

The setting is idyllic: 70 acres of rolling meadows, lawns and formal gardens; daffodils, tulips, primroses and lots of blue forget-me-nots; a secluded path winding around a lake past geese, wildflowers and ferns.

ignominy   *IG nuh mi ni*
(*public shame or humiliation*)

A well-spoken woman in her 30's, she said she was married and worked in a doctor's office. Her offense was her failure to produce her registration or proof of insurance coverage when stopped for a traffic infraction. After she was put into a cell, a matron entered and demanded that the "suspect" remove all her clothing preparatory to a body search. In tears, the woman resisted, pleading to be spared such a search, but was told flatly: "Either you remove your clothes, or we'll have to hold you down and remove them for you." The woman then suffered the ignominy of a search.

In "The Scarlet Letter," Roger Chillingworth confronts his wife, Hester Prynne, with the fact that he has seen her standing in punishment before the townspeople, holding her illegitimate infant: "I might have known that, as I came out of the vast and dismal forest, and entered this settlement of Christian men, the very first object to meet my eyes would be thyself, Hester Prynne, standing up, a statue of ignominy before the people."

---

illiteracy   *i LI tuh ruh si*
(lack of education or culture, especially an inability to read or write)

The report says bluntly that "from the preoccupations of the popular culture with the paranormal, the psychic, the mystic, and the occult, it is apparent that an alarming number of American adults cannot tell sense from nonsense." Scientific illiteracy in a world in which science and technology play so great a part seriously undermines the citizen's capacity to understand society and to help keep it prosperous and strong.

illusory   *i LOO: suh ri*
(deceptive; unreal; illusive)

Many prominent scientists in the past described ball lightning as illusory. In 1839 the great physicist Michael Faraday announced his conviction that ball lightning was nothing more than an afterimage on the retina of the eye, produced by the nearby flash of ordinary lightning.

imbue   *im BYOO:*
(to permeate, pervade or inspire)

The current popularity of sex therapy is poignant testimony to the fact that many of us were not allowed as children to express ourselves in sexually healthy ways, that many were imbued with feelings of guilt, inhibition and restricted beliefs about what "normal" sexual thoughts and behaviors are.

impassive   *im PA siv*
(not feeling or showing emotion; placid; calm)

As the bearded defendant, a resident of Bradford in northern England, stood impassively in the oak-paneled dock, the 20 verdicts were individually called out. In addition to the convictions for the 13 murders, Mr. Sutcliffe was charged with the attempted murder of seven other women.

impeach   *im PEECH*
*(to challenge the practices or honesty of; accuse: especially, to bring a
public official before a tribunal on a charge of wrongdoing)*

The Iranian Parliament today declared President Abolhassan Bani-Sadr
politically incompetent, thus paving the way for his dismissal from office
by Iran's supreme leader, Ayatollah Ruhollah Khomeini. The impeach-
ment vote, a triumph for Mr. Bani-Sadr's Moslem fundamentalist enemies in the Government, was 177 to 1, with 1 formal abstention and 11
legislators not voting.

impeccable   *im PE kuh buhl*
(without defect; faultless; flawless)

Lady Diana, the daughter of the eighth Earl Spencer, a wealthy
Northamptonshire landowner, has an impeccable social background suitable for someone who may one day be queen.

impede   *im PEED*
(to hinder the progress of; obstruct or delay)

South African drivers characteristically assume that they have the right of
way in nearly all circumstances. They pass impartially on the left or right.
They indicate their desire to pass by driving as close as possible to the
car that is impeding their progress, sometimes coming within half a car
length at speeds of over 60 miles an hour, and they seldom slow down
as a courtesy to another driver.

imperceptible   *im per SEP tuh buhl*
(so slight, gradual or subtle as not to be easily perceived)

Swirling in for a landing at La Guardia, the pilot banked into a 90-degree
turn, dropped the helicopter down 200 feet and made an imperceptible
touchdown.

impervious   *im PER vi uhs*
(incapable of being penetrated or affected by)

The armor—stainless steel jackets designed to fit around the money
box at the bottom of each phone, making it impervious to knives,
fists, hammers, fireworks and even explosives with a force of a
quarter stick of dynamite—has already been placed on the 5,000 most-
vandalized phones in the city and will be put on the rest during the
summer.

implacable   *im PLAY kuh buhl*
(*unalterable, inflexible; unappeasable*)

China's view of Southeast Asia is dominated by implacable hostility to Vietnam's conquest of Cambodia and a conviction that the event was part of a Soviet quest to encircle China and threaten the rest of the world.

implicit   *im PLI sit*
(*suggested or understood, although not expressly stated; implied*)

In his recent speech on crime, President Reagan quoted approvingly from an Esquire magazine article by a man who decided to defend against neighborhood crime by buying guns for himself and his wife. As the President was giving this implicit support to the proliferation of private firearms, Administration officials were preparing to dismantle the Treasury Department's Bureau of Alcohol, Tobacco and Firearms, the Federal agency that controls illegal possession and trafficking in guns.

impotent   *IM puh tuhnt*
(*ineffective, powerless or helpless*)

The Chief Justice said that crime is reducing the United States to "the status of an impotent society whose capability of maintaining elementary security on the streets, in schools and for the homes of our people is in doubt."

imprimatur   *im pri MAY ter*
(*sanction or approval: originally, an official license to print or publish a book, pamphlet, etc., especially such permission granted by a censor of the Roman Catholic Church*)

RIYADH, Saudi Arabia—When Citibank sold a majority stake in its bank here to Saudi nationals last July, the new organization found itself without the imprimatur and vast resources of a leading international bank.

———

Imprimatur is Latin for *let it be printed.*

———

impromptu   *im PRAHMP too:*
(*without preparation or advance thought; offhand*)

Leon Spinks promises to be on time tomorrow night and Larry Holmes promises to knock him out in a heavyweight title fight that both promise will be even more intense than their impromptu dance contest at a Las Vegas party nearly three years ago, when more than a hundred people stood on tables and chairs to watch.

impudent   *IM pyoo duhnt*
(shamelessly bold or disrespectful; saucy; insolent)

Improvisational comedy is essentially impudent madness. Because virtually all of it is created at the moment, often out of current experience and usually at the suggestion of audiences, it has little time for such niceties as taste and taboos. Improvisational comics must be fast on their feet and quick with their tongues. Inventiveness and situations count, not gags.

impugn   *im PYOO:N*
(to oppose or challenge as false or questionable)

In 1933, Shawn founded his Men Dancers company at the 75-acre farm he owned in the Berkshires, now the site of the dance school and festival. His aim was to convince the world that men could dance without impugning their virility, and to that end the group of nine male dancers—"God's gift to the women's colleges of America," as one reporter put it—crisscrossed the country performing in dances choreographed for them by Shawn and members of the company. It was a happy day for Ted Shawn when an Atlanta newspaper ran a review on its sports page.

impunity   *im PYOO: nuh ti*
(exemption from punishment, penalty or harm)

"It's time for honest talk, for plain talk. There has been a breakdown in the criminal justice system in America. It just plain isn't working. All too often repeat offenders, habitual lawbreakers, career criminals, call them what you will, are robbing, raping and beating with impunity and, as I said, quite literally getting away with murder. The people are sickened and outraged. They demand that we put a stop to it." [Ronald Reagan]

in absentia   *in ab SEN shi uh*
(although not present: Latin, in absence)

Two men who were convicted in absentia of international trade in weapons with terrorist organizations were each sentenced yesterday to 17 ⅔ to 53 years in prison. They are believed to be out of the country.

inadvertent   *i nuhd VER tuhnt*
(unintentional)

In fact, the revelry was at such a pitch that by the time of the wedding, many people, hung over and exhausted, inadvertently slept in the warm morning sunshine of St. James's Park right through the spectacle that they had come to watch.

incarnate *in KAHR nit*
(in human form; personified)

It's no secret that Mr. Hines may be the best tap dancer of our day, but he's never had a chance to show himself to quite the advantage that he does here. Wearing slick-backed hair, a series of sleek evening outfits and a raffish smile, he's more than a dancer; he's the frisky Ellington spirit incarnate.

incensed *in SENST*
(very angry; enraged)

Bill Gleason knew what he was doing when he raised three of his daughters to be lawyers. When the Chicago Hustle of the Women's Pro Basketball League tried to dismiss Gleason as coach last weekend, he had a phalanx of legal help that was as incensed as he was.

incessant *in SE suhnt*
(constant)

In a misguided effort to impart a sense of service (or perhaps because they are Aquarians), some waiters become incessant water pourers, reaching across tables with pitchers every time a sip is taken.

***

Aquarius, the eleventh sign of the Zodiac (January 21 to February 18), is symbolized by a man pouring water from a vessel. *Aquarius* is Latin for *waterbearer*.

***

inchoate *in KOH it*
(not organized; lacking order)

At two hours and 40 minutes, the production seems unduly long, and there are inchoate passages in the staging, as there are in the play itself. However, "Jungle of Cities" offers the Brooklyn Academy of Music company a fertile environment for exploration. For the first time this season, with Americanized Brecht, the company has found a general compatibility between actors and characters.

incisive *in SIGH siv*
(keen; penetrating; acute)

"The school systems are now dealing with a population that does not think that language is the primary means of thinking," said Leon Botstein, the president of Bard, a liberal arts college in Annandale-on-Hudson. "The major instrument of thinking—language—is no longer taught in a coherent relationship with thinking. Language becomes ritualistic, even with the best of students, rather than being used to think incisively.

incognito   *in KAHG ni toh*
(with true identity unrevealed or disguised: Italian, unknown)

Supreme Court Justices Lewis F. Powell Jr. and Byron R. White dine incognito among out-of-towners at the Supreme Court cafeteria. Once, a tourist, not recognizing Justice Powell, asked him to take a picture of his family.

incommunicado   *in kuh myoo: ni KAH doh*
(detained, residing or imprisoned without communication with the outside world: a Spanish term introduced at the time of the Spanish Civil War—1936–39)

The romance toppled a crown, shook an empire and titillated the world. It is history now. The Duke of Windsor is dead, the Duchess ill and incommunicado in Paris.

incongruous   *in KAHNG groo uhs*
(inconsistent; contrary; inappropriate; unsuitable)

It seemed incongruous for a transit system skidding toward bankruptcy, but there they were: dollar bills, hundreds of thousands of them, like ants at a picnic, covering the tables and floors in a Chicago Transit Authority counting room and piling up at a rate that threatened to bury the employees counting them.

incremental   *in kruh MEN tuhl*
(becoming greater or larger; gaining; growing; increasing)

To prepare the retarded for the world outside, two counselors, Martin R. Roth and Gary P. Hermus, have written a 600-page outline, step by tiny step, of the thousands of incremental steps involved in learning the daily maintenance of life. From this book, they have been able to reduce the young man's level of skills to a series of percentages and graphs. He has mastered, for instance, the 18 steps required to apply spray deodorant under his arm. He functions at 100 percent in shoe tying, 63 percent in washing his hair, and 76.2 percent in the use of an electric can opener.

incursion   *in KER zhuhn*
(a sudden, brief invasion or raid)

The French are not particularly receptive to foreigners on their fashion turf. But since they are convinced that they are the leaders, they will tolerate some incursions from outsiders who want to take advantage of the huge audience of buyers from throughout the world that the French fashion shows attract. The operating rule, however, is that visitors maintain a low profile and do not try to seize center stage.

indefatigable   *in di FA ti guh buhl*
(not yielding to fatigue; untiring)

Actors are indefatigable, even as fate and casting agents buffet them into assuming alternate occupations. There are actor-waiters, bartenders, typists, cabdrivers, housecleaners and salesmen. One actor-waiter zoomed from serving up fettuccine Alfredo to playing opposite Richard Burton in "Equus" on Broadway.

indigenous   *in DI juh nuhs*
(native)

A formal complaint filed recently with the United Nations accuses Paraguay of actions calculated to destroy an indigenous tribe of 700 Indians known as the Toba-Maskoy.

indigent   *IN di juhnt*
(in poverty; poor; destitute)

Last year, Mr. Buchbinder and his 399 colleagues in the Legal Aid Society's criminal defense bureau represented 162,656 indigent defendants in New York City assigned to them by the courts.

indignant   *in DIG nuhnt*
(angry or scornful at unjust or mean treatment)

When the Metropolitan Opera tried to present the Paris Opera Ballet last year, they felt that the only way they could sell the company to a supposedly sophisticated New York dance audience was to feature Rudolf Nureyev as guest star. Naturally, the indignant French dancers, stars in their own right, refused to appear.

indisputable   *in di SPYOO: tuh buhl*
(that which cannot be disputed or doubted; unquestionable)

Rosa Ponselle, indisputably one of the greatest operatic talents this country has ever produced, died of a heart attack yesterday in her Baltimore mansion, Villa Pace, at the age of 84.

indissoluble   *in di SAH lyoo buhl*
(undissolvable; lasting; permanent)

A great sadness, however, has intruded on Mr. Menuhin's sunlit world—the death early in January of his sister, Hephzibah. Four years his junior, Hephzibah Menuhin began playing the piano publicly with her brother at 13. It was an association, both musical and personal, that remained indissoluble; and several generations of music audiences will remember them as they came out on stage together hand in hand.

ineffable   *in E fuh buhl*
(too overwhelming to be expressed or described in words; inexpressible)

By the end of the play, the apparently passionless character, a woman without biography, has communicated to us a feeling of ineffable loneliness. There is no solace or interruption in her regimen—no friends, phone calls or even solicitors or burglars. She does not have the grace of music, literature or self-indulgence. Through an accumulation of details and objects, we arrive at a point of complete empathy with the woman as she heads toward her inevitable conclusion.

inept   *in EPT*
(awkward; clumsy; incompetent; unskillful)

The Time-Life production of "The Search for Alexander the Great," currently running on WNET/13 on Wednesday evenings at 10, offers four hours of generally inept drama. With James Mason reading lengthy narrations while strolling around the ruins of a Greek amphitheater, the production rarely becomes more than an illustrated lecture.

inertia   *in ER shuh*
(a tendency to remain in a fixed condition without change; disinclination to move or act)

"I'm very, very lazy," conceded Mr. Bergman. "I love to sit in a chair and look out the window and do nothing. Writing is boring, very boring, and it takes so much patience." Yet, Mr. Bergman has overcome this self-proclaimed inertia, frequently with the aid of a vision that comes to him while seated in his "lazy" chair, doing "nothing."

inexorable   *in EK suh ruh buhl*
(*unrelenting; unalterable*)

Breathing coal dust for 20 or 30 years slowly, but inexorably, strangles miners: Their hardened lung tissue no longer transfers enough oxygen into the blood.

Not for the mightly hen such trifling speculation as whether she or the egg comes first. She knows too well the inexorable decree of nature that the egg comes first, being served at breakfast, while the chicken is reserved for dinner.

Russell Baker

---

inextricable   *in EK stri kuh buhl*
(*incapable of being disentangled or untied*)

President Reagan said today that he had "no intention" of involving the United States inextricably in the fighting in El Salvador, but he declared that his Administration would continue to support the Government there against those committed to its "violent overthrow."

infallible   *in FA luh buhl*
(*incapable of error; never wrong*)

It has been observed here before now that no matter how deficient an umpire may be in physical beauty, personal charm and social grace, he is infallible on balls and strikes and matters of faith and morals.

infidel   *IN fuh duhl*
(*a person who does not believe in a particular religion*)

TEHERAN, Iran, May 27 (Reuters)—Ayatollah Ruhollah Khomeini warned feuding Iranian officials today to halt their grab for power. In a strongly worded speech, the revolutionary leader told critics of the clergy-dominated Government to "go back to Europe, to the United States or wherever else you want." He warned that anyone intentionally ridiculing Iran's doctrinaire Moslems would be considered an infidel. "His property must be confiscated and he must be killed," he said.

infighting   *IN figh ting*
(*intense competition or conflict, often bitterly personal, as between political opponents or within an organization or group*)

Iran's bitter political infighting has grown even fiercer since the release of the American Embassy hostages, casting doubt on the future course of the revolution, which is two years old this week.

influx   IN fluhks
(a flowing in; a continual coming in of persons or things)

The American shrimpers contend that the influx of Vietnamese fishermen has overcrowded the bay, threatening both their livelihoods and the shrimp crop.

inform   in FAWRM
(to give form or character to; be the formative principle of)

Dickens's earliest aspirations, in fact, were focused on the theater, and his passion for drama would unconsciously inform all his later work.

infrastructure   IN fruh struhk cher
(a substructure or underlying foundation, especially the basic installations and facilities on which the continuation and growth of a community, state, institution, etc., depend)

The physical infrastructure of a city, its system of water supply, sewers, bridges, streets and mass transit, is the underlying component of its economic base, and is vital to its economic health.

infuse   in FYOO:Z
(to put into as if by pouring; instill; fill)

One of the most common safety tests for cosmetics and other consumer products—and one heavily criticized as inhumane—was developed by the United States Food and Drug Administration. It measures irritation in the eyes of albino rabbits that are infused with an array of products ranging from perfumes to oven cleaners.

Society is infused with the vain idea that now is best, or worst or most important. If medieval society was geocentric, believing that all else revolved around the earth, we might be called neocentric—obsessed with now.

inherent   in HI ruhnt
(basic; built-in; innate)

Projecting from current trends, the agency and other safety officials estimate that automobile traffic deaths will increase by 30 percent by 1990, or to about 35,000 a year from about 27,000 a year, almost exclusively because of the inherent vulnerabilities of smaller cars.

injunction   *in JUHNGK shuhn*
(command)

"We are willing to go to jail for our version of the truth," Philip Berrigan said before the group, known as the Plowshares Eight, was sentenced. The group was named for the biblical injunction to beat weapons into plowshares.

innate   *i NAYT*
(existing naturally, rather than acquired)

The four foods that seem to lend themselves most naturally to no-salt cookery are tomatoes, onions, mushrooms and eggplants. These vegetables have an innate flavor that is more pronounced when they are cooked, and if treated properly their flavor gratifications need not be enhanced by salt.

innocuous   *i NAH kyoo uhs*
(harmless; inoffensive; dull and uninspiring)

There is also a special "Bionic Briefcase" that is bulletproof and theft-proof, contains both a bug and tape-recorder detector, and a device to sniff out bombs. "It's an innocuous-looking briefcase, but it can be made to do most things in a security field," Mr. Jamil said. "You just pack your bomb sniffer, your homing device and pajamas and you're ready to go."

innuendo   *in yoo EN doh*
(an indirect remark or reference; insinuation)

Between songs, the slick, flirtatious D.J.'s manipulate the sensibilities of female listeners with innuendo and suggestion.

insatiable   *in SAY shuh buhl*
(constantly wanting more; unsatisfiable)

The destruction, both vocal and personal, came about partly owing to Miss Callas's own insatiable desire for celebrity and a need to be close to power. But the chief instrument of ruin most certainly was the late Mr. Onassis, who from this book's detailed testimony was a remarkably crude, trivial and nasty man.

* * *

Anyone who knows teen-age boys knows that they are bottomless pits. Six ears of corn mean nothing; four pork chops, mountains of spaghetti. Seconds and thirds. Then half an hour after dinner I'd find them at the kitchen table eating a bowl of cereal. Anything loose in the refrigerator disappeared down their insatiable gullets; they'd eat anything.

The Bottomless Pit is the name given to Hell in Revelations 20:1–3. "And I saw an angel come down from heaven, having the key of the bottomless pit and a great chain in his hand. And he laid hold on the dragon, that old serpent, which is the Devil, and Satan, and bound him a thousand years. And cast him into the bottomless pit, and shut him up, and set a seal upon him, that he should deceive the nations no more, till the thousand years should be fulfilled: and after that he must be loosed a little season."

insidious   *in SI di uhs*
(stealthily treacherous; more dangerous than seems evident; proceeding inconspicuously but with grave effect)

Nine-year-old Eric is allowed to watch television only one hour a day, although he can choose whatever program he wants. "We've never really controlled how much Eric watched before," Mrs. Plent said. "Most of the kids in our neighborhood watch most of the time. Finally I came to see how insidious it was. For Eric—and us—it was a time filler-upper, a habit."

insipid   *in SI pid*
(without flavor; tasteless; dull; lifeless)

Under the mistaken impression that American country-pop music is "serious" concert fare, Miss Mouskouri also performed recent pop hits like "When I Dream" and "The Rose" with the same elocuted politeness with which she delivered the pop adaptation of the "Costa Diva" from Bellini's "Norma." It was all terribly insipid. Miss Mouskouri should have devoted more energy to exploring her Greek heritage and less time aspiring to American kitsch.

As for the thin and watery yogurt drinks, Le Shake and Sippity (more appropriately renamed, perhaps, Insipidity), both tasted like milk of magnesia blended with jam.

insomnia   *in SAHM ni uh*
(inability to sleep, especially when chronic; sleeplessness)

Some of the physicians who deal with insomnia do so because they themselves are, or have been, insomnia sufferers. They know, and can describe, the helplessness, even the panic that accompanies a sleepless night.

insouciant   *in SOO: si uhnt*
(blithely indifferent; free from concern; calm and unbothered)

At rehearsals, in sneakers and sweatshirt, a cigarette dangling from his lips, [Peter] Martins looks like an insouciant Nordic basketball coach. He beats time with his foot; he whistles between his teeth to the dancers. He is cool.

insular   *IN suh ler*
(like an island; detached; isolated)

The impoundment of the livestock represents the latest step in the Federal Government's efforts to move thousands of Navajos off their rugged ancestral homelands in northeast Arizona, one of the most insular and physically isolated regions of the country.

intangible   *in TAN juh buhl*
(a personal asset that cannot be seen, such as a character trait)

There have been few defensive ends who could match Willie Davis in the physical attributes of speed, agility and size, plus the intangibles—intelligence, dedication and leadership.

intercourse   *IN ter kawrs*
(communication or dealings among people, countries, etc.; interchange of products, services, ideas, feelings, etc.)

To suggest, as Professor Segal does, that because all the fantasized projections of the 1939–40 World's Fair in New York did not materialize, world exhibitions in general "have no serious social and cultural pretensions" is to ignore the fundamental objective of international fairs, which is to create a fertile ground for the intercourse of ideas despite unpredictable results.

"Our country! In her intercourse with foreign nations may she always be in the right; but our country, right or wrong."
Stephen Decatur (1779–1820), American Naval
Commander. Toast given at Norfolk, April 1816.

---

intermittent   *in ter MIT uhnt*
(stopping and starting again at intervals; periodic)

A White House official said Mr. Reagan's temperature was less than 100 degrees this morning. Mr. Reagan has had a fever intermittently since Thursday.

intermodal   *in ter MOH duhl*
(combining different ways of transportation into one system)

Two tractor-trailer trucks loaded with dried fruit from Taiwan became the first shipment to move through the city's intermodal rail terminal, which allows easy transfer of ship cargo to rail lines and trucks, United Press International reported.

internecine   *in ter NEE sin*
(pertaining to conflict within a group; mutually destructive)

For years the hospital, founded in the last century by Protestant missionaries, had treated the injured from all sides of Lebanon's internecine bloodletting with fine impartiality.

interpolation   *in ter puh LAY shuhn*
(to insert between or among others; interpose)

Except for a couple of interpolations designed to expand dancing opportunities, the ballet sticks fairly close to the traditional fairy tale.

intimidate   *in TI muh dayt*
(to make timid; make afraid; overawe)

The most pervasive confusion exists on menus printed entirely in French or Italian, generally in upper-class establishments where a certain air of intimidation prevails with staff as well as on the menu. The idea in such cases must be that those who have to ask what dishes are do not belong there anyway, a hint that customers might well consider taking.

intone   *in TOHN*
(to utter in a singing tone or in prolonged monotones)

BELFAST, Northern Ireland, Sept. 9—The judge, resplendent in a scarlet robe, sits facing the defendant, who is guarded by two policemen. The lawyers wear curly gray wigs and starchy white dickeys, and the crier opens the trial by intoning, "God Save the Queen."

intractable   *in TRAK tuh buhl*
(stubborn; obstinate; resisting treatment or cure)

Widespread hunger remains intractable throughout the world and is exacting a high human toll. About half a billion individuals are still crippled by hunger, and a billion or more others should have a more varied diet, according to nutritionists. The great majority of the under-nourished—some 80 percent, by World Bank estimates—are women and children.

intransigent   in TRAN si juhnt
(uncompromising; inflexible)

Improvisation of that kind is what Mr. Matthau enjoys most about film acting. "When you get an intransigent director and writer who complain if you change a single comma, that is very unconducive to doing comedy. Shakespeare never described what happens in a scene. He just put the words down, like a good playwright, and then he died."

Many words found in Shakespeare's works are now obsolete: for example, *accite* (to summon), *bollen* (swollen), *coistrel* (knave), *shunless* (inevitable) and *twire* (twinkle). On the other hand, Shakespeare provided the language with more currently used words (either coined by him or found in his works for the first time) than any other writer. They include:

accommodation	gull (dupe)
apostrophe	gust
aslant	heartsick
assassination	hint
barefaced	hot-blooded
baseless	hurry
call (visit)	impartial
control (the noun)	import (the noun)
countless	inauspicious
courtship	indistinguishable
dawn (the noun)	lackluster
denote	laughable
disgraceful	leapfrog
dislocate	lonely
distrustful	lower (the verb)
dress (the noun)	misanthrope
dwindle	monumental
educate	needlelike
eventful	obscene
expellent	pedant
exposure	premeditated
fitful	reliance
fretful	submerged
frugal	summit
grovel	

---

intrusive   *in TROO: siv*
(intruding; coming unbidden or without welcome)

Some of the waiters affect a style that they seem to think is breezy but which is really intrusive and insolent. There is also a tendency to use the kindergartenish "we." Spilling wine on a cloth and menu, the waiter soothed an annoyed patron with, "We're not going to let that spoil our evening, are we?"

intuition   *in too I shuhn*
(the direct knowing of something without the conscious use of reasoning; immediate apprehension or understanding; keen and quick insight)

Intuition, says Ingmar Bergman, is the essence of creativity and the foundation of his unparalleled success as a film maker. "I make all my decisions on intuition," said the 62-year-old Swedish director. "But then, I must know why I made that decision. I throw a spear into the darkness. That is intuition. Then I must send an army into the darkness to find the spear. That is intellect."

inundate   *I nuhn dayt*
(to flood; cover with water)

Last year, heavy snows in the western mountains and torrential rains in central China resulted in flooding along the Yangtze. To prevent the river cities of Wuhan, Nanjing and Shanghai from being inundated, dikes and levies were opened or broke under pressure, flooding millions of rural residents out of their homes.

Since she appeared in last month's three-part television adaptation of John Steinbeck's "East of Eden," Jane Seymour has been inundated with scripts, according to the actress, who said most of the offerings called for her to play "evil women."

inure   *in YOOR*
(to make accustomed to; toughen or harden through exposure to; habituate)

In 1977, attorneys for a 15-year-old Florida youth argued that six to eight hours' worth of daily television viewing had so inured him to violence that he had lost the ability to distinguish right from wrong, and therefore should not be convicted of fatally shooting his next-door neighbor, an 82-year-old woman, during a robbery attempt. Elements of one episode of the boy's favorite television show, "Kojak," were said to resemble the actual slaying.

invective   *in VEK tiv*
(a violent verbal attack; insults; curses)

Kevin Martin, one of four Irish nationalists charged with disorderly conduct for shouting political invective at Prince Charles at the Metropolitan
Opera House on Wednesday night, was at Liffey's bar in Elmhurst,
Queens, last night celebrating what he called "our victory." Mr. Martin
had stood up and begun shouting "Victory to the I.R.A." from a seat that
he estimated was no more than 20 feet from the Prince and Nancy
Reagan.

inveigh   *in VAY*
(to make a violent verbal attack; talk or write bitterly)

The novel, "The Book of Ebenezer Le Page," was begun in the 60's by
G.B. Edwards. It is a story told by a bandy-legged, crotchety old bachelor
who inveighs against any signs of change on the Channel Island of Guernsey, where he has lived his entire life.

inventory   *IN vuhn taw ri*
(the store of goods on hand)

The Salvadoran Navy lists 11 boats in its inventory. Two are capsized
hulls, four have been stripped for parts, and of the rest, only three are
operational.

(to make an appraisal, as of one's skills, personal characteristics, etc.)

In an interview a couple of months ago, I was reported to have said that
burnout can be a productive time for people, a time to inventory life's
satisfactions. My interview with the reporter sounded actually enthusiastic about the benefits of burnout. I hope I didn't leave anyone with the
impression that depression can be fun.

invertebrate   *in VER tuh brit*
*(an animal without a backbone, or spinal column; any animal other
than a fish, amphibian, reptile, bird or mammal)*

Instead of working on all endangered species simultaneously, the department will concentrate on higher species. This means that mammals will
be given top priority and such invertebrates as insects and mollusks lower
priorities.

invidious   *in VI di uhs*
(causing animosity, resentment or envious dislike)

In 1979 the Senate Judiciary Committee adopted a policy statement declaring it "inadvisable for a nominee for a Federal judgeship to belong to a social club that engages in invidious discrimination."

invoke   *in VOHK*
(to resort to or put into use, as a law, ruling, penalty, etc.)

But golf has a history of conscience. Golfers often have invoked penalties against themselves for a violation that only they saw or knew. The late Babe Didrikson Zaharias once disqualified herself from a tournament for having hit the wrong ball out of the rough. "But nobody would have known," a friend told her. "I would've known," Babe Didrikson Zaharias replied.

invulnerable   *in VUHL nuh ruh buhl*
(incapable of being wounded, hurt or damaged)

The digital disc will also render unnecessary all kinds of fussy record care. No more brushes and cleaners—and you needn't hesitate to lend your records to fumble-fingered friends. The laser beam searches out the music from beneath a plastic coating that makes the record virtually invulnerable.

Although *laser* is an acronym composed of the initials of the words describing the device (*l*ight *a*mplification by *s*timulated *e*mission of *r*adiation), it has become a part of our common vocabulary, not thought of as *standing* for something but as *being* something. We may say NOW, UNICEF, CORE, HUD and OPEC as word units, but we're still conscious of them as groups of initials. Other words in the *laser* class are *radar* (*ra*dio *d*etecting *a*nd *r*anging), *scuba* (*s*elf *c*ontained *u*nderwater *b*reathing *a*pparatus) and *snafu* (*s*ituation *n*ormal *a*ll *f*ouled *u*p).

---

irascible   *i RA suh buhl*
(easily angered; quick-tempered)

When you feel like some Wagner after everyone else has gone to bed, or if you have thin walls and irascible neighbors, earphones are instruments of domestic peace.

irredeemable   *i ri DEE muh buhl*
(that cannot be reformed; hopeless)

"Nickleby" as a novel is rich in Dickensian sentimentality, and it is if anything intensified on the stage. The good characters are angelic, the evil irredeemably bad.

irrepressible   *i ri PRE suh buhl*
(incapable of being repressed or restrained)

The "Popemobile," an open vehicle such as the one he was riding in when he was shot yesterday, has become a symbol of his mobility. Before his weekly audiences in the square, he stands in the vehicle as it winds through the crowds. The act is a byproduct of his instinctive showmanship and his irrepressible desire to bring the church to the people.

jejune   *ji JOO:N*
(without interest; dull; insipid)

Here is the fearless forecast for Phase II of the Reagan Revolution, wherein ideas that were considered jejune in January will, this fall, become the top ten items on the nation's domestic agenda.

jerry-built   *JER ee bilt*
(built poorly, of cheap materials; unsubstantially built: a mid-19th century British slang word of uncertain origin)

The majority of the fresh fruit and vegetable markets in eastern Long Island are relatively small and vary in structure and produce. Some are on wagon beds, some in jerry-built shacks that seem to be put together with a few boards, hammers and nails.

jettison   *JE tuh suhn*
(to throw away as useless or a burden: originally, to throw overboard to lighten a ship in an emergency)

The Americans managed to withdraw their army to Manhattan, but the British crossed the East River, landed in the area of the East 30's and pushed crosstown, slicing through demoralized rebel troops. Near Lexington Avenue and East 42d Street, where people still rush about, Washington was outraged by the behavior of his troops, who jettisoned their arms and fled. It was here that he threw his hat on the ground and cried, "Are these the men with whom I am to defend America?"

When last heard from in September, Anita Bryant, having ended her marriage of 20 years, had left Miami and returned to her native Oklahoma. She jettisoned her religious crusade against equal rights for homosexuals and said she had decided she believed in "live and let live."

jibe   *jighb*
(a jeer; taunt: a variant spelling of gibe)

In a rare personal jibe, Mr. O'Neill said that Mr. Reagan called Vice President Bush into a meeting today with Republican lawmakers to discuss the budget "because he had to have someone explain it for him."

jocular   *JAH kyoo ler*
(joking; humorous; full of fun)

Mr. Young's high spirits showed time and again in an understated jocularity that caused laughter in the audience of reporters and Johnson Space Center employees. Once Captain Crippen was asked if his pulse rate of 130 at liftoff, against Mr. Young's 90, meant he was more excited. "You betchum I was excited," he said. Mr. Young added, "What you don't understand is, I was excited too. I just can't make it go any faster." Mr. Young is 50 years old, seven years older than his partner.

joie de vivre   *zhwah duh VEE vruh*
(delight at being alive; enjoyment of life: French, joy of living)

It was 1953, and Paris was inexpensive and romantic, and it was possible then, as it had been possible in Hemingway's time, to make writing not only a vocation but an entire way of life. And so a group of young Americans went to Paris, where they wrote and drank and played tennis and sat up all night at cafes, and where they started a little magazine that ran on talent and enthusiasm and a youthful joie de vivre.

josh   *jahsh*
(to tease good-humoredly: colloquial American since the 1880's; origin uncertain)

The droll, witty Harvard Lampoon staff, the prime joshers of the Ivy League, have selected People magazine for their next parody effort.

journeyman   *JER ni muhn*
(a competent, experienced but not brilliant worker or performer)

Wayne Merrick's magnificent obsession has always been with the Stanley Cup itself, never with any of the other old, polished silverware that the National Hockey League presents for individual glory. As a journeyman center, he has always considered the team trophy to be the extent of his dream, a dream that came true.

juncture *JUHNGK cher*
(a critical moment in the development of events; crisis)

The moment of truth arrives in Congress today for the President's tax bill and that of his Democratic opponents. Or perhaps one should call it the moment of untruth. Both Republicans and Democrats are going to have trouble keeping a straight face hailing either bill as just what the nation needs at this juncture in economic history.

junket *JUHNG kit*
(a trip at public expense, ostensibly with a public purpose, such as that of a Congressional investigating committee, which in reality the members are taking principally for pleasure)

It is unfortunate that many would probably agree with Mr. Reagan that a trip to Hawaii to study issues involving native Hawaiians is a junket, as Mr. Reagan reportedly described the commission's fact-finding mission. These same individuals are undoubtedly unaware, as the President may be, of the role that the Government played in the overthrow of the Hawaiian monarchy, the takeover of lands from the Hawaiian kingdom, and the continuing decline of a culture.

juxtaposition *juhk stuh puh ZI shuhn*
(the placement or location of things side by side or close together)

The juxtaposition of old and new is widespread in Africa. But in Nigeria, oil wealth has burnished the glitter of new things in an obvious sort of way: The man who wears the traditional robes is just as likely to be sporting Gucci loafers and a gold Rolex.

kamikaze   *kah mi KAH zi*
(a suicide attack by a Japanese airplane pilot in World War II; the airplane or pilot in such an attack)

Several of the Marine guards held hostage in Iran had plans to sacrifice their lives next month in a "kamikaze mission" intended to kill as many of their captors as possible, one of those involved in the plot said today. "It wasn't going to be a breakout, it was going to be a kamikaze mission," Sgt. James M. Lopez told reporters at a hometown news conference. "We had been there a year and we'd be damned if we'd stay there another year. We were going to get this thing over with one way or another."

"I Won't Dance," which was unveiled at the Helen Hayes yesterday afternoon, can take its place alongside such other recent Broadway kamikaze missions as "Animals" and "Inacent Black."

Kamikaze, the name applied to Japan's World War II suicide air squadrons, originated in 13th-century Japan. In 1274, Kubla Khan, the first Mongol to rule all of China (his grandfather was the warrior Ghengis Khan) attempted an invasion of Japan, but was stopped by heavy losses. His second attempt, in 1281, failed when 1,000 of the 4,400 invading warships were destroyed by typhoons. The Japanese called the seemingly God-sent storms kamikaze, or divine winds.

---

ken   *ken*
(mental perception)

Thomas Hart Benton, the American regionalist painter who was Jackson Pollock's teacher and Harry S. Truman's favorite artist, has long been associated in the public ken with the earthy art and people of his native Missouri and Middle West. The muralist depicted farmers scything hay, gaunt Ozark hillbillies, black sharecroppers, soldiers in honkytonks, miners hunched over from years in the pits and riverboats on the Mississippi.

kinetic   *ki NE tik*
(pertaining to motion)

This is one of the best performances by any dancer in recent memory, both sensitively shaped and kinetically exciting. As Mr. Parsons keeps dancing with beautifully bright flair, Miss York attempts to run after him. But the speedy pirouettes and distorted barrel turns in the air—the total virtuosity—stop her, as they do the hearts of the audience.

kiosk   *ki AHSK*
(a small structure open at one or more sides, used as a newsstand, bandstand, subway entrance, etc.)

There are lines for almost everything in Poland. Lines at kiosks for newspapers in the morning become lines for cigarettes later in the day. There are lines for bread, lines for vodka, lines for plane tickets, linoleum and detergents. Lately, lines for gasoline have meant waits of one to two hours.

kitchen cabinet   *KICH in KA buh nit*
(a group of unofficial advisers which a President may assemble and on which he relies heavily: the term was first used for such a group advising President Andrew Jackson in 1829)

The meeting was organized by the President's "kitchen cabinet," an informal advisory group that includes wealthy Californians who are long-time friends of Mr. Reagan.

kitsch   *kich*
(slickly professional art, writing, etc., calculated for popular appeal, but artistically shallow or vulgar)

In the weeks leading up to the wedding, Britain has been drenched in kitsch as manufacturers rush to turn out souvenirs, many of them blithely ignoring the Lord Chamberlain's pleas for good taste. There are 42 different designs of commemorative mugs, and one mail-order firm is offering more than 200 items, ranging from pin cushions to table lighters to a jigsaw puzzle of the parade route to a special brick to throw at the family television set if the coverage gets too boring.

kosher   *KOH sher*
(honest; legal; legitimate; reliable; trustworthy; authentic; ethical; approved: Hebrew, clean and acceptable according to Jewish dietary laws. In British and American slang, new applications of "kosher" occur regularly.)

Mayor Koch, who saw the film ["Fort Apache, The Bronx"] at a preview, described it as "racist" because of the antisocial manner in which it depicts Puerto Ricans and blacks: "I saw it as a fascinating film in terms of excitement, but a racist film in the following way: There was not one Puerto Rican personality that was without some major character defect." He noted that the most prominent Puerto Rican in the film, a nurse, turns out to be a "junkie." But, Mr. Koch said, he doubted the movie would injure the city's image. "People can smell something that is not kosher," he added. "This film is not kosher."

labyrinth   *LA buh rinth*
(an intricate network of winding passages hard to follow without losing one's way; maze; a complicated, perplexing arrangement, course of affairs, etc.)

Merchants of the Teheran bazaar, a sprawling labyrinthine collection of shops and stalls that is the largest in the Middle East, financed the movement that overthrew the Shah in 1979.

———

In Greek mythology, the labyrinth was an underground maze of great complexity that the architect Daedalus built for King Minos of Crete. In it, Minos confined the Minotaur, a monster with the body of a man and the head of a bull, which every year devoured seven youths and seven maidens whom Minos placed in the labyrinth. The Minotaur was finally slain by Theseus, who unwound a ball of string as he began to wander through the maze and in that way was able to find his way out again after he had accomplished his mission.

———

lace   *lays*
(to add a dash of alcoholic liquor to)

Don't pass up the torta De Medici, which has a layer of sponge cake topped by a frothy cloud of chocolate mousse laced with rum—it melts in your mouth.

lachrymose   *LA kruh mohs*
(tearful; sad)

Everyone showed their stuff at the 64th Street reviewing stand, where Governor Carey, wearing several shades of green, sang "Danny Boy" as a band played the lachrymose air.

lackey   *LA ki*
(a follower who carries out another's orders like a servant; toady)

Ayatollah Ruhollah Khomeini today characterized the assassination of his personal representative in Tabriz as the work of United States "lackeys" and vowed that "the people would take revenge," the Teheran radio reported.

laggard   *LA gerd*
(a slow person who is always falling behind)

The laggard in children's programming this season is NBC, which has produced no new dramas for its "Special Treat" series.

laid back   *layd bak*
(calm, cool and relaxed; nonchalant; low-keyed: a slang term)

One of the more colorful and lively places offering the limited but entertaining range of Texas dishes is the Cottonwood Cafe on Bleecker Street, just east of Bank Street. The style here is so laid back that you'll feel overdressed in anything more elaborate than a cotton shirt and jeans, but after one of the huge and marvelous frozen tequila and lime juice margaritas, you would be likely to feel at home in anything, even white tie and tails.

languid   *LANG gwid*
(lacking in vigor or vitality)

Modigliani is one of the most familiar 20th-century artists. His melancholy faces and languid nudes occupy an entire corridor in the museum without walls. His works have been reproduced so often that they were a part of us before we knew his name.

languish   *LANG gwish*
(to undergo neglect; live under distressing conditions)

After years of languishing in small, chilly arenas, figure skating has become hot stuff as a spectator sport. The world championships are a sellout, a 15-city North American tour after the world event will play the largest indoor facilities, and ice shows and skating exhibitions now are regularly seen on network television.

lares and penates   *LAI reez and pi NAY teez*
(the treasured belongings of a family or household: Latin)

The shelterless people are visible all over the West Side. They sit on the benches of the Broadway malls. They sleep in doorways, often surrounded by the bulging shopping bags that are filled with the lares and penates of their homeless existence. Many talk to themselves. Some are abusive. Most look gentle and vacant.

The penates were the personal gods of each Roman household that watched over the family's welfare and prosperity. The lares were also household gods, but they were the deified spirits of ancestors who watched over and protected their descendants' homes. The *lar familiaris* was the spirit of the founder of the house which never left it. There were also public lares—guardian spirits of the city, the fields, the highways, the sea, etc. Each home had a shrine in which stood images of its lares and penates, and to which the family prayed. On special occasions offerings were made to them of wine, cakes, honey and incense.

---

largess *lahr JES*
(*a generous bestowal of gifts; liberality in giving*)

A million-dollar jury verdict for an injured client is a trial lawyer's Oscar, his laurel wreath, his grand slam, his jackpot and his badge of success. It commands the respect of his fellows and entitles him to tell them how he coaxed such largess from the jury.

lassitude *LA suh too:d*
(*a state of being tired or listless; weariness*)

Fever and lassitude are the symptoms to look for when checking for tick bites, but physicians in the Hamptons sometimes begin treatment before they have a definite diagnosis.

latent *LAY tuhnt*
(*lying hidden and undeveloped within a person or thing, as a quality or power*)

The secret of chess is that it's a killer's game, requiring above all the will to win. It brings out latent aggression even in the mildest of people, and turns grown men into children when a blunder leads to defeat.

latitude *LA tuh too:d*
(*freedom from narrow restrictions*)

In 1952, Mr. Sauter joined forces with Bill Finegan, who had been chief arranger for Miller and Dorsey, to form an orchestra that would carry out their innovative writing ideas. "We agreed that it would not be brass and saxes all over again," Mr. Sauter explained. "We'd had that. We wanted a different combination of instruments. We came up with one that gave us lots of latitude—from piccolo to tuba. It gave us space to make the lines come out so you don't always have a wad of sound thrown at you."

lax   *laks*
(loose; not strict; careless; negligent)

Security around the gleaming black and white missiles is lax. A Syrian soldier yawns as he glances at the documents of some travelers in cars. It is possible to take pictures.

layman   *LAY muhn*
(a member of the laity; a person not of the clergy: any profession can also refer to those outside it or not skilled in it as lay persons)

The word came from the Vatican: "Politics is the responsibility of laymen, and a priest should be a priest." So after 10 years in the House of Representatives, Robert F. Drinan, the liberal Jesuit priest from Massachusetts, gave up his seat last Jan. 1.

leery   *LEE ri*
(on one's guard; wary; suspicious)

Wall Street has always cherished its eccentrics and been leery of them at the same time: It is hard to tell, after all, what an off-beat individualist with a lot of hustle might be up to. Take an outspoken, Budapest-born securities analyst and stock promoter named Andrew G. Racz.

legalese   *lee guhl EEZ*
(the language of legal forms, documents, etc., often thought of as incomprehensible to anyone but lawyers)

The back of a typical auto rental contract contains the conditions, but they are usually in legalese that virtually defies comprehension by anyone but a lawyer.

———

Legalese: "If the insured is a mortgagee, this company's right of subrogation shall not prevent the insured from releasing the personal liability of the obligor or guarantor or from releasing a portion of the premises from the lien of the mortgage or from increasing or otherwise modifying the insured mortgage provided such acts do not affect the validity of priority of the lien of the mortgage insured. However, the liability of this company under this policy shall in no event be increased by any such act of the insured."

From the Title Insurance Policy for the author's home.

_____

legion   *LEE juhn*
(a large number; multitude)

Excitement or preoccupation with an activity may block perception of pain. Stories are legion of athletes who do not realize until the end of the game that they have broken bones.

lèse-majesté   *LEEZ MA ji sti*
(an offense against a ruler's dignity as head of the state: French, from the Latin, læsa majestas, injured majesty, used by the 4th-century historian Ammianus)

He supported Ronald Reagan for President when that was lèse-majesté in a New York party that was under the thumb of Mr. Rockefeller.

lethargy   *LE ther ji*
(a great lack of energy)

Drawn to nature, thousands of New Yorkers are about to renew the summer custom of leaving work early on Friday afternoons. Gripped by lethargy, normally productive members of the labor force will find themselves not at their work stations, but behind the wheels of automobiles heading for retreats.

leverage   *LE vuh rij*
(power to act effectively)

Most believe that the Kremlin has not exhausted attempts at a political resolution of the Polish issue. But the fact remains that whatever leverage the Russians may still have derives not from the persuasiveness of their ideological arguments but from the ever-present threat of military intervention.

leviathan   *luh VIGH uh thuhn*
(a whale; anything of immense size and power, as a huge ocean liner: originally, a biblical sea monster, thought of as a whale or crocodile)

There are whales in the waters off Long Island, and there are whale-watchers, too—a weekend navy that scouts the still-chilly ocean for descendants of the leviathans whose oil and skin were the most precious products of Long Island's economy early in the 19th century.

lexicon   LEK si kahn
(a dictionary; the vocabulary of a particular author, subject, profession, language, etc.)

Love and forbearance figure high in the lexicon of Baptist virtues, but at this year's annual convention of Southern Baptists, held in Los Angeles last week, some serious rifts disrupted the mood.

liaison   LEE uh zahn
(a close relationship)

Rarely in France are you served pâtés, terrines and sliced cold meats, such as salamis, without the pickles known as cornichons—and often mustard —as an accompaniment. In this country, sauerkraut is a perfect liaison for a frankfurter on a bun, and cole slaw in many places is the inevitable side dish with hamburgers.

libidinous   li BI duh nuhs
(full of lust: from libido, the sexual urge or instinct; Latin, lubet, it pleases)

When Ned Racine (William Hurt), the libidinous, slightly down-at-the-heels lawyer, who is the movie's hero, meets Matty Walker, she drives him wild. Matty (Kathleen Turner) is a rich and unhappily married beauty in a clinging white dress, and she means to arouse in Ned a sexual longing so powerful it will make him absolutely ruthless.

Lilliputian   li luh PYOO: shuhn
(tiny: from Lilliput, a land in Swift's "Gulliver's Travels" inhabited by people six inches tall)

Rose growers are learning that small is beautiful. In the last six or seven years sales of Lilliputian rosebushes have increased from limited production for hobbyists to a booming multimillion-dollar business.

limpid   LIM pid
(perfectly clear; transparent; not cloudy or murky)

Some of the calm, limpid coves are perfect for snorkeling among Mediterranean fish in a rocky submarine landscape.

linchpin   *LINCH pin*
(*a central or cohesive element*)

One of the linchpins of the city's 10-year capital plan, according to Mr. Koch, will be the ability of the city to go to the bond market annually with the announced goal of selling $1 billion in city bonds by 1986.

lingua franca   *LING gwuh FRAHNG kuh*
(*a standard language that is widely used as a general medium of communication; a hybrid language used for communication between different peoples, as pidgin English*)

Collage as a way of making great art has been around for 70 or so years. Not only is it part of the lingua franca of 20th-century art, but it also seems almost to have been bred into us, like table manners or brushing our teeth. For this reason, the fallacy is now widespread that almost anyone can make a good collage if he puts his mind to it.

The original lingua franca (Italian, Frankish language) was a hybrid language of Italian, Spanish, French, Greek, Arabic and Turkish elements, spoken in certain Mediterranean ports beginning in the 17th century for the purpose of facilitating business and trade. It consisted mostly of Italian words without their inflections.

---

lionize   *LIGH uh nighz*
(*to treat as a celebrity*)

French interest in American dance is not unprecedented. It was the French who first lionized Loie Fuller in 1892, making her revolutionary dances of colored lights and billowing fabric the toast of the Folies Bergeres.

Lionize, to treat someone as a celebrity who is unaccustomed to being treated that way, came into use in the early 1800's, after an exhibit of lions at the Tower of London attracted people from far and wide who had never seen a live lion.

---

listless   *LIST lis*
(*feeling no inclination toward or interest in anything; spiritless; indifferent*)

When Michael is briefly estranged from his wife, he is too listless to do anything but watch the game show "Family Feud" on television.

litany　　*LI tuh ni*
(a repetitive and almost predictable recital of things, as in a ritual: originally, a form of prayer in which the clergy and the congregation read responsively in a fixed order)

At Maybe's recent meeting, the litany of children's problems today was recited: drugs and drinking, alcoholic parents, split homes, abortions, schizophrenia, vandalism, shoplifting and burglary, among other things.

literally　　*LI tuh ruh li*
(actually; in fact)

The Mayor of Norwalk, Conn. is running again, this time literally, and has offered to take on about half the town in the race. Anyone who beats him does not take the Mayor's job, but gets an official certificate saying the Mayor was defeated.

literati　　*li tuh RAH ti*
(persons of literary attainment; scholarly or learned people: Latin, learned)

Northern New Mexico has been an oasis for writers, artists and photographers since D.H. Lawrence and Georgia O'Keefe settled here in the 20's. The literati have been well established for decades, but now the glitterati are moving in and, much to Santa Fe's dismay, the town is fast becoming an open secret. The most notable new arrivals are probably the Duke and Duchess of Bedford, who have purchased a home in the nearby village of Tesque that was listed for $1.1 million, according to Lee Head, a real estate agent.

lithe　　*lighth:*
(limber; supple)

At 54, Mr. Belafonte is lean, lithe and as strikingly handsome as he was when he first appeared in the 1950's and helped give folk music a period of mass appeal.

litigation　　*li ti GAY shuhn*
(the process of carrying on a lawsuit; a lawsuit)

Damage claims by workers exposed to asbestos and by their families now constitute the largest, and potentially most costly, block of product liability litigation ever to confront American industry. About 25,000 people who believe they are victims have already filed 12,000 suits against 260 companies that manufacture, use or sell asbestos products, according to Michael Mealey, editor of the Asbestos Litigation Reporter.

litmus test   *LIT muhs test*
(a decisive test: from the use of litmus paper to test a solution for acidity or alkalinity. An older term with the same meaning is acid test)

If the Republicans make the tax vote a "litmus test" of party loyalty, Mr. Gephardt added, it will be very hard for the Democrats to win any Republican defectors.

loath   *lohth*
(unwilling; reluctant)

VERKHOYANSK, U.S.S.R.—Whatever the temperature, Siberians are loath to admit it's cold, but here they have no choice—there simply aren't many colder places on earth. Dawn is still far off at 9 A.M.; it's 60 degrees below zero.

lobotomized   *loh BAH tuh mighzd*
(dulled or deadened, suggesting the aftereffects of a lobotomy, in which part of the brain is surgically removed in order to blunt the emotions of a severely disturbed psychotic)

"The Best of Friends," which will be shown Sunday night at 8 on Channel 5, is billed as a screen adaptation of an Ernest Hemingway short story titled "The Three Day Blow." In fact, it bears no resemblance to the story, which is just as well. "The Best of Friends" is Hemingway lobotomized for dopes, something straight out of the "Bad Playhouse" parodies on "Saturday Night Live."

loggerheads   *LAH ger hedz*
(in a head-on dispute; quarreling: usually used with "at")

The border dispute long kept the two Asian [nations] at loggerheads, but in the last few years both have tried to establish normal contacts and resolve their differences by negotiations.

lollygag   *LAH li gag*
(to waste time in trifling or aimless activity; fool around: a slang word of obscure origin)

If you don't have to rush around making a living today, Bryant Park, that often abused greensward between West 40th and 42d Streets, just behind the Public Library on Fifth Avenue, is bursting with opportunities for musical lollygagging.

longueur   *lahn GER*
(a long, boring section in a novel, play, musical work, etc.: French)

After some longueurs, the weight of Mr. Wise's expertise helps build a head of steam that rushes the reader along, past implausible parts and bits of clumsy writing, as the conflict between Travis and Black moves to a cosmic Washington showdown.

lounge lizard   *LOWNJ LIZ erd*
(a sleek adventurer frequenting lounges in the expectation of women, their money and caresses)

In "Zorro," Mr. Hamilton looks like what your grandma used to call a lounge lizard. Small black mustache, slick polished hair and a slightly crazed glint in the bedroom eyes.

Lounge lizard was coined in the 1920's, and depending upon in what reference work one seeks its meaning, can take on greater or lesser noxious connotations. "Webster's Third" defines it as a "ladies' man, fop, social parasite," and lets it go at that. The "Oxford English Dictionary" has "one who spends his time in idling in fashionable society." Other general dictionaries are more or less in agreement with Eric Partridge, whose definition, in his "Dictionary of Slang and Unconventional Usage," appears with the entry here. An interesting and quite different one appears in the "Dictionary of American Slang": "A ladies' man, often characterized as stingy, who calls upon girls and women but does not entertain them away from their own homes. The lounge lizard's interest is in necking." G.P. Krapp, an outstanding historian of the English language, predicted in 1925 that *lounge lizard* would be dead within a generation.

---

lowest common denominator
LOH ist KAH muhn duh NAH muh nay ter
(that which is accepted, understood or appreciated by the broadest mass of people)

As a rule, prime-time television has not been terribly receptive to concepts like "the conflict of ideas." Escapism is usually favored over authenticity; sexual titillation and automobile chases over the exploration of subtler relationships and social issues. "Lou Grant" is one of the few shows—"M*A*S*H," "The White Shadow," "Hill Street Blues" and "Barney Miller" are others—that critics have agreed consistently aims above the lowest common denominator.

lucid   *LOO: sid*
(clearheaded; rational)

Sinn Fein said that 25-year-old Kevin Lynch, fasting for 53 days, was "extremely weak and suffering pain" but was still lucid.

lug   *luhg*
(a fellow, especially a stupid or dull one: a slang word)

Mr. Caan is most convincing as a none-too-bright lug with a talent for thievery and a desire for the conventional life that is forever beyond his reach.

————————

Calling a dull or stupid fellow a *lug* may be our unwitting homage to the stereotype of the caveman's brutish treatment of his woman. *Lug* derives from the Scandinavian *lugga*, which literally means *to pull by the hair.*

————————

lumber   *LUHM ber*
(to move heavily, clumsily and, often, noisily)

Even at its earnest, lumbering best, Paul Hindemith's expertly constructed but pedestrian music can be a chore to listen to.

luminary   *LOO: muh ne ri*
(a famous person)

In 1980 the City Council passed 73 measures that became law. Twenty of them name some piece of New York City—a park, a street, a traffic island or a playground—after a local or national luminary or foreign leader.

luminosity   *loo: muh NAH suh ti*
(brightness)

Janacek's orchestra scores are notoriously tricky, but the orchestra played with taut discipline and dazzling luminosity.

luxuriant   *luhg ZHOO ri uhnt*
(growing in great abundance; lush; rich)

In recent seasons, Rosalind Elias, the Metropolitan Opera mezzo-soprano, has spent considerable time wearing a luxuriant beard as Baba the Turk, the bearded lady of Stravinsky's "The Rake's Progress."

macabre   *muh KAH bruh*
(gruesome; grim and horrible; ghastly)

Soon after the suicide or murder of 913 men, women and children on Nov. 18, 1978, James Reston Jr. visited Jonestown and found the tapes. U.S. officials confiscated them, but Reston got most of them back under the Freedom of Information Act: more than 900 macabre hours.

Macabre came into English in 1842 from the French *danse macabre,* which was an allegorical representation of Death (in the form of a dancing skeleton or corpse) leading all sorts and conditions of humanity to the grave. It is first found in the 14th century, and there is a series of woodcuts on the subject by Hans Holbein the Younger (1497–1543). W.H. Auden's poem "The Dance of Death" was published in 1933; and what music appreciation teacher would be without Camille Saint-Saën's "Danse Macabre" (1875), that quintessential piece that conjures up images of graveyard frolics.

------

machination   *ma kuh NAY shuhn*
(an artful or secret plot or scheme, especially with evil intent: usually plural)

As Miss Swit sees it, people do not have to be knowledgeable about the film industry to enjoy "S.O.B." "It could be about any big business, like General Motors," she said. "They all have the same machinations and the same wheeling and dealing and the same big egos. It's not just our industry that's like this."

magnanimous   *mag NA nuh muhs*
(noble in mind; high-souled; generous in spirit and in overlooking injury or insult)

To the Editor: I have been noting with mounting disgust the media's attempts to discredit Frank Sinatra and their criticism of our President for any relations he might have with him. I have never had the pleasure of meeting Mr. Sinatra, but I have carefully studied his philanthropic record. This man has magnanimously given of himself—his talent, his time, his energy and sizable fortunes from his own pocket—to support good causes. What a pity that the media cannot adopt a balanced attitude toward people!

magnate   *MAG nit*
(a powerful or influential person, especially in business or industry)

One film magnate flew his favorite caterer over from New York on the Concorde for a party last Saturday at the Hotel du Cap in Antibes.

magnum opus   *MAG nuhm OH puhs*
(a person's greatest work or undertaking)

In 14th-century Yemen, then a thriving place along trade routes to the Orient, there was a king with an intellectual bent. He wrote numerous scientific tracts, including one dealing with the cultivation of grains, and was knowledgeable in health and astronomy. But his magnum opus was a six-language dictionary, a work of impeccable scholarship.

mainstay   *MAYN stay*
(a chief support: on a sailing vessel, a mainstay is a line supporting the mainmast and holding it in position)

With the peak tourist time of the year coming up, the strikes have already dealt a serious blow to the tourist business, Bermuda's economic mainstay. The Government has urged tourists to cancel reservations at the hotels.

makeshift   *MAYK shift*
(serving as a substitute)

In the bright sunshine, small children in Beirut's Moslem neighborhoods shoveled earth from vacant lots into plastic garbage sacks for makeshift sandbags that are stacked around storefronts, homes and gas pumps.

malinger   *muh LING ger*
(to pretend to be ill or otherwise incapacitated in order to escape duty or work; shirk)

All pain is real, whether caused by a tumor pressing on a nerve or by tension that tightens muscles or by fear that constricts arteries. Gastrointestinal cramps triggered by anxiety can be just as painful—and are just as real—as those due to amoebic dysentery or colitis. The only "fake" pain is not pain at all; it is a deliberate lie told by a malingerer.

malleable   *MA li uh buhl*
(capable of being changed, molded, adapted, etc., as metals can that are hammered or pressed into various shapes without breaking)

"Democracy in our part of the world is a portmanteau word malleable enough to take all shapes and postures," Chanchal Sarkar, an Indian columnist said this week, applying the lesson in India to the problem in Bangladesh.

———————

A portmanteau word is an artificial blend of two words in order to convey the combined meanings of both. We get *smog* from *smoke* and *fog; motel* from *motor* and *hotel; greige* from *grey* and *beige.* Lewis Carroll coined the term in "Through the Looking Glass," where Humpty Dumpty describes how two meanings get "packed up into one word," like a portmanteau, a valise that opens up like a book into two compartments. Carroll used several portmanteau words in "Jabberwocky," among them *slithy* (slimy + lithe), *mimsy* (flimsy + miserable) and *chortle* (chuckle + snort). Only *chortle* remains in use. Portmanteaus that have become standard English are *dumbfound* (dumb + confound), *splurge* (splash + surge) and *twirl* (twist + whirl). And of course there are *slimnastics, Exercycle, urinalysis, stagflation, beautility, Instamatic, sexploitation* and *broasted.*

———————

mammoth   *MA muhth*
(an extinct species of elephant with hairy skin and long tusks curving upward; hence, anything huge)

Former Chancellor Willy Brandt made a series of speeches in which he lumped the United States and the Soviet Union together as similar mammoths, both disagreeable and more or less equally responsible for the tensions of the world.

mandate   *MAN dayt*
(the wishes of voters expressed through an election and regarded as an order)

Mr. Reagan said that he and other officials elected in November had "an overwhelming mandate to rescue the economy" by reducing spending and cutting Federal income taxes.

(to order or command authoritatively)

HARTFORD, May 28—Two gun-control bills that will go into effect Oct. 1 were signed into law today by Gov. William A. O'Neill. One mandates a five-year prison sentence for using a firearm while committing a serious crime and the other requires a one-year term for carrying a handgun without a permit.

mandatory *MAN duh taw ri*
(authoritatively commanded or required; obligatory)

Jefferson believed in the mandatory teaching of science to all American citizens, and wrote, "Science is important to the preservation of our republican government and it is also essential to its protection against foreign power."

manifest *MA nuh fest*
(evident; obvious; clear)

Mohammed Anwar el-Sadat was born Dec. 25, 1918, in Mit Abul Kom, a cluster of mud-brick buildings in Minufiya Province between Cairo and Alexandria. He was one of the 13 children of Mohammed el-Sadat, a Government clerk, and his part-Sudanese wife, a heritage manifest in the boy's skin, darker than the average Egyptian's.

manifesto *ma nuh FE stoh*
(a public declaration of motives and intentions by a government or by a person or group regarded as having some public importance)

The Russian-born painter Wassily Kandinsky (1866–1944) has long been acknowledged to be one of the central figures, if not indeed the central figure, in the creation of abstract painting. His treatise called "On the Spiritual in Art," published in Munich in 1911, was the first major manifesto of the movement, and the paintings themselves initiate a tradition that can be seen to embrace the work of Miro, Gorky, Pollack and the whole Abstract Expressionist School.

manifold *MA nuh fohld*
(having many and various forms, features or parts)

"Being here in Alaska, so richly endowed with the beauties of nature, one so rugged and yet so splendid, we sense the presence of God's spirit in the manifold handiwork of creation." [Pope John Paul II]

marathon *MA ruh thahn*
(a long contest or task with endurance as the primary factor: after the 26-mile 385-yard racing event held at the Olympics and elsewhere)

John Bickford, president of the sales group for the Westmorland Coal Company, recalled the marathon sessions during which he and officials of the Israeli Electric Company sat bleary-eyed trying to agree on a 30-year contract to deliver steam coal to the utility.

I will not bore my readers with yet another retelling of how the Olympic marathon was instituted to memorialize the victory of the Greeks over the Persians at Marathon in 490 B.C., the result of which was announced at Athens by a courier who fell dead on arrival, having run nearly 23 miles. I *will* inform my readers, however, that an *apophasis* is the mentioning of something by saying that it will not be mentioned.

---

marshal *MAHR shuhl*
(arrange; organize)

"American culture is a business culture," said Barry J. Kaplan, an urban historian at the University of Houston. "We have marshaled our resources to create a business culture. If that's true, Houston is the epitome of what America can do."

martial *MAHR shuhl*
(warlike: Latin, martialis, *of Mars, the Roman god of war)*

In a speech that combined the tough, martial language of his campaign speeches with appeals to West Point's tradition, the President underscored his call for more arms by attacking the Soviet Union as a nation of prisoners and an "evil force" bent on destroying the United States.

masochist *MA suh kist*
(one who derives pleasure from suffering physical or psychological pain, either self-inflicted or caused by others)

"I was running when marathon running was not fashionable. Maybe part of the reason my first wife divorced me was that I was obsessed with running. To be great in anything, not just the marathon, you've got to have compulsive, obsessive tendencies and a little bit of the masochist. Maybe it's more so for marathon runners. You really have to hurt yourself to run, not only physically but also psychologically."

maudlin   *MAWD lin*
(foolishly and tearfully sentimental; mawkish: derived from Mary Mag-
dalene—her English name was Maudlin in the 1500's—who appeared
in paintings and statuary with eyes red or swollen from weeping at the
tomb of Jesus)

His first successful song was "Brother, Can You Spare A Dime," written
with Jay Gorney in 1932, in the Depression. "I thought that work out
very carefully," he told an interviewer, Max Wilk. "I didn't make a maudlin lyric of a guy begging. I made it into a commentary. It was about
the fellow who works, the fellow who builds, who makes railroads and
houses—and he's left empty-handed. This is a man proud of what he
has done but bewildered that his country with its dream could do this to
him."

mausoleum   *maw suh LEE uhm*
(a large, imposing tomb)

"Anyone going out for a quiet evening wants a restful place. But those
who want to go to a really in spot to be seen want to feel they are in the
thick of the action. If the restaurant were as quiet as a mausoleum, they
would walk right out."

maverick   *MA vuh rik*
(a person who takes an independent stand, as in politics, refusing to
conform to party or group)

Poland is not Czechoslovakia. Intervention here would mean war or
something very much like it. The problem for the Kremlin is not a handful
of maverick party leaders pushing the country in a liberal direction but
a widespread demand for radical change that commands the unquestion-
ing support of a majority of the 37 million people.

Samuel A. Maverick (1803–1870) was a Texas lawyer who accepted 400 head of cattle in lieu of a $1,200 debt. Having little
interest in cattle ownership, he left the cattle unbranded, and
little by little most of them found their way into other people's
herds and received their brands. Maverick caught on as a name
for any stray, unbranded cattle. Since the 1880's the name has
been applied to politicians who did not acknowledge any party
leadership (they could not be branded "Democrat," etc.). But
Sam Maverick, too, was a maverick, since he didn't adhere to the
conventional practice of branding.

---

mayhem   *MAY hem*
(the offense of committing violent injury upon a person)

There must be hoodlums who attend the theater or opera or ballet as well as baseball, football and hockey games, but they never throw things at the actors, and only certifiable crackpots try to slash the Mona Lisa or take a hammer to Michelangelo's Pietà. Customers who wouldn't dream of jeering at Barbra Streisand or Luciano Pavarotti seem to feel that a ticket to the grandstand or the bleachers is a license to commit mayhem on the entertainers.

mecca   *ME kuh*
(a place that many people visit or hope to visit: from Mecca, the birth-place of Mohammed in Saudi Arabia, a holy site to which Moslems throughout the world make a pilgrimage)

Also, New York, apparently cured of its most serious fiscal ills, has be-come more than ever a mecca for international business. There are about 150 foreign-owned banks in the city and trendy Italian and French bou-tiques increasingly dot midtown streets.

mélange   *may LAHNZH*
(a mixture; hodgepodge: French mêler, to mix)

The faces and costumes of the market afford an instant introduction to Xinjiang's ethnic mélange. Uygurs in embroidered skullcaps mingle with ruddy-cheeked Kazaks in flared coats and baggy pants tucked into high riding boots. The donkey carts of Mongols in furry hats bump along the street, competing for traffic lanes with the bicycles of the ethnic Chinese in blue or green peaked caps, the native garb of eastern China.

meld   *meld*
(to blend, merge, unite)

As the former hostages gradually meld back into American life, more details of their long ordeal are emerging, bringing into sharper focus a picture of deprivation, humiliation and terror, spiked with occasional physical attacks.

melee   *may LAY*
(a noisy, confused fight or hand-to-hand struggle among a number of people: French, a mixing)

"What saved us was the passengers and crew on the airplane. When they rushed the gunmen, there was a big mad scramble, and everyone was all over the place; it was a melee." One terrorist fired several shots before he was subdued. Five hostages were reported wounded—three Turks and two Japanese.

melisma   *muh LIZ muh*
(a succession of different notes sung upon a single syllable)

In her brief solo, Miss Marie proved to be the most powerful white female soul singer that this observer has ever seen. Capable of executing great whooping melismas in perfect pitch, this tiny red-headed woman passed one of the ultimate tests for a pop singer in being able to deliver a ballad —Donny Hathaway's "Someday We'll All Be Free"—in a large arena and keeping the audience riveted.

ménage à trois   *may NAHZH ah TWAH*
(an arrangement by which a married couple and the lover of one of them live together: French, household of three)

There we were, we panda fans, our eyes fixed on Washington's National Zoo and last spring's unfortunate ménage à trois: Ling-Ling, Chia-Chia and Hsing-Hsing. We hoped for progeny; what we got was the spectacle of one female (L-L) being brutalized by one male (C-C) and ignored by the other (H-H).

_____

Ménage à trois? Three pandas? A ménagerie à trois, perhaps.

_____

menial   *MEE ni uhl*
(pertaining to unskilled work)

Several lunchtime smokers, asked why they used marijuana, said they did it for the same reasons "other people drink"—to improve their mood, or from habit. Workers in menial or repetitive jobs sometimes spoke of marijuana as if it were a hedge against boredom.

mentor   *MEN tawr*
(a wise, loyal adviser; a teacher or coach: in Homer's "Odyssey" Mentor was the loyal friend and adviser of Odysseus and the teacher of his son, Telemachus)

When he was 10 years old, he was apprenticed to a medicine man, or traditional healer, in his native Ghana. Yesterday, at the age of 29, he graduated from the Cornell University Medical College. Dr. Atta-Mensah still has respect for the techniques he learned as a child, helping his mentor gather roots and herbs for curative potions.

mercurial   *mer KYOO ri uhl*
(quickly changeable; fickle; erratic: from the Roman god Mercury—in Greek, Hermes—famous for his fleetness and quick-wittedness)

One of the few hard and fast rules of thumb in the otherwise mercurial restaurant business is that a Chinese restaurant will have the best chance of success if it opens in a Jewish neighborhood.

meretricious   *me ruh TRI shuhs*
(lacking sincerity; alluring by false, showy charms)

At her best, Edna St. Vincent Millay expressed a "passion for identification with all of life which few poets of her generation have possessed; she made ecstasy articulate and almost tangible," wrote Louis Untermeyer, poet and critic. But the passing years have not been kind to her reputation, as critics have noted her many borrowings and the meretricious posturing of much of her verse.

meshuguhnuh   *muh SHOO guh nuh*
(a crazy, mad or insane person: Yiddish)

Would Israel attack a Libyan reactor? "Let us deal first with that meshuguhnuh, Saddam Hussein," Mr. Begin remarked to laughter. Meshuguhnuh is a Yiddish word for "crazy person." Saddam Hussein is the President of Iraq, whom Mr. Begin yesterday called "evil" and a "tyrant."

messiah   *muh SIGH uh*
(any expected savior, liberator or leader: in Judaism, the promised and expected deliverer of the Jews; in Christianity, Jesus, regarded as the realization of the Messianic prophecy)

In general, Mr. Springsteen is less than convincing when he seems to be buying the image admiring critics and fans have created for him, the image of the rock messiah whose songs are eternal verities carved in stone. No rock artist can afford to take himself that seriously and, in any case, Mr. Springsteen's writing is too uneven and too musically limited to bear up under the sort of scrutiny that is routinely lavished on holy writ.

metamorphose   *me tuh MAWR fohz*
(to change in form or nature; to undergo metamorphosis: Greek, meta, over + morphe, shape)

At the end of the fifth stage, the larva becomes a pupa and then metamorphoses into a moth, which lays egg clusters on trees in the fall. The eggs hatch in the spring.

(to undergo a marked or complete change of character, appearance, condition, etc., as radical, figuratively, as that undergone literally by animals such as butterflies and frogs)

The metamorphosis of Chinese women this summer, from being wrapped in cocoons of baggy trousers and formless shirts to wearing colorful and relatively revealing dresses and skirts, even miniskirts, has transformed China into a land not only of beauty but also of beauties.

metastasize   *muh TA stuh sighz*
(to spread to other parts of the body, as cells of a malignant tumor by way of the blood stream or lymphatics)

There are approximately 100 different kinds of cancer, and the treatment and prognosis for cure will be based on the type and whether it is still confined to one area or has already metastasized.

meticulous   *muh TIK yoo luhs*
(extremely or excessively concerned with details; scrupulous or finicky)

First drafts of his books consist of black loose-leaf binders filled with lined white paper, meticulously covered with peacock-blue script—no blots, no scratchings-out.

miasma   *migh AZ muh*
(an unwholesome or befogging atmosphere, influence, etc.: literally, a vapor rising from marshes, formerly supposed to poison and infect the air, causing malaria, etc.)

In neighborhoods all around this blossoming metropolis, thousands of families, black and white, have been experiencing an agonizing, unwanted change in their daily lives. A common thread underlies the new living patterns: fear. It rises like a miasma from the 16 unsolved cases of Atlanta's missing and murdered children, in defiance of a generally declining crime rate.

microcosm   *MIGH kroh kah zuhm*
(a world in miniature; a community, village or other environment regarded as a miniature or epitome of a larger world or of the world)

In a "touch tank," set up as a microcosm of the Great South Bay, children can handle horseshoe and hermit crabs, sea stars (which destroy scallops), urchins and other salt-water invertebrates.

mien   *meen*
(appearance)

A man of sharp features and severe mien that is not softened by his black turban, thick spectacles or dark beard, Hojatolislam Khamenei is known to acquaintances as Vajabi, which roughly translates as "Tom Thumb."

milieu   *meel YOO*
(environment, especially a social or cultural setting: French, middle)

Frontiers traditionally attract two kinds of people: the enterprising and energetic, and those escaping from somewhere else. This is the milieu that produced Ronald Reagan. He was among millions of people who emigrated to California in the Depression with little more than their ambition, and he was among the enterprising and energetic who made their fortune here.

When we enter water we enter an alien milieu. As a child and a teen-ager, I always had a vague sense of foreboding when swimming in bay, sound or ocean. Dark shapes—some still, some moving—were below me and tendrils of seaweed or the soft, undulating forms of jellyfish touching me often brought a spurt of fear.

millennium   *mi LE ni uhm*
(a thousand years)

Under the name of Changan, the city was the seat of 11 dynasties, spanning a millennium.

ministrations   *mi ni STRAY shuhnz*
(the act of giving help; service)

Having undergone the ministrations of three different directors, and as many choreographers, before it finally reached Broadway, "Sophisticated Ladies" is the kind of show that costume designers are apt to view with something akin to horror. Willa Kim, the musical's Tony Award-winning costume designer, agrees. "It was a pain in the neck," she says. "All the directorial changes," explained Miss Kim, "meant that numbers, and therefore costumes, were constantly being cut and added."

ninutiae   *mi NOO: shi uh*
(small, unimportant details)

Bits, pieces, minutiae, the commonplace all go into the journal because "someday they'll be of interest," he says. "I always include the price of things, the names and addresses of restaurants. I write routine stuff because I never know what will interest the historians, and it's often the obvious stuff that gets lost."

misconstrue   *mis kuhn STROO:*
(to take in a wrong sense; misunderstand; misinterpret)

There is something ominously misconstrued about the phrase "idle curiosity." The most idle brain, any scientist or artist will tell you, is often the most fertile ground. Playing around with formulas or paints or phrases is the way that science and art and poetry are made.

miscreant   *MI skri uhnt*
(a criminal)

Strenuous efforts have been made to bring the park back to a place suitable for ordinary civilians, as against ne'er-do-wells, idlers and miscreants who had occupied large swatches of it.

misgivings   *mis GI vingz*
(a disturbed feeling of doubt, fear, apprehension, etc.)

Despite his misgivings about the nation's state of preparedness, General Doolittle has hope. "America," he said, "seems to have gotten lazy, selfish and immoral, but is in the process of correcting it."

mishmash   *MISH mash*
(a hodgepodge; jumble)

The playwright has merged the most memorable scenes from James Whale's 1931 Hollywood version with random scraps from the 1816 Shelley novel only to end up with a talky, stilted mishmash that fails to capture either the gripping tone of the book or the humorous pleasure of the film. This "Frankenstein" has instead the plodding, preachy quality one associates with the lesser literary adaptations of public television.

misogyny   *mi SAH juh ni*
(hatred of women, especially by a man)

"Cheaper to Keep Her," which opened yesterday at the Criterion Center and other theaters, has a strain of misogyny that's part of a larger cynicism it displays. Miss Lopez, though she does it with delicious animation, plays a scheming woman who won't bed down with Mr. Davis until he buys her an expensive dinner. And the alimony plot offers plenty of opportunity for similar observations about women and their motives.

Misogyny derives from the Greek *miso* (hatred) + *gyno* (woman), and is one of a number of English words prefixed with *miso* or *mis* and meaning the hatred of something. Those likely to be encountered in general reading are *misanthropy*, hatred of people (*anthropos*, a man) and *misogamy*, hatred of marriage (*gamy*, marriage).

modicum   *MAH di kuhm*
(a small amount; bit)

Palestinians are a talented, industrious, and cultured people. We are not terrorists. We were severely traumatized when a Jewish state was created in our midst. We ask only a modicum of justice. We, too, need a home, a flag and passports.

mogul   *MOH guhl*
(a powerful or important person, especially one with autocratic power: the Moguls were the Mongol conquerers and rulers of India who held power from the 16th to early 18th centuries)

What young pianist does not secretly hope that a great mogul in the management world will hear him, realize that the next Rubenstein or Horowitz has appeared, and rush to him with fat contracts and a promise of unending fame?

mollify   *MAH luh figh*
(to soothe the temper of; pacify; appease)

WASHINGTON, Oct. 26—In an atmosphere of deep crisis, a delegation of nearly 100 leaders of American science met here today with top Reagan Administration officials to discuss the fate of science in anticipation of further cuts in Federal support for research. The officials attempted to mollify the scientists, assuring them that science remains a top priority even if economic conditions require cutbacks. But there was no meeting of the minds, and indeed the session seemed in some ways to deepen the sense of apprehension that is sweeping the scientific community.

monastic   *muh NA stik*
(characteristic of monastery life; ascetic; austere)

To write, William Faulkner said, the tools he needed were "paper, to-bacco, food and a little whisky." The question is, what sort of food? Should it be severe and monastic, a meal of canned tuna and tea? Should he pick at dishes such as Alice B. Toklas's Salade Aphrodite, yogurt, apples and celery, "for poets with delicate digestions"? Or, like Balzac, is he nearly killing himself with black coffee, ground at frequent intervals from a grinder attached to the desk?

monetarist   *MAH nuh tuh rist*
(one adhering to the theory of monetarism, which holds that economic stability and growth are determined primarily by the maintenance of a steady rate of growth in the supply of money)

What Wall Street now wants is a stricter budget and fiscal policy, which would remove some of the burden from tight money and high interest rates. The traditional conservatives of Wall Street, including many prag-matic monetarists, are calling for major cuts in the military budget, amounting to $30 billion or more, by fiscal 1984, as well as further cuts in nonmilitary programs.

monolith   *MAH nuh lith*
(a single massive block or piece of stone, or something that calls such an image to mind)

There are some signs that Iranians may be tiring of clerical rule. The clergy itself is by no means monolithic. There are a small but influential number of senior clergymen who are becoming increasingly dissatisfied with the course of the revolution.

The old McGraw-Hill building, Raymond Hood's dazzling green mono-lith on 42d Street, has always fared better as a symbol of New York's sophisticated urban landscape than it has in the city's office market. The building has not been fully occupied for more than a decade, since the publishing company left it for larger offices in Rockefeller Center.

monotheism   *MAH nuh thee i zuhm*
(the doctrine or belief that there is only one God)

CAIRO, March 8—The fate of the contents of the Royal Mummy Room at the Egyptian Museum continues to spark discussions among Govern-ment officials, museum personnel and antiquities experts. President Anwar el-Sadat ordered the museum exhibit closed in early October because, he said, Egypt's monotheistic creed is against the public dis-play. The museum's gallery of 30 or more mummies of Pharoahs, on public view since 1958, was immediately put under lock and key, and a committee was appointed to study the problem of the future of the mummies.

montage   *mahn TAHZH*
(the art, style or process of making one pictorial composition from many pictures or designs, closely arranged or superimposed upon each other: French, mounting)

Condon's has a long bar, at the end of which is the bandstand that faces the row of tables that lines the other wall, beneath a montage of photographs of greats that have blared and muted in the annals of jazz.

moot   *moo:t*
(open to debate; unresolvable)

It is a moot point as to whether blondes have more fun, but millionaires certainly do, especially Malcolm S. Forbes, who is the chairman of Forbes magazine. Mr. Forbes is not what one would call a reticent type. He enjoys himself smack in the public eye, and balances such unmillionaire-like activities as ballooning and motorcycling with the more genteel pursuits of collecting Faberge and yachting.

moratorium   *maw ruh TAW ri uhm*
(a temporary, authorized stopping of an activity)

Former President Jimmy Carter, abandoning what aides described as his moratorium on criticism of his successor, has made a wide-ranging attack on President Reagan's economic, environmental and foreign policies.

mordant   *MAWR duhnt*
(biting, cutting, caustic or sarcastic, as speech, wit, etc.)

The highlight of the picture is a mordantly funny monologue by Mr. Sahl, whose comedy is as nervily fresh and irreverent as it ever was, whether he's defining what he calls "social Democrats"—"people who worry about whales, the atmosphere and women"—or recalling a painful appearance on Johnny Carson's "Tonight Show" with John Davidson as host—"a $35 haircut on a 15-cent head."

moribund   *MAW ruh buhnd*
(having little or no vital force left; stagnant)

Whitney Young was one of the leading figures on the American scene as executive director of the National Urban League from 1961 to 1971.

The league, founded in 1910 by white and black social workers and philanthropists, had become moribund. Under his leadership, the league grew tremendously and its activities, power and influence were revitalized.

mortified MAWR tuh fighd
(embarrassed, ashamed or humiliated as the result of an unpleasant experience)

I went into a Chinese restaurant with three of my friends, and one of them could not decide about his order. Finally, he said to the waiter, "Oh, just bring me a bowl of Chinks." We were mortified. The waiter was impassive. When he returned with our food, he placed in front of my friend a number one combination, chicken chow mein, egg roll and fried rice, which was exactly what my friend wanted.

mosaic moh ZAY ik
(a picture or decoration made of small pieces of inlaid stone, glass, etc., or something resembling this kind of construction)

Property owners in some parts of Fire Island's 32-mile mosaic of developed and undeveloped land are upset by the Federal Government's continuing efforts to acquire their land, demolish their houses and enlarge the amount of territory that is protected from future growth.

motif moh TEEF
(a dominant or recurring theme, idea, feature, element, etc.)

Many of the plays and stories of that celebrated esthete Oscar Wilde shared a dominant motif—the exposure of a secret sin, followed by humiliation and disgrace.

Amsterdam Avenue, for all its distinguished architectural pockets, is a tribute to the tenement, and its continuing motif from one end to the other is the fire escape, mostly in standard, straightforward metal, but occasionally displaying a coquettish bellying out to relieve the uniformity.

mot juste moh joo:st
(the right word: French)

Miles Davis, in the words of Gil Evans, the arranger who collaborated in the creation of five important recordings, "was the first man to change the sound of the trumpet since Louis Armstrong." As early as the 1950's, critics vied among themselves on his album liners and in magazine articles for the mots justes to describe the Davis sound.

muckrake   MUK rayk

to search for and publicize in newspapers, etc., real or alleged scandal, corruption by public officials, industrialists, etc.)

Virtually alone among Indian journalists, Mr. Shourie, an editor of The Indian Express, the nation's largest circulation daily newspaper, has organized and written muckraking exposés on such scandals as the blinding by policemen of 31 suspects awaiting trial, the selling of women and the detention for years of poor people awaiting trial on minor charges.

The term *muckraker*—a crusading journalist whose goal is to uncover corruption in business and politics—originated with Theodore Roosevelt. In a 1906 speech, he said, "The men with the muckrakes are often indispensable to the well-being of society; but only if they know when to stop raking the muck." The source of Roosevelt's muckrakers appears to be a character in John Bunyan's 1684 allegorical novel, "Pilgrim's Progress." In it, those who seek only worldy treasure, while oblivious to life's spiritual riches, are symbolized by "A man that could look no way but downwards, with a muckrake in his hand."

---

mundane   MUHN dayn

commonplace; everyday; ordinary)

A former thoroughbred race horse, now retired to more mundane work carrying riders on Central Park bridle paths, apparently sought to return to his old glory yesterday. The horse, a 20-year-old chestnut gelding named Paramount, threw his rider at the western edge of the park near 90th Street and raced off through the Upper West Side. The police finally caught up with him in Riverside Park, where he had paused to graze.

nabob   *NAY bahb*
(a very rich or important person: originally, a European who made a large fortune in India or another Eastern country)

Joseph Wharton (1826–1909) was a man of wealth who, like many of the nabobs of his time, was also a philanthropist and a supporter of causes —in his case education and a protective high tariff.

nadir   *NAY der*
(the lowest point; time of greatest depression or dejection: Arabic, opposite the zenith)

"It was the nadir of my life," Mr. Vickery recalled. "Paris, 1971. Broke. A string of stupid jobs. A tortured love affair. I was getting nowhere. I asked myself: 'What do I know how to do?' I had done plays in college, and it was really what I liked to do. So, I decided to be an actor."

naïveté   *nah EEV tay*
(the state of being naive; artlessness; ingenuousness: French)

A wide-eyed, strawberry blonde, with a marvelous deadpan quality, Miss McArdle sings such classics as "Blue Skies," "White Christmas" and "They Say It's Wonderful" with a purposeful naïveté that underscores the songs' innocence.

narcissism   *NAHR si si zuhm*
(self-love; excessive interest in one's own appearance, comfort, importance, abilities, etc.)

Changing seats three times so that a photographer can shoot his "good" side, Mr. Vidal arranges his face—a face he once described as that of one of Rome's "later, briefer Emperors"—in a mirror, turns sharply to a visitor and offers another definition. "I suppose you'll call me a narcissist," he says. "Well, a narcissist is someone better looking than you are."

Because she chattered incessantly, Echo, a wood nymph, was rendered voiceless by Juno, except to repeat what others said to her. When she fell in love with beautiful Narcissus, she could not convey her feelings, but only mimic his words. One day, however, hearing Narcissus call, "Let us join one another," she repeated it, then rushed to his arms. Narcissus recoiled. Crushed, Echo sulked in caves and on cliffs, fading away till only her voice remained (remained, remained, remained). Soon another rejected nymph prayed that Narcissus, too, might know the pain of unrequited love. Vengeance was hers. Narcissus, stooping over a river's brink, fell in love with his image in the water. He talked to it, tried to embrace it, languished over it, pined away and died. Even on its way to Hades, his shade leaned over the boat to catch one last glimpse of itself in the river Styx. The local nymphs prepared a pyre on which to burn the youth's body, but it was gone. In its place a flower grew, purple and white, called to this day—Narcissus.

---

ne'er-do-well   *NAIR doo wel*
(an irresponsible and unsuccessful person; good-for-nothing)

Nita Longley looks like a child herself, with her big eyes and skinny body and pale freckled face. But she is a mother: she has two small sons, and her handsome, ne'er-do-well husband has left her to raise them alone in a small Texas town.

nemesis   *NE muh sis*
(an agent of retribution or punishment: in Greek mythology, Nemesis is the goddess of retributive justice, or vengeance)

Ralph Nader, often portrayed as the nemesis of corporations, says he wants to help them save some money.

neophyte   *NEE uh fight*
(a beginner; novice)

Becoming an inspector for the Guide Michelin is not easy. The apprenticeship lasts five years because the neophyte must work in every corner of France and visit virtually every restaurant listed in the guide, and all his reports are checked by senior staff members. "It's a long time," said Mr. Trichot, "but we must be sure of the man and he must become one of us."

nepotism   *NE puh ti zuhm*
(favoritism shown to relatives, especially in appointment to desirable positions)

John D. Simpson, the president of the Transit Authority, in an interview, did not dispute Mr. Regan's figures on employment of relatives. But he denied that frequency of close kinship ties suggested nepotism. "Nowhere does he demonstrate that the sons or daughters of present employees were treated any differently than any other applicants for the job," Mr. Simpson said.

nocturnal   *nahk TER nuhl*
(functioning or active during the night: the opposite of "diurnal")

The interview took place at 1 A.M. today, in deference to Mr. Arafat's nocturnal working habits, in the warren of Palestinian guerrilla headquarters on the edge of West Beirut. Outside, the darkened streets of the Fakhani neighborhood, heavily bombed by Israel last month, were patrolled by strongly armed young guerrillas in camouflage uniforms and platform shoes.

nomadic   *noh MA dik*
(wandering from place to place, in the manner of a nomad, a member of a tribe or people having no permanent home, but moving about constantly in search of food, pasture, etc.)

A dollar, tip included, is what the nomadic bootblacks who ply their trade in office buildings are paid by most of their customers.

nom de plume   *nahm duh PLOO:M*
(a pen name; pseudonym: French, pen name)

"Edward I. Koch, Mayor," is a nom de plume of Evelyn Strouse, poet, teller of children's tales, and professional correspondent, one of 12 people who work full time answering about 1,000 letters the Mayor receives daily.

Nom de plume is a French term, and yet it is *not* a French term. It was coined by English-speaking people to give themselves a French term for "false name." The French themselves don't even use it. They use *nom de guerre* (war name), a term that originated in the days when every entrant into the French army assumed a name. Herewith, a short list of writers and others who used noms de plume, noms de guerre, pen names or pseudonyms (your choice) during part or all of their careers, with the real name coming first: Mary Ann Evans/George Eliot; François Marie

Arouet/Voltaire; Eric Blair/George Orwell; Aleksei Peshkov/ Maxim Gorky; Jean Baptiste Poquelin/Molière; Émile Herzog/ André Maurois; Lev Davidovich Bronstein/Leon Trotsky; Marie Henri Beyle/Stendhal; Karen Blixen/Isak Dinesen; T.J.K. Korzeniowski/Joseph Conrad.

---

nomenclature   *NOH muhn klay cher*
(the act or process of naming)

The nomenclature of various dishes is fascinating, for things are, to borrow a phrase, seldom what they seem. There is a crisp puff-pastry desert called pig's ears; a Mont Blanc is a "mountain" of puréed chestnuts; and eggs in the snow, or les oeufs à la neige, are poached meringues floating in a vanilla custard.

nominal   *NAH muh nuhl*
(in name only; not actually; so-called)

Throughout the Springboks' tour, thousands of New Zealanders protesting South Africa's policy of racial separation have demonstrated in an attempt to halt the South Africans' visit. The team, representing a private club, is nominally integrated, with one mixed-race coach and one mixed-race player among its 40 members.

Count Basie and his orchestra were the nominal stars March 20 at the third of three jazz concerts at Carnegie Hall celebrating the auditorium's 90th year. But Sarah Vaughan was the life of the party.

nonchalant   *nahn shuh LAHNT*
(coolly unconcerned; casually indifferent)

"We talked and laughed for 10 hours. He got to know me, the person, and apparently liked what he heard. When it was time to become intimate, I very nonchalantly mentioned: 'By the way, I just had both my breasts removed. Does that matter to you?' I knew I was taking the biggest chance of rejection of my life," she continued, "but it was now or never. His mouth dropped, his eyes dilated. He was absolutely silent for a minute. Then he said, 'So what.' "

nondescript   *NAHN di skript*
(a person or thing with no outstanding or distinguishing features)

In a matter of hours from the instant when the President flinched from the gunfire, different people around the country offered the first hurried identifications of Mr. Hinckley. They talked of the son of a Denver oil executive, a mostly nondescript dropout from social routine, an individual easily forgotten, a man whose life was marked in private by psychiatric troubles and in public by a reported involvement with neo-Nazis.

nonpartisan   *nahn PAHR tuh zuhn*
(not supporting any particular party or side)

In a rare display of nonpartisan solidarity, Agustín Rodríguez Sahagún, president of the governing Union of the Democratic Center; Felipe González, leader of the Socialist Party; Santiago Carrillo of the Communist Party, and Manuel Fraga Iribarne of the rightest Democratic Coalition walked side by side.

non sequitur   *nahn SE kwi ter*
(a remark having no bearing on what has just been said: Latin, it does not follow)

Dr. Harvey A. Rosenstock, a Houston psychiatrist, suggests ending arguments with teen-agers by deliberately introducing a non sequitur that, being irrelevant and unanswerable, usually provokes a smile. For example, when you've reached an impasse, suddenly say, "What do you think of the Australian Government?"

nosh   *nahsh*
(a snack; in Leo Rosten's words in "The Joys of Yiddish," "Anything eaten between meals and, presumably, in small quantity: fruit, a cookie, 'a piece cake,' a candy": Yiddish, from the German, nachen, to eat on the sly)

In the old days we had only the blue and orange umbrellas denoting the hot dogs of Sabrett, plus pretzel and ice cream vendors. Today the peripatetic nosher can choose from Mexican tacos, Middle Eastern felafel, Greek souvlaki, Chinese Fu Manchu stew, Japanese tempura, so-called New York-style steak sandwiches and true New York-style hot dogs and egg creams, Afghanistan kofta kebabs and Caribbean beef or chicken curry.

novel   *NAH vuhl*
(new and unusual)

When John and Carilyn Redman had trouble finding a buyer for their $113,000 home in northern Virginia earlier this year, they hit on a novel solution to beat the high mortgage rates: They decided to raffle it off.

novice   *NAH vis*
(a person new to a particular activity; beginner)

Last October, Salazar predicted he would run 2 hours 9 minutes in the New York City Marathon, his first race at that distance. To the astonishment of many who had dismissed him as a naïve novice, he won in 2:09:41.

noxious   *NAHK shuhs*
(offensive)

Besides causing noise and noxious odors, raccoons and squirrels can rip up attic insulation and make "doorways" the size of a grapefruit on or around a roof.

nuclear family   *NOO: kli er FAM uh lee*
(a basic social unit consisting of parents and their children living in one household)

The nuclear family seems to be splitting into ever smaller particles. According to 1980 census figures released last week, the size of American households has declined sharply since 1970—a drop caused by a lower birthrate and by the record numbers of adults living alone.

nullify   *NUH luh figh*
(to make valueless or useless; remove the effectiveness of)

Whatever his age, it's beginning to show on Ken Norton's face and in the hint of a bald spot. But in order to get a title shot against either Larry Holmes, the W.B.C. champion, or Mike Weaver, the World Boxing Association champion, he must first nullify Gerry Cooney's left hook, the punch that has produced a 24-0 record with 20 knockouts.

numinous   *NOO: muh nuhs*
(having a deeply spiritual or mystical effect)

One of the very few things about African art on which everyone is agreed is that, at its best, it has a numinous quality. It was not meant for collectors and dealers or even for disinterested enjoyment. It was meant, as Miss Vogel reminds us, to give exalted pleasure, but [also] "to express and support fundamental spiritual values that are essential to the survival of the community."

numismatist   *noo: MIZ muh tist*
(*a coin collector*)

American numismatists tend to be chauvinistic about their hobby, viewing United States coins as the ultimate in rarity and value. This type of smugness was jolted several weeks ago when two Michigan dealers announced that they had purchased a rare Canadian coin for $325,000, a price exceeded by few American issues.

obeisance   *oh BAY suhns*
(*a gesture of respect or reverence*)

Before Vice President Bush's celebrated Presidential-inauguration toast to Ferdinand E. Marcos—"We love your adherence to democratic principle and to the democratic processes"—passes forever into the satirists' domain, let us not forget that this startling obeisance is a natural expression of President Reagan's foreign policy. The United States, in supporting any dictator who proclaims himself anti-Communist, apparently has forgotten an important lesson: Right-wing dictatorships, by driving the moderate opposition underground, are the fastest breeders of radical movements.

obesity   *oh BEE suh ti*
(*fatness*)

Our culture's attitude toward obesity is so degrading and humiliating that fat people today are allowing their bodies to be cut open by the surgeon's scalpel; spending billions of dollars a year on diet gimmicks, pills and books; literally losing their lives on dangerous fad diets—*anything* to lose weight and satisfy society's demands.

obfuscate   *AHB fuh skayt*
(*to muddle; confuse; make unclear or obscure*)

If I seem hypersensitive to recipe obfuscations, it is probably because I was scarred at an early age, when my mother gave me a recipe for one of her coffeecakes. For baking time it said, "The longer it bakes, the better." When I asked her if she meant an hour, a week, or a year, she answered, "A sane person can't have a decent conversation with you." To this day I have not made the cake, wondering just how much time I must set aside for its baking.

obligatory   *uh BLI guh taw ri*
(having the nature of an obligation; virtually a requirement)

Mayor Daniel K. Whitehurst of Fresno today made the obligatory dawn-to-dusk state tour to announce his candidacy for the Democratic nomination for the United States Senate.

oblique   *oh BLEEK*
(not straight to the point; indirect)

The only reference Maureen Reagan made to her father in a commercial she filmed for a mail-order acne lotion was oblique. "Let me tell you," she said, "it certainly made my life easier during that frantic election campaign."

oblivious   *uh BLI vi uhs*
(unaware or unconscious)

In the second-floor family quarters, Mr. Reagan was said to be studying his briefing books, oblivious to the commotion downstairs. It wasn't until 7:49, when he stepped off the elevator and his old friends shouted "Surprise," that he appeared to realize what was going on. As the guests sang "Happy Birthday Dear Ronald," the President's face registered amazement.

obscurantist   *uhb SKYOO ruhn tist*
(opposing human progress or enlightenment)

Mr. Bani-Sadr pictured his own role as President as a losing struggle against the obscurantist and fanatical groups that Ayatollah Khomeini eventually allowed to take over. "It was a struggle between the mullahs and the intellectuals," he said. "After the takeover of the American Embassy the mullahs began to manipulate things, and this change of power was decisive."

obstinate   *AHB stuh nit*
(stubborn)

A teen-ager may be warm and loving one minute, hostile and rejecting the next, flexible and cooperative today, obstinate and self-centered tomorrow.

Occident   *AHK suh duhnt*
(the western part of the world, especially Europe and the Americas)

Orient meets Occident in the bathroom, with a familiar Western-style sink and toilet, deep, round tiled Korean bathtub with shower fixture, large basin and sloping tile floor with drain.

ocher   *OH ker*
(dark yellow: ocher is an earthy clay colored by iron oxide, usually yellow or reddish brown, and used as a pigment in paint)

From an airplane, Egypt appears to be a ribbon of water, girded by green and placed in an endless expanse of parched, ocher desert.

odious   *OH di uhs*
(arousing or deserving hatred or loathing; disgusting; offensive)

Mrs. Shields is also given, like many stage mothers, to odious comparison. In a single breath, she will compare her daughter to Elizabeth Taylor and Natalie Wood, saying that her daughter "has more appeal than Liz had or has," that her daughter's voice cracks "just like Natalie Wood's," and taking her daughter's hand, kissing it three times, concludes with, "I know you'll marry the men you go to bed with, just like Liz did."

"Is it possible your pragmatical worship should not know that the comparisons made between wit and wit, courage and courage, beauty and beauty, birth and birth, are always odious and ill taken?"

Cervantes, "Don Quixote"

---

odyssey   *AH duh si*
(an extended wandering or journey: after the Greek victory against the Trojans, Odysseus had ten years of adventures and wanderings before returning to his island kingdom of Ithaca and resuming his rule)

A fairly complete picture has emerged of his remarkable odyssey from a maximum-security prison outside Istanbul in November 1979 to the Vatican on May 13—an odyssey that led through Iran, Yugoslavia, Bulgaria, Austria, Switzerland, Tunisia and Spain, and perhaps through Hungary, West Germany, France, Belgium and Britain as well.

officious   *uh FI shuhs*
(meddlesome, especially in a high-handed or overbearing way)

Mr. Zane is short and chunky, with a buoyant, strutting walk and the very funny look of an officious floorwalker in a second-rate department store.

offshoot   *AWF shoo:t*
(something that branches off or derives from a main stem)

Bluegrass music, with its commercialized offshoots, is a thriving American subculture, not just in the South, where it originated, but in the New York area as well.

off-the-cuff   *AWF thuh KUF*
(impromptu; without preparation)

United States Government officials concede that the Russians have also been made uneasy by President Reagan's latest off-the-cuff comments that the prolonged turmoil in Poland represents "the first beginning cracks" in Soviet domination of Eastern Europe.

oligarchy   *AH li gahr ki*
(a government in which the ruling power belongs to a few persons)

President Francois Mitterrand said today that he had "serious reservations" about United States' policies in Central America. "The people of the region want to put an end to the oligarchies that, backed by bloody dictatorships, exploit them and crush them under intolerable conditions," he said. "A tiny part of the population owns almost everything," Mr. Mitterrand went on. "How is it not possible to understand this popular revolution?"

omnipresent   *ahm ni PRE zuhnt*
(present, or seeming to be present, in all places at the same time; ubiquitous)

The omnipresent and ever-verbal Mayor Koch will narrate Prokofiev's "Peter and the Wolf" at Town Hall on Saturday afternoon.

omnivorous   *ahm NI vuh ruhs*
(eating both animal and vegetable food)

Why not, we reasoned, learn all we could about what lures a sea robin likes? We quickly discovered that the fish's omnivorous eating habits lead it to hit virtually everything. Sinking plugs, spoons, metal jigs, bucktail jigs—even a weighted fly—all were seized with alacrity.

onus   *OH nuhs*
(responsibility; burden)

The onus is on the restaurant to have sufficient expertise to recommend a likable wine and to have the grace to take it back if the recommendation is rejected.

opaque   oh PAYK
(not letting light pass through; not transparent or translucent)

It is a cloud of pollution that smears the crisp, desert sky above Phoenix with a puffy, opaque crown of dirty air reminiscent of a giant chef's cap. On many days it can be seen more than 40 miles from the city.

operative   AH puh ray tiv
(a spy)

Mr. Kalp, who spent 374 days in solitary confinement, more than any other hostage, has denied that he is a Central Intelligence Agency operative. He has said that his alleged role as a spy had nothing to do with his harsh treatment in the hands of the Iranians; that, he said, stemmed from his unwillingness to cooperate and his attempted escapes.

opulent   AH pyuh luhnt
(rich; abundant)

Seven of the Copeland songs were sung by Marilyn Horne, as one more observance of the composer's 80th birthday season. She seemed to be trying to subdue her opulent operatic voice by adopting a quasi-folk approach, and that produced lovely results at times, as in "Long Time Ago."

orthodox   AWR thuh dahks
(conforming to the established and traditional beliefs and rules, as in religion, politics, a field of art, etc.)

Mikhail A. Suslov, a top member of the Soviet Union's ruling Politburo and a symbol of Kremlin orthodoxy, arrived in Warsaw today and began talks with Polish Communist leaders, presumably on the pace and scope of liberalization measures.

oscillate   AH suh layt
(to swing back and forth)

"The real challenge is how to structure a policy that is genuinely responsive to global complexities. This applies not only to East-West relations;

the dilemma concerns our relationship with the third world, too. We tend, as a country, to oscillate." [Zbigniew Brzezinski]

osmosis   *ahz MOH sis*
(a gradual absorption of knowledge, a skill, etc., by contact with it rather than through formal study or training)

Nell Dorr's father was a photographer, and she learned the craft from him by osmosis and by direct instruction.

ostensible   *ah STEN suh buhl*
(given out as such; seeming; professed; supposed)

After his evening appearance in "Fifth of July," the actor [Richard Thomas] was lured by his wife, Alma, to La Méditerranée, a Second Avenue restaurant, ostensibly to meet a couple of out-of-town friends. What he found was about 60 mostly in-town friends who had gathered for a surprise party that he insisted was truly a surprise. Mr. Thomas, it turned out, had a surprise of his own. The baby his wife is expecting in September, he confided to some of the guests, is actually twins.

ostentatious   *ah stuhn TAY shuhs*
(show-offy, as with knowledge, material possessions, etc.; pretentious; meant to impress others)

No one who watched the embarrassing spectacle of Maria Callas in her declining years could fail to see that the soprano was being slowly but certainly eaten alive by the ostentatiously wealthy and vulgar society that surrounded her.

ostracize   *AH struh sighz*
(to bar; exclude)

I.F. Stone has rejoined the pack. Mr. Stone, the premier loner and dedicated maverick of American journalism, was welcomed back into the National Press Club yesterday after having been ostracized by that section of the journalism Establishment for trying to take a black friend to lunch at the club 40 years ago.

Ostracism was originally the method of banishing citizens of ancient Greece whose power was considered dangerous to the state. *In a secret ballot taken in the Assembly, the* accused's name was written on a piece of pottery, called an *ostrakon.* In Athens, a majority of at least 6,000 voting members of the Assembly had to vote "yes" for someone to be sent into exile, which was usually a period of 10 years. During the 90 years this practice existed in Athens, only 10 persons were banished.

---

overweening   *oh ver WEE ning*
(exaggerated; excessive; arrogant)

Mrs. Shields also possesses the overweening attention of all stage mothers and managers, commenting, with some concern, that her daughter's face is beginning to change, to look a "little sculpted." "You mean square," said Brooke.

pacesetter   *PAYS se ter*
(a person, group or thing that leads the way or serves as a model)

While explicit honor systems exist only on relatively few campuses, they are generally viewed as pacesetters of undergraduate ethics.

pacify   *PA suh figh*
(to make peaceful or calm; in military usage, to seek to neutralize hostility or win over people in an occupied area)

"In the past two years alone, one country in the area, Afghanistan, has been brutally invaded and occupied but not pacified. Afghan freedom fighters continue their determined struggle for their country's independence." [Jeane J. Kirkpatrick]

paleontology   *pay li uhn TAH luh ji*
(the science that deals with prehistoric forms of life through the study of fossils)

"But Jefferson virtually founded the science of paleontology," Mr. Bedini said. "He collected fossil bones, sometimes failing to identify them correctly. But he stimulated other investigators and lent respectability to the fledgling science."

palmy   *PAH mi*
(flourishing; prosperous)

The palmy days of the cowboy lasted only from about 1865, when the big cattle drives north from Texas to the Rocky Mountain grasslands began, until the late 80's, when famous blizzards, barbed wire, overgrazing and plunging cattle prices ended the great days of the open range.

palpable   *PAL puh buhl*
(tangible; perceptible)

In the 60's, new albums from the Beatles, the Rolling Stones, Bob Dylan, and a few other performers were genuine cultural events. These albums seemed to fuse the rock audience into a palpable coherent community. They were messages from the community's seers, to be savored and probed for hidden meanings and listened to again and again, with joy and reverence, until the group's next album came along.

panacea   *pa nuh SEE uh*
(a remedy for all ills; cure-all)

Will the microcomputer transform the school or is it destined to join the teaching machine and other technological gimmicks in the graveyard of failed panaceas?

panache   *puh NASH*
(an air of spirited self-confidence or style; dashing elegance of manner)

"That's about $185,000," Philip B. Miller, the president of Neiman-Marcus, observed coolly as a voluminous skin-on-skin sable wrap was modeled with appropriate panache. Other six-figure sables, with scalloped edges, were tossed dramatically over leather pants. That's the new order of fashion: ultimate luxury worn as casually as a sweater.

pandemonium   *pan di MOH ni uhm*
(wild disorder, noise or confusion)

Then the rockets hit. Within seconds, the beach front in West Beirut emptied in pandemonium, people fleeing into the streets, horns blaring. Gunfire crackled as the gunmen of half a dozen factions fired pistols and Kalashnikov rifles in the air.

Pandemonium was coined from the Greek *pan* (all) and *daimon* (demon) by John Milton (1608–1674) for the name of the capital city of Hell, the site of Satan's palace, in "Paradise Lost" (1667).

---

panoply   *PA nuh pli*
(magnificent array)

All the panoply of monarchy was deployed on this, one of the great days in the history of the House of Windsor: the stirring music of Handel and Purcell and Elgar; the Household Cavalry, in their burnished breastplates and helmets with red plumes; the stately royal horses, caparisoned in silver; almost all the reigning sovereigns of Europe, come in their finery to share in the happy occasion, and the royal bride herself, resplendent in a gown of pale ivory, with puffy sleeves and a train 25 feet long.

paparazzo   *pah puh RAH tsoh*
(an aggressive freelance photographer who pursues celebrities to take their pictures wherever they go: Italian)

Ron Galella, the party paparazzo, was seated much of the evening: "When *he's* sitting down, you *know* there's nobody around," someone said.

paradigm   *PA ruh dim*
(a pattern, example or model)

If a string quartet, as many players say, is a paradigm of human relationships, then the Juilliard Quartet is the most modern of marriages. Now celebrating its 35th anniversary with a concert tomorrow night at Carnegie Hall, the Juilliard thrives on the kind of emotional intensity that sends most people running for space and has, despite five divorces, three residencies, and a schedule that would drain an athlete, lasted longer and been praised more lavishly than any other American quartet performing today.

paradox   *PA ruh dahks*
(a seeming contradiction)

"The real reason why the monarchy survives," wrote Lord Blake, Provost of The Queen's College, Oxford, in The Financial Times last week, "is because the British people want it to survive. In that sense it is not only the oldest, but also, paradoxically, the most democratic of our institutions."

paragon   *PA ruh gahn*
(a model of perfection)

In revival, led by Rex Harrison, "My Fair Lady" endures as a paragon of wit, romance and musicality. Every song is a winner. Need one add, with regret, that they simply do not write shows like this anymore?

parlance   *PAHR luhns*
(a way or manner of speaking; language; idiom)

In industry parlance, a "good" picture has nothing to do with a critically acclaimed picture. As Gordon Weaver, senior vice president for world-wide marketing at Paramount Pictures, defines it, the good picture is "the picture people will pay money to see."

parochial   *puh ROH ki uhl*
(*small in scope; narrow; provincial*)

I have long since lost the parochial feeling that there is no other worth-while cuisine in the world except that of my native France.

paroxysm   *PA ruhk si zuhm*
(*a convulsive or violent outburst; fit*)

A little more than a decade ago, women went through paroxysms as they shortened their dresses, as much as an inch or two a month, thinking each time they did so they looked a little younger. But the search proved as futile as Ponce de Leon's, and hemlines soon came tumbling down—first to the knees, then the calf, then even lower.

parry   *PA ri*
(*to turn aside a question, criticism, etc., by a clever or evasive reply*)

The Governor and Miss Gouletas parried questions about their plans, but when asked if he had any declarations of affection to make, Mr. Carey said, "You betcha," and kissed Miss Gouletas on the lips. As television cameras whirred, she looked up and wiped a smudge of lipstick from his lips.

parse   *pahrs*
(*to separate a sentence into its parts, explaining the grammatical form, function and interrelation of each part*)

Mr. McKellen is an actor-scholar. He took Macbeth's "tomorrow and tomorrow" soliloquy and gave it a thick Scots burr, turning it into a comic monologue. Then he parsed the same speech for meaning, analyzing it with the erudition of an Oxford don. Finally, he spoke it, beautifully, in the context of the play, surrounded by other soliloquies.

parvenu   *PAHR vuh noo:*
(*upstart; a person of newly acquired wealth or power who is not fully accepted by the social class into which he or she has risen: French*)

The average consumer, presented with the trim little containers and the fancy French names, might well be confused, wondering what differences, if any, there are between the parvenu yogurts and the originals. Having tasted the three new yogurts plus two yogurt drinks and having compared them with conventional yogurts, I can report that the substantive differences are minor.

pate *payt*
(the top of the head: a humorous or derogatory term)

One night, wandering in the audience during a second-act skit, Mr. Rooney paused to pat the head of a bald theatergoer: "Pardon me, sir," he said, "I thought you were sitting upside down." Mr. Rooney now singles out a new pate to pat at each performance.

patent *PAY tuhnt*
(obvious; plain; evident)

Perhaps there's nothing wrong with "Under the Rainbow" that more laughs couldn't have cured. But it also seems that Mr. Rash takes his material too seriously, so that he winds up pursuing all the plot's loose ends, instead of succumbing happily to their patent silliness.

paternity *puh TER nuh ti*
(fatherhood)

A new blood testing procedure is revolutionizing the way courts determine the identity of a child's father in paternity cases, medical and legal experts say. The testing is known as H.L.A., for human leukocyte antigen. It identifies inherited genetic "markers" in the blood's white cells, allowing a laboratory to match a child with its biological father in almost all cases.

patina *PA tuh nuh*
(a thin, outer covering, like the fine greenish crust or film on bronze or copper formed by natural oxidation and often valued as being ornamental: here used figuratively)

Time can put a patina of significance and value on improbable objects: an Etruscan coin, an Art Deco cocktail shaker, a beer-bottle cap. Or, perhaps, on Leonard Bernstein's "Mass"?

patois *PA twah*
(a dialect spoken in a particular district, differing substantially from the standard language of the country: French, clumsy speech)

The book is written in a variant of the English patois common to Guernsey, a British possession 30 miles west of the Normandy coast of France.

patriarch   *PAY tri ahrk*
(a founding father of a religion, group, business, etc.; a venerable old man)

If the producer of "Dallas" has his way, no one will replace Jim Davis, who died yesterday, in the role of Jock Ewing, patriarch of a Texas oil dynasty.

patrician   *puh TRI shuhn*
(noble; aristocratic: in ancient Rome, originally a member of the citizen families, later a member of the nobility)

An amiable Boston aristocrat, Roger Nash Baldwin was for decades the country's unofficial agitator for, and defender of, its civil liberties. With patrician dispassion, he battled ceaselessly for the concept that the guarantees of the Constitution and the Bill of Rights apply equally to all.

patrimony   *PA truh moh ni*
(inheritance from one's father or ancestors)

German 19th-century music was a part of our universal patrimony, and prized as such even at the worst moments of World War II.

paucity   *PAW suh ti*
(scarcity; dearth; insufficiency)

Both are clever acts with strong musical ties to mid-1960's English rock. But both use the styles of a bygone era to evoke a surface hipness that masks a paucity of originality.

Hep had its time in the sun prior to the late 1950's. It has been completely superseded by *hip* among jazz enthusiasts, but both have meant informed, knowing, wise to things.

----

payload   *PAY lohd*
(the cargo, warhead, bombs, etc., carried by a rocket or aircraft, having to do with its objective but not related to its operation: originally, any cargo producing income)

According to the space agency's plan, the payload for the second mission will be installed in the Columbia by June 29. The payload is an array of experimental instruments for geological mapping by imaging radar and infrared sensors, for observing plankton in the ocean, for optical studies of lightning discharges and for locating and identifying vegetation on the earth's surface. The Columbia carried no research payload on its first flight.

pedagogue *PE duh gahg*
(a teacher—a word with contradictory connotations, used as a term of ridicule for a narrow, petty and dogmatic educator, but also to describe a master teacher: Greek, a leader of children)

Ivan Galamian, an internationally known violin pedagogue at the Juilliard School for 35 years and the teacher of many of today's best-known violinists, died, apparently of heart failure, yesterday morning in his Manhattan apartment. He was 78 years old and had been active until the end, having given his normal schedule of lessons on Monday.

pedantic *pi DAN tik*
(teacherish, in the negative sense of the word, that is, adhering rigidly to rules without regard to common sense; stressing minor or trivial points; showing off scholarship)

"The Complete Book of Pastry" is admirably detailed and scholarly without being pedantic.

pedestrian *pi DE stri uhn*
(ordinary and dull)

The books ranged from the profound to the pedestrian. Under the same canvas roof as Proust and Shakespeare were entire tables devoted to Cliff's Notes, the outlines used by students who procrastinate, and Reader's Digest condensed novels.

peer *peer*
(an equal; someone or something of similar rank, quality, ability, value, etc.)

Horseradish will never win a garden competition for its looks. But as a zesty condiment to excite the digestive juices and enhance the flavor of fish and meat dishes, it has no peer.

penchant *PEN chuhnt*
(a strong liking or fondness; inclination; taste)

Prince Charles's penchant for outdoor activities is legendary, including polo, skiing, riding, shooting and wind-surfing.

penultimate   *pi NUHL tuh mit*
(*next to the last: Latin,* paene, *almost*)

The film's penultimate sequence, about Tony, now a junkie-bum, and his illegitimate son, Pete, is grimly funny, sad and scary.

peregrinations   *pe ruh gri NAY shuhnz*
(*travels from place to place; wanderings; journeys*)

Mr. Bodkin easily fields requests for almost any type of music, a result of his own piano-playing peregrinations that have brought him to hotels in Amsterdam, Teheran, Tel Aviv and other far-off lounges.

perfidy   *PER fi di*
(*treachery; a breaking of trust*)

That morning, [Balanchine] had led a one-hour company class, where he had warned the dancers about the perfidy of the mirror. Dancers always stare in mirrors; it is their preoccupation. Balanchine, however, had told them, "The mirror is not you. The mirror is you yourself looking at yourself."

perfunctory   *per FUHNGK tuh ri*
(*done routinely, with little care or interest; without real concern; indifferent*)

Service is best when the restaurant is least crowded—week nights and afternoons—when waiters and managers offer patient explanations and show a desire to please. Friday and Saturday night and all day Sunday can be hectic and customers may be treated perfunctorily.

perimeter   *puh RI muh ter*
(*the outer boundary of an area*)

A year ago, the Moroccans began building a 280-mile wall of sand, six feet high and sprinkled with mines and barbed wire, enclosing what is called the "useful Sahara." Initially ridiculed by some, this perimeter, known as a berm, was finished early this year and seems to have hampered the rebels' ability to flee across the desert after striking isolated Moroccan positions.

peripatetic   *pe ri puh TE tik*
(*moving from place to place*)

"I made more in one month with 'Island in the Sun' than I did in 40 years of writing with about 38 books and countless stories," Mr. Waugh said the year after the book was published. The money he earned enabled the author to live the sort of peripatetic life that intrigued him from the time he left school at 17 to join the army.

Peripatetic derives from the Greek word *peripatein* (to walk around) and was first applied to the philosophy or followers of Aristotle, who walked about as he taught his students in the covered walk of the Lyceum.

---

permeate   *PER mi ayt*
(to pass into and affect every part of; penetrate and spread)

It is abundantly clear that rampant crime is permeating every aspect of society, threatening our leaders, families and neighbors.

per se   *per SAY*
(in or by itself: Latin)

Aside from possible physical discomfort, however, there is nothing about menopause per se that should disrupt a woman's sexual desire or activity since estrogen, the ovaries and the uterus have no direct effect on libido.

persona   *per SOH nuh*
(the outer personality or facade presented to others by an individual)

I don't think the nation ever hung on the words of Walter Cronkite. He is not exceptionally insightful or witty. Primarily, he brought a reassuring presence and persona to whatever the news happened to be that day. And I suspect even Mr. Cronkite would wince at his works being called a "heroic service."

persona non grata   *per SOH nuh nahn GRAH tuh*
(a person who is not acceptable or welcome; a foreign diplomat unacceptable to the government to which he is sent: Latin)

"I'd be happy to have him in the neighborhood," one homeowner said. "All I can say is I'm glad he picked Saddle River," said another. The subject of these comments was Richard M. Nixon. Persona non grata when he tried in 1979 to buy two New York City cooperative apartments, the former President eventually settled for a Manhattan townhouse. Last week, an aide said Mr. Nixon now is buying a $1 million home in Saddle River, N.J.—and with no complaints from the neighbors.

personify   *per SAH nuh figh*
(*to represent an abstraction in the form of a person; embody*)

Dated Feb. 1, 1981, the unpublished memoir says: "I was 22 years old when we began filming 'Gone With the Wind.' The role of Melanie meant a very great deal to me, for she personified values very much endangered at the time. The source of her strength was love. For a little while, as I lived her life, I felt her love, felt her trust, felt her faith, felt her happiness."

petrifaction   *pe tri FAK shuhn*
(*a turning into stone; a benumbed state*)

Part burlesque sketch, part gospel service and all silly, this play is remarkable mainly for its ability to reduce any reasonably adult onlooker to a state of instant and total petrifaction.

phalanx   *FAY langks*
(*a compact or closely massed body of people or things: the phalanx was an ancient Greek military formation of infantry in close and deep ranks with shields joined together and spears overlapping*)

Even before the Columbia had stopped its landing roll, a convoy of 21 service vehicles whose operators had been training for that moment for almost three months, was moving in a phalanx toward the craft, stirring up a cloud of dust like a battalion of tanks moving over the Sahara before battle.

phantasmagoric   *fan taz muh GAW rik*
(*dreamlike; magical*)

Since the eighth-century poet Li Po celebrated the phantasmagoric beauties of Huang Shan, a mountain of oddly-shaped peaks, pines and clouds, the Chinese have considered it one of the wonders of nature.

phoenix   *FEE niks*
(*in Egyptian mythology, a beautiful, lone bird which lived in the Arabian desert for 500 or 600 years and then consumed itself in fire, rising renewed from the ashes to start another long life: it symbolizes resurrection, renewal or immortality*)

Rising like a phoenix from the site of a former pornographic movie theatre, the Hollywood Twin Cinema, on Eighth Avenue at 47th Street, has been renovated by three movie buffs who hope to revive not only good old films but the street as well.

picayune   *pi ki YOO:N*
(trivial or petty: French, picaillon, small coin, halfpenny)

Robert S. Kane, who is revising his "A to Z" guidebooks with a new publisher, Rand McNally, avoids specifics, such as prices, but categorizes hotels and restaurants as luxurious, first class or moderate. "I don't go into picayune details that change all the time," he said, "and that people can get from their travel agents."

pickup   *PIK up*
(assembled or organized informally or hastily)

A handful of the nation's governors grinned, grunted and groaned through a pickup basketball game in a parking lot today in the cause of charity.

_____

As a noun, *pickup* has been a versatile term, meaning among other things, the fielding of a rapidly rolling ball; the acceleration of a car; a stranger briefly befriended for the purpose of sex; an improvement in business; a small truck; a stimulating drink or snack; a hitchhiker; an out-of-the-studio broadcast; a phonograph arm; and an arrested person.

_____

piéce de resistance   *pyes duh ray zi STAHNS*
(the principal dish of a meal; the main item or event in a series: French, piece of resistance)

The world's rarest and most valuable stamp, the British Guiana 1856 1-cent black on magenta, was the piéce de resistance of last year's Rarities of the World sale and many highly knowledgeable figures were predicting that it would bring a million dollars.

pinnacle   *PI nuh kuhl*
(the highest point; acme)

The British invented summer pudding, a ruby-red molded dome made with currants, blackberries and raspberries that is the pinnacle of their summer desserts.

pirate   *PIGH rit*
(to publish or reproduce without authorization, especially in violation of a copyright)

"There's quite a bit of outright pirating of the Calvin Klein name," he said. "Our biggest problem is in the Philippines, where someone is not only manufacturing but exporting under our name."

* * *

It seems that unscrupulous Taiwan businessmen have published a pirate edition of his book, "Kingman's Watercolors," without paying royalties.

pittance   *PI tuhns*
(a small or barely sufficient allowance of money)

Her budget on "Sophisticated Ladies" was $175,000. Like other successful theatrical designers, she now has assistants who worry about getting the shoes and accessories. The "Sophisticated Ladies" budget, however, seems a pittance when compared to that of "42nd Street," which had a costume budget of over $500,000, the highest on record for a Broadway show.

pivotal   *PI vuh tuhl*
(crucial; central)

Electronic detection and tracking devices played a pivotal part in the Battle of Britain, and since then, the rapid development of radar and antiradar technology has come to dominate human warfare.

placate   *PLAY kayt*
(to stop from being angry; appease; pacify)

Labor unions are the most powerful force in Argentina outside the military, which since coming to power in a coup five years ago has sought to placate them by keeping unemployment down and wages high.

placebo   *pluh SEE boh*
(a substance having no pharmacological effect, but given to a patient who supposes it to be a medicine; a substance used as a control in testing the efficacy of another, medicated substance)

Fully a third of pains can be relieved by a placebo, or sugar pill, if the patient believes it to be an active pain-killing drug. Recent studies suggest that placebos work by triggering the release of the body's own morphine, endomorphine.

Placebo (I shall be acceptable) is the first word sung in response to the priest's words in the Roman Catholic Church's vespers for the dead. The full line is "Placebo Domino in regione vivorum" ("I will walk before the Lord in the land of the living"), and is from Psalm 116. Because people who sought favors from relatives of the departed sometimes made sure they were seen singing this line at vespers, *to sing placebo,* as early as the 14th century, came to mean to play the flatterer. The earliest citation in the "Oxford English Dictionary" of *placebo* as we use the word today is from Hooper's "Medical Dictionary" of 1811. It defined *placebo* as a name "given to any medicine adapted more to please than benefit the patient."

___

placid   *PLA sid*
(*calm; tranquil; quiet*)

Some Chinese parents worry that the tough regimentation of nurser school and kindergarten tends to make their children too placid an uncreative. A professor at Peking University said he was concerned tha his 5-year-old son, whom he boards in kindergarten, just sits quietly an doesn't speak when he comes home.

plastic   *PLA stik*
(*capable of changing or adapting*)

"Heredity, shmeredity! You have to do something," says Dr. Reuve Feuerstein in answer to the endless argument over whether disadvar taged children do poorly in school because of inherited traits or becaus of their environment. The human organism, he says, "is an open system very plastic. It can be changed and modified." The question is whethe educators have the will, the confidence and the instruments to "do som thing."

platitude   *PLA tuh too:d*
(*a commonplace or trite remark, especially one uttered as if it were fresh or original*)

Last week, President Reagan gave a mishmash of a commencement a dress to the West Point cadets. He served a themeless pudding on platter of platitudes, calling for spiritual revival and promising high pay; he denounced "shrill voices" in a determinedly unshrill voic and proved to every doubter that the White House contains a book quotations.

plebian   *pli BEE uhn*
(*characteristic of the common people: the plebians were members of the ancient Roman lower class*)

Where oysters are posh, and summon up images of costly elegance, clar are plebian and suggest a more casual, less self-conscious if no le rapturous pleasure.

plebiscite *PLE buh sight*
(an expression of the people's will by direct ballot on a political issue)

Mr. Cabangbang, a retired colonel of the Philippine Air Force and major of the United States Air Force, is opposing Mr. Marcos for the presidency next Tuesday on the ticket of his Federal Party. Its goal is to defeat the President and then, in a plebiscite to be held later this year, convert this former American colony into the 51st state.

plenary *PLEE nuh ri*
(for attendance by all members)

The theme of the gathering of the N.A.A.C.P., "A dual society is an unequal society," was addressed in dozens of workshops, plenary sessions, committee meetings and speeches.

plethora *PLE thuh ruh*
(overabundance; excess)

Noting that last-minute cancellations "never panic me at all," Mrs. Buckley went on to say that she does try to avoid either "a plethora of men or a plethora of women" at large dinners. "We always try," she said, firmly. "I know there are people who say it's ridiculous to worry about having an equal number but I happen to think it's important."

ploy *ploi*
(a maneuver or strategem to gain the advantage)

Channel 13 has hit upon the nifty ploy of rerunning productions so old that they can be marketed as "classics" rather than repeats. The gimmick applies not only to movies but also to documentaries.

plunder *PLUHN der*
(to rob of goods or valuables by open force, as in war or hostile raids)

ZAMBOANGA, the Philippines, Sept. 2 (UPI)—Philippine navy ships searched the Sulu Sea today for pirates who plundered a trading vessel of more than $500,000, killed 10 merchants and took an undetermined number of people hostage.

pluralism *PLOO ruh li zuhm*
(the existence within a society of groups distinctive in ethnic origin, religion, cultural patterns or the like)

The president of Yale University attacked the Moral Majority and other conservative groups yesterday as "peddlers of coercion" in "a radical assault" on pluralism, civil rights and religious and political freedoms in the United States.

plutocrat *PLOO: tuh krat*
(a person who has power or influence because of wealth: the word derives from Plutus, the Greek god of wealth, whom the Romans incorporated into Pluto, their god of the underworld)

The public-financing law was designed to free Presidents, and to a lesser extent Congressmen, from obligations to a handful of plutocrats by placing limits on the amounts they could contribute in election campaigns.

ply *pligh*
(to sail or travel regularly back and forth between places)

A group of fishermen who ply the ocean off New York and New Jersey asked the Supreme Court to allow them to sue for damages to fish caused by the dumping of sewage.

———————

Sewage is the waste matter carried off by sewers or drains. Sewerage is the system of sewers that carries off waste matter.

———————

pogrom *puh GRAHM*
(an organized persecution and massacre, often officially prompted, of a minority group, especially of Jews in Czarist Russia: Russian, destruction*)*

Most of Argentina's Jews are second- and third-generation descendants of those who arrived around the end of the last century after fleeing the pogroms of eastern Europe and Russia. They found a young country rich in opportunity and similar in geography and culture to Europe.

polyglot *PAH li glaht*
(composed of several languages)

Just a few feet from the boulevard, however, is a newer face of Los Angeles. Tens of thousands of immigrants, most of them from Asia and Latin America, are crowded into what city planners call the Wilshire Corridor, and these polyglot neighborhoods are stunning evidence of the relatively recent waves of refugees from abroad that have turned this city into the nation's new melting pot.

polyphonic   *pah li FAH nik*
the simultaneous sounding of different notes in harmony)

Bach being Bach, it should surprise nobody that his Cantata No. 50, though the briefest piece on the program, also was the best. This polyphonic jewel for eight-part double chorus, only one movement of what probably was meant to be a longer work, is a miracle of intricate design but simply irresistible.

ponderous   *PAHN duh ruhs*
massive; bulky; heavy)

For so huge a creature, the California gray whale is ponderously graceful, erupting from the Pacific swells in easy arcs, so big the sea itself bulges as it lifts to the surface, breaking the blue-green water with an audible cascade.

pontificate   *pahn TI fi kayt*
to speak in a pompous or dogmatic way)

Knowing, feeling, viable human life has always been cheap—in war zones, refugee camps, even in sorrowful pockets of our own cities. So isn't it hypocritical, however well-intentioned, to pontificate about the right to life of a fertilized egg? Of course, it *is* a lot easier than worrying about born babies. Ask any mother.

popinjay   *PAH pin jay*
a person given to vain displays and empty chatter; fop: from an old Arab name for a parrot, signifying grand plumage and empty squawk-ing)

France, for Liebling, was Western civilization. His account of the removal of its popinjay Government from Paris to Tours as the Nazis advanced makes Jean-Paul Sartre, in his "Roads to Freedom" trilogy, sound sanguine.

portent   *PAWR tent*
omen)

It was a nervous moment. Nine fractious 2-year-old colts were circling the walking ring in Belmont Park's paddock. Hundreds of undecided bettors crowded the rail of the ring, looking for some portent of how to wager on a race full of first-time starters. Several edgy trainers carefully watched each step taken by their young horses.

portly *PAWRT li*
(large and heavy in a dignified way; stout)

Baldish, portly and faintly rumpled, Charles Kuralt is one of television's most familiar faces.

posh *pahsh*
(luxurious and fashionable; elegant)

Mrs. Fenwick spoke up, loud and clear. She is a remarkable woman, slimly elegant, her blue-gray hair perfectly groomed, a picture of what I imagine in the poshest New Jersey country clubs, until she puffs thoughtfully at her pipe a moment and then raises her voice.

posit *PAH zit*
(to set down or assume as fact; postulate)

People are not always kind to the beluga whales at the New York Aquarium. Sometimes they throw pennies into their pool, as though Amy Lou and Blanchon were marble fish on the Trevi Fountain, not mammals that some scientists posit may have intelligence greater than that of the average tourist.

posterity *pah STE ruh ti*
(all future generations)

Arriving in Guyana shortly after the story of the mass suicide and murder stunned the world, Mr. Reston discovered the existence of some 900 hours of tapes, made for posterity because Jim Jones always considered himself a historic figure.

posthumous *PAHS choo muhs*
(published or presented after the creator's death)

Sounding like a character in one of his autobiographical short stories, Mr Saroyan called The Associated Press five days before his death to leave a posthumous statement: "Everybody has got to die, but I have always believed an exception would be made in my case. Now what?"

potable *POH tuh buhl*
(something drinkable; beverage)

Mr. Dutond downed three pounds four ounces of Maroilles, arguably France's smelliest cheese, in 10 minutes. Half the contestants were eliminated in the first round by proving unable to consume a pound of the cheese in five minutes, unaided by bread, water or wine. During the second half potables were permitted, dispensed by gendarmes enlisted to insure the moral tone of the event.

potboiler   *PAHT boi ler*
A piece of writing or the like, usually inferior and uninspired, done quickly for money: so-called because it brings in money for food and other necessities)

Mr. Crichton, age 38, is not only that rare combination of successful novelist and screenwriter, he is also that rare writer who made the leap from writing potboiling paperbacks to literary respectability.

pother   *PAH th:er*
an uproar; commotion; fuss)

When I went to Ireland for a longish stay some 10 years ago, I thought it would be nice to have something Irish in my name, so I dropped the middle name Harrison and substituted Rossa. Oddly enough you can do this with no legal pother whatsoever.

potpourri   *poh poo REE*
a mixture; miscellany: French, rotten pot)

LONDON, July 24—Prince Charles and Lady Diana Spencer have invited a potpourri of personal friends and people whom they have never met to their wedding Wednesday—kings and gamekeepers, presidents and comedians, generals and charwomen.

Olla-podrida (OH luh puh DREE duh) is the name of a traditional Spanish meat and vegetable stew. It translates literally as *rotten pot,* and is called that probably because the stew is slow-cooked. When the French adopted this Spanish dish, they gave it their own name for *rotten pot: potpourri.* In English, both *potpourri* and *olla-podrida* mean an incongruous or miscellaneous mixture of any kind. In English, a potpourri is also the name of an aromatic blend of flower petals and spices stored in a jar.

---

precarious   *pri KAI ri uhs*
dangerously insecure or uncertain; risky)

The acting Archbishop of San Salvador, Arturo Rivera y Damas, faces a daily reminder of the precariousness of his post. An oil portrait of his predecessor, Archbishop Alvaro Oscar Romero, stares at the altar from

the transcept of the Metropolitan Cathedral where the body of the pre-
late, murdered 14 months ago, is buried.

precious   *PRE shuhs*
(overrefined or affected, as in language or behavior)

The point is this: The drinking of wine in America, particularly American
wine, is on the brink of becoming inbred and precious. Wine enthusiasts,
including we writers, who should know better, ape the jargon of the trade
and feel special when we exchange arcane trivia about grape crushers, red
spiders and who is opening next week's winery.

precipitate   *pri SI puh tayt*
(to bring on; cause)

Instead of expressing these feelings openly and constructively and thus
dissipating them, they tense their head and neck muscles, precipitating
a headache.

precipitately   *pri SI puh tit li*
(rashly; impetuously)

When Mary Larkin decided to give up her job at the Mercer Rubber
Company in Trenton, effective July 31, she was hardly acting precipi-
tately. Miss Larkin, who is 93 years old, went to work for the company
in 1905 and was continuously employed there for 76 years.

precipitous   *pri SI puh tuhs*
(steep, like a precipice)

From the beginning, there has been difficulty in recognizing toxic shock
syndrome, which is commonly characterized by the acute onset of high
fever, as in some cases of influenza; scaling or peeling of the skin, as in
scarlet fever; and a precipitous dropping of blood pressure.

preclude   *pri KLOO:D*
(to make impossible, especially in advance; shut out; prevent)

Q. Mr. President, I know you said earlier that you were not thinking of
revenge toward Iran, but does that preclude any punishment whatsoever
for what they've done? A. Well, again, I have to ask your forbearance and
wait until we've finished our study of this whole situation, as to what we're
going to do. I don't think any of us have a friendly feeling toward the

people that have done what they have done. But, I think it's too complex for me to answer until we've had time to really study this.

precocious   *pri KOH shuhs*
(developed or matured beyond what is normal for the age)

Mozart, one of the most precocious composers in history—the others were Mendelssohn and Saint-Saëns—had completed 13 symphonies by the time he was 12.

precursor   *pri KER ser*
(forerunner; predecessor)

In the zaniness of its humor and the frantic rigors of its live weekly production schedule, "Your Show of Shows" was a precursor of such hit variety series as "That Was the Week That Was" and "Saturday Night Live."

Zany derives from the Italian *zanni*, a clown or buffoon, which derives from Giovanni, the Italian equivalent of John, the most common male name not only in Italian, but also in German (Johann), French (Jean), Spanish (Juan), Russian (Ivan), Dutch (Jan) and other languages. They all derive ultimately from the Hebrew Yohanan, a contraction of Yehohanan, which means "God (Yoh, from Yahweh) is gracious."

---

predatory   *PRE duh taw ri*
(living by exploiting others)

"So Fine" is somewhat marred by an unpleasant attitude toward its female characters, every single one of whom is made out to be sexually predatory. While the men congratulate themselves on their prowess, sex-starved women eye them acquisitively, and it doesn't take long for this to become nasty.

predilection   *pree duh LEK shuhn*
(a preconceived liking; partiality or preference)

At bottom, Brendan Behan was an entertainer, a performer whose notoriety, as well as much of his charm, was based on a lethal predilection for bringing out the worst in himself. Early in life he wrote awfully well; later in life he became everyone's favorite drunk. He died at 41, his public decline attended by enchanted journalists and other voyeurs, and he left behind him not so much a body of work as a reputation for being what he most certainly was not. For all the posturing about life, he was in love with death.

predisposed   *pree di SPOHZD*
(*inclined to something in advance; made receptive beforehand*)

There are composers and performers who become cultural heroes or villains by virtue of their political stance. When we hear the music of Hindemith or Schoenberg or the conducting of Toscanini, we cannot help being predisposed toward them, partly because Hitler was not.

preeminent   *pree E muh nuhnt*
(*excelling others; outstanding*)

Irene Worth, one of the preeminent Shakespearean actors of our generation, recalled recently that during the first season of the Stratford, Ontario, Shakespeare Festival, she and Alec Guinness would work on breath control by trying to declaim an entire sonnet without stopping to breathe.

pre-empt   *pree EMPT*
(*to take action before anyone else can*)

The Israelis destroyed two tanks, five other vehicles, an underground arms depot, machine guns, houses and tents, according to the statement. The tanks, Soviet-made T-34's, were said to have been acquired recently from Hungary. The military command described the raid as a pre-emptive strike to disrupt preparations for terrorist raids against Israel.

premise   *PRE mis*
(*a proposition from which a conclusion is drawn; basis*)

It is an idea whose time came thousands of years ago, went out for Western civilization two centuries ago and now seems on the verge of a comeback. The premise: that women were intended to give birth sitting or squatting and not lying down as they have done ever since 1738 when François Mauriceau, obstetrician to the Queen of France, proposed facilitating the physician's task by having patients recline for delivery.

premonition   *pree muh NI shuhn*
(*a forewarning; foreboding; presentiment*)

When the Nazi's closed in on Berlin's Jewish community in 1939, Charlotte Saloman, a 21-year-old artist, fled to the home of her grandparents in Ville-franche-sur-Mer, in the south of France. There, with a premonition of doom, she furiously began to paint the story of her life just as Anne Frank in Amsterdam had written intimately about herself in the famous diary. In late summer 1942, Miss Saloman was picked up and sent to Auschwitz, where she died the next year.

prenatal   *pree NAY tuhl*
before birth)

A baby who would probably have died because of a genetic defect in its ability to use the vitamin called biotin was diagnosed early in its prenatal life and was treated successfully by giving the mother large doses of the substance daily for the final three months of her pregnancy.

preponderance   *pri PAHN duh ruhns*
superiority in quantity, weight, power, importance, etc.)

Others have faulted Mr. Reagan for failing to name long-range conceptual thinkers to key policy jobs. They argue that his Administration may suffer from a preponderance of officials experienced in carrying out but not in designing foreign policy.

prerogative   *pri RAH guh tiv*
an exclusive right or privilege)

For the nude scenes in "Endless Love," Mrs. Shields exercised her prerogative as manager and mother to select the stand-in. "I picked the girl who would be nude," she said. "Since I am the only person who's ever seen Brookie nude, I was the best person qualified to find the double. Her arms and hands were similar but her nails were longer. But she had a pimple on her rear end which no one saw, so $14,000 was spent retouching every frame. I said you can't let that in there."

primordial   *prigh MAWR di uhl*
(existing from the beginning; primitive; primeval)

Now part of the town finds living here like existing on some primordial planet where the earth belches noxious gases and where the ground sometimes opens up under the tread of unwary feet. "It was awful scary," said Todd Domboski, 13 years old, describing his escape last month from a 250-foot hole that had opened in his grandmother's yard and almost swallowed him.

pristine   *PRI steen*
(unspoiled; untouched; pure)

Through the pristine wilderness of northwestern Wisconsin flows the Flambeau River, one of the best white-water and quiet-water canoeing rivers in the Midwest.

procrastinate   *proh KRA stuh nayt*
(to put off to a future time; postpone habitually)

On the topic of lunch, artists are sharply divided. There is a group for whom it is an irritation, a waste of valuable time that is to be dispensed with as quickly as possible. Others seize upon the meal as a clever way to procrastinate; ideas may still come as cucumbers are sliced or as bacon hisses in the frying pan.

procreation   *proh kri AY shuhn*
(the producing of young; reproduction)

SAN FRANCISCO, July 2—The hardy, prolific and devastatingly destructive Mediterranean fruit fly appears to have survived a $22 million eradication program south of the Bay area, which included extensive stripping of fruit trees, ground spraying of insecticide and the release of millions of sterile males to thwart their procreation.

procure   *proh KYOOR*
(to obtain; secure)

Markets run by Koreans have been cropping up in neighborhoods all over the city, and special effort seems to have been made by them to procure exceptionally fresh greens and display them attractively.

Was the reporter intentionally punning when she wrote that markets are "cropping up," or am I finding wordplay where none was meant to exist?

---

prodigious   *pruh DI juhs*
(enormous; huge)

After the defeat of the French in Canada at the hands of the British in 1759, the French population in Canada increased so prodigiously in the 19th and early 20th centuries that the phenomenon came to be called "the revenge of the cradle." But since the end of World War II, the birth rate of French Canadians has dropped precipitously, and English-speaking Canada has grown much faster.

prodigy   *PRAH duh ji*
(a child of highly unusual talent or genius, but also, any person so
extraordinary as to inspire wonder)

A hockey prodigy who began playing the game at the age of 5 and entered
the N.H.L. as a heralded 18-year-old, Orr lived up to his extravagant
notices, dazzling elder competitors and teammates with his skating, his
puck control and his sense of the game.

profligate   *PRAH fluh git*
(extremely wasteful; recklessly extravagant)

For sheer, profligate waste of energy, it's hard to beat "Louis," the new
musical in a workshop presentation at the Henry Street Settlement's New
Federal Theater. This show, an ostensible account of the early career of
Louis Armstrong, boasts more talented, hard-working performers than
some Broadway musicals—and not one of them is put to good use.

profuse   *pruh FYOO:S*
(in great amount)

One of the last scenes in the movie shows an Elvis so bloated he's almost
unrecognizable, sweating profusely and so obviously drugged that he
can't remember song lyrics; he's in a huge arena, but he barely seems to
know the audience is there.

progenitor   *proh JE nuh ter*
(an ancestor in a direct line)

He's not considered a member of Britain's Royal Family, but like the
Queen, Walter Lee Sheppard Jr. claims direct descent from Edward III
and other royal progenitors.

progeny   *PRAH juh ni*
(offspring)

The captured salmon are being removed—gently, for they are a hypersensitive fish—to a holding facility in Barkhampsted, Conn. During the
natural spawning time in November, the eggs of the females and the milt
of the males will be removed for artificial spawning, and the progeny will
later be returned to the rivers.

prognosis   *prahg NOH sis*
(a forecast, usually of the course and outcome of an illness)

The superintendent of Gemelli Hospital said today that although Pope John Paul II had been moved out of intensive care his condition was still guarded and that a prognosis about his recovery would not be possible for a few more days.

The prognosis for Mr. Silverman's future at NBC is not good; trade speculation about the network president has shifted from "if he will leave" to "when he will leave."

proliferate   *proh LI fuh rayt*
(*to multiply rapidly; increase profusely*)

More and more women are playing as well as singing rock-and-roll, and bands that consist entirely of women are proliferating.

prolific   *pruh LI fik*
(*producing in large quantity*)

Mr. L'Amour, said to be one of the most widely read writers in the world, is so prolific that he can't remember whether his latest book is number 78 or 79. "I do about three a year by writing practically every day of my life," he said.

prolix   *proh LIKS*
(*overly long; tiresome; long-winded: usually with reference to writing*)

"The Firebird" is the one of Stravinsky's "big three" early ballet scores that is probably better heard in the form of a suite than in its rather prolix complete version.

prosaic   *proh ZAY ik*
(*dull and ordinary*)

There was a 13th-century minnesinger named Walther von der Vogel-weide—what a name for a poet, a poem in itself! I was jealously contemplating it one day, thinking bleakly of my own bald, prosaic, easily forgotten name, when this couplet came to me:

> My name looks mighty plain beside a
> Walther von der Vogelweide

Minnesingers were lyric poets, or troubadours, of 12th- to 14th-century Germany who specialized in love songs (*minne* was at that time *love* in German). They were aristocrats by birth and operated within guilds. They were succeeded in the 14th to 16th centuries by the meistersingers (master singers), who were members of the merchant class. Almost every German city had a meistersinger guild, one of which is the subject of Wagner's comic opera "Die Meistersinger."

----

proscribe *proh SKRIGHB*
(to forbid the practice or use of)

Modern governments have a muddled record when it comes to legislating against sin. Killing, proscribed by the Commandments, is punishable by law if undertaken as a private enterprise, but not if done professionally —as a soldier or an executioner, say—in the service of the state.

proselytize *PRAH suh li tighz*
(to try to convert to one's religion, beliefs, way of life, etc.)

The Baha'is have also infuriated the Islamic clergy because they are one of the few religious groups that attempt to proselytize among the Moslems.

prostitute *PRAH stuh too:t*
(to sell for unworthy or degraded purposes)

The actor [Philip Bosco] says he refuses to do television commercials. "I hate to sound pompous and holier-than-thou," he explained, "but I feel very strongly as an artist that this is not the kind of thing I want to do, because it's not acting. It's being a salesman. I choose not to use the word prostitute because it's too strong. But I think that's essentially what it is. It's being dishonest, being less than true to what you hold dear."

Holier-than-thou is a phrase from Chapter 65 of the biblical book of Isaiah. God has been provoked to anger at the sight of Jews who are sacrificing animals, burning incense and eating swine's flesh, and who say to others: "Stand by thyself, come not near to me; for I am holier than thou."

----

protean *PROH ti uhn*
(very changeable; quickly taking on different shapes and forms, as did the sea god Proteus of Greek myth)

What helps make the choreography of Dana Reitz so remarkable is its protean nature. Just as one thinks one has perceived the basic shape of a movement, that movement immediately becomes something else. Miss Reitz's choreography is a choreography of perpetual metamorphosis.

protocol   *PROH tuh kahl*
(the forms of ceremony and etiquette observed by diplomats and heads of state)

New social aides are given tours of the White House to familiarize themselves with its history and background, and they are supplied with a manual that spells out the formalities of diplomatic protocol, the customs of different countries and the rules governing formal introductions.

prototype   *PROH tuh tighp*
(the first thing of its kind; model; original)

BOLINGBROOK, Ill., March 25—Old Chicago opened here in 1975 as America's first hybrid of shopping center and amusement park. Fifty million dollars, a bankruptcy and a foreclosure later, the prototype seems to argue against its own concept.

providence   *PRAH vuh duhns*
(divine guidance; fortune; luck)

"And to me it has been providential to be an artist, a great act of providence that I was able to turn my borderline psychosis into creativity—my sister Rose did not manage this. So I keep writing. I am sometimes pleased with what I do—for me, that's enough." [Tennessee Williams]

provincial   *pruh VIN shuhl*
(limited in perspective; narrow; unsophisticated)

German 19th-century literature had a token status even among people who had never read a word of it. But German 19th-century art was thought of as provincial, second-rate, secondhand and altogether beneath discussion.

proviso   *pruh VIGH zoh*
(a condition or stipulation)

If you want to go up to Broadway, says the brain, it's okay by me, but I've got one proviso. No shows about show business. "Well," say I, after scanning the theater ads, "that rules out 'A Chorus Line,' 'A Day in Hollywood/A Night in the Ukraine,' 'Ain't Misbehavin',' 'Amadeus,' 'Barnum,' 'Dancin',' '42nd Street,' 'They're Playing Our Song,' 'Sophisticated Ladies'. . . ."

provocateur *pruh vah kuh TER*
(*a person hired to join a labor union, political party, demonstration, etc.,
in order to incite its members to actions that will make them or their organization liable to penalty: the full French term is* agent provocateur)

Two leaders of the Socialist Workers Party have testified that Federal
agents used false charges, anonymous letters and undercover provoca-
teurs to disrupt their political activities.

proxy *PRAHK si*
(*someone with authority to act for another; deputy*)

The United States has been deeply concerned about Libya's international
activities for some time. It has been worried that the Libyans were serving
as an indirect Soviet "proxy" in Africa by interfering militarily and politically in various countries.

prudent *PROO: duhnt*
(*showing good judgment; cautious or discreet in conduct; not rash*)

But the casinos want much more freedom than a prudent state would
grant. They would like the state to ease its rules on the size of each
casino's staff and on "junkets"—organized gambling excursions. They
also want to operate around the clock, and seek relaxation of other rules.

pseudonym *SOO: duh nim*
(*a fictitious name*)

"We do not depend on any nation's support," said one of the guerrilla
leaders, who called himself Marcos. "United States support to the Government is prolonging the conflict." The four, who appeared to be mostly
in their 20's, used pseudonyms and said they were political and military
commanders directing the fighting in each of the four fronts inside El
Salvador.

puckish *PUH kish*
(*full of mischief; impish*)

Injury or no, Danny Kaye, at 68, could still be mistaken for Hans Christian
Andersen or Merry Andrew—older perhaps, but the traces of puckish-
ness lurk nonetheless behind the sober manner.

Puck, also known as Robin Goodfellow, was a merry prankster of
English folklore, an elf who delighted in tricking and confound-

ing people. He was Shakespeare's model for Puck in "A Midsummer Night's Dream," and lent his name, in a slightly changed form, to the breed of dog known as the pug.

---

puffery   *PUH fuh ri*
(exaggerated praise, as in advertising or chamber of commerce boosterism)

Some who have seen the new museum might consider it a work of art in its own right. Texas Monthly, a magazine not generally known for puffery, wrote of the museum that "it will undoubtedly be celebrated as one of the most original architectural projects ever undertaken in Texas," and said its design "creates some stunning effects."

punchy   *PUHN chi*
(groggy, dazed or dizzy: originally from punch-drunk, a condition resulting from numerous blows on the head, as in boxing)

Like most people at Cannes, Miss Burstyn said she was a bit punchy from seeing two films a day.

punctilious   *puhngk TI li uhs*
(very exact; scrupulous)

On this day in New York, Danny Kaye was not feeling very funny. Maybe it was because he had expected his visitor to arrive earlier and he is punctilious about keeping appointments.

punctuate   *PUHNGK choo ayt*
(to break in on here and there; interrupt)

As directed by Richard Loncraine, "The Haunting of Julia" is virtually scareless, and the camera angles provide advance tipoffs to the few frightening episodes that punctuate the dull ones.

pundit   *PUHN dit*
(an expert or authority in a particular field; a person who makes judgments or comments in a solemnly authoritative manner)

When the Soviet Union invaded Afghanistan, pundits agreed that guerrilla resistance would be more difficult than in, say, Vietnam. Why? Without jungle ground cover, insurgents have no place to hide. It would be a piece of cake for Soviet helicopters to pick off the rebels.

pungent   *PUHN juhnt*
(*sharp to the taste or smell*)

For many people, though, working at American Chicle has not been just
another job. Most of the employees say they like the place, the pay and
the supervisors. They even like the smell—a pungent, sinus-clearing
blend of peppermint, cinnamon and sugar.

purge   *perj*
(*the process of ridding a nation, political party, etc., of individuals held
to be disloyal or undesirable*)

Forty-five more executions were reported from Iran today as the Islamic
Government continued its purge of leftist opponents.

puritan   *PYOO ruh tin*
(*a person regarded as extremely or excessively strict in matters of morals
and religion, as America's 17th-century Pilgrims were said to be*)

Pete Seeger has always described himself, and has been described by his
friends, as a puritan: he doesn't smoke, he doesn't drink, he disapproves
of gambling and there is every reason to believe that he was innocent of
sex until he married Toshi Ohta, his wife of 40 years.

purple patch   *PUR puhl PACH*
(*a passage of obtrusively ornate writing that stands out from the style
of writing around it and reveals the author's attempt at being impressive
or poetic*)

The most powerful segments of "Anatomy of a Volcano" are, of course,
the mountain in eruption, the landslides, floods and the scarcely credible
flattening and stripping of mature Douglas firs many miles away. . . . The
narration, written by Stuart Harris of the BBC and spoken by Frank
Donlan, wisely does not try to match this extraordinary event with purple
patches, but is a model, by and large, of low-key lucidity.

putative   *PYOO: tuh tiv*
(*reputed; supposed*)

The production is at the scrappy collegiate rather than the professional
workshop level. While all the principals sing and dance well, some of
them go wildly and noisily out of control during their putative comic or
dramatic moments.

quack   *kwak*
(a fraudulant or incompetent medical doctor; anyone who pretends to have knowledge or skill in a field but does not; charlatan: short for quacksalver, one who quacks, or boasts, as snake oil and liniment vendors did about their products at fairs)

The nutritional quack often cloaks his information in scientific language, supported by references in the scientific literature. Most people are in no position to check the accuracy of the claims against the original references. More often than not, they are distortions or unwarranted extensions of the true findings.

Quack is a *clipped form,* a word formed by clipping off the front or back of an older word. Clips are the natural result of people wanting to say or write something in a shorter way. Clips like *mod*(ern) and *demo*(nstration) will probably always be colloquial, while others, like *zoo*(logical park) and (omni)*bus* are standard usage and rarely thought of or used in their original forms. Among the more recent clips are *stereo*(phonic), *limo*(usine), *condo*(minium), *disco*(thèque), *sit*(uation) *com*(edy) and *narc*(otics detective). More traditional clips are *ad*(vertisement), *vet*(erinarian), *coop*(erative), *lab*(oratory) and *pro*(fessional). Students are traditionally prolific clippers, as witness *dorm*(itory), *math*(ematics), *gym*(nasium), *eco*(nomics), *psych*(ology), *bio*(logy), *poli*(tical) *sci*(ence) and *grad*(uate) school. Back clips are far more numerous than front clips, probably because of the practice of retaining the most important part of the word and dropping the suffix. Two of our most common words, however, (air)*plane* and (tele)*phone* are front clips. One popular clip gets snipped from back and front—(in)*flu*(enza).

---

quagmire   *KWAG mighr*
(a difficult or inextricable situation; literally, a bog or swamp)

The invasion of Afghanistan lowered Soviet standing with Moslems and created a military quagmire which Moscow probably did not expect.

qualm   *kwahm*
(*an uneasy feeling or pang of conscience; misgiving*)

Ivan Fisher is a successful lawyer who defends major narcotics dealers, earns large fees for his work and makes no apologies for it. He has no moral qualms about handling drug cases, Mr. Fisher said, expressing vehemently a view shared by several other New York lawyers who were interviewed about their defense of narcotics traffickers. "Personally," he said, "I find some white-collar defendants more reprehensible—at least a drug dealer takes money from a drug user or from another drug dealer."

quandary   *KWAHN dri*
(*dilemma; perplexing situation*)

Nevertheless, despite the professions of loyalty to Israel, the Reagan Administration has found itself in a public dispute with Israel over arms sales to friendly Arab nations. This is the same quandary that faced the Ford and Carter administrations when they began to step up arms sales to the Arab world.

quantitative   *KWAHN tuh tay tiv*
(*capable of being measured*)

By running roaches on a treadmill, three scientists at the State University of New York at Buffalo have performed what they believe is the first quantitative study of energy consumption and efficiency in a running insect, and only the second such study of an invertebrate of any kind. (The first examined the energy budget of a big land crab.)

quarry   *KWAW ri*
(*something hunted or pursued; prey*)

Blanda was a quarterback, and the quarterback is the marked man on any team, the quarry of 350-pound pass-rushers hungering to pluck him off his feet and ram his head into the ground.

quash   *kwahsh*
(*to quell or suppress; put down*)

The Detroit office of the Internal Revenue Service is moving to quash a burgeoning tax revolt reported among 3,500 Michigan workers, many in the automobile industry, who have avoided having income taxes withheld by claiming as many as 99 dependents.

quasi   *KWAY sigh*
(seemingly; in a sense; resembling; in part: Latin, as if)

The particular charm of North Carolina's mountain stream trout fishing is the wilderness or quasi-wilderness backdrop. One meets few anglers on most streams and none on others, and I, for one, would rather catch a nine-inch trout under such conditions than a five-pound, hatchery-reared fish on a crowded river or reservoir.

Quasi takes a hyphen when joined to an adjective (quasi-public); used with a noun, it should remain a separate unit (quasi corporation). *Quasi* is an element in only a small number of established English terms: *quasi contract* and *quasi-judicial*, for example. But it has a sound and sense to it that, when joined with most words, makes the combination seem standard usage, as in these New York Times examples: *quasi-operatic* rock singing; a play with a *quasi flashback* structure; a *quasi-religious* society; from *quasi Cockney* to indeterminate mid-Atlantic; information of a *quasi-classified* type; the *quasi-private* Corporation for Public Broadcasting; a general atmosphere of *quasi-sexual* horror. The combinations are limitless, and the results are almost always genuine aids to expression.

---

quay   *kee*
(a wharf, usually of concrete or stone, with facilities for loading and unloading ships)

Prince Charles and his new Princess will arrive in Gibraltar by plane late in the afternoon on Aug. 1. They will drive slowly through the tiny crown colony to the quay where the Britannia will be berthed and board her. She will depart only an hour and 40 minutes after the royal couple's plane has touched down.

quell   *kwel*
(to put an end to; crush)

The disturbance was quelled when guards flooded the high-rise prison with tear gas and then used clubs and shields to force the inmates back into their cells.

queue   *kyoo:*
(to form in a line or file while waiting to be served; wait in—or on— line: the use of "up" following "queue" is optional)

Miss Horne opened at the Nederlander Theater on Tuesday night, and for the last two days people have queued outside the box office to buy tickets.

quibble   *KWI buhl*
(to argue, criticize or object in a petty fashion)

While Mr. Reagan lay with a bullet in his lung, two senior Cabinet officers quibbled about who was in charge.

quid pro quo   *KWID proh KWOH*
(one thing in return for another: Latin, something for something)

Los Angeles is no place for a woman. Out here, a woman is a nonperson unless she is under 21, powerful or a star. In this quid-pro-quo town, the flip side of an aging female without box-office clout or her own daily newspaper is an aging man, without the power to hand out parts, on a date with an actress.

quintessence   *kwin TE suhns*
(the most perfect embodiment of something)

The use of fire is the quintessence of the human condition, even more so than the use of tools, since some animals at least use sticks as primitive tools but only man uses fire.

———

"What a piece of work is a man! how noble in reason! how infinite in faculties! in form and moving how express and admirable! in action how like an angel! in apprehension how like a god! the beauty of the world, the paragon of animals! And yet to me what is this quintessence of dust?"

Hamlet, Act II Sc. II

———

quip   *kwip*
(a witty remark or reply; jest or gibe)

Judges have often tried to assert control by imposing injunctions, or even dispatching troops to troubled coal towns. But John L. Lewis's quip—"You can't mine coal with bayonets"—is as widely quoted as proverbs in Bibles that sit on tables in most miners' livingrooms.

quixotic   *kwik SAH tik*
(romantically idealistic; visionary; having impractical, improbable goals from noble motives: like Don Quixote, the hero of Cervantes' 1605 novel, who set out to correct the wrongs of the whole world)

No doubt George F. Kennan will be widely considered quixotic for calling attention at this time to the "collision course" on which he believes the nuclear superpowers are embarked, and for urging the immediate reduction by 50 percent of American and Soviet nuclear arsenals.

rabid   *RA bid*
(fanatical or unreasonably zealous in beliefs, opinions or pursuits)

MOSCOW, May 10—The Soviet press reacted quickly and angrily today to a speech in Syracuse yesterday by Secretary of State Alexander M. Haig Jr., terming it an exercise in "rabid anti-Sovietism and anti-Communism."

raconteur   *ra kahn TER*
(a person skilled at telling stories or anecdotes: French, recounter)

The late Francis Robinson, that amiable raconteur who ended up his many years at the Metropolitan Opera as tour director and consultant, used to have a lovely Milanov story. Zinka, he said, came to the Met to hear Mirella Freni as Adina in "L'Elisir d'amore." No competition there. Freni was a light lyric. (With dramatic sopranos Milanov could be merciless.) Anyway, said Robinson, Milanov came to his office at the end of the second act, dissolved in tears. "Francis," she sobbed. "Francis, Francis, she's beautiful. She sings like a a young *me.*"

racy   *RAY si*
(somewhat indecent; suggestive; risqué)

In his Hollywood days, for example, Mr. Reagan was known to be partial to handsome women and off-color jokes, and he does not shy from a mildly racy line now. Middle age, he asserted last night, is "when you're faced with two temptations and you choose the one that will get you home by 9 o'clock."

rancor   *RANG ker*
(a continuing and bitter hate or ill will)

MERANO, Italy, Sept. 30—Two angry men, Viktor Korchnoi of Switzerland and Anatoly Karpov of the Soviet Union, will face each other in the world chess championship match beginning here tomorrow. Korchnoi, the challenger, thrives on rancor, developing instant aversion for every opponent he plays; Karpov, probably with generous help from the Soviet Chess Federation, has learned from him.

rankle   *RANG kuhl*
(to cause keen irritation or resentment in)

"I have close blood ties with the people of Israel and a special feeling about them, as anybody would about their antecedents," Mr. Koch says. The Mayor had rankled a number of Israeli officials prior to his trip because he had criticized aspects of Israel's settlement policies on the occupied Arab lands of the West Bank, calling them "irritants."

rapport   *ruh PAWR*
(a close or sympathetic relationship; harmonious feeling)

Learning to identify and harvest wild edibles is not, for nearly all of us, a way to reduce the food budget or a passport to survival. It is, if it appeals, another passageway to a deeper rapport with the natural world and with the dwellers of a less sophisticated time.

rapprochement   *ra prawsh MAHN*
(an establishing, or especially a restoring, of harmony and friendly relations: French, rapprocher, bring together)

What development of recent years has done the most to assure Israel's long-term security? The answer surely is the rapprochement with Egypt. The most important of Israel's Arab neighbors is no longer an enemy.

rapt   *rapt*
(completely absorbed or engrossed)

Row G, on the aisle, at the National Theater for the exuberant opening night of "Evita." Alejandro Orfila, an Argentine who is Secretary General on the Organization of American States, and his German-born wife, Helga, sat rapt, watching the musical on the rise of Eva Perón. Mr. Orfila served as Juan Perón's last ambassador to the United States, from 1973 to 1975.

rash   *rash*
(too hasty or incautious in acting or speaking; reckless)

Leonid I. Brezhnev, the Soviet leader, warned today that a rash step in the Middle East could engulf the entire region in war.

(a sudden appearance of a large or excessive number; plethora: originally, the sudden and temporary eruption of red spots on the skin)

The rash of unfounded bomb threats and false reports of bombs continued yesterday in New York City as investigators reported no substantial progress in their efforts to find those responsible for Saturday's fatal blast at Kennedy International Airport.

The *rash* that means *recklessness* derives from the German *rasch*, meaning dashing or lively. The *rash* whose literal meaning is *a skin eruption* derives from the Latin *rasica*, which has also given us *rasp*, to scrape or rub, as with a file.

---

raucous   *RAW kuhs*
(harsh, grating and loud)

To the raucous sputter of a chain saw, the elm branches were falling in Riverside Park this week, sinking almost lazily to the ground from 45 or 50 feet up as a few joggers and passers-by craned their necks.

ravage   *RA vij*
(to destroy violently; devastate; ruin)

ROSEAU, Dominica—It has been nearly two years since Hurricane David ravaged this Eastern Caribbean nation of 80,000 people, turning its green mountains brown and tearing off nearly every roof.

raze   *rayz*
(to tear down completely; level)

Some American analysts doubt that northern Israel can ever be completely secure. Even if Israeli troops take and raze Beaufort Castle, an observation point for the guerrillas, and the guerrillas retire to the Beirut-Damascus highway as demanded by the Israelis, groups of two or three guerrillas will be able to infiltrate south.

rebuke   *ri BYOO:K*
(to blame or scold sharply; reprimand)

A popular Soviet playwright has been rebuked in the Soviet press for ideological deviation in his latest hit, a long-running play at the Moscow Art Theater that takes an unblinking look at the corrupt and shoddy aspects of Soviet life and milks them for laughs.

recalcitrant   *ri KAL si truhnt*
(resisting authority or control; not obedient; hard to manage)

The trip was uneventful until a fight developed in the rear of the bus between the conductor and a recalcitrant fare. Not knowing any Indian language, I relied on the gestures and increasing volume of screaming to determine that an old man claimed he was broke and could not pay his fare.

The film has some choice bits of comic business that no one else could have invented, for example a scene in a Chinese restaurant where Mr. Matthau argues philosophy with Jill Clayburgh while trying to snare a recalcitrant dumpling with a pair of unwieldy chopsticks.

recant   *ri KANT*
(to formally or publicly renounce one's beliefs or former statements)

SAN FRANCISCO, Feb. 25—A Roman Catholic priest who is a homosexual has been notified that he will be expelled from his religious order unless he resigns or recants his criticism of the vow of priestly celibacy.

recapitulate   *ree kuh PI chuh layt*
(to restate briefly; summarize)

In the den two teen-agers, one a boy with only one leg and the other a girl walking with crutches, were recapitulating the week's action on "General Hospital."

recidivism   *ri SI duh vi zuhm*
(repeated relapse, especially into crime)

My 13-year-old daughter's feminist credentials are impeccable. Her babysitting empire and use of creative accounting methods whenever she gets an advance on her allowance should render her financially independent before she can vote. Jane even gets Ms. magazine (she won the subscription at a roller-skating fund-raiser). Yet in one respect she remains recidivist: she loves the Miss America contest.

recision   *ri SI zhuhn*
(an act of canceling or voiding)

At this very moment, the program is threatened by a recision of $8 million —a small amount compared to the years of work, planning and fund-raising that many groups and agencies have engaged in to build lives and neighborhoods.

reckoning   *RE kuh ning*
(the settling of an account)

El Salvador has long been a violent society. Before the war, some 2,000 people died each year in political or personal blood reckonings.

recluse   *ri KLOO:S*
(one who lives a secluded, solitary life)

Only occasionally did the alligator poke its snout above the muddy surface of the pond, and these appearances often provoked a barrage of rocks and bottles. As a result, the alligator became reclusive, spending most of its time in the muck at the bottom.

rectitude   *REK tuh too:d*
(correct conduct according to principles; uprightness)

Since he has always had a reputation for moral rectitude, it may come as no surprise that Roger Staubach, who retired last year as the Dallas Cowboys' quarterback, has lent his name to a fund-raising drive for an organization [Morality in Media, Inc.] that fights what it calls smut on television.

red herring   *RED HE ring*
(something used to divert attention from the basic issue: from the practice of hunters drawing a red herring—i.e. one dried, smoked and salted— across the fox's trail to distract the hounds)

Senator Helms, saying that the abortion issue was rooted in the Judeo-Christian tradition and the Ten Commandments of Mount Sinai, rejected arguments that up to 15,000 pregnancies result from rape each year. "This is a red herring," Senator Helms declared, as a full gallery of tourists watched from above, "a red herring whereby people come up four months later and say, 'Oh, by the way, I was raped four months ago.' "

redolent   *RE duh luhnt*
(smelling [of]; suggestive or evocative [of])

Although Sidney Lumet's "Prince of the City" has an atmosphere deeply redolent of crime and corruption, very few specific misdeeds are ever shown on the screen. They don't have to be. Mr. Lumet's film offers such a sharply detailed landscape, such a rich and crowded portrait, that his characters reveal themselves fully by the ways they move, eat, speak, listen or lie.

red tape   *RED TAYP*
(official forms and routines; strict application of regulations and routines, resulting in delay in getting business done)

Americans who travel abroad will soon be issued a new passport that can be read by a machine in an effort to speed up the passage of travelers through red tape at borders and to reduce fraud.

Charles Dickens is said to have originated the term *red tape*, from the red tape commonly used by British lawyers and government officials to tie their papers.

redundant   *ri DUHN duhnt*
(needlessly repetitive; superfluous)

Q. You often specify corn or vegetable oil in your recipe. To me this sounds redundant. Corn is a vegetable and is, therefore, a vegetable oil. Why do you indulge in such a redundancy?
A. This has been pointed out to me on numerous occasions. I repeat "corn or vegetable" oil because some jars of oil are labeled corn and others vegetable. It is to simplify things for readers, to reassure them, in other words, that the oils marked corn or vegetable are interchangeable.

Montgomery Ward, the troubled retail subsidiary of the Mobil Corporation, is reportedly preparing to offer a program of widespread early retirements with incentives to redundant senior and middle-rank executives in an effort to sharply cut administrative costs.

refurbish   *ree FER bish*
(to renovate; polish up; brighten)

In Connecticut, New York and New Jersey, the high price of oil is leading to the refurbishing of small, abandoned, vandalized hydroelectric stations. They are once again becoming commercially feasible installations and making small dents in the nation's foreign payments for oil.

regale   *ri GAYL*
(to delight with something pleasing or amusing)

Already this week, British readers have been regaled with the news that 500 million people in 50 countries are expected to watch the spectacle on television, that Lady Diana wore "figure-hugging yellow dungarees" to watch her fiancé play polo on Sunday and that a Baptist minister has advised the couple to "take time to make love."

reiterate   *ree I tuh rayt*
(to say over again; repeat)

Governor Carey today backed away from a proposal he made last month to keep some bars open 24 hours a day, but reiterated his support for the sale of wine and spirits in supermarkets.

remiss   *ri MIS*
(negligent; careless or slow in performing one's duty, business, etc.)

"I would feel guilty and remiss if we took a trip without Louis," William A. Spiegler, director of communications for the C.W. Post Center of Long Island University said of his 12-year-old son. "I couldn't take a trip that I knew would be fun and educational without him."

renaissance   *RE nuh sahns*
(revival; rebirth)

Alligators were once in a dramatic decline in Louisiana, the result of unrestricted killing. Now, with the help of state and Federal regulations, the animal has made a strong comeback, and signs of its renaissance are conspicuous in busy canals, bayous and rivers, in cypress swamps and residential districts and in the soup, potage alligator au sherry, at Antoine's.

rend   *rend*
(to tear, pull apart or split with violence)

Saudi Arabia's economic planners believe they can successfully link the West's technology and the Islamic faith without rending society, but acknowledge they face a challenge.

render   *REN der*
(to cause to be or become; make)

The John C. Mandel Security Bureau once sent a karate-trained female to protect a former Olympic male wrestling champion rendered temporarily defenseless by a racing car accident.

rendezvous   *RAHN duh voo:*
(to meet or assemble at a certain time or place: French, betake yourselves)

As if to punctuate their emergence from America's shadow, the Europeans will launch in 1985 an unmanned mission to rendezvous with Halley's Comet.

renege   *ri NIG*
(to back out of an agreement; go back on a promise)

Mr. Sands was the negotiator for the seven Roman Catholic prisoners who gave up a long hunger strike just before Christmas, as several of them neared death. He later maintained that the British had reneged on promises they made to him then, and so he began a hunger strike of his own on March 1 in support of the same demand—that I.R.A. prisoners be granted political status, with the right to wear their own clothes, for example, rather than being treated as common criminals.

renounce   *ri NOWNS*
(to cast off or disown; refuse further association with)

Maxim Shostakovich, the Soviet conductor, and his 19-year-old son, Dmitri, who defected to the West nearly two weeks ago, renounced their Soviet citizenship today and said they would become United States citizens.

repast   *ri PAST*
(a meal)

We were fed overabundantly three times a day. Even breakfast, if one chose the Chinese version, was a large repast of hot rice gruel, steamed breads and cold sliced meats.

repercussion   *ree per KUH shuhn*
(an indirect or remote effect of some action or event)

A right-wing military junta in power in Madrid would also put enormous strains on Portugal's fragile democratic institutions, in the view of many Western European diplomats, and the repercussions would be felt in Italy and Greece.

A junta was originally a Spanish or South American government council. Today, however, *junta* is applied to small groups of people, usually from the military, who rule a country after seizing political power, usually through a coup d'état. *Junta* is derived from the Latin *juncta,* to join.

---

repertoire   *RE per twahr*
(the entire range of things in a particular field or art: French, catalogue, inventory)

Pitching machines that cost around $1,500 have been refined to the point where they can deliver any of the pitches in a major league pitcher's repertoire—including a devastating knuckle ball—at varying speeds and in different locations around the strike zone.

replete   *ri PLEET*
(well-filled or plentifully supplied)

When "Lolita" opened its pre-Broadway tryout engagement in Boston, some reviewers and theatergoers were outraged by other, non-Nabokovian touches added by Mr. Albee. For one thing, the stage version of "Lolita" arrives replete with four-letter words in its vocabulary. There are none in the novel.

repository   *ri PAH zuh taw ri*
(something serving as a center of accumulation or storage)

The Nuclear Regulatory Commission today proposed safety standards for the long-term storage of highly radioactive atomic waste, such as spent reactor fuel, in a proposed underground repository.

requisite   *RE kwuh zit*
(required, as by circumstances; necessary; indispensable)

At a party the poet and anthologist Oscar Williams was introduced to the wife of the actor George Segal. She was wearing a remarkably low-cut dress and had the requisite figure. After acknowledging the introduction, Mr. Williams unbuttoned his shirtfront and pulled it open. "I too," he said, "have a perfectly hairless chest."

rescind   *ri SIND*
(to revoke, repeal or cancel)

In 1954 a general meeting of the Duke faculty voted 61 to 42 to rescind the offer of an honorary doctor of laws degree to Mr. Nixon, who was then the Vice President.

resolute   *RE zuh loo:t*
(firmly resolved or determined; showing a fixed, firm purpose)

But it is difficult to witness anybody doing anything resolutely in sweltering Peking, with the possible exception of kissing, snoozing and trying to buy beer.

respite   *RE spit*
(an interval of rest or relief)

This year the New Yorker League for Cerebral Palsy will conduct an evening tour, "City Nights, City Lights," to six Manhattan residences between Central Park South and East 57th Street. A wine and cheese respite will be offered at one of the stops.

resplendent   *ri SPLEN duhnt*
(gleaming; splendid)

King Juan Carlos, a military man by training and Commander in Chief of the armed forces, appeared on television after the sprawling studio complex was retaken by loyal troops. Wearing full-dress uniform resplendent with medals, he denounced the seizure of Parliament and pledged his faith in democracy.

restorative   *ri STAW ruh tiv*
capable of restoring or renewing health, strength, vitality)

To give up clams would be to give up the food that is most symbolic of childhood summers, when, after being parched by the salt and sun of Brooklyn beaches, we crossed the footbridge over Sheepshead Bay and swallowed clams more rapidly than they could be shucked at Lundy's open-air bar. The saline clams, as coolly restorative as an ocean breeze, satisfied both thirst and hunger, and stand in memory for the best and most carefree summers of my life.

reticent   *RE tuh suhnt*
not inclined to speak freely; reserved)

For the last six months, Samuel R. Pierce Jr. has remained one of the most reticent members of the Reagan Cabinet, earning the name "Silent Sam" among his own staff. Today, Mr. Pierce broke his silence.

Most Americans think of flowers as the centerpiece but never the main course. We like to see them, pick them, sniff them. But eat them? Not likely. Other cultures are less reticent about eating flowers.

retrenchment   *ri TRENCH muhnt*
(a cutting down or reducing; curtailing)

DENVER, July 4—Protecting gains made by blacks in a conservative atmosphere of Government retrenchment was the major task set before the 72d annual convention of the National Association for the Advancement of Colored People, which ended here last night.

retribution   *re truh BYOO: shuhn*
(deserved punishment for evil done)

Asserting that the criminal justice system has collapsed, Mr. Reagan made it clear that his Administration intended to put public safety ahead of offenders' rights. He criticized social thinkers for popularizing the idea that poverty and bad environment produced crime, and he called for a system of swift retribution for criminals.

retrospective   *re truh SPEK tiv*
(a representative exhibition of the lifetime work of an artist or of a particular period of art)

Beginning Saturday, the museum will celebrate its birthday with a retrospective honoring artists who have contributed to the growth of American crafts since World War II.

reverberate   *ri VER buh rayt*
(to re-echo or resound)

KOUROU, French Guiana, June 19—Western Europe's Ariane rocket rose from its jungle launching pad here today, the reverberations rolling across the wild coastal savanna, and successfully boosted two satellites into orbit around the earth.

revere   *ri VIR*
(to regard with love, deep respect and awe; venerate)

Jamaica was an island in mourning today following the death in Miami of the country's revered reggae star Bob Marley, whose music combined pop with protests against poverty and oppression.

revile   *ri VIGHL*
(to think or speak of with contempt)

CHIHUAHUA, Mexico, July 7 (AP)—Luz Corral de Villa, the widow of Pancho Villa, the Mexican general who was reviled as a bloodthirst bandit and revered as a revolutionary hero, died last night in this city in northern Mexico. She was 89 years old.

rhapsodic   *rap SAH dik*
(*extravagantly enthusiastic; ecstatic*)

Reviews of the massive book were generally rhapsodic, with one reviewer saying, "The three best novels I read this year were 'Gone With the Wind.' " J. Donald Adams, in The New York Times Book Review of July 5, 1936, wrote: "This is beyond a doubt one of the most remarkable first novels produced by an American writer. It is also one of the best. I would go so far as to say that it is, in narrative power, in sheer readability, surpassed by nothing in American fiction."

ribald   *RI buhld*
characterized by coarse or vulgar joking or mocking, especially dealing with sex in a humorously earthy or direct way)

Angel Cordero often screams and sings, and the other jockeys hurl ribald but friendly insults at one another. But Vasquez sequesters himself in front of his locker or beats his valet at backgammon in the jockeys' lounge, as he did yesterday while waiting for the Wood Memorial at Aqueduct.

rife   *righf*
abounding)

Most of the American musical idioms that preceded and shaped rock-and-roll were regarded "the Devil's music" at one time or another—especially the blues. Early blues lyrics are rife with satires on preachers, who are depicted as hypocrites with their minds on adultery and financial gain, and often the most uncompromising blues have suggested their own pragmatic value system as an alternative to Christian values.

"Music can stir the appetite for food, rebellion, immorality, indecency, dope addiction, filthy bodies and all the rest that goes with the devil's crowd. Parents should get acquainted with this because it is even creeping in through some well known Gospel Quartets and Gospel Music, because they are adopting the beat that is associated with the rock groups. This is not just speculation but bare facts, and can be proven. So if youth is rebelling better check the music it is listening to."

From The Budget, the Amish and
Mennonite newspaper, April 12, 1973.

---

riffle *RI fuhl*
(to leaf rapidly through, as by letting the edges or corners of the pages slip lightly across the thumb)

Mr. O'Neill, dressed in golf shirt and slacks, riffled through a heavily marked copy of the thick Republican budget bill and considered the final impressive volley of Presidential lobbying. "It was the old Lyndon Johnson style," he said. "Johnson knew how to move and these fellows know how to move."

rinky-dink *RING kee dingk*
(small-time; not modern or up-to-date; corny: a slang term)

What? Watch tug-of-war? "I thought it was going to be some rinky-dink competition," said Lynne Cox, manager of the United States women's water polo team, "but I stayed, mainly out of curiosity. And the thing really surprised me."

riposte *ri POHST*
(a sharp, swift response or retort: originally, a fencing term for a quick thrust after parrying a lunge)

Mr. Brezhnev gave his speech a conciliatory tone, with few echoes of the polemics that have issued from Washington and Moscow alike in the last few weeks. He chose, for example, to make no riposte to Mr. Reagan's rather sharp attack on the morality of the Soviet leadership.

risible *RI zuh buhl*
(laughable, amusing)

Meredith Monk's music, like nearly all the various manifestations of her art, can seem moving, exciting, beautiful and profoundly original—once one overcomes the impulse to find it pretentiously risible. Miss Monk i so earnestly strange in her precociously talented little-girl way that i takes a while to accept her premises and to appreciate her properly. Bu it's worth it to take that time.

roil *roil*
(to agitate; make angry; rile)

Whatever judgment is ultimately made of his performance, Mr. Koch remains, unless every opinion poll is dead wrong, the most popula mayor in two generations—a roiling, thumb-in-the-eye persona who ha come to typify a city that thrives on its self-image as an abrasive toug guy.

oman à clef   *raw MAHN ah KLAY*
a novel in which real persons appear under fictitious names: French,
ovel with a key)

In November, [Mr. Levin's] novel "The Architect," a roman à clef about the life of Frank Lloyd Wright, will be published by Simon & Schuster. It is described as the story of a Wisconsin youth who comes to Chicago in an era of robber barons and muckrakers and reshapes the American landscape.

oustabout   *ROW stuh bowt*
an unskilled or transient laborer, as on a ranch or in an oilfield)

Gulf takes 362,000 barrels of oil a day out of Nigeria. About 86 percent of its work force is Nigerian. A way had to be found to satisfy the 14 percent that is not Nigerian. The incentive that was worked out amounts to $2,000 a month tax-free for the lowest roustabout, and free flights to and from anywhere in the world that is home, in exchange for less than six months of labor a year.

ubato   *roo: BAH toh*
rhythmic flexibility within a musical phrase or measure: Italian, short
or tempo rubato, stolen time)

"In my conducting, I try not to be exaggerated," [Klaus Tennstedt] says. "It's just not necessary. There is rubato in all music, even Mozart, but it should not affect the outer flow of the music; it should be an expression of the inner unrest of every score. A compromise between head and heart is the alpha and omega of music."

Rubato involves varying the mechanical regularity of notes or phrases by lingering longer over some of them than the written music indicates, and making up the time by hurrying over others. The underlying tempo is maintained, as though a metronome were continuing to tick it off, but the musicians or singers are free to depart from the timing of notes and phrases as they have been set down in the written music. Just how rubato is employed in any performance depends upon the sensitivity and personal taste of the performer or conductor.

---

ubberneck   *RUH ber nek*
to stretch one's neck or turn one's head to gaze about in curiosity, as
a sightseer)

It is still enough to advertise a new play with little more than a photograph of Glenda Jackson's bony face. It is still enough for her merely to

walk through a downtown restaurant on the way to a table to throw th
entire bar into a frenzy of rubbernecking.

rube   *roo:b*
*(a naive, unsophisticated person from a rural region: slang nickname of
Reuben, a rustic name)*

Orchard and its network of satellite streets—Allen, Ludlow, Rivingto
Grand, Hester and Broome—are the closest thing New York has to
bazaar. And it is a bazaar in the real sense, for on Orchard Street ther
is no such phrase as "list price" and if you should fail to bargain you ris
revealing yourself as some sort of urban rube.

rubric   *ROO:brik*
*(a heading or title. In early books and manuscripts, a rubric was a
chapter heading, initial letter, or first sentence printed or written in red,
decorative lettering: Latin,* ruber, *red.)*

People are troubled by Mr. Sadat's arrest of many dissenters who wer
not directly involved in religious matters. Presumably, many of them fa
under the rubric of having "indirectly" fostered "sectarian sedition." Bu
the rationale has not been spelled out, and there is a tendency to see M
Sadat's crackdown as extending to all his vocal critics.

rudiments   *ROO: duh muhnts*
(fundamentals)

When the Lehmans enrolled their daughter in a music program at th
Henry Street Settlement on Manhattan's Lower East Side, they wer
encouraged to learn the rudiments of their child's instrument—the violi
—to help with practice at home.

rue   *roo:*
(to wish something undone or unmade; regret)

The Administration's attempt to lend decorum to Presidential news cor
ferences by choosing questioners by lot from President Reagan
jellybean jar was rued as an experiment in tepidness today. "I thir
old-style pandemonium is preferable," said Helen Thomas of Unite
Press International.

ruminate   *ROO: muh nayt*
*(to turn something over in the mind; meditate on: a mental chewing of
the cud, as ruminant animals like cattle, goats, deer and camels do)*

"I am working, not at the pace I used to take, but at a pace. Now is the time to ruminate, assess. I have more time with my children. And I have more time with Marian. Getting reacquainted with your wife is a nice thing to have happen to you." [Jacob K. Javits]

saccharine   *SA kuh rin*
(too sweet or syrupy: Latin, saccharum, *and Greek,* sakharon, *both sugar)*

"Good Morning America" affects a saccharine chumminess that might be comforting in a late-afternoon spot, when John Davidson and Merv Griffin woo the lonely. But in the morning, this much affability is too much.

sacred cow   *SAY krid KOW*
(anything treated as immune from criticism or change: an allusion to the fact that the Hindus hold the cow sacred)

In looking for ways to help cut the Federal budget, Secretary of Education Bell needed to look no farther than his department's most sacred cow—college student aid. His assault is heresy to colleges and parents who have run up the program to an annual cost of nearly $5 billion. Tuition assistance has grown by 150 percent in just three years, epitomizing the Government's loss of control over spending. Mr. Bell is looking in a fair and proper place.

sacrosanct   *SA kroh sangkt*
(very sacred, holy or inviolable)

"Judges are not sacrosanct," the Mayor said yesterday in an early morning WNYC radio broadcast. "They believe they are above any kind of criticism by the Mayor. They are not."

salacious   *suh LAY shuhs*
(erotically stimulating; pornographic)

Condemned as salacious trash by some critics but praised as a master piece by many others, Nabokov's "Lolita" became an instant best-selle and soon gained wide recognition as one of the classics of modern literature—a brilliant evocation of one man's obsessional search for paradise lost amid the wilderness of roadside America.

salad days   *SAL ad DAYZ*
(one's fresh, vigorous, early years of life)

In my salad days, I used to fasten my speared fish to a line at my waist and keep on swimming. Now I go ashore with each fish.

"My salad days, when I was green in judgment" is spoken by Cleopatra in Shakespeare's "Antony and Cleopatra." Shakespeare created dozens of other phrases and expressions still used today. Among them: led by the nose, wear the heart on the sleeve, the naked truth, eat out of house and home, flaming youth, fancy free, too much of a good thing, at one fell swoop, forever and a day, play the fool, it was Greek to me, itching palm, die a slow death and truth will out.

---

salmagundi   *sal muh GUHN di*
(a mixture: originally, of minced veal, chicken or turkey; anchovies or pickled herrings; and onions, all chopped together and served with lemon juice and oil)

The 30's, keyed to songs from or about movies, leans on warm nostalgia —Fred Astaire, George Gershwin, "Gone With the Wind"—and the 40's is a mixture of wartime sentimentality and the emergence of Latin music from south of the border. This musical salmagundi is carried off by a versatile and tremendously hard-working cast of two women and three men who are simultaneously waiting on tables while they are performing.

salvo   *SAL voh*
(a simultaneous discharge of firearms)

The opening salvo in the bidding war for Conoco Inc. was fired on Thursday, June 25, when Joseph E. Seagram & Sons, the American subsidiary of the huge Canadian liquor company, offered $73 a share in cash for 35 million shares, or 40.7 percent, of Conoco's 86.8 million shares.

sanctimonious   *sangk tuh MOH ni uhs*
(pretending to be pious or righteous)

Needless to say, most treatments of sex-and-violence subjects are couched in the rhetoric of noble motivations. The film or news report is always offered as an exercise in consciousness-raising, designed to alert the country to some festering social problem. In fact, television seems to have entered what might be called an era of sanctimonious sensationalism.

sanguine   *SANG gwin*
(cheerful and confident; optimistic; hopeful)

A Western diplomat in Moscow not known for his sanguine views of Soviet intentions toward Poland was mildly optimistic last week. "They've got the safety catch on," he said. "But we'd better keep listening for that click."

sartorial   *sahr TAW ri uhl*
(pertaining to clothing or dress, especially men's)

If a player who last played tournament bridge half a century ago returned to the fray today he would be struck not so much by the improvement in bidding conventions as by the deterioration in sartorial conventions. Black ties have given way to T-shirts and blue jeans.

savage   *SA vij*
(to attack in a violent way)

A 3½-hour version of "Heaven's Gate" was withdrawn last November after it was savaged by critics. The new 2-hour 25-minute version received equally negative reviews.

savoir-faire   *sa vwahr FAIR*
(knowledge of just what to do in any situation: French, knowing how to do)

Then the lights dimmed and Connie Cook, the fresh-faced model with the short blond hair, sauntered down the runway with the savoir-faire of Fred Astaire. Like the dancer, she wore white tie and tails.

savvy   *SA vi*
(shrewd; in-the-know; discerning: Spanish, sabe usted, *do you know?)*

A savvy, middle-class Warsaw resident mapped out the city like a battle zone: On this side of Marszalkowska Street you can usually find bread; over here the meat lines aren't so long; vegetables are better here.

saw   *saw*
(an old saying, often repeated; maxim; proverb)

The old saw that it is easy to stop smoking—as Mark Twain said, "I ought to know because I've done it a thousand times"—is all too familiar to millions of smokers who would like to kick the habit.

Saw: A trite popular saying, or proverb. So called because it makes its way into a wooden head.
Ambrose Bierce, "The Devil's Dictionary," 1911.

---

scapegoat   SKAYP goht
(a person, group or thing upon whom the blame for the mistakes or crimes of others is thrust)

Because it has roots in Islam, [Baha'i] has been viewed as heretical by the Islamic clergy. What has made Baha'is more vulnerable is their relative prosperity and professional success—tempting scapegoats in a revolutionary country with a floundering economy and an aimless war.

Scapegoat, meaning the goat that escapes, was coined in 1530 by the English biblical translator William Tyndale (1494–1536), whose translations formed the basis of the Authorized Version of the Bible and thus one of the foundations of modern English. He was imprisoned in 1535 for his professed Lutheran beliefs and his attacks on papal supremacy, and, condemned for heresy, was burned at the stake.

The scapegoat was a goat over whose head the high priest of the ancient Jews confessed the sins of the people on the Day of Atonement, after which it was allowed to escape into the wilderness.

---

scatological   ska tuh LAH ji kuhl
(obscene; dirty)

"The Choir Boys," a lousy movie, was a wonderful novel, and almost impossible to review in a family newspaper. The language of cops who have seen too much of the corruption of the world, and have done some corrupting themselves, is necessarily scatological.

---

schlock   shlahk
(anything cheap or inferior; trash: Yiddish)

If you ask Samuel Klein what Klein's of Monticello, 105 Orchard, specializes in, he'll tell you, "We don't have any bottom-of-the-line children's schlock here." And he hasn't. This is a children's wear store with piles of Izod, Cardin, John Weitz, Gant and Quoddy.

schmooze   *shmoo:z*
(*to have a friendly, gossipy, prolonged, heart-to-heart talk: in "The Joys of Yiddish," Leo Rosten says, "I have never encountered a word that conveys 'heart-to-heart chit-chat' as warmly as does schmooze"; Yiddish*)

"Idle time is something he's never learned to live with," his close friend John Trubin once said. "He has an agenda for everything—even relaxation. He's not a guy who can sit around and schmooze."

scourge   *skerj*
(*a cause of serious trouble, affliction or calamity*)

Epidemic typhus, the scourge of many of the armies of World War I, has been a rarity in this country since the early 1920's.

scrupulous   *SKROO: pyuh luhs*
(*minutely careful*)

It was clear in interviews that the former hostages were scrupulously trying to avoid criticizing one another, and it was equally clear that, although many interviews were detailed, aspects of the story are yet to be told.

scurrilous   *SKER uh luhs*
(*using indecent or abusive language; coarse; vulgar*)

It was a mock television commercial for the fictitious "United Chemical Company" of the very real Piscataway, N.J., and it portrayed a supposedly brain-damaged worker eating his lunch amid clouds of noxious chemical dust. The skit, on NBC's "Saturday Night Live" on March 7, did not seem funny to the folks in Piscataway, where Mayor Robert Smith called it a "scurrilous attack" that had "damaged my town and its national reputation."

seamless   *SEEM luhs*
(*with no noticeable separation; perfectly cohesive*)

One of the unusual things about Mr. Matthau's performance in "First Monday in October" is that he blends comic and serious moments seamlessly. In one scene he delivers a eulogy over the grave of a dead Justice, and yet he also includes many comic flourishes.

sedition   *si DI shuhn*
(*the stirring up of discontent, resistance or rebellion against the government in power*)

AMRITSAR, India—A 49-year-old former teacher sits cross-legged in the room he dares not leave for fear of arrest and explains passionately if seditiously how he advocates the creation of a Sikh nation to be wrenched violently from India.

seethe   *seeth:*
(to be violently agitated or disturbed; boiling)

Mr. Sands, who spent a third of his life in jail for terrorist crimes, had joined the I.R.A. at the age of 18. And the teen-agers of Twinbrook, seething with a hatred that passes from generation to generation, still provide a pool of potential talent for the illegal organization.

segue   *SAY gway*
(to proceed without pause from one musical number or theme to another, or from one scene into another, as in film or radio drama)

"Kent State" opens with a documentary collage of 1960's images—John F. Kennedy and hula hoops, Martin Luther King and the Beatles, moon walks and Woodstock, the Vietnam "living room war" and peace marches, all of which segue into the Thursday, April 30, 1970 television speech in which President Richard M. Nixon announced the secret bombings of Cambodia.

seminal   *SE muh nuhl*
(like a seed in being a source)

Professor Longhair, the New Orleans pianist and singer who played a seminal role in the development of rhythm and blues and, later, rock-and-roll, died of a heart attack in January 1980, but his music lives on.

semiotic   *se mi AH tik*
(pertaining to signs)

In "Family Photographs: Content, Meaning and Effect," Julia Hirsch teaches us to read, semiotically, the expressions, groupings, activities, gestures and relationships in such photographs. She observes that the formal family photograph is based on Renaissance portraiture filtered through 19th-century sentimentality, which leaned toward the "romantic agony" look of generalized longing.

send-up   *SEN duhp*
(a parody; takeoff; spoof: originally, British public-school slang meaning to send a boy to the headmaster to be punished)

In Blake Edwards's movie "S.O.B.," most of the actors give portrayals that are devastating send-ups of people connected with the Hollywood film industry. Perhaps none is more devastating than that of Loretta Swit, who plays Polly Reed, a powerful, ruthless, screeching, foulmouthed gossip columnist known as "the mouth of Hollywood."

sequester   *si KWE ster*
(to keep separate, secure or secluded)

State Department officials said Colonel Qaddafi, who once freely walked the streets of Libya, playing soccer with children, had virtually sequestered himself. His barrack in the Tripoli suburb of Aziya is ringed with antiaircraft artillery, machine guns and tanks.

seraglio   *si RA lyoh*
(harem)

A television audience confronted with quality goods is as unnatural as an archbishop in a seraglio. The natural instinct is to run.

seraphic   *suh RA fik*
(angelic)

What needs to be established right away—for those still afflicted with the image of Mr. Shankar as some seraphic guru for the millions—is that he is not only the greatest living master of the sitar, but also one of the most masterly instrumentalists of any sort in the world today.

serendipity   *se ruhn DI puh ti*
(an aptitude for making fortunate discoveries accidentally)

In 1977, when American scientists traveled to the Indian Ocean to observe the occultation of a star by Uranus, they made a serendipitous discovery. They saw that Uranus had at least six faint rings around it. Later observations detected nine rings.

———

Occultation, in astronomy, is an eclipse in which the apparent size of the eclipsed body is much smaller than that of the eclipsing body.

———

serrated   *SE ray tid*
(having sawlike notches along the edge)

For those who cannot even be bothered juggling four pieces at a summer lawn party, Hammacher Schlemmer has come up with the all-purpose dinner-size buffet utensil, which it advertises as a combined fork, knife and spoon, albeit in stainless steel. It resembles the old ice cream fork with the added advantage of having a serrated edge. And a plastic version of this, called a spork, is making its way through school cafeterias.

shoal   *shohl*
(*a large school of fish*)

Riding the tides of summer once again are great shoals of jellyfish, which flourish in the warm coastal shallows through the brief season of their maturity.

short list
(*a narrowed-down list of applicants or candidates from which a final selection will be made, especially for a job or position*)

White House and Justice Department officials have produced a "tentative short list" of possible nominees for the Supreme Court and plan to interview some candidates before making a recommendation to President Reagan, Administration officials said today.

showboat   *SHOH boht*
(*to show off; be an exhibitionist*)

"It was during the N.I.T. at Madison Square Garden," Auerbach said. "His talent for dribbling caught my eye—behind his back and between his legs, an extraordinary feat for someone 6-8. I'll tell you this, the kid was not showboating, I know showboating when I see it. He had great body control, quickness and very fluid moves."

showcase   *SHOH kays*
(*to exhibit or display*)

WIMBLEDON, England, June 28—On the same day that John McEnroe threw a temper tantrum on the No. 1 court, a woman sat in the umpire's chair for the first time on center court at the All England Club. No place showcases the shifting, unsettled world of professional tennis better than Wimbledon.

shtick   *shtik*
(*a gimmick, act or routine, especially in a show or performance: Yiddish, a piece*)

The walk-around is the little routine done twice, maybe three or four times, as the clowns parade around the three rings between the acts, such as a shtick that involves a slip on a big banana peel repeated for each side of the house.

simplistic   *sim PLI stik*
(making complex problems unrealistically simple; oversimplified)

Some Presidential scholars like James David Barber of Duke University discount Mr. Reagan's upbeat speeches as simplistic and unrealistic cheerleading without clear purpose and vision. They expect him to be a fairly passive President, a throwback to the conservative, probusiness quietism of Warren G. Harding or William Howard Taft.

sine qua non   *SI nay KWAH nohn*
(an essential condition; indispensable thing: Latin, without which not)

Living in the desert for 8,000 years, one must develop some skills with which to cope. The Bedouins, a declining 700,000 people in Saudi Arabia who live in the deserts of the Arabian Peninsula, have mastered their environment. They can predict the weather, the sine qua non of an outdoor existence, and tell from footprints a person's size and sex and, if the footprints' owner is female, whether she is pregnant.

sinuous   *SI nyoo uhs*
(bending, winding or curving in and out; serpentine)

At its center is the Paseo del Rio, or Riverwalk, a cozy, old-world collection of restaurants, sidewalk cafés, nightspots and hotels strewn like jewels along the sinuous San Antonio River as it flows through the downtown area 15 feet or so below street level.

skulduggery   *skuhl DUH guh ri*
(sneaky, dishonest behavior; trickery)

And the requirement that high-level casino jobs "go first to New Jersey residents" invites political skulduggery.

skulk   *skuhlk*
(to move about stealthily; sneak)

British rock bands make New York debuts frequently these days, but most of them sort of skulk into town, victims of record-company austerity and the new wave's own antipretensions. Not so Spandau Ballet, which gave its New York first local performance Wednesday night at the Underground with a full, nostalgically old-fashioned blast of hype, complete with a London vanguard fashion show and a disco full of exotically costumed trendies.

skunk   *skuhngk*
(to defeat overwhelmingly in a game or contest, especially while keeping the opponent from scoring: a slang word)

Obviously, the President has no intention of again taking all the heat for trimming Social Security benefits, not after his Administration's proposal to cut early retirement pensions was skunked, 96-0, in the Senate.

smorgasbord   *SMAWR guhs bawrd*
(a wide variety of appetizers and other tasty foods served buffet style: Swedish; here used figuratively)

With little fanfare, a few major insurers have been experimenting with group auto coverage in the expectation that it will eventually take its place on the corporate smorgasbord of employee benefits.

snipe   *snighp*
(to direct an attack in a sly or underhanded way)

The significance and goal of the visit, the officials said, was in creating what one American called "good mood music" between Mr. Reagan and Mr. Schmidt so that the political sniping between Bonn and Washington that marked the term of President Carter would stop.

sniper   *SNIGH per*
(one who shoots at an enemy from a hidden position: originally, a sniper was a hunter of snipe, a tasty bird of marsh and swamp that is so wary that hunters must often lie concealed for hours before they can bag one)

A sniper attack on a convoy of coal trucks left two drivers injured yesterday as striking members of the United Mine Workers tried to close nonunion coal operations in Kentucky, the police said.

sobriquet   *SOH bri kay*
(a nickname)

When the building opened, it was only 25 percent rented, earning it the sobriquet of the Empty State Building. It did not really begin to fill up until after the Depression.

A sobriquet is a nickname so closely attached to a person, place or thing as to be understandable when used in its place. Examples follow:

Eternal City (Rome)
Empire State (New York)
Emerald Isle (Ireland)
Great Emancipator (Abraham Lincoln)
Great White Way (Broadway)
king of beasts (the lion)
redcoats (British soldiers)
Big Apple (New York City)
Frisco (San Francisco)

Yankees (Americans)
Sol (the sun)
Uncle Sam (U.S.A.)
Paris of the East (Saigon)
Little Flower (Fiorello La Guardia)
Schnozzola (Jimmy Durante)
Stan the Man (Stan Musial)
Brown Bomber (Joe Louis)
Dixie (the South)

sodden   SAH din
(*heavy or soggy as a result of improper cooking or baking*)

It's fashionable and fun to put down British cooking. Americans love to make jokes about sodden brussels sprouts and dishes with names like Toad in the Hole.

soigné   swah NYAY
(*carefully or elegantly done, operated or designed; well-groomed: French*)

Not many years ago it was hard to imagine a sharper contrast than Manhattan and Secaucus, N.J. On one side of the river stood gleaming towers, marking the very latest in soigné sophistication. On the other side were the swine, 250,000 of them in 55 Secaucus piggeries. Manhattan had That Look. Secaucus had That Smell.

sommelier   sah muhl YAY
(*a wine steward: French, originally a person in charge of pack animals*)

Mr. Rowan knew which wine he wanted to order, but the process took far longer than it should have. Finally the bottle arrived, and the sommelier uncorked it with a flourish and presented the cork for inspection, whereupon Mr. Rowan put it in his mouth and chewed it up. He sagely nodded his head, indicating that the cork had been approved, and motioned for the horrified sommelier to pour the wine. As the glasses were filled, Mr. Rowan kept spitting out bits of cork and nodding his head in approval. "The guy never even smiled," he said, "but the others at his table were practically falling off their chairs."

sonority　　*suh NAW ruh ti*
(full, deep or rich: said of sound)

Mr. O'Riley likes big sonorities, and attacks the keyboard energetically. When he played the Brahms F-minor Piano Quintet, he all but made a little concerto out of it. He is a pianist with temperament and a big style.

sophomoric　　*sah fuh MAW rik*
(self-assured, intellectually pretentious and opinionated, though imma-ture and superficial: Greek, sophos, *wise* + moros, *foolish)*

Some of the people who make pop music just want to be entertaining and to make money, but even the ones with the loftiest ambitions, the ones who want to make art, want to make *popular* art. Any discussion of the vitality of popular music has to take the vitality of what's popular into account, and when what's popular is mostly sophomoric, played-by-the-book hard rock, along with the usual smattering of sentimental pop ballads, popular music just could be in trouble.

sotto voce　　*SAH toh VOH chi*
(in a low voice, so as not to be heard: Italian, under the voice)

On another occasion, in a group of people, I said that my daughter's name was Cambria—"Latin for Wales," I added, and I heard a woman say to another, sotto voce, "Imagine naming your daughter after a fish!"

soupçon　　*soo:p SOHN*
(a tiny amount; slight trace: French, a suspicion)

The staggeringly high prices are staunchly defended by Mr. Tannen. The famous "21" hamburger, for example, which is priced at $13.50, contains only the finest sirloin and tenderloin, with a soupçon of celery, he says, all of which is lovingly hand-mixed and hand-patted.

Spartan　　*SPAHR tin*
(having only the bare necessities; austere: the people of the ancient Greek city-state of Sparta were noted for their frugal, highly disciplined and rigorously simple way of life)

The most imposing building is the Kun Lun Hotel, where we stayed. It has a somber gray facade, Roman-style pillars in the lobby and Cyrillic letters on the elevator buttons, a sign of Russian technical assistance. Our room was Spartan, its one touch of luxury a locally woven rug that partly covered the painted wooden floor.

spawning ground   *SPAW ning GROWND*

(a place where fish or other water animals lay their eggs or produce their young; figuratively, a place where an idea or movement is born)

Berkeley, the spawning ground of the Free Speech Movement, student revolt and the antiwar movement, has in recent years become something of a laboratory for leftist municipal government. The city passed an initiative against police enforcement of marijuana laws, offered asylum to draft resisters and sent its mayor on trips to Cuba, Mexico City, Vienna and Madrid in pursuit of leftist causes.

sporadic   *spaw RA dik*

(happening at irregular intervals; scattered; appearing singly or apart from each other)

The eerie nighttime howls that are being sporadically heard more and more often near suburban homes in the eastern United States are signs to wildlife biologists that the coyote, which once freely roamed eastern America in the Pleistocene Epoch and later was driven out, has returned.

spurious   *SPYOO ri uhs*

(not genuine; false; counterfeit)

Note: I've just eaten a large plate of crow. I am now satisfied that the document on El Salvador discussed in my column last Friday, which I believed was an official paper, was indeed spurious, as the State Department later said. Many of the facts checked out, but it wasn't a Government paper. I'm abashed.

To eat crow is to undergo the embarrassment or humiliation of having to retract a statement or admit an error. Brewer's "Dictionary of Phrase and Fable" says: "The expression derives from an incident during an armistice of the War of 1812. A New Englander unwittingly crossed the British lines while hunting and brought down a crow. An unarmed British officer heard the shot and determined to punish the offender. He gained hold of the American's gun by praising his marksmanship and asking to see his weapon. The Britisher then told the American he was guilty of trespass and forced him at the point of the gun to take a bite out of the crow. When the officer returned the gun the American in his turn covered the soldier and compelled him to eat the remainder of the crow."

----

staid   *stayd*

(settled and steady)

In midlife, Paul Gauguin left his wife, family and a staid bank job to live in the South Seas and paint.

stalemate   *STAYL mayt*
(an unresolved situation in which further action is impossible or useless; deadlock)

Egypt and Israel recently resumed their stalemated talks on autonomy for the 1.3 million Palestinian Arabs in the Israeli-occupied West Bank and Gaza Strip. More meetings are scheduled, but the assassination of Mr. Sadat may defer them.

stamp   *stamp*
(a distinctive mark or character)

Meanwhile, Mrs. Reagan and her co-hosts had telephoned invitations to 120 people. The guest list had a definite West Coast stamp and included Mrs. Reagan's hairdresser and her interior decorator.

stanchion   *STAN shuhn*
(an upright bar, beam or post used as a support)

In old comic books it was simple: When Clark Kent needed to turn into Superman, he stepped into a phone booth. But in the 1978 Superman movie he pauses at a pay phone only to find that, alas, it offers no privacy: It's mounted on a stanchion, and below waist level it's completely open to public view.

stasis   *STAY sis*
(a state of equilibrium, balance or stagnancy)

MOSCOW, March 5—"The word for it is stasis," a Western diplomat said. "No new people, no new ideas. . . ." He was referring to the 26th Congress of the Communist Party of the Soviet Union, the fourth such gathering presided over by Leonid I. Brezhnev, the party leader. The congress ended this week in a glow of unanimity and confirmation of the Soviet status quo.

state of the art   *STAYT uhv thi AHRT*
(the level of scientific or technological development in a given field or industry at the present, or at any designated time)

The quaint and cramped 425-seat Old Globe is being re-created as a 580-seat, $6.5 million, state-of-the-art theater with removable walls, dressing-room space for 52 actors and a thrust stage that can convert to a proscenium.

stentorian   sten TAW ri uhn
(*very loud: Stentor, a Greek herald in the Trojan War, is described in the "Iliad" as having the voice of fifty men*)

Sometimes Mr. Jagger reaches for notes that aren't there, but the Rolling Stones have never been a letter-perfect band. The current vogue for stentorian quasi-operatic rock singing, as exemplified by performers like Pat Benatar or Meat Loaf, is foreign to their idea of what rock-and-roll is supposed to be.

stereotype   STE ri uh tighp
(*a fixed or conventional notion or conception of a person, group, idea, etc., held by a number of people, and allowing for no individuality or critical judgment*)

"A significant number of the Miami rioters were not poor or unemployed or members of the criminal class," the study contends. "Many held jobs and did not otherwise fit the stereotypical image of a 'rioter.' "

stigma   STIG muh
(*a mark of disgrace or reproach; a stain, as on one's reputation*)

He stressed that going to a vocational college apparently still carried a stigma, despite high salary possibilities for experienced machinists. "Many kids are downplayed—pushed down—by advisers and parents saying that, if they don't do well in English and math, they can go to a vocational college," he said.

stipple   STI puhl
(*to dot or fleck*)

It was 5:30 A.M. when Mr. Wood, in hip waders and yellow suspenders, and John Bartow, in a plaid shirt and jeans, navigated their skinny gray clam boat through the maze of marshes stippling Hempstead Bay.

stipulate   STI pyuh layt
(*to require as an essential condition in making an agreement*)

Salmon was once a cheap fish, as prevalent as chicken today. It was so plentiful that servants in Colonial America had clauses in their contracts stipulating that they could not be served salmon more than a certain number of times a week.

stoic   STOH ik
(unemotional; impassive)

Female Secret Service agents, like males, tend to wear raincoats, business suits, dark glasses and stoic expressions.

stoicism   STOH i si zuhm
(impassiveness under suffering, bad fortune, etc.)

Besides discussing the comforting of dying people and their families, Dr. Kübler-Ross also brings up the often-neglected question of the hospital staff and their emotional needs. Their professional stoicism, she says, is just another one of the masks we put on to hide from death, and they ought to be free to grieve too, in their special ways.

Zeno of Citium (334?–262 B.C.) was the founder of the school of philosophy known as Stoicism, called that because Zeno taught his followers in the Stoa Poikite, or Painted Colonnade, a building at the foot of the Acropolis in ancient Athens. Stoicism stresses virtue as the highest good, and the strict control of the passions and appetites. Indifference to the external world and to passion, Zeno taught, leads to an inner happiness and self-mastery.

---

stolid   STAH lid
(unemotional; impassive)

In firm and clear English, the Pope spoke in generalities that nevertheless plainly applied to Mr. Marcos's decision to suspend civil rights and rule under martial law from 1972 until last month. "Even in exceptional situations that may at times arise, one can never justify any violation of the fundamental dignity of the human person or of the basic rights that safeguard this dignity," the Pope declared as Mr. Marcos sat stolidly on one of the thronelike gilt chairs on the stage.

strident   STRIGH duhnt
(harsh-sounding; shrill; grating)

As every feminist knows, those women who bide their time and are silent often live to reap the benefits won for them by others who spoke out and were called strident.

Stygian   *STI ji uhn*
(dark or gloomy: like the hellish region of the river Styx, in Greek mythology. The shades of the dead were rowed across the Styx to their eternal home in Hades, the underworld.)

Just west of the Hilton Hotel's northern wall is Eddie Condon's, a re-incarnation in name of the old Condon's of 35 years ago on West Street. This Condon's is a long, narrow and dark, but not Stygian room at No. 144, just a few doors east of the block's other jazz retreat, Jimmy Ryan's.

stymie   *STIGH mi*
(to hinder or obstruct: originally a golf term for the condition that exists on a putting green when an opponent's ball lies in a direct line between the player's ball and the hole)

The state Fair Political Practices Commission had asked district attorneys here [Los Angeles] and in Sacramento to review evidence that Brown aides had altered or destroyed documents, including 3,000 name and address cards, and withheld others in an effort to stymie a commission inquiry into whether a computer system leased with state money had been used for political purposes.

subculture   *SUHB kuhl cher*
(a group having social, economic, ethnic or other traits distinctive enough to distinguish it from others within the same culture or society)

Though most large cities have their garish honky-tonk sections where prostitution, drugs and other vices can be found late at night, West 42d Street seems to stand apart with its entrenched lawless subculture that threatens outsiders—with the exception of a small group of "alumni" who hold down jobs but return to the street to partake of the excitement and see old friends.

subservient   *suhb SER vi uhnt*
(submissive; obedient; compliant)

Instead of advising the women who are listening to them to "Stand By Your Man," as a more traditional country singer like Tammy Wynette would do, Miss Cash and Miss Carter encourage them to be true to themselves. They challenge the decorous and often subservient roles women have traditionally played in country music by singing songs that assert their independence and that are relatively explicit sexually, and by mixing their country music with jolting rock-and-roll.

substantive   *SUHB stuhn tiv*
(of considerable amount or quantity; substantial)

Time Inc. said today that it had received a handful of inquiries but no substantive purchase offers for The Washington Star, which is to cease publication in two weeks.

subterfuge   *SUHB ter fyoo:j*
(a plan or action used to hide one's true objective or evade a difficult or unpleasant situation)

When we were recognized, it became impossible to order the duck or pheasant pâtés. On three attempts we were told they were not fresh, yet both were on display and both were being served to other guests. Finally, through a bit of subterfuge, we did manage to try both. Though the duck proved acceptable, the pheasant was indeed stale.

succès de scandale   *suhk SE duh skan DAHL*
(notoriety gained by something scandalous, as a shocking play, movie, novel, etc.: French, success of scandal)

Over the years, many of Mr. Malle's films have proved controversial indeed. His second feature film "The Lovers," which brought him early fame at the age of 26, created something of a succès de scandale when it won a special prize at the Venice Film Festival in 1958. Portraying a woman who leaves her husband for a young lover, it was condemned by censors for what were then regarded as dangerously explicit sex scenes.

succès d'estime   *suhk SE de STEEM*
(an artistic work receiving acclaim from professional critics, often without being a financial success: French, success of esteem)

Though the benefit was a succès d'estime, its financial intake was something less than the $20,000 hoped for.

succinct   *suhk SINGKT*
(clearly and briefly stated; terse)

At an awards luncheon at the Harvard Club, Mr. Steig was succinct. "I'm a writer, not a talker," he said. "Thank you."

succumb   *suh KUHM*
(to yield or submit; die)

Post-mortem studies of birds that lived on such rivers as the Thames, Trent and Avon showed that more than 50 percent of the birds had succumbed to lead poisoning after ingesting lead fishing weights. The rest had up to three times the normal amounts of lead in their blood.

Where desserts are concerned, almost everyone I know is guilty of succumbing to one alluring vice or another.

suffuse   suh FYOO:Z
(to overspread)

Since the tall Gothic church was built over a century ago, it has been the center of the quiet village and within its walls the lives of the people have been suffused with the rituals and teachings of the Roman Catholic faith.

sully   SUH li
(to soil or stain by disgracing or dishonoring)

There are boxing people and fans who feel that passing scandals cannot seriously smirch a sport that has thrived in a state of sullied reputation for as long as punches have been thrown for pay in this country. A man enjoying a mudbath is intrepid when threatened with mudslinging.

summarily   suh MAI ruh li
(promptly and without formality)

At least two dozen of Mr. Bani-Sadr's aides were detained. About 40 people who demonstrated in his support last weekend were arrested and summarily killed. A poster at the Justice Ministry offered "a place in heaven" to anyone with information leading to Mr. Bani-Sadr's arrest.

superannuated   soo: per A nyoo ay tid
(discharged from service, especially with a pension, because of old age or infirmity; antiquated)

One striking thing to be noticed in this biography is the qualitative change over the years in Miss Callas's circle of associates. Increasingly, her days and nights were spent in the company of the world's silly people: the Elsa Maxwells, the superannuated princes, the dress designers, the perfume heiresses.

superficial   soo: per FI shuhl
(on the surface; shallow)

The whale had first tried to beach itself on Coney Island Wednesday night, but it was nudged back out to sea by a police launch. Early the next morning, it was discovered off Oak Beach. A gash on the side of the whale was found to be superficial, apparently caused when it scraped against the ocean bottom.

Mr. Denver has a strong, steady folk-pop baritone, but his mechanical style of declamation turns almost everything he sings into a semiformal campfire sing-along. Even though his 30-song repertory included country, folk, pop, blue grass and Stephen Foster, Mr. Denver and his nine musicians made only superficial stylistic distinctions.

supernumerary   *soo: per NOO: muh rai ri*
(a person considered extra; someone superfluous)

Until Mr. Hoffa tapped him as his temporary stand-in when he left for prison, Mr. Fitzsimmons, a chubby, rather inarticulate man, was something of a figure of ridicule in the teamsters' hierarchy. He was known as Mr. Hoffa's "gopher," the supernumerary who would go for coffee or hold chairs.

supersede   *soo: per SEED*
(to cause to be obsolete; replace; supplant)

The book, "The World Challenge," predicts that industrial society will be superseded in the 1980's by a computerized society in which microchips will replace manpower.

supple   *SUH puhl*
(easily bent; flexible; pliant)

A strong contender for the niftiest new hat in town is made in England of soft brown felt, has a pigskin band, is supple enough to stuff in an attaché case and is $39.50 at Paul Stuart, Madison Avenue at 45th Street.

surfeited   *SER fuh tid*
(filled to excess or overflowing)

The Pope had been shot—a consummate act of terror in a world surfeited with it.

surreal   *suh REEL*
(bizarre; fantastic; grotesque)

In Guyana, the People's Temple becomes a surreal setting for paranoia, sinister threats and outright insanity. Followers approach the Jones throne to swear that they will kill themselves and their children rather than surrender to the "capitalists" or "fascists."

Surreal derives from *Surrealism,* a modern movement in art and literature, in which an attempt is made to portray and interpret the workings of the unconscious mind as manifested in dreams: it is characterized by an irrational, noncontextual arrangement of material. Salvador Dali (b. 1904) is the best known painter of the Surrealist movement, whose roots can be traced as far back as the Dutch painter Hieronymus Bosch (1450?–1516).

---

surreptitious   *suh ruhp TI shuhs*
(acting in a secret, stealthy way)

Sergeant Lopez found that "day-to-day life was pretty much boredom." But he enlivened it for his fellow captives by sketching cartoons that, said Mr. Morefield, "became a tremendous morale factor. Some of them were just devastating," he said. At first, the sketches were passed around surreptitiously. Then the captors—who presumably did not understand some of the nuances—permitted them to be posted on a wall near where hostages would be taken to watch propaganda films on videotape.

surrogate   *SER uh git*
(substitute)

Lord Mountbatten, who was killed by Irish republican terrorists in 1979, was a cousin of the Queen and a kind of surrogate grandfather to Prince Charles.

suzerainty   *SOO: zuh rin ti*
(control over something, in the manner of a suzerain, or feudal lord)

Some date the current travails of the city's subway system to 1971, a period when Dr. William J. Ronan's suzerainty over the Metropolitan Transportation Authority was total. That year the voters rejected a $2.5 billion transportation bond issue, an act, according to these historians of our decrepit system, that hastened the decline and stall of the wholly Ronan empire.

swan song   *SWAHN SAWNG*
(the last act or final creative work of a person: from the false belief that the swan sings beautifully just before it dies. Various species of swan do honk, croak or emit a whistle-like sound. Some never utter a note. But none sings.)

It was Judge William Hughes Mulligan's final decision before leaving the United States Court of Appeals in Manhattan. The case involved smuggling rare swans from Canada, and so, in what he called his "swan song," Judge Mulligan filed a 12-page decision this week peppered with painful puns and other attempts at judicial humor. Calling the appeal a *rara avis*, Judge Mulligan said the two suspects had worked "hand and claw" in what he called a nefarious practice.

A *rara avis* (Latin, a rare bird) is an unusual or extraordinary person or thing; a phenomenon; a rarity. The term was first applied by the Roman poet Juvenal (60?–130?) to the black swan of Australia.

---

sweatshop   *SWET shahp*
(a shop or factory where employees work long hours at low wages under poor working conditions)

While sweatshop conditions vary, there is a grim sameness to the basic appearance: rows of women bent over sewing machines, separated by narrow aisles often made impassable by dress racks and piles of piece goods.

sybaritic   *si buh RI tik*
(fond of luxury and self-indulgence; hedonistic: the people of Sybaris, a Greek colony in southern Italy, were known for their love of luxury and pursuit of pleasure)

A few years ago ready-to-wear boutiques were opening so fast that even the most inveterate shopper could not keep track of them. Now it is lingerie shops. Not corset shops. Not hosiery shops. Simply places where women can indulge their Sybaritic urges for lace teddies, silk nightgowns, satin negligees and marabou bed jackets.

symbiotic   *sim bee AH tik*
(interdependent, as in an association of two forms of life to their mutual advantage. For example, some species of birds feed on the insects they find on the backs of rhinoceroses and other wild animals.)

Movies and electronic games have a symbiotic relationship. Theater owners make extra dollars by installing two or three games in the lobby.

synergism   *SI ner ji zuhm*
(the simultaneous action of separate agencies which, together, have greater total effect than the sum of their individual effects: said especially of drugs)

In an interview, Dr. Lewin said that the combination of alcohol, which is also a depressant, with other sedatives or hypnotic drugs often created a synergistic effect that could cause a collapse of the central nervous system, with resulting coma and respiratory or cardiac failure.

synthesize   *SIN thuh sighz*
(to form by bringing together separate parts)

The Mujahedeen, most of them young, who tried to synthesize Islamic religious traditions and modern Socialist thought, have been severely attacked by Ayatollah Khomeini and the clerics.

tableau   *ta BLOH*
(*a representation of a scene, picture, etc., by a person or group in costume, posing silently without moving: French, short for* tableau vivant, *living picture.* Tableaux *is the plural.*)

Dolls have been making a whimsical journey in a fantasy world at the Museum of the City of New York, Fifth Avenue at 103d Street. They don't actually move, but in a series of tableaux they are to be seen waking up, packing their trunks, traveling through forests, a jungle and a desert to an ocean, and finally arriving at their destination: the museum itself.

tabula rasa   *TA byoo luh RAH suh*
(*the mind before impressions are recorded upon it by experience: Latin, scraped tablet*)

A tabula rasa is what I'm after, and if that sounds as though I were simply trying to dodge an honest day's labor before betaking myself to the playhouse, so be it. Call me truant, say I'm goldbricking. My vote still goes to the man who doesn't prepare himself for the theatrical experience he's about to have. He's the man most likely to have it.

tacit   *TA sit*
(*not expressed or declared openly, but implied or understood*)

Few gestures are taken as personally as the acceptance or rejection of food, most especially if it has been prepared by the giver. By overtly or tacitly registering dislike for food served in a home, one invariably, if unintentionally, expresses at least a certain amount of disapproval of the cook and often of an entire family and its way of life.

taciturn   *TA suh tern*
(*almost always silent; not liking to talk; uncommunicative*)

Until now, Mr. Mubarak has been the butt of popular jokes in Egypt, pictured as a smiling and silent nonentity at the right hand of the President. But his taciturnity has been viewed by some as a survival tactic in a country where overly popular military figures are often quickly shuffled off to posts away from the centers of power.

take out   *tayk owt*
(to destroy; get rid of; kill: U.S. military slang originating during the Vietnam War)

Praising the Israeli air attack that last Sunday destroyed an Iraqi nuclear plant, he said it had helped to slow the production of nuclear weapons at least temporarily. "Anything that takes out a nuclear installation, I'm in favor of," Senator Moynihan said.

tantalize   *TAN tuh lighz*
(to tease by keeping out of reach)

But the most tantalizing issue remaining from the settlement of the 50-day strike was exactly what manner of season will be resumed one week from Monday. Will the schedule simply be picked up after a loss of 713 games? Or will the remaining eight weeks constitute a miniseason, with second-half pennant races of its own?

Tantalize derives from Tantalus, a son of Zeus, whose punishment after death was eternal hunger and thirst. In Hades, he was placed in a pool of water that would recede whenever he lowered his head to drink. Above Tantalus' head hung luscious fruits, which a breeze would sweep beyond his grasp whenever he reached for one. The crime for which he suffered so is variously given as his attempt to serve to the gods a banquet of his own son's flesh; his theft of nectar and ambrosia from the table of the gods; and his divulging of secrets entrusted to him by Zeus.

---

tantamount   *TAN tuh mownt*
(equivalent)

Mr. Lippman said his articles had not identified many of the people he quoted or associated with because "it would be tantamount to having them arrested."

tautology   *taw TAH luh ji*
(needless repetition of an idea in a different word, phrase or sentence; redundancy: for example, necessary essentials)

"A Stranger Is Watching" is about a crazy murderer (if you excuse the tautology) who keeps a television newscaster imprisoned in the catacombs under Grand Central.

Past history openly reveals the true fact that redundant tautologies reoccur again and again when individual persons join together similar synonyms. Here, then, is a varied mixture of word pairs, each of which the reader is invited to reduce down to one single word: free gift, present incumbent, invited guests, final conclusion, complete monopoly, temporary recess, personal friend, past experience, original source, attach together, hoist up, necessary requisite, return back and swallow down.

---

teetotaler   *tee TOH tuh ler*
(one who abstains completely from alcoholic drinks)

CORRECTION—An article March 19 on lobbying efforts in behalf of the arts misidentified a man sipping wine at a reception given by the National Symphony. The man remains unidentified; he was not Senator Jake Garn, Republican of Utah, who is a teetotaler.

telescope   *TE luh skohp*
(to slide one into another, like the concentric tubes of a small, collapsible telescope; condense)

For his birthday, they bought him one of those small, expensive telescoping umbrellas to tuck into his briefcase.

temerity   *tuh MAI ruh ti*
(foolish or rash boldness)

Treasury Secretary Donald T. Regan, the former chairman of Merrill Lynch & Company now in his first government post, recently called in some political aides for advice on handling Congress. As they talked, he sank one of their ideas with the curt judgment: "No, I don't think that will work on the Hill." Quickly he broke into laughter at his own temerity. "Here I am," he chortled, "spouting off to you guys about politics."

temper   *TEM per*
(to bring to the proper texture, consistency, hardness, etc., by mixing with something or treating in some way)

Writings found in Asia Minor said that to temper a Damascus sword the blade must be heated until it glows "like the sun rising in the desert." It

then should be cooled to the color of royal purple and plunged "into th
body of a muscular slave" so that his strength would be transferred to th
sword.

tenacity   *ti NA suh ti*
(firmness in holding fast; persistence)

A blue crab's tenacity is often the cause of its demise. A fish head c
carcass or a chicken neck attached to a string and tossed into the wate
sooner or later will be seized by a crab. If one retrieves the line slowl
the crab will often hang on until a net is slipped under it.

tendentious   *ten DEN shuhs*
(showing or having a definite tendency, bias or purpose)

Lucy S. Dawidowicz's "The War Against the Jews, 1933–1945" was indis
pensable reading. Her "Holocaust Reader" was a scar that glowed in th
dark. "The Holocaust and the Historians" is a peculiar and—to use on
of her favorite words—tendentious essay, creating more confusion tha
it dispels. She believes that the Holocaust, in which two-thirds c
Europe's Jews were murdered, has for the most part been neglected c
ignored by contemporary historians.

tenet   *TE nit*
(a principle or belief held as a truth)

It may seem curious that an American black woman with a degree in socia
work from Columbia has embraced Rastafarianism, the religion that i
adhered to by most reggae musicians. Among other things, Rastafariar
ism teaches that women should serve their men and look after thei
homes; its tenets are not very compatible with feminism.

tensile   *TEN suhl*
(capable of being stretched)

Mr. Breuer's Cesca and Wassily chairs truly changed the way our centur
looked at furniture. Before Mr. Breuer began bending tubular steel an
adding some leather slings to it to make seats, we thought of furnitur
as massive, voluminous, heavy; the Wassily chair made it suddenly clea
that furniture could be something tensile and light and alive.

tenure   *TE nyer*
*(status granted to an employee, usually after a probationary period,
assuring permanence of employment)*

"We have no security; tenure is unknown," said Dorothy Ozog, a fourth-grade teacher in a Catholic school in Detroit.

pid   *TE pid*
kewarm)

I can race through two or three smutty novels and a half-dozen gossip magazines and hear the Top Forty playing on the stereo in the background while the television viewer is wasting three hours and getting nothing but the tepid, watered-down stuff afforded by three or four sitcoms and an evening soap opera.

rse   *ters*
ee of superfluous words; concise; succinct)

In theory, the strikers are seeking political status, which Mrs. Thatcher refused last week to grant with the terse comment, "Crime is crime is crime." Mr. Sands is serving a 14-year sentence for the illegal possession of arms.

stament   *TE stuh muhnt*
roof or tribute that serves as evidence of something)

China is justly famous for its inventions. Gunpowder, paper and one of the world's great cuisines are but a few testaments to Chinese innovation.

sty   *TES ti*
ritable; peevish)

The current issue of Harper's contains a testy article on our current literary biggies, people like Joyce Carol Oates, William Styron, Norman Mailer, John Updike and so on and on, the burden of which is that they are only 13th-raters whose skill at promotional flimflam has persuaded the world and themselves that they are a new race of Tolstoys.

Flimflam, says Eric Partridge in "A Dictionary of the Underworld," is "the generic name for the various dodges by which a thief, in changing money (paper or coin), obtains more than he gives, whether from tradesmen or even from tellers in banks." Partridge's earliest citation is from 1881. A flimflam today can be any sly trick or deception of a con artist.

---

te-à-tête   *TAY tuh TAYT*
private or intimate conversation between two people: French, head-to-ad)

"The President and I had a tête-à-tête," Mrs. Thatcher said after leavin the Oval Office. That private meeting was followed by two larger gather ings that included Secretary of State Alexander M. Haig Jr. and Lor Carrington, the British Foreign Secretary.

theocracy   *thee AH kruh si*
(the rule of a state by God, whose laws are interpreted by ecclesiastical authorities; government by priests claiming to rule with divine authority)

Fundamentalist religion is gaining strength in the United States. But I d not believe it follows that religious Americans want a theocracy as thei form of government. Many, even of the strongest personal beliefs, woul hold to the country's tradition of diversity in faith and separation c religion from government.

theorem   *THEE ruhm*
(a general statement or rule, not self-evident, that cannot be proved to be true)

Halston continued to build the Halston mystique, which boils down to a uncomplicated theorem: clothes should be simple by day, extravagant b night.

threshold   *THRESH hohld*
(the point at which a stimulus is just strong enough to be perceived or produce a response)

Age and sex affect the perception of pain: As you get older your sensitiv ity to pain is likely to decline; women tend to have a lower pain threshol than men.

thwart   *thwawrt*
(to prevent from accomplishing a purpose; frustrate; defeat)

LA PAZ, Bolivia, June 27 (AP)—Bolivia announced today that an effor to topple its President, Gen. Luis Garcia Meza, had been thwarted with out bloodshed and that the Bolivian Army commander and Chief of Sta had been arrested as plotters.

time warp   *TIGHM wawrp*
(the condition or process of being displaced from one point in time to another, as in science fiction)

"You have to remember that Philadelphia politics are caught in a time warp," said a Philadelphian familiar with the city's politics. "In voting on Congressional races people here don't vote for national issues, they vote for constituent services. They vote on who can get their potholes fixed."

titillate   TI tuh layt
to excite or stimulate pleasurably)

One of the demands we properly make on our political leaders is that they amuse and entertain us. Without such titillation, our spirits would be overcome by subway fires, gridlocks and blackouts, and we would fall into profound melancholy.

titular   TI chuh ler
existing only in title; in name only; nominal)

After the embassy luncheon, Prince Charles, who will someday be titular head of the Church of England, participated in services at the National Cathedral, where the primates of the Anglican Communion are meeting.

topiary   TOH pi ai ri
the art of trimming and training shrubs or trees into ornamental shapes)

The topiary gardens, with 80 figures of lions, camels, giraffes and other forms carved out of California privet and golden boxwood, was begun more than 60 years ago and is operated today by the nonprofit Preservation Society of Newport County.

torpor   TAWR per
a state of being dormant or inactive; sluggishness; apathy)

Some relief from the torpor inflicted by desert air, which makes you taste sand when you lick your lips, came Wednesday night when a young Egyptian soccer team won the Africa Cup by beating Cameroon, 2-0.

torrid   TAW rid
passionate; ardent)

It seems only yesterday that Mayor Fiorello H. La Guardia, cleaning up Times Square, ran burlesque out of 42d Street, clear to Union City, N.J. Actually that happened more than 40 years ago. It is something of a commentary too that Ann Corio, once a supreme practitioner of the

torrid striptease art, has brought her stage memoir, "This Was Burlesque," back to Times Square, to the Princess Theatre, and it has an
almost uplifting effect on the neighborhood.

totter   *TAH ter*
(to rock or shake as if about to fall; be unsteady)

No doubt the penny has become an endangered species, along with
the whale, the whooping crane, the snail darter. But, tottering as it is on
the brink of extinction, must it go the way of the dinosaur and the dodo
bird?

Totter and *teeter* both refer to the in-place movement of an object
in an unstable position. But *teeter* implies an impending fall from
one plane to another, such as from a table to the floor, while *totter*
implies a fall onto the plane the object is standing upright on,
such as a floor lamp tottering back and forth and crashing onto
its side. Totter also refers to unstable walking, as from old age,
infirmity or inebriety.

----

touchstone   *TUHCH stohn*
*(a test or criterion for determining genuineness or value: from a type of
black stone formerly used to test the purity of gold or silver by the streak
left on it when it was rubbed with the metal)*

"You want to destroy the country," the Ayatollah told the rival factions.
"The nation must not listen to those who are arguing against each other
and must condemn those who are weakening each other. This nation
should be united as it was at the start of the revolution," he said. But unity
seemed far away. And Ayatollah Khomeini himself, the touchstone of
revolutionary legitimacy, avoided, as he has in the past, coming down
hard on one side or the other.

tour de force   *toor duh FAWRS*
*(an unusually skillful or ingenious creation, production or performance:
French, feat of strength)*

In something of a tour de force for an actress making her starring-role
debut, Miss D'Obici plays Fosca with shrewd, merciless consistency, without an ounce of pity, which is as it should be and is the major strength
of the film.

tract   *trakt*
*(a propagandizing pamphlet, especially one on a religious or political
subject)*

Several of the songs on "Wild Gift" (Slash records), X's new album, champion monogamy. "White Girl" is a kind of tract on the pitfalls of sexual temptation, and "Adult Books" is a caustic indictment of pornography, swinging singles and other examples of contemporary sexual mores.

anscendent   *tran SEN duhnt*
oing beyond ordinary limits; exceeding; supreme)

As it happened, about a dozen of the club's elderly members had gathered around the television to watch the last match of the cricket series between England and Australia, an event of transcendent interest, to be compared with the Super Bowl or the last game of the World Series.

ansgression   *tranz GRE shuhn*
breaking or overstepping of a law or rule; sin)

FORT LAUDERDALE, Fla., March 1—When Reggie Jackson arrives in the Yankee camp, he will learn that inflation has hit the cost of reporting late to spring training. Jackson reported late a year ago, and the transgression cost him $500 a day. He is late again, but this year, George Steinbrenner announced, he will be fined $2,500 a day.

ansient   *TRAN zi uhnt*
aying for only a short time; temporary; passing through)

Pain can be sharp, throbbing or dull, mild or severe, transient or prolonged, continuous or intermittent.

ansmogrify   *tranz MAH gruh figh*
o transform, especially in a strange or grotesque manner)

Turning a good book into a bad movie is child's play. Any fool can do it; many have. But it has lately become commonplace to find awful novels transmogrified into movies that are even worse, and surely this is a phenomenon worth looking into.

rappings   *TRA pingz*
dornments; accouterments)

For all of the religious trappings, the cult primarily offered a curious mixture of socialism and blasphemy. By the time of the move to South America in the summer of 1977, critics and investigators were beginning to close in on Mr. Jones.

travail   *truh VAYL*
(hardship; suffering; anguish)

Legions of soap opera fans tuned in to the travails of Stella Dallas, th
beautiful daughter of an impoverished farmhand who had married abov
her station in life.

Travail comes from the Latin, *tripalium*, an instrument of torture
composed of three stakes: *tri*, three + *palus*, stake. In addition to
its meaning hardship, suffering and anguish, as in the Times
passage above, *travail* also means labor or childbirth pains, toil
or intense pain.

---

traverse   *truh VERS*
(to travel across, over or through)

The four carriage processions that will carry the royal family on th
wedding day will traverse a route laden with history.

travesty   *TRA vi sti*
(a crude, distorted or ridiculous representation of something)

Of all the dishes we tried none was so dreadful as choucroute garni
The sauerkraut itself was acceptable if a little greasy, but the real traves
ties were the meats: a skinless, supermarket variety frankfurter; a dark
dried-out, paper-thin slice of ham, and a piece of meat that was proba
bly some form of pork, but was almost too hard to pierce with fork o
knife.

tremolo   *TRE muh loh*
*(in music, a tremulous or quivering effect produced by the rapid reitera-
tion of the same tone)*

The eerie call of the loon is one of earth's most unearthly cries. Its wailin
and tremolo calls are regarded by many as the most thrilling and distinc
tive symbol of the northern wilderness.

trenchant   *TREN chuhnt*
(keen; penetrating; incisive)

Mort Sahl is back, at least for two weeks, at Marty's and at the age of 5
his humor is as it ever was—highly political, trenchantly topical, occasion
ally venomous, equally savage toward Republicans, Democrats, liberals
conservatives and all ideological stops between.

trepidation   *tre puh DAY shuhn*
(fearful uncertainty; anxiety)

Although for years I watched my mother, a terrific cook, entertain with apparent ease, I approached my own first dinner party with trepidation.

tropism   *TROH pi zuhm*
(a movement or action in response to a stimulus)

BONN—This is the time of year when Germans, as if seized by a communal tropism, are drawn into the woods to gather wild mushrooms. Again and again, they are told to be careful. Again and again, it seems, an extraordinary number of people do not listen. Since the mushroom hunting season started in the middle of August, nine persons have died from eating a poisonous variety called the death cup.

truculent   *TRUH kyuh luhnt*
(pugnacious; belligerent; defiant)

Mr. Marchais has increasingly adopted a truculent, brawling manner, making gleeful hash of the tradition of genteel television interviews here —though recently the interviewers have begun to show their own teeth.

truism   *TROO: i zuhm*
(a statement the truth of which is obvious and well known; commonplace)

It is a truism that all stars were once sidemen and all sidemen want to be stars. An equally accurate but less widely recognized truism is that stars are musicians who have made clever career moves or been lucky, and that sidemen are often equally talented musicians who haven't had the breaks.

truncate   *TRUHNG kayt*
(to shorten by cutting off a part)

The New Jersey Symphony Orchestra, which has not performed since August 1980 and which seemed in danger of disappearance, has returned to life. The orchestra will present a truncated, 14-week season starting Nov. 1, and hopes to resume more normal operations in 1982–83.

trundle   *TRUHN duhl*
(to push or propel on wheels; roll; wheel)

Every Tuesday and Friday, Giovanna Conti trundles her old-fashioned shopping cart, a bulging basketwork container on two wheels, to the outdoor market on the Via Trionfale near her home and fills it with potatoes, fresh vegetables and fruit.

tryst   *trist*
(a secret meeting between lovers)

A tryst with Lira sends Bobby escaping the jealous husband by dashing home in nothing but Lira's angora sweater, fluffy slippers and tight jeans.

turbulent   *TER byuh luhnt*
(violently agitated or disturbed; tumultuous; chaotic)

The main international topic of discussion at Camp David seems certain to be the turbulent situation in Central America. Mexico and the United States are in stark disagreement over both the causes of and the solutions to the region's political violence and instability.

turpitude   *TER puh too:d*
(baseness; vileness; depravity: the word is usually preceded by "moral")

Under immigration law, convicted felons or those convicted of a crime of moral turpitude, such as prostitutes, embezzlers and petty thieves, cannot be admitted to the United States and must be returned "to the country whence they came."

tutelage   *TOO: tuh lij*
(instruction; teaching)

School begins promptly at 7 A.M. as dozens of budding Escoffiers don their tall white hats and spotless aprons, ready to peel, wash, chop and simmer under the tutelage of master chefs.

tycoon   *tigh KOO:N*
(a wealthy and powerful industrialist)

The most expensive inaugural festivities in the nation's history are providing the backdrop for the wealthy industrialists and assorted tycoons who constitute much of the Reagans' social circle.

———————

Tycoon came into use in the 1850's as the title by which foreigners knew the shogun of Japan. The Japanese *taikun*, mighty lord, was derived from the Chinese *ta*, great + *kiun*, prince.

———————

Type A

a behavior pattern associated with a tendency to develop coronary heart
disease, and characterized by total involvement in one's job, a constant
striving for achievement, inability to relax, impatience and tenseness:
coined in 1972 by Meyer Friedman and Roy H. Rosenman, American
cardiologists)

The Type A behavior pattern, an aggressive, struggling, rushed action-emotion complex that is associated with heart disease, may also be associated with superior scientific work, according to Karen A. Matthews, assistant professor of psychiatry at the University of Pittsburgh.

ubiquitous   yoo: BI kwuh tuhs
(present, or seeming to be present, everywhere at the same time; omnipresent)

Many a hostess would love to have one or two, and the White House has 36: white-gloved military social aides who help smooth the way at White House social occasions. Quietly ubiquitous, they direct the flow of traffic, help greet guests at state dinners and luncheons, move people along receiving lines at receptions, make small talk at teas and dance with any guest who appears to be stranded.

ukase   YOO: kays
(an authoritative order or decree; an edict: Russian, ukaz, edict—originally, in Czarist Russia, an imperial order or decree having the force of law)

Conversations at a [men's] club may wander from the disturbing situation in Poland to the Jets' need to get back into the National Football League race, but in most two subjects are barred: women and professional matters. The late Peter Fleming, an amateur of social history, held that this rule was an extension of the Duke of Wellington's ukase against discussion of these subjects in an officers' mess on the ground that they were the most likely to lead to violent argument and ultimately a duel.

unabashedly   uhn uh BA shid li
(unashamedly)

Mr. Sinatra is not an opera singer. He uses a microphone and his stylistic idiom is unabashedly popular. But for a man of 65 years his technique is remarkable; in fact, every time this writer has heard him in recent years his voice has seemed more secure and wider in range both for dynamics and pitch.

unassuming *uhn uh SOO: ming*
(modest; unpretentious)

Though Mr. Rush's folk baritone isn't powerful, he has an unassumingly authoritative manner that works nicely in a small club like the Lone Star.

unbridled *uhn BRIGH duhld*
(unrestrained; uncontrolled)

To be sure, the Italian campaign in Libya remains as an example of unbridled imperialism beside which the operations of the British in India and the French in Morocco seem like nursery tales.

underling *UHN der ling*
(a person in a subordinate position; inferior: usually contemptuous or disparaging)

Federal workers who thought they had seen everything in the bureaucracy are now being shown Government films that dramatize how right-thinking civil servants are expected to behave. One film urges underlings to track their supervisors' comings and goings and to speak out—"blow the whistle" is too hard-core a term for this Federal cinéma vérité—when the boss takes three hours for lunch.

————

Why, man, he doth bestride the narrow world
Like a Colossus; and we petty men
Walk under his huge legs, and peep about
To find ourselves dishonorable graves.
Men at some time are masters of their fates:
The fault, dear Brutus, is not in our stars,
But in ourselves, that we are underlings.
        William Shakespeare, "Julius Caesar"

————

unequivocally *uh ni KWI vuh kli*
(plainly; clearly; unambiguously)

Having warned Poland unequivocally to reverse its course toward democratization and having publicly demonstrated its loss of confidence in Warsaw's leaders, the Soviet Union faces the approach of the critical Polish Communist Party Congress next month with anxiety and with sharply reduced options.

unflappable *uhn FLA puh buhl*
(not easily excited or disconcerted; imperturbable; calm)

Lemon, who failed as an infielder and an outfielder with Cleveland befor
becoming a pitcher in 1946, is a secure, unflappable man who seems no
to have an enemy in baseball. "I've had a hell of a life," he said durin
his first term as Yankee manager. "I've never looked back and regrette
anything. I've had everything in baseball a man could ask for. I've bee
so fortunate. Outside of my boy getting killed. That really puts it i
perspective. So you don't win the pennant. You don't win the Worl
Series. Who gives a damn? Twenty years from now, who'll give a damn
You do the best you can. That's it."

ungrudging   *uhn GRUH jing*
(*without resentment*)

Still, the Norway maple does have redeeming values. An alien, it ha
made itself very much at home over here and is often mistaken for it
American cousin, the sugar maple. If it is not sweet, however, it is sturdy
growing ungrudgingly in poor soil and shrugging off the city's grime.

unilateral   *yoo: ni LA tuh ruhl*
(*one-sided*)

Anwar el-Sadat is never far from the minds and eyes of the 42 millior
Egyptians he governs all but unilaterally.

unmitigated   *uhn MI tuh gay tid*
(*out-and-out; absolute*)

Helen Lawrenson, in the March issue of The Dial, the public television
magazine, writes of Miss Hepburn: "A personality? Yes. An actress? No
On the set she was an unmitigated pain in the neck."

unobtrusive   *uhn uhb TROO: siv*
(*not calling attention to oneself; inconspicuous*)

During the general audiences that Pope John Paul holds in St. Peter's
Square during the warm months, plainclothes agents of the Italian
carabinieri and state police unobtrusively mingle with the multilingual
crowds to keep an eye out for pickpockets and possible troublemakers.

unprepossessing   *uhn pree puh ZE sing*
(*unimpressive; nondescript*)

Consider the ratfish. Plagued by unprepossessing looks and a name that
invites universal ridicule, his is a woeful life. The ratfish's misery is as-

suaged only by the company of other equally disadvantaged deep-sea acquaintances, such as the grunt, the gag, the hogsucker and the lizardfish.

unremitting   uhn ri MI ting
(ceaseless; without letup; never relaxing)

Isaiah Thomas (1749–1831) was the leading publisher of his day and an unremitting foe of British rule.

upbraid   uhp BRAYD
(to rebuke severely; censure sharply)

The editors and their friends overflowed the 600-seat main hall, however, for a session entitled "Sex, Sexism and the Sexes," at which they were upbraided for the fact that their organization has only 34 female members.

upscale   UHP skayl
(in the upper levels of a particular category, especially one relating to the standard of living: coined in the late 1960's to refer to people in the upper levels of income, education and social standing)

"Unlike Kentucky Fried Chicken, the distinct leader, Sisters is an upscale fast-food experience. It's going after the dining-room market as well as the carry-out business."

ursine   ER sighn
(bearlike)

To begin with, Gianfranco Ferre was in town, which caused enough hub and bub to get everyone going. Mr. Ferre, who is 36 years old, Milanese and appealingly ursine, has been producing clothing under his own name for only three years, and is currently one of the few fashion talents intent on exploring new ideas in clothing design.

usurp   yoo ZERP
(to take or assume—power, position, property, rights—and hold in possession by force or without right; encroach)

Despite the proliferation of credit cards, no one has been able to usurp the American Express card's stronghold in the travel and entertainment market.

utilitarian   *yoo ti luh TAI ri uhn*
(aiming for utility or usefulness, rather than beauty, ornamentation or pleasantness)

Window shopping is not a widespread practice in Moscow, where shops, for the most part, are bleak and utilitarian outlets for scarce goods. Window displays are usually unimaginative pyramids of faded goods, working hours are roughly stenciled onto ill-fitted doors and store names are usually confined to stark descriptions of offered wares: "meat," "shoes," "produce," "books."

Utilitarianism encompasses two related doctrines: one, that actions are right in proportion to their usefulness or their tendency to promote happiness; and two, that the purpose of all action should be to bring about the greatest happiness of the greatest number. The English philosopher Jeremy Bentham (1748–1832) coined the term and promoted this philosophy along with James Mill and his son John Stuart Mill. Bentham, himself, remains useful to this day: his skeleton, dressed in his clothes and with a model head, stands at University College, London. It was his wish.

utopia   *yoo: TOH pi uh*
(an ideally perfect society: Greek, ou, not + topos, a place; an imaginary island in Sir Thomas More's "Utopia," a 1516 novel about a society with a perfect political and social system)

The Mayor of Fort Myers, Ellis Solomon, 60, dressed in a white suit and red and white shoes, counts himself among the optimists. "As long as the sun shines, this is an absolute utopia for a family to move to and enjoy themselves," he said.

vacuum   *VA kyoo uhm*
(a state of being sealed off from external influences; isolation)

No amount of planning and preparation by the Secret Service, no bullet-proof car, no armed bodyguards can guarantee the safety of a public figure if an assassin is willing to risk capture or death. Especially in America, the occupant of political office cannot survive in a vacuum. He has to mingle with the electorate and take his chances.

(a space left empty by the removal or absence of something usually found in it; void; emptiness)

One of the most basic human instincts is the need to decorate. Nothing is exempt—the body, the objects one uses, from intimate to monumental, and all personal and ceremonial space. It is an instinct that responds to the eye, for pure pleasure; to the rules of society, for signals of fitness and status, and to some deep inner urge that has been variously described as the horror of a vacuum and the need to put one's imprint on at least one small segment of the world.

Vacuum is among the hundreds of Latin words adopted into English unchanged. Some others are: acumen, affidavit, alibi, aorta, bonus, cornea, elixir, emporium, explicit, gratis, genius, inertia, innuendo, item, memento, minutia, panacea, recipe, requiem, tarantula, status, stimulus, verbatim, veto and vim.

---

vagary   *vuh GAI ri*
(an unpredictable occurrence, course or instance)

Sitting back after lunch, Mr. Sommers commented on the vagaries of the 5,000 foot altitude, which require a sensitive—and patient—cook: More flour may be needed than a recipe calls for; steaks take 20 minutes to broil —rare—and eggs require six minutes to soft boil.

vanguard   *VAN gahrd*
(the leading position or persons in a movement: originally, the part of an army which goes ahead of the main body in an advance)

While Mrs. Reagan is fashion-conscious, her tastes are too conservative to place her in the fashion vanguard.

vantage   *VAN tij*
(a position or situation likely to provide superiority or advantage)

There is little indication that I.R.A. prisoners in Northern Ireland will abandon their hunger strike. From their morbid vantage, it has proved a winner. With six dead, and two more dying, they have finally found a way to make their cause a passionate concern that can even bring down a Dublin Government.

variegated   *VAI ri uh gay tid*
(having variety in character or form; varied; diversified)

As it did a few years ago when it focused on "classics in action," Lord & Taylor has gathered together the variegated strands of current fashion, added some notes of its own and dubbed the package "the new heroines."

vaunted   *VAWN tid*
(boasted or bragged about)

By the time of the first spacecraft encounter with Mars, however, no one seriously believed any more in the vaunted Martians who were said to have built a global system of canals. These turned out to be figments of the imagination of astronomers of the late 1800's.

vector   *VEK ter*
(an animal, as an insect or mite, that transmits a disease-producing organism from one host to another)

Dog ticks can be vectors of Rocky Mountain spotted fever, a usually mild but sometimes serious infection that is now prevalent throughout the country, particularly in suburban and rural areas.

vehement   *VEE uh muhnt*
(characterized by forcefulness of expression or intensity of emotion, passion or conviction; emphatic; fervent)

Someone had written to Shaw asking for his autograph to which, Mr. Lowe said, Shaw replied with vehemence that he did not give autographs, doesn't believe in autograph hunters nor autograph collecting, a pastime he described as "despicable." He concluded with both a flat refusal to give his autograph and a threat—if he ever bothered Shaw again, the playwright wrote, he would regret it. "Very sincerely yours. G. Bernard Shaw."

vehicle   *VEE uh kuhl*
(a play, role or piece of music used to display the special talents of one performer or company)

It may have taken a long time for her to get to Broadway, but she has arrived in high style. In Lillian Hellman's "The Little Foxes," Elizabeth Taylor has found just the right vehicle to launch her career as a stage actress.

vendetta   *ven DE tuh*
(a prolonged feud or seeking for vengeance)

It is difficult to understand the vendetta that the writers of The Living Section are conducting against iceberg lettuce ("All That Is Lettuce Is Not Iceberg," July 8). There are those of us who like and enjoy eating this wonderful vegetable. Why are they constantly putting down this pleasant, tasty, crisp green leaf?

veneer   *vuh NIR*
(an attractive but superficial appearance, hiding the true nature of what lies beneath it)

The veneer we call social order is a very thin membrane indeed—it is the mutual contract we make with our neighbors to respect each other's place and space.

venerable   *VE nuh ruh buhl*
(worthy of respect or reverence because of age, dignity, character, position, etc.)

CBS-TV announced yesterday that it planned to add five hours of news programming a week to its daytime schedule, including an afternoon program and an expanded version of its morning news program, which will replace a half-hour of "Captain Kangaroo," the venerable children's show.

venomous   *VE nuh muhs*
(*poisonous; malignant*)

On the broad avenue of Takht-E-Jamshid outside, the throng of 450 angry young protesters had appeared at 7:30 A.M., as it had for days to take up its venomous chant: "Death to the Shah!" "Death to Carter!" "Death to America!"

venture capital   *VEN cher KA puh tuhl*
(*funds invested or available for investment at considerable risk of loss in potentially highly profitable enterprises*)

Coca-Cola will establish a $1.8 million venture capital fund to help develop black-owned companies and investment groups set up to buy into existing bottling franchises or to purchase wholesale distributorships. The funds will be lent with interest; thus Coca-Cola will make money on this aspect.

verdant   *VER duhnt*
(*green and lush*)

New Orleans looks and feels like a humid Caribbean metropolis, with its colonial architecture, its verdant tropical foliage, and its relaxed pace.

verisimilitude   *vai ruh si MI luh too:d*
(*the appearance of being true or real*)

WILLIAMSBURG, Va., May 2—Prince Charles and a royal entourage of embassy officials, personal aides and security personnel swept into town for about three hours today to pick up an honorary fellowship at William and Mary College and tour the reconstructed Colonial buildings. During an address at the college, Prince Charles joked about being a "genuine Redcoat" who had come to Williamsburg "to add a little verisimilitude to your proceedings."

Verisimilitude is usually used to describe the quality in a work of fiction that makes its events, characters and setting seem possible or believable to the reader. Daniel Defoe's "Journal of the Plague Year" (1722) is a prime example. Written in the form of a narrative of a Londoner during the Great Plague of 1664–65, the supposed eye-witness story is so vivid, forceful and accurate that some modern librarians and bookstore owners, either reading or scanning the book, have placed it in their nonfiction sections.

---

vermiform   VER muh fawrm
(wormlike)

Few magazine articles have transfixed so many readers as Jacobo Timerman's prison memoir in The New Yorker of April 20. Understandably. There is no more devastating account of Argentine repression, and no more vivid depiction of the vermiform creatures who inhabit that country's murderous security forces.

vernacular   ver NA kyuh ler
(the style of architecture and decoration peculiar to a specific culture)

Fans of 20th-century Americana should not miss John Margolies's color photographs of vernacular architecture, such until recently unappreciated structures as diners and filling stations, which can be seen at the Hudson River Museum (511 Warburton Road, Yonkers) through Sept. 13.

vestige   VE stij
(a trace, mark or sign of something that once existed but has passed away or disappeared)

That curious and somewhat exotic vestige of the 1960's, the waterbed, currently ebbing and flowing in its second decade, has emerged, despite occasional opposition to it, as a very big business indeed in these early days of the 1980's.

viable   VIGH uh buhl
(physically fitted to live; capable of living: said of fetuses that have developed sufficiently within the uterus to be able to live and continue normal development after birth)

To be viable, frog eggs must be fertilized immediately after laying, so a scientist will squeeze the frogs, causing them to eject their eggs, and quickly apply frog sperm.

(workable and likely to survive)

What is left to be said about Caruso? His name, even now, is synonymous with opera, and there has never been a time over the past 80 years when his records were not before the public. He was the first big record-seller —a good case could be made for the fact that Caruso singlehandedly turned the phonograph from a mechanical toy into a commercially viable artistic medium.

vicarious   *vigh KAI ri uhs*
(shared in or experienced by imagined participation in another's experience)

Getting students to develop reasoning abilities early is considered vital and Mr. Lipman's approach for elementary school pupils permits youngsters the security of vicarious reasoning. They read about characters their own age in works of fiction in which reasoning concepts are strewn lavishly through the pages.

vicissitudes   *vi SI suh too:dz*
(unpredictable changes; ups and downs)

His current success notwithstanding, the 34-year-old actor is also resigned to the inevitable vicissitudes of the theater business. "I've been 'discovered' an awful lot. What happens? Nothing," he says with a rueful smile. "I think you have to be discovered around nine times before you start to make a living at this."

vie   *vigh*
(to compete)

One competition has youngsters vying in a mannequin-modeling contest, with models striking poses for 15 minutes without moving—no blinking, smiling, twitching or stretching.

vignette   *vin YET*
(a short literary or dramatic sketch)

Mr. Bergquist's play, which he described as a series of satirical vignettes about contemporary life with an emphasis on the popularity of various schools of psychotherapy, has been playing on and off in Stockholm for the last six years.

vilify   *VI luh figh*
(to use abusive or slanderous language about; revile; defame; slander)

President Abolhassan Bani-Sadr was impeached and vilified by the clerics last week, and if words could kill he would surely be as dead as the dozens of Iranians who were summarily executed for protesting his ouster.

vindication   *vin duh KAY shuhn*
(a clearing from criticism, blame or suspicion; the evidence that serves to justify a claim or deed)

WASHINGTON, April 14—To the millions of citizens who watched the space shuttle Columbia glide to its flawless landing today, the newest space exploit was sweet vindication of American know-how. The automobile industry may be beset by Japanese competition and the military establishment may feel that Moscow has gained the advantage of momentum in the strategic arms race, but the nifty two-wheeled touchdown in the Mojave Desert provided a quick, jubilant lift for a nation that has been suffering from technological self-doubt.

vindictive   *vin DIK tiv*
(vengeful in spirit; inclined to seek vengeance)

Yesterday Mrs. Montenegro said: "We want the judges and all to know that we do not come to the courts for vindictiveness or vengeance. We want only justice. We ask that the victims also be heard in the court. We are tired of being nonpersons in the courtrooms."

vintage   *VIN tij*
(being of a past era)

A special Art Deco display will highlight this weekend's semiannual exhibition for collectors of vintage posters and postcards. Appraisals of antique cards and postcards will be offered.

The term *Art Deco* derives from the Exposition Internationale des Arts Decoratifs et Industriels Modernes, held in Paris in 1925. The Art Deco style is characterized by geometric forms, strong colors and a streamline effect in art and architecture. New York City's Chrysler Building and Radio City Music Hall are major Art Deco creations, both built during the height of the style's popularity, the late 1920's and early 1930's. Art Deco saw a revival in the late 1960's among artists, architects and industrial designers that is still flourishing.

---

virtuoso   *ver choo OH soh*
(a person displaying great technical skill in some fine art, especially in the performance of music)

Mr. Burns does not want to start out as a third trumpet in a small out-of-town orchestra, work his way to first trumpet at the New York Philharmonic, and eventually land solo engagements. He plans to be a soloist immediately, a virtuoso within a matter of years. And if he does not succeed, he says he will go into another line of work.

visage   *VI zij*
(face; aspect; appearance)

The manager said that Mr. Monberg could be "one of the guys" in a social setting, but in public he adopts a stern, investment-banker type visage.

viscera   *VI suh ruh*
(the internal organs of the body: here used figuratively)

Mr. Rushdie, whose other novel, "Grimus," I haven't read, was born in Bombay and now lives in London. Bombay is the viscera of this novel, as Danzig was for Günter Grass in "The Tin Drum."

visceral   *VI suh ruhl*
(emotional or instinctive, rather than intellectual; earthy)

It is still possible to buy a White Mountain ice-cream maker that is hand-cranked. Then you can have the enjoyment—and I really do think it gives some people a good, visceral feeling to do things the hard way—of cranking the dessert for about 25 minutes.

vista   *VI stuh*
(a distant view)

The Negev, which encompasses 60 percent of the area of Israel proper, is an arid and barren stretch of wilderness with quiet vistas of hills and mountains and canyons in some places.

vituperative   *vigh TOO: puh ray tiv*
(verbally abusive and bitter)

Although the Soviet publications and broadcasts have mounted an impressive and vituperative campaign against American production of neutron weapons, Mr. Brezhnev avoided specific reference to the weapon today.

vociferous   *voh SI fuh ruhs*
(loud, noisy or vehement in making one's feelings known)

As a group, he found, those of Irish background tend to deny pain while so-called Yankees take a matter-of-fact attitude. Ethnic Italians tend to be vociferous about their discomfort and want it relieved immediately, he said, and Jewish patients are vocal but worry more about the significance of the pain than its alleviation.

vogue *vohg*
(the accepted fashion or style at any particular time; general favor or acceptance; popularity: French, a fashion)

Chèvre, that tangy, aromatic cheese formed from pure goat's milk, is suddenly in vogue. As if out of nowhere, a staggering and mysterious variety of chèvres have appeared on the scene, replacing Brie as *the* imported cheese in demand.

void *void*
(an empty space or vacuum)

After taking 25 minutes to read his 1982 budget message at the start of a news conference the other day, Mayor Koch asked if there were any questions. He got one of the longest moments of silence at City Hall in some time. Finally, the Mayor filled the void. "Let me say this," he said with some amusement. "I know a balanced budget is a bore."

volatile *VAH luh tuhl*
(vaporizing or evaporating quickly)

Hundreds of people were forced out of their places of work and traffic was backed up for miles on major roadways near Newark International Airport early this morning after a railroad tank car containing 26,000 gallons of a volatile toxic chemical caught fire at the Oak Island Conrail freight yards.

(likely to shift quickly and unpredictably; unstable; explosive)

The volatile Pennzoil shares advanced nearly $5 a share on Monday and Tuesday, only to fall back by about the same amount on Wednesday and yesterday.

voluminous *vuh LOO: muh nuhs*
(enough to fill volumes)

But Jefferson kept voluminous records of anything that could be measured. He designed and commissioned the building of several elaborate hodometers, which were instruments attached to carriage wheels to measure distance. He measured miles, paces, degrees, hours and even the number of shovels of earth required to fill in the grave of a friend.

voracious *vaw RAY shuhs*
(very greedy or eager in some desire or pursuit; insatiable)

The offshore oil industry's appetite for workers is voracious. Because of the huge monetary investment in equipment and drilling expense, the facilities, both on shore and off, operate around the clock seven days a week, 365 days a year.

vulgar   VUHL ger
(lacking taste; coarse; crude)

When the new Bonwit Teller store on East 57th Street was still a-building, it was covered by a seven-story-high billboard bearing the store's celebrated trademark of purple violets. Such a huge sign might ordinarily seem to be a vulgar commercial intrusion on genteel 57th Street, but somehow this sign was special—it was a breath of fresh air and color on the street, a surprise element at enormous scale that enlivened its entire block.

vulnerable   VUHL nuh ruh buhl
(open to attack)

Although military planners believe that 75 percent of the B-52's in an attack could get through Soviet defenses today, they say the planes will become more vulnerable in the mid-1980's.

waft *waft*
(*to float, as on the wind*)

After 11 months of captivity in which mob denunciations of the United States had become routine, the hostages suddenly heard a most outlandish sound waft into their cells one day: a stirring band recording of the quintessentially American march "Stars and Stripes Forever."

wag *wag*
(*a comical or humorous person; joker; wit*)

It wasn't long after Richard Thomas, who used to play John Boy Walton on television, became the father of triplet daughters Wednesday that wags started calling the new arrivals John Girl I, John Girl II and John Girl III.

wane *wayn*
(*to grow gradually less; fade; decline; weaken*)

This has been, in my own case, a banner year for growing tomatoes and, of all the things that come from my garden, it is one of the only vegetables of which I never tire. My enthusiasm for an overabundance of zucchini or green beans may have waned as the summer progressed, but for tomatoes, never, whether in salads, sandwiches, sauces or casseroles.

wanton *WAHN tuhn*
(*sexually loose or unrestrained*)

Survivors of childhood's rainy afternoons will recall the hours passed looking up racy words in the dictionary. The same parents who'd hidden "Tropic of Cancer" from innocent eyes never seemed to have grasped the wanton possibilities of a walk through Webster.

(senseless, unprovoked or unjustifiable)

Capt. Roy Baughman of the Green Brook police said that vehicular homi-
cide charges in New Jersey require proof that a driver "operated a motor
vehicle carelessly and heedlessly in a willful or wanton disregard for the
rights of others."

war-horse   *WAWR hawrs*
*(a symphony, play, opera, etc., that has been performed so often as to
seem trite and stale: an allusion to a horse that has been in battle many
times and is trotted out again and again for its dependability)*

Back in the old days, 25 to 30 years ago, the City Opera was a haven for
the adventurous. But after its move to Lincoln Center in 1966, the company began more and more to stage the same war-horses that dominated
the repertory across the plaza at the Metropolitan Opera.

wastrel   *WAY struhl*
(an idler or good-for-nothing)

"Stripes" stars Bill Murray, who says his achievements make his mother
happy "not because I'm successful, but because I didn't turn out to be
a complete wastrel."

wean   *ween*
*(to withdraw someone gradually from a habit, occupation, object of
affection, especially by substituting some other interest)*

Drugs are regarded as only a temporary solution to tension headaches.
For some patients, weaning from heavy doses of strong pain killers, such
as those containing narcotics, is the first crucial part of treatment, since
prolonged use of the drug can result in a reduced tolerance to pain and
may cause other health problems.

wellspring   *WEL spring*
(a source of abundant and continual supply)

The challenge is monumental. For this son of Hollywood has captured
the Presidency at a time when the wellsprings of national confidence had

nearly run dry and the yearning for America to regain control of its destiny is palpable across the land.

welter   *WEL ter*
(confusion; turmoil)

The nation's most sensitive political issue expanded in a hot welter of speculation and uncertainty yesterday, about what development the next few days might bring for the 52 Americans held hostage in Iran.

white elephant   *WIGHT E luh fuhnt*
(a possession unwanted by the owner but difficult to dispose of and expensive to keep or maintain)

"Just last month I was on the Norway, which used to be the great French liner France—the grande dame of the twilight years of the North Atlantic runs. She sat for five years, a big white elephant, and the Norwegians took her and she's completely rejuvenated."

———————

Many centuries ago in Siam, now Thailand, each white or albino elephant captured or born in captivity was considered sacred. It became the property of the king and was not allowed to work. If the king wanted to punish someone he didn't like, he would present the unlucky person with a white elephant. One could not refuse a gift from the king, and it wouldn't be long before the white elephant had brought its new master to financial ruin, eating him out of house and home.

———————

white lie   *WIGHT LIGH*
(a lie concerning a trivial matter, often one told to spare someone's feelings)

Social Security was sold to the public as the alternative to depending on children or charity. The truth, though, is subtly different. Social Security is not considered a handout only because society winks at the resemblance. It is a system of white lies. Social Security payroll taxes have never paid for more than a small fraction of the benefits promised. The system only muddles through by taxing today's workers to pay for today's retirees.

windfall   *WIND fawl*
(any unexpected acquisition, gain, or stroke of good luck: like something blown down by the wind, as fruit from a tree)

When the Speaker of the House, Representative Thomas P. O'Neill Jr., emerged from a White House meeting today with President Reagan he denounced the President's tax proposals as "a windfall for the rich" and said the Democrats were concerned with "the working class."

winnow   *WI noh*
(to separate out or eliminate; sift; extract: grain is winnowed by tossing it into the air and letting the wind blow the chaff from it, or by exposing it to a forced current of air)

An Administration official said today that the "short list" contained fewer than five names, winnowed by Attorney General William French Smith from a "long list" of about 25 names. The official declined to say how many people on the "short list" were women.

wiseacre   *WIGHZ ay ker*
(an offensively self-assured person; smart aleck: Dutch, wijssegger, *soothsayer)*

In the beginning, Joe De Filippis considered calling his clothing shop for men 5 feet 8 inches and under the Short Stop, the Small Shop or the Little Store. One tall wiseacre even suggested the Masculine Munchkin.

wistful   *WIST fuhl*
(full of melancholy yearning; longing)

One of the most wistful of Brooklyn dreams—the return of the borough's baseball Dodgers to their home turf—received a daylong elaboration in parties and proclamations yesterday. By order of Governor Carey, a statewide Brooklyn Dodger Day was designated.

wither   *WI th:er*
(to lose a once-possessed freshness; shrivel; languish)

The withering of black studies programs has left James Baldwin, Ralph Ellison and Toni Morrison the only black writers receiving much academic attention.

wizened   *WI zuhnd*
(shriveled; withered)

Near the boy sat two wizened old men. One was apparently crippled by arthritis, his broken body wrapped in an old shawl. The second man, slightly younger, sat on a blanket gazing absent-mindedly at the nearby hills.

wolf   *woolf*
(to eat ravenously)

Having fasted since the previous midnight, they wolf down the chicken soup and crackers, cookies and hot chocolate that they are offered.

wrangle   *RANG guhl*
(an angry, noisy dispute or quarrel)

After an angry political wrangle, the board of the Metropolitan Transportation Authority voted 8 to 6 yesterday to pave the way for a probable July 1 fare increase. Board members shouted at each other across a conference table before they reached their decision.

wrath   *rath*
(intense anger; rage; fury)

Martin, who has often demonstrated his wrath against umpires by screaming obscenities, kicking dirt and hurling his cap, went into that act in the fourth inning of a game that the A's lost to the Blue Jays, 6-3.

wry   *righ*
(drily humorous, often with a touch of irony)

Betsy Cronkite, discussing the wry sense of humor of her husband, Walter, recalls in an interview in the February issue of McCall's that after a national magazine asked Mr. Cronkite to write his own obituary for it, he sent one in immediately. The obituary read in full: "Walter Cronkite, television and radio newsman, died today. He smothered to death under a pile of ridiculous mail which included a request to write his own obituary."

(a temporary twisting of the facial features in expressing distaste)

The 750 instrumentalists at Juilliard sacrifice their social life, their youth and—some add with a wry smile—their sanity toward one goal: becoming a professional musician.

wunderkind   *VOON der kint*
(a child prodigy or one who succeeds at something at a relatively early age: German, wunder, wonder + kind, child)

Prince, the 21-year-old Minneapolis-bred wunderkind of black music, put on an electrifying performance at the Ritz last Sunday night. Four months ago, when Prince played the same club, it was half-empty. But word of mouth and widespread critical acclaim for his third album, "Dirty Mind," insured that the show would be sold out.

Xanadu   *ZA nuh doo:*
a fabled city built during the 13th century by Kubla Khan, the Mongol
emperor of China, and depicted in Samuel Taylor Coleridge's poem,
"Kubla Khan")

[Robert Moses'] first great achievement was the erection of Jones
Beach, for which he took an almost unused sandbar and at vast expense
transformed it into an elaborate seaside Xanadu for the masses, complete
with bathhouses, restaurants and a tower inspired by a Venetian bell
tower.

Samuel Taylor Coleridge (1772–1834) fell asleep one afternoon
in the summer of 1797 while reading about Xanadu in a travel
book, and dreamt, he said, a 200- to 300-line poem. Upon awak-
ening, he began to write it down, but after 54 lines he was interrupted by a visitor and could never again recall more of the
poem. Its opening lines are: In Xanadu did Kubla Khan/A stately
pleasure-dome decree:/Where Alph, the sacred river, ran/
Through caverns measureless to man/ Down to a sunless sea.

---

xenophobia   *ze nuh FOH bi uh*
fear or hatred of strangers or foreigners: Greek, xenos, *strange or*
foreign + phobos, *a fear)*

France became the latest hate object of Iranian xenophobes and plot-
mongers Aug. 29, when it gave ousted President Abolhassan Bani-Sadr
refuge, the same courtesy it once extended to Ayatollah Ruhollah
Khomeini.

yahoo   *YAH hoo:*
a rough, coarse or uncouth person: in Swift's 1726 book, "Gulliver's
Travels," the Yahoos are a race of beastly human creatures. Their
masters are the Houyhnhnms, a race of horses of the highest intelligence
and rational thought)

"Beatlemania," which opens today at the Ziegfield and other theaters, is even more about its audience than it is about the Beatles, who of course were not willing participants in this venture. While the four Beatle stand ins launch perfunctory versions of Beatle hits, the extraneous footage recalls the viewer's lost youth. In the purest yahoo spirit, the audience is encouraged to cheer for the things they used to dig, and boo the things they didn't. Richard M. Nixon gets boos, which isn't surprising. And there are cheers for Dustin Hoffman, Janis Joplin, marijuana and LSD.

zealot   ZE luht
(a person zealous to an extreme degree; fanatic: with capital Z, among the ancient Jews, a member of a radical political and religious sect who openly resisted Roman rule in Palestine)

At 9 o'clock on Sunday, ABC begins presenting its eight-hour, multimillion-dollar "Masada," which will be shown over four consecutive evenings. Filmed on location in Israel, this is the story of how, in the year A.D. 73, 960 Jewish Zealots killed themselves rather than surrender to the 5,000 Roman soldiers who were invading their fortress.

zenith   ZEE nith
(the highest point; culmination; peak; summit: Arabic, path above the head. In astronomy, the point in the sky directly overhead. Its antonym is "nadir")

Mr. Brinkley, whose star was at its zenith in the 1960's and early 70's when he was co-anchor of the evening newscast with the late Chet Huntley, stunned NBC last Friday with the sudden announcement that he would be leaving next month.

zero in   zi roh in
(to concentrate attention on; focus on: a riflery term meaning to adjust the sight settings of a rifle by calibrated firing on a standard range with no wind blowing)

Very deliberately, Mr. Reagan zeroed in on a single theme—uncontrolled government spending had sapped America's economic vitality and forced the urgent need to shift to a new approach to tame inflation. And with folksy examples and informality, he drew his audience into his line of thinking.

More Ways
to Use English
Effectively

Verbs of Action
Giving Language Life

The verb is life. Without it nothing breathes, nothing moves, nothing *does* anything. Nothing can *be,* nothing can *do,* nothing can *happen* without a verb. And nothing animates and invigorates one's written or spoken expression more than well-chosen verbs.

But forceful, vigorous and vivid verbs are the most underused and underrated words in the language, and take a back seat to adjectives in the work of many writers; they think that the number of adjectives one uses is a mark of good writing. The idea of verbs seems to strike these people as arid, while the idea of adjectives seems lush. Yet adjective-loaded writing tends to be overdone and under-whelming, while verb-loaded writing tends to be vital and animated.

In the eight and a half months that I was immersed in *The Times,* hunting passages for *Words That Make A Difference,* no aspect of journalistic writing impressed me more than the talent newspaper people have for selecting verbs that bring a scene or an idea to life: Anwar Sadat is *bristling* with indignation; a sportswear designer *catapults* to the top of the fashion world; an alligator *clambers* over a fence; a prisoner is almost *plucked* from the roof of a jail by a friend in a helicopter; the shuttle blast-off *spewed* a fine tan dust over everything. These are verbs with almost a moving-picture quality about them.

Bristling and *catapult* are used figuratively, and *clambers, plucked* and *spewed* are used literally, but each evokes a specific movement for us, and that is the main reason the reporters used them. As in any other aspect of writing, the key is to choose the precise word to communicate the message. But why do so many people think that five showy, ornate, glittering, elegant and imposing adjectives will be more effective than a single verb that sizzles? In *The Verb Finder,* Kingsbury M. Badger says, "Every day writers strive vainly to ornament and enrich their expression before they have learned to animate and strengthen it. The result of their striving is more often mere prettiness with no vigor beneath it."

No one is more aware of the dangers of pretty but dead language than journalists, for, above all, their profession is devoted to describing action—what people are doing and what's going on—so thei readers can imagine being there. Wars, catastrophes, accidents, cele brations, sporting events, speeches, negotiations, crimes, strikes, dis coveries, deaths, marriages, coronations, performances, elections— endlessly and in infinite variety, things are happening, and the mos valuable tool the journalist has for conveying these events to th reader is the verb.

Interestingly, among the most active verbs are those derived fror nouns (to *carpet* a room; *shoe* a horse; *table* a proposal; *book* an ac *carpool* to work; *mainstream* a student; *cycle* to town). The reason thes verbs are so animated is that they are describing the action and th thing in one word, and *that* is powerful imagery. Let's use anothe example: You can put wallpaper up, or you can paper the wall. In th first instance, there is an unmoving object, *wallpaper*, accompanied b a plain verb, *put*. In the second instance, *paper* becomes the objec *and* the action, and you've eliminated the plain verb. *Cycle* calls t mind both the action of riding a bicycle and the bicycle itself; *carpo* conveys the idea of a group of people in a car as well as the movemen of the car.

The following selection of words can be used as both nouns an verbs. An added dimension of these words is that they are all exam ples of onomatopoeia: words that sound like the object or action the signify. This gives each of them three dimensions. It *represents* a thing it conveys the *action* of that thing, and it *sounds* like that thing. That' very heavy duty for one word, and it emphasizes how even the short est, simplest words can superbly serve the person who knows how t use them. Try devising your own sentences for these words, first a nouns and then as verbs. (An example would be this pair: *There wa a splash below. Something splashed below.*) I'm sure you'll note the addi tional punch each word has when you use it as a verb.

bang	clang	hiss	splash
bark	clatter	murmur	whack
blare	clink	plink	whisper
blast	crackle	plunk	whiz
boo	crash	roar	
boom	creak	scratch	
buzz	growl	sizzle	
chirp	grunt	snap	

Puns

The Lowest Form of Wit, Says Who?

Puns have traditionally been called the lowest form of humor, but the tradition is carried on only by people without the talent for making puns. They're jealous. Punning is a natural act of people who like to play with words and who have the impromptu verbal dexterity to make strange, but often pointed, associations from plainly spoken statements. Their minds work like Las Vegas one-armed bandits, with plums and cherries and oranges spinning madly upon someone's utterance, searching for the right combination to connect on a pun.

Most people groan when they hear a pun. But that too is a traditional, learned response. They feel it's expected of them, and would rather appear sophisticated to their fellow learned-response groaners than give the punner the satisfaction of laughter.

Those who do laugh at the puns of others are people who understand and appreciate the mental gymnastics required in the creation of a play on words. For, unlike jokes, which may take time to devise, and can be retold, a pun is a one-time thing, manufactured on the instant, suiting only the present occasion, and rarely recycled. It is the most evanescent form of wit.

Puns in literature, however, can become classics read and enjoyed through the years. In the *Odyssey*, composed about 800 B.C., a sea goddess, seeing the shipwrecked Odysseus adrift on a raft, says (in Homeric Greek, but translatable into English as the same pun), "Poor Odysseus! You're odd I see, true to your name!" In *Romeo and Juliet*, Mercutio can't resist a pun, even when he's dying: "Look for me tomorrow," he says, "and you will find me a grave man."

I think that punning is the act of brave people, people unafraid of the inevitable groans and upturned eyeballs. On second thought, it isn't quite fair to call it bravery—that's giving punners a little too much credit—it's compulsiveness. They can't help themselves. Punners are practically forced to say Hamlet was a good egg, or that, even when they're optimistic, proabortion lobbyists have a defetused attitude.

Here is a brief selection of puns and other wordplays that have appeared in *The Times*. Note that in a newspaper, wordplay must advance the story as well as be humorous.

Even those who prefer smooth peanut butter are now faced with a crunch.

Bird watchers from as far away as Denver have flocked to the Merritt Island Wildlife Refuge.

Natick Lab's recommendations, if accepted, would allow full-scale fish testing to begin as early as this fall.

The presence of Prince Charles will add a fillip to an evening-long celebration of the Royal Ballet's 50th anniversary at Lincoln Center.

After two and a half slow-gaited years, the "horse licensing and protection measure" galloped through the City Council on July 21, passing 40–0.

A racy sitcom called "Soap" once sent Baptists and other church groups into such a lather that several sponsors pulled out.

Bluegrass music, with its commercialized offshoots, is a thriving American subculture.

Balloons have become a high-flying business and sell at inflated prices.

Mr. Koch, who sometimes refers to himself as Mayor Culpa when he feels apologetic, tried to make amends yesterday—in his fashion. "I love Greenwich, Conn.," he said. "Why is she angry at me?"

Slang
The Outer Edge of Language

Slang is the most fertile, creative and restless part of our language, and is spoken by people in all levels of society and in every situation imaginable.

A teenager refers to two groups in her school as "the jocks and the burnouts"; Joe Torre, after being fired as manager of the New York Mets baseball team, calls it a "screwed-up" season; Mayor Edward Koch says he is furious at the way the State Legislature "ripped off" New York City; Flora Lewis, a *New York Times* columnist, writes that she hopes the Poles will "hold their cool."

Slang is often the most forceful and expressive way to communicate, and when we are excited, upset or outraged we tend to reach for slang, sometimes even surprising ourselves when we come out with a word we have never uttered before. In the early 70's, when *ripoff, hassle* and *uptight* were the possessions of the Woodstock generation, I never used them, nor did I imagine I ever would. But recently, when my porch furniture was stolen, I told a friend it had been ripped off; when I waited two hours for baggage following a thirty-minute plane flight, I complained about the hassle; and when I get irrationally angry when caught in traffic, I regularly wonder why I'm so uptight.

It probably won't be long before these three words pass from the realm of slang to colloquial language. And one day, perhaps a century from now, if they survive, they may simply be general entries in the dictionary. A sign of how accepting a newer generation is of words such as these was brought home to me startlingly when I mentioned them to my thirteen-year-old daughter. "They're not slang, are they?" Rachel asked. "Uptight's just a compound word, isn't it?"

Almost palpably, I was seeing a word that was introduced in my time as slang becoming accepted as conventional English. And that has been the case with many English words over the centuries, despite the efforts of some influential people to prevent them from taking hold. Samuel Johnson, who intended his 1755 *Dictionary* to be the final word on what was pure in the English language, raged against such barbarous slang as *wobble, swap, budge, coax, touchy, stingy, fib, chaperon* and *fun*—obviously unsuccessfully. And Jonathan Swift tried to boot *sham, bubble, bully* and *banter* out of the language. Other words of ours that began as slang hundreds of years ago are *mob, joke, nowadays, workmanship* and *downfall.*

If slang is on the outer edge of language, that's because it's usually the product of groups on the outer edges of society—groups like teenagers, rock and jazz musicians, narcotics addicts, prisoners, soldiers and the Mafia. Subcultures are hotbeds of slang. Their members are people who are not only isolated, but whose lives are filled with turmoil, insecurity, uncertainty, tension, innovation and rebellion. So that much of their vocabulary, while not thought of by them as being anything unusual, has been generated precisely because of life-styles that are lived on a more heightened level than the rest of society's. Then there's the jargon we inherit from professional subcultures: *hype* comes to us from Madison Avenue; *bottom out* from Wall Street.

Eventually, however, a lot of slang takes hold on the general population that either didn't know it existed or didn't want anything to do with it. Through repetition in newspapers, magazines, radio, television and the movies, slang has a way of working itself into our psyches. Time appears to be its arbiter, as it is of all language, and if what we once thought was coarse and inappropriate shows us that it can fill a gap in our communication, we make it ours.

I close this chapter with a selection of slang words and terms that were popular during the 60's and 70's. Which of them did you have no trouble accepting and using? Which have slowly but surely come to have a place in your vocabulary? And which are you absolutely certain no one will ever catch you saying? If some of these words aren't recognizable to you as slang, no sweat!

grass	hack it	scuzzy
freak	hangup	shrink
flipped out	kinky	soul
funky	klutz	turnon
grungy	off the wall	where it's at
zit	out of it	twerp
nebbish	blew my mind	wimp
gut reaction	rap	

Nonce Words

Here Today, Gone Tomorrow—But Not Always

Some words are coined for a particular occasion, the speaker or writer having no idea that they will ever be used beyond that speech, article, or literary work. These are called *nonce words*, because they are invented just for the nonce, the moment. And most of them do serve their creators for one time only. Others, however, catch on, usually because they serve to communicate an idea for which previously existing words have not been satisfactory.

Nonce words come and go frequently, serving to get a thought across for a particular moment and then, almost always, disappearing forever. A drama critic changes the letter of a well-known word to give us a new one when he refers to a character in a play as an "ambisextrous philanderer." A mayoral candidate who doesn't come across well on television is said by a columnist to lack "telegenic charisma," the term replacing (for the nonce) "photogenic."

Using the Greek root *kratos,* meaning rule, a reporter says that at a modeling agency party at a discotheque, "the beautocracy reigned supreme." A food writer adds good-humored stature to someone skilled in the use of leftovers by coining the term "leftouvrier." And a Brooklyn pastor accuses Jerry Falwell, the leader of the Moral Majority, of practicing "micro-ethics" because he opposes abortion but sanctions military actions.

Inventing a word requires not only familiarity with language and an extensive vocabulary, but a sense of ease around words, a confident approach that allows you to be unafraid to fool with them.

Shakespeare was among those unafraid to approach words. He is said to have had the largest vocabulary of his time, with the exception of one Philemon Holland, a translator. Yet Shakespeare was apparently never quite satisfied with the words at hand and created new ones continually—more than 1,500 in all. Some of them, true nonce words, never went further than their appearance in his plays, but others—like *suspicious, critical* and *hurry*—are essential parts of our vocabulary today.

But, in a sense, all coined words were nonce words to begin with, because their inventors had no way of knowing, and probably didn't care, whether they would catch on. It still amazes me that words so integral a part of our thinking and communication were actually invented by someone, any more than grass or flowers were invented. They are so much a part of our language that they seem to have sprung from the earth to answer the need that human beings have to express themselves. Among their inventors were John Milton (1608–1674): *impassive, earthshaking, lovelorn, pandemonium;* Sir Thomas More (1478–1535): *anticipate, exact, explain, fact, insinuate;* Sir Thomas Elyot (1490?–1546): *dedicate, maturity, protest, irritate;* and William Tyndale (1494?–1536): *beautiful* and *brokenhearted.*

And there has been no end to it. The word-making process continues, and only time can tell which words will fall by the wayside at the end of an era, or after a few months, or even when today's newspaper is thrown out with the garbage; and which will survive to become indispensable. *The Barnhart Dictionary of New English Since 1963*, published in 1973, and its companion volume, *The Barnhart Second,* published in 1980, contain more than 10,000 words and terms that are either completely new to the language (such as *cryonics, nebbish, deprogram, laid back, circadian* and *groupie*) or that have acquired additional meanings in the last two decades *(launder, cosmetic, charisma, in, soul* and *rap).*

Some of those words—*cryonics,* for example—will always be around, but never used much. Others, like *nebbish,* are still used but are being supplanted by newer slang—*nerd,* in this case. And still others seem to be waiting around for their popularity to rise again. *Launder,* for example, was popular during the Watergate investigations of 1972–1974, when it was learned that funds contributed to the Nixon campaign had first been deposited in a Mexican bank (the laundry) and then drawn to finance illegal campaign activities. But *launder* now lies dormant. Perhaps it's just a matter of time before another large-scale, shady financial transaction is discovered, and *launder* is recycled.

Beyond the Comma
Using the Colon, Semicolon, Dash and Parenthesis

The skillful handling of punctuation is as important to precise, clear and lively communication as the skillful employment of words. And because four punctuation marks in particular—the colon, semicolon, dash and parenthesis—are underused, misused or avoided by most people, I thought a brief chapter on their functions and applications would be valuable to many readers.

The comma, of course, is the most useful and necessary internal punctuation mark, but if it has been the only internal punctuation mark you use, you have been placing unnecessary limits on the way you express yourself in writing.

I hope this chapter will encourage the use of these four punctuation marks among people who have tended to consider them the property only of grammar experts who are familiar with countless rules governing their use. There is no mystique to the semicolon, colon, dash and parenthesis. Familiarity with them comes simply from observing the way other writers use them, and then beginning to incorporate them into your own writing.

The Semicolon

The semicolon is intimidating. People tend to avoid it; they think only accomplished writers and grammar experts know how to use it. But being comfortable with the semicolon is a matter of familiarity with it, and that comes from examining its use in the writing of others and then beginning to use it on your own.

There are five major uses of the semicolon, and once they are understood, the mark should lose its forbidding reputation.

1. The semicolon is used when you must have a stronger break in a sentence than a comma, but feel a period will be too strong, as in this case:

I don't think we need any more firewood; we already have enough for the winter.

In this case, a comma would be incorrect; the result would be a run-on sentence (also called a *comma splice*). A period, on the other hand, would be correct, but too strong; the writer wants to show a closer connection between the two parts. We see, then, an important use of the semicolon: It indicates closer connections between thoughts than a period does. Another example:

That filter-down theory hasn't worked in India; rich people just don't spend money to help the poor.

Again, the second part of the sentence could have been a separate sentence, but the writer wanted to show its close relationship to the first part.

2. The semicolon is used to replace coordinating conjunctions, such as *and* and *but,* for the purpose of tighter writing. In these next examples, the semicolon has replaced such a conjunction:

(, but)
Gina wouldn't admit that she had sent me the letter; neither would she deny it.

(,but)
Slocum took the train and was home by 9 P.M.; Hadley took the bus and didn't get home until midnight.

(, because)
Only rarely has the okapi been sighted by people; its secretive nature keeps it deep within the jungle.

Basically, the rule is: Whenever two sentences seem so closely connected in thought that you don't want to separate them, but also don't want to use a conjunction, you can join them with a semicolon.

3. Semicolons are the perfect midpoint between two balanced statements:

All that is positive about his children, he credits to his effect on them; all that is negative, he credits to his wife.

I don't see frustration with Mr. Reagan; I see frustration with Congress.

It's a beginning, but nothing is resolved yet; you don't become cured after just one meeting of Alcoholics Anonymous.

4. Ordinarily, a comma is used between sections of a sentence that are joined by a coordinating conjunction (*and, but, for, nor, yet, or*):

Bill Finn was first in line for the manager's job, but he was passed over after his division lost the B.L.T. account.

But when a coordinating conjunction joins sections that themselves have commas, a semicolon helps to distinguish the sentence's major divisions:

Bill Finn, one of our sharpest salespeople, was first in line for the manager's job; but when his division lost the B.L.T. account, he was passed over.

5. The semicolon is used to separate elements in a series when the elements contain internal commas:

The high scorers were Bud Chester, 24 points; Stan Nye, 20 points; Lew Tuck, 14 points; and Jesse Abt, 12 points.

We spent a week in Berne, Switzerland; two weeks in Milan, Italy; and a week in Dusseldorf, Germany.

In these sentences, the semicolon has neatly separated items which commas would have thrown together confusingly.

The Colon

The colon is an introducer. Most of us probably used it for the first time when we learned how to write the salutation of a business letter. Indeed, when we write "Dear Mr. Stewart:" the colon is introducing our message to him.

1. The colon is among the most sophisticated and helpful punctuation marks. Those two dots say the equivalent of *for example, as follows, this is what was said,* or *this is what is meant:*

I remember how he looked when we left him: downhearted and frail.

Costa Rica's condition can be tersely summed up: worthy, democratic and broke.

Nevertheless, Mr. Boas observed: "These people manage to subsist on an income that permits only the barest necessities."

Clara has a heavy but stimulating schedule in school this term: physics, chemistry, algebra, French and psychology.

Flanagan was dumbfounded: Wherever he went, bad weather seemed to follow.

The Mayor's present stance goes something like this: If he can get both Westway and an equivalent amount of money for mass transit, then he will take both.

Note that the first word after a colon is not capitalized if what follows the colon is not a complete sentence. If a colon *is* followed by a complete sentence, that sentence may or may not be capitalized: That choice is up to the writer or the editor. Usually, a particularly strong statement following the colon will be capitalized.

2. Another major function of the colon is to separate main clauses when the second clause explains or amplifies the first:

Journalists are stimulated by a deadline: they write worse when they have time.

I am a simple drama critic: I refuse to do more than make general assertions about music and painting.

They covered only three miles on the fourth day: rocky ground and continual breakdowns made their bicycles almost useless.

3. The third major use of the colon is to introduce quoted material of more than one sentence or paragraph. In the normal flow of journalistic and other prose writing, quotes are introduced by commas, as here:

The Governor said, "I will not be a candidate this year."

However, a colon should be used when a quote will be several straight sentences or paragraphs of direct quotation, as here:

In outlining his reasons for not seeking reelection, the Governor said: (followed by five paragraphs of direct quotation).

The Dash

Dashes can be lively, brash or dramatic. Like colons, their major function is to introduce, but they do it in a more spirited and informal way. A colon is a momentary obstacle—a "Stop" sign; a dash is a momentary skid. A colon is a stone wall that falls away in an instant to let you pass; a dash is a gap that you catapult yourself across.

1. The dash, almost always, suspends you for an instant—then throws the rest of the sentence in your lap. "Take my wife—please" isn't the newest joke in the world, but printing it points to the implicit presence of the dash in jokes that have punch lines.

In one way or another, the dash is an attention getter. While the colon is a rather sedate and formal introducer that implies *this is what I mean* or *for example,* dashes quite often seem to say *Get this!, Are you ready for this one?,* or *This may surprise you,* as in these sentences:

For Costa Rica to borrow so heavily was surely unwise—but it was encouraged by Washington and eager commercial banks.

What bothered him most, though, was that the thief turned out to be the person he had the greatest trust in—his partner.

Management doesn't talk to workers or care about how its workers feel—until now, that is, when it wants us to sacrifice.

Frank's the kind of guy who'll do anything for a friend—and never stop talking about it.

Notice how each dash in these sentences is followed by something f a surprising, startling or revealing nature.

2. A dash may also replace a colon when you're looking for an ᵻformal air for what would be too solemn or stiff with a colon:

The trip wouldn't have been as enjoyable without our poodles—Muffy, Quincey and Ralph.

We covered a lot of territory in two weeks—Spain, Italy, France, Germany and Switzerland.

3. Dashes in pairs function much the same way as parentheses. But arentheses usually enclose supplementary information or asides, hile dashes usually set off material that is more central to the mean-ᵻg of the sentence, as in these examples:

France is not obsessed—as America now is—with the need to act always in concert with her allies.

Mrs. Milligan—even though she was my mother she required me to call her Mrs. Milligan—was rather formal for a parent.

Mr. Sartre's points of view were less heeded—although still respected—in the 1970s as he became a maverick political outsider on the extreme left.

In these sentences, the material between the dashes speaks just as ᵼud as the rest of the sentence, which was precisely the writers' ᵻtention. Were parentheses used instead, they would have muted ᵻe material within them.

4. Dashes should be used instead of commas to avoid confusion ⸱hen the elements of a sentence would run into each other, as in this ᵉntence:

The boats—catamarans, runabouts, sunfish, and dinghys—were thrown high onto the beach by the storm.

If a comma were used after *boats,* it would at first seem to the reader that boats *and* catamarans were being talked about, instead of *boat* as the category under which catamarans, runabouts, etc., fall. Although the reader would quickly catch on, it would have been an unnecessary hitch in the reading. In addition, that comma and its partner after *dinghys* would have resulted in a five-comma sentence something to avoid. Dashes have given us a clearer sentence with a clean, crisp look.

These examples further illustrate the clarity and crispness you can get when you replace commas with dashes:

> *The cafeteria food—the hot plates as well as the sandwiches—was awful*

> *However, two familiar faces—Gov. Carey and Senator Daniel Moynihan —may not be delegates, because party rules require delegate hopefuls to declar their presidential preferences in order to vote at the conclave.*

5. Dashes also indicate a break in thought, as in these cases:

> *Oh, no, I forgot to bring my—oh, wait, here it is.*

> *What I dislike most about Ferdy is—but why should I burden you with my problems?*

> *Sylvia, you are the world's biggest—please, let's just drop the whole thing all right?*

> *He began: "Dearest Felicia, I suppose you've been wondering—" but crushed the paper in his hands and threw it away.*

Use the dash sparingly. It's a versatile mark, and one so meaning ful it comes close to being a word itself. But, like the exclamation point, it has a tendency to be overused by its biggest fans. Overuse dilutes its effect, and readers begin to find it an intrusion rather than an aid. Precisely because it is so expressive, it should be reserved for the times when it will do the most good.

The Parenthesis

The parenthesis is used to enclose material that is not essential to understanding a sentence but in some way enhances it. It may contain an illustration, explanation, definition or additional piece of information. But we have all come to expect that a parenthesis will *not* contain information vital to a sentence, but only supplementary or incidental

> *Orantes (pronounced O-RANN-tays) became a ball boy at the age of ten at the Royal Tennis Club of Barcelona.*

> *The President's physicians said his temperature was normal (98.6 throughout the night.*

Fifty varieties of sausage are available (from $2 to $12 per pound).

Mrs. Henderson left the courtroom saying only "c'est la vie" (that's life) to the waiting reporters.

Information that *is* essential should appear out of parenthesis, as part of the sentence, or in a separate sentence of its own:

Raymond had the best of excuses for not attending the game (his house had burned to the ground that day).

This should be two sentences, the second beginning with *His.*

Readers approach a parenthesis expecting to hold the sense and structure of the first part of the sentence in abeyance until they are past the closing parenthesis, at which point they're ready to resume the original flow. For that reason, parenthetical material should be as short and clear as possible, with few or no punctuation marks.

Like the dash, the parenthesis should be used sparingly. Each parenthesis is, after all, an interruption, and the fewer the better.

A parenthetical statement within a sentence, even though it is a complete sentence in itself, does not take an initial capital letter or final period. That's because every sentence can begin only once, and a parenthesis and its contents are really part of a sentence-in-progress:

Spaghetti (my mother's always tasted better on the second day) is still my favorite dish.

However, if the parenthesis begins an entirely new sentence, its sentence takes a capital and a period:

Spaghetti is my favorite dish. (My mother's always tasted better the second day.)

When parenthetical material comes at the end of a sentence and is part of it, place the period outside the closing mark:

He called to me from his new car (a blue Datsun with a yellow side-stripe).

If the parenthetical material is independent of any other sentence and requires a period, place the period inside the closing mark:

He called to me from his car. (It was a Datsun with a yellow side-stripe.)

Do not place a comma before a parenthesis. If you would have placed a comma immediately before the parenthetical material, then place it after the closing parenthesis:

The dessert (chocolate pudding), he said, was too fattening.

Allusions
Less Is More

"I love the Metropolitan Opera," said Leontyne Price, one of it
star singers. "For me, it's a total Shangri-la." All we have to read i
the name of that utopian Buddhist community in James Hilton'
novel, *Lost Horizon,* and we know how perfect a place Miss Price
considers the Met. She has reminded us of something we already
know and can compare the Met to.

Indirect references like this are called allusions, and they play
an important part in creating associations, impressions and emotions in readers. Allusions link what we are reading with what we
have read, heard or seen in the past, enhancing new material with
old associations. Shangri-la is a word with a meaning of its own
and most people know what it means even if they haven't read *Lost
Horizon.* But for those who have read the book it evokes a much
greater image: The whole place seems to appear before the mind's
eye.

This is the way of an allusion, getting us to experience a word or
two levels at once. Mythology, drama, literature, the Bible and history are the major sources from which writers draw when they wish
us to associate and incorporate material that they are newly presenting with what we have read or experienced in the past.

Biblical and mythological allusions abound in Shakespeare's plays
and poems. Today we need footnotes to help us understand them
but the Elizabethan audience probably had little difficulty in understanding what Mark Antony means when he refers to "Caesar's spirit
ranging for revenge, with Ate by his side." Ate, Shakespeare's audience would have known, is the goddess of revenge.

Shakespeare's works themselves have been a major source of allusions for hundreds of years, with writers and speakers using expressions like "star-crossed lovers" and "Et tu, Brute?" to add far more
meaning to what is being discussed because of their associations with
Shakespearean characters. The name Romeo, by itself, is an allusion
used to describe a young man ardently in love.

Allusions appearing in contemporary books still tend to derive rom the traditional sources because books are written to be read next year, a decade from now, or far into the future. Journalists, however, writing for tomorrow's paper, are free to grab at contemporary allusions. Since newspapers are so ephemeral, being thrown away by most readers within a day, the reporter or columnist needn't worry whether an allusion will be understood even a week past its appearance in the paper. Reporters can allude to such short-lived creations as television commercials and such unlofty things as popular songs. Perhaps you remember a television commercial for Sasson jeans in which members of the New York Rangers hockey team skate to an abrupt halt before the camera and sing (off key), "Oooh la la, Sassoon." When that commercial was still on the air, a sports columnist began his piece with a combined pun-allusion that could not have been better timed:

> While the Islanders shop for a new supply of silver polish for the Stanley Cup that they should defend successfully in the next two weeks, the Rangers are out of the playoffs. Oooh la la, so soon.

(By the way, subsequently, the jeans manufacturer was enjoined from allowing the name of the jeans to sound like Sassoon, since that was the name of another, more prestigious designer brand, and the commercial was shelved.)

With the greater latitude given to journalists to select allusions of a culturally transient nature comes the responsibility of choosing allusions that won't throw readers who don't "get" them, and thus impede their understanding of the story. Readers who did not understand the Sasson allusion, for example, because they weren't familiar with the commercial, would still have found meaning in the literal words, "Oooh la la, so soon."

One of the most startling and cleverly concocted allusions I've seen was the invention of Lane Kirkland, the president of the A.F.L.-C.I.O., who, in February 1982, charged the Reagan Administration with practicing "Jonestown economics" with a budget that "administers economic Kool-Aid to the poor, the deprived and the unemployed." He was alluding, of course, to the suicides and murders in Jonestown, Guyana, in 1978, of more than 900 followers of the Reverend Jim Jones, who, at his urging, drank a fruit-flavored drink laced with cyanide. Mr. Kirkland's chilling allusion brought to mind the picture of hundreds of bodies lying in the midst of a huge jungle clearing.

The allusion is one of the most effective literary devices writers can use because with a single word (Hercules) or phrase (a thumbs-up verdict) they are doubling the impact of their message. But there's

another, more subtle reason why allusions are so affecting: The
create intimacy between writer and reader.

The impressions they create depend upon readers meeting writer
halfway, not only understanding the allusion, but filling in what ha
been left unsaid. Often, there's a little nod of recognition within us
a response to the fact that the writer has shared part of our literar
or cultural experience. The writer who says, "As Charles Dicken
wrote in *A Tale of Two Cities,* it is the best and worst of times," i
weakening the point of the statement by giving us too much informa
tion. In writing, as in so many other things, less is more, and sugges
tion often strikes deeper and more memorably than direct statement

But if less is more, why am I going on and on like this about wha
allusions are and aren't? The following passages from *The Time*
contain allusions that you can figure out for yourself.

Perhaps the unkindest cut of all is a poll of ten Confederate state
showing that Mr. Kennedy would carry every one of them, includ
ing Georgia, in primaries against Mr. Carter.

"Raindrops keep falling . . ." but what if they don't? And what i
there are water-use restrictions?

Wall Street analysts converged on the Polaroid Corporation a
Cambridge, Mass., last week with sugar plums dancing in thei
heads. When they emerged, the sugar plums had turned a bit sour

James Bond, the film superspy, got a message today from Russi
without much love. An official Soviet newspaper criticized the new
Bond film, "Moonraker," saying it proves again that agent 007 wa
a pillar of Western culture whose adventures answer the dictate
of bourgeois ideologists.

Paul Bloom, the former Energy Department lawyer who turned
over $4 million in Federal funds to four charities to help the poor
pay their heating bills, said today that he had not been trying to
play Robin Hood with oil company money.

Jonathan Swift, meet the Rev. John J. O'Connor. A few weeks ago,
Father O'Connor made a modest proposal: If Asian refugees in the
San Francisco area had a taste for dogs or cats (it had been reported that some did), why not let them draw on the humane
society's larder?

The Providence & Worcester Railroad Company is trying to prove
it is the little engine that can provide profitable freight service in
southern New England without governmental help.

National magazines, thrilled to discover another Cinderella among cities, have filled their pages with color photographs of Baltimoreans sitting in chic new cafes and shopping for exotic produce in expensive new markets.

Zbigniew Brzezinski thinks that you can go home again—and he tried it for the day yesterday. The former Assistant for National Security Affairs under President Jimmy Carter returned to the Columbia University campus, where he has been a professor for the better part of the last 20 years.

Much as I hate to admit it, since I enjoy the game so much, tennis has a "Catch-22" that is frustrating to a great many players. And the unfortunate thing about it is that there really doesn't seem to be an easy solution.

What is the Catch-22 of tennis? Just this: To improve your game, you must play with better players. But the better players won't play with you until you improve your game.

Such soaring rates of inflation are so new that a retiree would have needed the foresight of a Cassandra to prepare for the consequences.

Now, without being quite ready to lie down like the lion and the lamb, these top business and labor leaders say they want to work together for the national interest.

Ever since the apple episode, delving into secret knowledge has been a risky business.

It's a moot point whether blondes have more fun, but millionaires certainly do, especially Malcolm S. Forbes, who is the chairman of Forbes magazine.

One needlepoint pillow was stitched with "Old sailors never die, they just get a little dinghy."

E Pluribus Unum
The Melting Pot of English

English has always been a blend of tongues. In 1066, the year of the Norman Conquest, England's language was Anglo-Saxon (or Old English), a blend of tongues introduced by the Angles, the Saxons, and other Germanic and Scandinavian tribes that settled in England during the fifth century.

The Lord's Prayer in its Anglo-Saxon form will give you an idea of how different that language was from modern English.

> *Faeder ure thu the eart on heofonum, si thin nama gahalgod.*
> (Father our, thou that art on heavens, be thy name hallowed.)
> *Tobecume thin rice.*
> (Become thy rich.)
> *Gewurthe thin willa on eorthan swa swa on heofonum.*
> (Worth thy will on earth so so on heavens.)
> *Urne gedaeghwamlican hlaf syle us to daeg.*
> (Our daily loaf sell us to-day.)
> *And forgyf us ure gyltas, swa swa we forgyfath urum gyltendum.*
> (And forgive us our guilts, so so we forgive our guiltings.)
> *And ne gelaed thu us on costnunge*
> (And not lead thou us on temptation)
> *Ac alys us of yfele. Sothlice.*
> (But free us of evil. Soothlike.)

Different, yet how similar. The strange spellings and archaic sounds of the words cannot mask the fact, especially when you read it out loud, that there is much that is familiar to an English-speaking person in that Anglo-Saxon prayer.

When the Normans conquered England, the next major period of English (Middle English) began, with Norman-French the new ingredient added to the blend.

Here is the Lord's Prayer again, this time in its fourteenth-century form. A translation is no longer needed.

> *Oure fadir that art in hevenes, halwid be thi name.*
> *Thi kyngdom cumme to.*

Be thi willa don as in heven and in erthe.
Gif to us this day oure breed over other substaunce.
And forgeve to us oure dettis, as we forgeve to our dettours.
And leede us nat into temptacioun
But delyvere us fro yvel. Amen.

The new words are French, many of them derived from Latin, such as *substance, debt, debtors, temptation* and *deliver.*

By 1450, Anglo-Saxon and Norman French had mixed so inextricably that together they had formed one language. The period of modern English had begun.

It is believed that the Anglo-Saxon language may have contained as many as 100,000 words. But 85 percent of them fell into disuse in the two centuries following the invasion, as Norman culture held sway and Anglo-Saxon literature and education died out. Because the Normans were the ruling class, their language dominated the church, the courts, the military, the government and the arts—all of England's important and vital institutions. In fact, the most telling proof of the influence of French on the English language is that almost every important term associated with England's institutions is of French derivation. Here are a few examples from each area:

From the church come *saint, clergy, miracle, mercy* and *faith;* from the courts, *jury, judge, crime, arrest, accuse* and *bail;* from government, *crown, state, country, tax, nation* and *parliament;* and from the military, *war, peace, battle, arms, soldier, navy, enemy, spy* and *assault.*

It is popularly thought that the one-syllable words of modern English derive mostly from Anglo-Saxon, the language of a relatively simple-living people. That is only partially true. While many basic concepts like *man, wife, child, house, bench, meat, grass, leaf, good, high, strong, eat, drink, sleep, live, fight* and *love* are, indeed, Anglo-Saxon in origin, many others are not. Some of the words the Normans contributed to everyday life are *air, sound, large, poor, real, cry, please, pay, quit, wait, age, face, use, joy* and *pen.*

It took centuries for Anglo-Saxon and Norman French to blend into a common tongue. Part of the reason was the normal length of time it takes for languages to fuse. But another reason was the resistance of the general Anglo-Saxon population to learning the language of their conquerors. As new generations were born, however, old memories died. By the middle of the fifteenth century they were no longer Anglo-Saxons and Normans. They were the English, a distinctive people with a distinctive language.

During the hundreds of years when Anglo-Saxon and Norman French were fusing into one language, the slow blending process caused the words of both languages to take on a uniquely English sound. That's why we detect no difference between words of Anglo-Saxon origin, such as *eat* and *sleep*, and those of Norman origin, such as *face* and *pen*.

In the centuries following its emergence as a modern language, English adopted thousands of words from other languages, especially as England became a nation of international merchants, traders, explorers and colonizers. Most of these words don't look or sound particularly foreign to us because their sounds and spellings were Anglicized. *Yacht, booze, easel* and *pickle* may hint slightly of their Dutch origin, but *nap, leak, toy, snap* and *kit,* also Dutch, don't seem at all foreign. Each of the following lists presents just a small sample of Anglicized loan words. From Arabic (either borrowed directly or via Italian, French or Spanish) come: *cotton, orange, sugar, almanac, alcohol, algebra, giraffe, magazine* and *zero.* From German we have: *noodle, seminar, bum, nix, halt, poker, swindler, stroll* and *sleazy.* From Italian are derived: *balcony, bandit, miniature, umbrella, cartoon, bank, cash, concert* and *attack.* From Spanish come: *cask, cargo, chocolate, guitar, plaza, tomato, patio* and *ranch.* Smaller contributions have come from Hebrew (*amen, jubilee, cherub, sabbath*); Hindi (*bungalow, pajamas, cot, loot, thug, jungle, shampoo*); Persian (*bazaar, caravan, magic, rice, rose, tape, tiger*); Portuguese (*albino, molasses, pagoda*); Pacific island languages (*bamboo, taboo, tattoo, gingham*); West African languages (*banana, jazz, banjo, tote, gorilla, yam*); and American Indian (*moose, raccoon, skunk, moccasin, mackinaw*).

Many foreign words have come into English more as contributions than as adoptions, since they were brought to the United States, or created here, by settlers and others who needed new words to describe their new environment and way of life. In this way English was enriched by the French (*gopher, pumpkin, chowder, bayou, butte, rapids, depot, shanty, toboggan, apache, lacrosse, levee*); the Spanish (*armadillo, corral, lasso, rodeo, stampede, bonanza, vigilante, canyon, mesa, tornado*); the Dutch (*cookie, waffle, sleigh, boss, caboose*); and the German (*delicatessen, frankfurter, pretzel, semester, pinochle, loafer, ouch, phooey*). Each word is Anglicized just enough to make it comfortable English, yet each retains the flavor of its original language.

So far, the words I've talked about have been those which have blended relatively smoothly into English. Thousands of other adopted words, however, have fully retained their foreign look and sound, and these are today properly called foreign loan words.

Avant-garde is such a word. Even though it has been used by English-speaking people since the fifteenth century, it still looks and sounds French. *Postscript* is, by contrast, a foreign word that has become fully Anglicized through the dropping of a few letters and the combining of two words. As a sixteenth-century Latin loan, it was *post scriptum*, and if it had stayed that way it would be as genuine a Latin loan today as *ad infinitum*, *per capita*, or *sub rosa*.

Sometimes, instead of adopting a foreign word, we find as close a literal translation for it as we can. The result is called a *calque*, a French word meaning an *imitation*. *Masterpiece* is a calque from the German *meisterstuck*. Other calques from German are *superman* (*Übermensch*), *chain-smoker* (*Kettenraucher*), and *academic freedom* (*akademic Freiheit*). *Gemütlichkeit* (see the "1,455 Words" entry) has remained in its German form because a suitable calque has not been found for it.

Thousands of foreign words and expressions are currently in use in English, from commonly understood expressions like the Latin *ad lib* and the French *faux pas*, to the more obscure *tabula rasa* and *chef d'oeuvre*, both "Treasury" entries. While some loans have been an integral part of English since the Middle Ages, such as the French *adieu* and *bon voyage*, others, like *macho* (Spanish), *ombudsman* (Swedish), and *apartheid* (Afrikaans) have become well known only since the 1960's.

The foreign entries in *Words That Make a Difference* range from the erudite *(lèse majesté)* to the slangy *(bubkes)*, but they have one major attribute in common: They fill a need that no English word satisfies.

Incidentally, word borrowing isn't a one-way street. Many English (especially American) words and phrases have gained worldwide currency, although their pronunciation has often been adapted for the other language. Japanese radio listeners will hear a *disuku jokii* playing *sutereo* records, while Spaniards may have a *coctel* before dinner and mix their whiskey with *lleneral* (ginger ale). An Italian will take off makeup with *colcream*, wear a *pulova*, play *futbol*, and tell a friend to *tegidizi*. In Paris, moviegoers will see a *trilleur*, in which a *sexi* woman in *des shorts* falls in love with a *teuf* gangster during *le holdup*.

These Americanisms (called *Franglais* by the French) are frowned on by the French Academy, which assiduously keeps them out of the Academy's dictionary, the country's major language arbiter, and discourages their use on radio and television.

But while the Academy continues to purge Franglais, millions of French citizens are buying *les blugines* and lunching at le *snacque-barre*. Others are sipping Cokes at one of the most popular spots along the Champs-Élysées—Le Drug Store.

Usage
The Good, the Bad and the Ugly

Since 1635, the French Academy, composed of eminent scholars and writers, has kept a sharp watch over the French language. In the words of its statutes, a major goal of the Academy was to "give definite rules to our language, render it pure, and establish a certain usage of words." For more than three hundred years the Academy has succeeded in preventing thousands of words and phrases from gaining a foothold in the French language, first by condemning them in speeches and journals, and then by denying them entry in the Academy's dictionary, a work of scholarship equivalent to the *Oxford English Dictionary*, and the final word in acceptability. Few French writers have dared to ignore the Academy or challenge its standards.

No such academy has ever existed in England or the United States. The English writers John Dryden and Jonathan Swift strongly advocated one, and Queen Anne showed some interest. But she died in 1714 and was succeeded by George I, a German, who showed little interest in English (he never even learned to speak it), and the Academy movement died.

It has fallen to individual English and American writers, teachers and scholars to act as self-appointed guardians of our language. And while the educational establishment in both countries has been generally successful in maintaining standards of *grammatical* correctness among educated people, those individuals who have attempted to screen *words* from the language, in the fashion of the French Academy, have knocked their heads against a brick wall.

Take the sixteenth-century English dramatist Thomas Nash, for example. In 1592, he called *ingenuity, notoriety* and *negotiation* "pathetic" words. Thomas Wilson, whose *Art of Rhetorique* (1553) was read by Shakespeare, termed *capacity, celebrate, native, fertile, relinquish* and *confidence* "affected" and "outlandish." He also condemned *splendidious* (splendid), *fatigate* (to cause fatigue) and *adnichilate* (to annul). But the last three didn't become obsolete because of Wilson. They lied from disuse: they lacked serviceability, while *relinquish, confidence* and the others were useful.

Closer to our time, there was Ambrose Bierce. He is known mainly for his bizarre short stories, but he was also the author of a little book on usage titled *Write it Right* (1909), in which he called *tantamount* an "ugly," "illegitimate" and "ludicrous" word. He also said that because *dilapidated* comes from the Latin word for stone, *lapis*, it "cannot properly be used of any but a stone structure." He called *gubernatorial* "needless and bombastic"; said that *laundry* is "a place where clothing is washed" and cannot mean "clothing sent there to be washed"; that there is "no such word" as *militate;* and that we must say "asylum for the insane" and not "insane asylum," for an asylum cannot be insane.

If this last stricture of Bierce's seems hard to take seriously more than seventy years later, consider what is happening today with *hopefully*, as in "Hopefully, the rain will soon stop." That use of *hopefully*, meaning *it is to be hoped*, has been the object of great scorn in recent years by writers and usage experts who say *hopefully* may only mean *in a hopeful manner*, as in "We waited hopefully for the rain to stop." How, they might ask, can rain stop in a hopeful manner? A majority of the usage panel of the *Harper Dictionary of Contemporary Usage* (1975) condemned the use of *hopefully* in that sense: Leo Rosten called it a "barbarism," Phyllis McGinley "an abomination" and Orville Prescott "illiterate jargon." The late Red Smith of *The Times* said, "I curse it." Yet, many of those most vehemently against the "incorrect" use of *hopefully* admitted that theirs was a losing fight.

So what will happen? I believe that *hopefully*, which is popular in its "incorrect" form because it succinctly means *it is to be hoped*, will eventually be accepted by all but the most puristic of writers. After all, if it is perfectly good usage to say "Luckily the gun misfired" or "Happily, autumn is here," it is no less logical (nor should it be any less acceptable) to say "Hopefully, the rain will soon stop." Whether the syntax of those three sentences is logical is less important than whether their meanings are clearly understood by all who read them. We cannot condemn a word simply because it is taking on a new function. We must allow our language to breathe—in the name of dilapidated log cabins, gubernatorial elections and dirty laundry.

There are, however, certain rules of usage that should always be adhered to; otherwise important distinctions between words break down and communication suffers. Some of them follow.

accept/except

Accept is always a verb meaning to take or receive: *Cyril would not accept the blame. Claudia was accepted at Yale.* As a verb, *except* is uncommon, and means to omit or exclude: *Please except me from your plans; I'm busy that day. Cordelia was excepted from her father's will. Except's* common use is as a preposition meaning but: *No insect can swivel its head except the praying mantis.*

affect/effect

Affect is always a verb (except for one noun use in psychology) and usually means to influence: *Tornadoes always affect my sinuses. Affect* also means to pretend: *Jake affected a limp in order to get our sympathy. Effect* is usually a noun meaning result: *Fontana's "Not guilty" plea had no effect on the jury. One effect of the transit strike was an increase in pedestrian traffic. Effect* is sometimes a verb meaning to bring about: *The mediator effected a quick settlement of the strike.* In the plural form, *effects* can mean property: *Stimson's personal effects were stored in the prison safe.*

afterward/afterwards

In the United States, *afterward* is preferred; in Great Britain, *afterwards: Hey, let's meet at Times Square afterward. I say, shall we meet at Grosvenor Square afterwards?*

aggravate

In its formal and strict sense, *aggravate* means to intensify or make worse: *Hot foods aggravate the pain of an abscessed tooth. Racial tensions were aggravated by the sit-ins.* When it is used to mean annoy or irritate, *aggravate* is considered informal or colloquial: *Get out of this kitchen and stop aggravating me, you rotten kid!* Some usage experts would banish that use of *aggravate* altogether. Most of them probably don't have children.

ain't

Some people who don't know any better argue that *ain't* is acceptable English because it's found in the dictionary. But some dictionaries list *all* words, acceptable or not, that are part of the language, including obscenities. *Ain't* remains an illiteracy, and should be avoided unless used intentionally for a humorous or other effect in front of people who know that you really do know better. Under no circumstances, however, should *ain't* be used during a job interview or in a letter of application for a Park Avenue condominium.

a lot/allot

A lot is a phrase that means many, and it is incorrect to write it as one word (alot): *Buzzy ate a lot of oysters. A lot of people wondered who she was. Allot* means to distribute in shares: *Buzzy allotted ten oysters to each guest. We can allot only ten gallons of gas to each car.*

all right/alright

There is absolutely only one correct way to say *all right,* and that's it. *Alright* is always all wrong.

already/all ready

Already is an adverb and means earlier or previously: *By the time the bus arrived I was already soaked through. It's already been decided that Carey won't run again. All ready* is an adjective meaning completely ready: *Plotkin was all ready by 3 P.M.*

although/though

Although and *though* may be used interchangeably. *Though,* however, is more commonly used in the midst of a sentence and is preferred at the end of one: *Although it was still drizzling, the ball game began. It was an exciting, though wet, game. We stayed the full nine innings, though.*

altogether/all together

Altogether means entirely, on the whole, or in all: *It's altogether too hot in here. That was an altogether rotten remark, my dear. All together* simply means everyone together, in a group, or all at once: *All together, there were ten of us. Ray gathered the tools all together and locked them up.*

alumna/alumnus/alumnae/alumni

An *alumna* is a woman graduate: *Katy is a Reed alumna.* An *alumnus* is a male graduate: *John is a Brooklyn College alumnus. Alumnae* are women graduates: *Lisa and Jill are Yale alumnae. Alumni* are male, or mixed, graduates: *Jack and Lenny are Emerson alumni. The alumni committee meets each winter.*

amiable/amicable

Amiable means friendly, pleasant or good-natured, and refers to people's dispositions: *Jack's cheerfulness makes him an amiable co-worker. Amicable* means friendly in feeling, showing good will or peaceable, and is used in connection with human relationships: *What had begun as a tension-filled meeting ended amicably.*

among/between

In general, *between* applies to two things, and *among* to more than two. *Stashu skied between the fir trees. Stella and I divided the malted between us. Among the eight of us, Sparky had the largest nose. Sedgewick swam gingerly among the jellyfish.* *Between* also refers to three or more things when each is considered in relation to the others as individuals: *Rivalry is great between the Ivy League football teams. Sean had to choose between Tel Aviv, Pago Pago and Tijuana as the location of his new motel.*

and/but

There's no reason why a sentence cannot begin with *and* as long as it is a complete thought and an effective piece of writing. In the first chapter of Genesis, thirty-three out of thirty-five sentences begin with *and.* Our teachers told us never to begin a sentence with *and* or *but* because they wanted us to avoid writing incomplete thoughts. But the rule should never have been an absolute one. Sentences beginning with *and* or *but* are found in virtually every book. Newspapers print dozens of sentences every day beginning with *and* and *but,* most of the time to break up long sentences for easier comprehension.

The police this morning questioned the two men who had been crossing the field with Mr. Voii when he allegedly shot Mr. Brugman. But they were not charged in connection with the shooting.

Thousands of people on probation in New York City are going virtually unsupervised because of severe budget and personnel cuts in the Probation Department, many probation officers and officials assert. And judges and department employees contend that the quality of presentence reports—another key responsibility for the agency—has deteriorated.

angry at/angry with/mad

Use *angry at* with things, and *angry with* with people: *Germaine was angry at having missed the train. Gert was angry with Gladys for ruining the fudge. Mad* is acceptable as an informal or colloquial alternative to angry, but inappropriate in formal use: *Boy, was I mad when the waiter dropped the quiche in my lap. Mad* is always properly used when it means insane or frenzied: *You think me mad, don't you, simply because I collect old light bulbs. Gordie made a mad dash for his foxhole.*

because

Many people are under the impression that one must never begin a sentence with *because,* yet a glance at any book or newspaper will reveal how mistaken that notion is. True, *because* is often the first word of a sentence fragment that belongs with the preceding or following sentence: *Because it was hot. Because it wouldn't do any good.* Those, of course, are sentence fragments and incomplete thoughts. But this isn't: *Because of the rain, we decided to stay home.* We have simply begun the sentence with the dependent clause. The test is to switch the clauses around, in this case beginning the sentence with *We.* If it works that way, it is all right to begin it with *because.*

bring/take

Bring denotes movement toward the speaker or writer: *Please bring me back an order of fried wonton. Take* denotes movement away from the speaker or writer, or any other movement that is not toward him or her: *Let's take this extra wonton over to Biff's place. San Francisco can be quite cold in August, so take warm clothes.*

canvas/canvass

Canvas is a kind of cloth; to *canvass* means to question or solicit.

capital/capitol

A *capitol* is always a building of one sort or another. *Capital* is used in every other sense.

carat/karat/caret

Gemstones are weighed by *carats: We priced a 2-carat diamond at Ludlow's.* The fineness of gold is measured in *karats. Pure gold is 24 karats.* A *caret* is an editing symbol (∧) that indicates something missing such as a letter or word:

for

It's time ∧ *a change.*

careen/career

Careen means to lean sideways, as a sailing ship before a high wind, or to lurch from side to side while moving rapidly. To *career* means to move at high speed, to rush madly.

climactic/climatic

Climactic refers to a climax: *Four major characters die in* Hamlet's *climactic scene. Climatic* refers to climate: *Climatic conditions make the Napa Valley ideal for grape growing.*

complement/compliment

To *complement* is to complete or make perfect: *Her pearl necklace and earrings complemented her black gown. Her photography complemented his writing, and the result was a beautiful book.* To *compliment* is to praise: *The judges complimented Bernie on his marmalade.* The words retain the same sense when used as nouns: *Her pearl necklace is a complement to her gown. Bernie appreciated the judges' compliments.* A *complement* is also a group or set: *The President sent a complement of Americans to the prime minister's funeral.*

could of/should of/would of

All of these are incorrect constructions when the writer means *could have,* etc., as in *"I could have danced all night."* The error springs from the contraction *could've* sounding as though it should be written *could of.* But there's simply no such grammatical construction. *Of* is not a verb; *have* is.

delusion/illusion

Delusions are more serious than *illusions.* A *delusion* is a false belief that is wholly accepted as true and guides one's actions. Under *delusions,* people spend lifetimes seeking the fountain of youth, trying to turn lead into gold, imagining they are Satan or Jesus or expecting gasoline prices to return to thirty-nine cents a gallon. Such *delusions* obviously contradict rational thinking. *Illusions* are basically false impressions that tend to dissipate or shatter with experience. Commonly shattered illusions are the belief that one's parents are perfect, that crime never pays and that "I'm not the marrying type."

desert/dessert

A *desert* is where the sand dunes are. It derives from a Latin word meaning forsaken or abandoned. *Dessert,* the final course of a meal, derives from a French word meaning to remove what has been served at table.

disinterested/uninterested

Disinterested and *uninterested* may look like two of a kind, but they have quite different meanings. *Disinterested* means objective, unbiased, impartial, fair and unprejudiced. It's the kind of attitude expected of a judge and the members of the jury, a labor arbitrator, a referee or an umpire, a news reporter or a parent when each child claims the other one started something. *Uninterested* means bored, uncaring, indifferent, apathetic. A disinterested judge may take notes; an uninterested judge may take naps.

elicit/illicit

To *elicit* is to call forth or invite: *The mayor's speech elicited both boos and applause. The lawyer elicited conflicting testimony from the witnesses. Illicit* means unlawful, improper or prohibited: *The judge's illicit involvement in the casino operation made the morning headlines. Illicitly sold cigarettes cost the state millions in taxes.*

empathy/sympathy

Empathy is feeling someone else's problems deeply because you have undergone similar experiences or because you are putting yourself in that person's place. *Sympathy* is pity or compassion for another's troubles, without necessarily sharing deeply in their feelings.

ensure/insure

Both words mean to make certain or to guarantee, but only *insure* may be used to mean to guarantee payment for loss or damage: *This cushioned package will ensure safe delivery of the china, but I'll insure it for $100 anyway.*

etc.

Etc. is usually a cover-up. The writer can't think of anything else, and *etc.* is added to give the opposite impression: *New York City's major problems are street crime, dirty subways, high rents, etc.* That's not fair to readers. How are we to know what the writer would have added? But writers also use *etc.* to avoid an unnecessarily long and obvious list: *Our camping gear was the usual: tents, sleeping bags, cooking utensils, etc.* This use of *etc.* is more acceptable because the unlisted items can, indeed, be assumed by most readers. But why should readers have to assume anything? For clear, precise and honest writing, the solution is to avoid *etc.* altogether. If you want to indicate that a list is partial, use constructions such as: *He had many pets, among them, a dog, a cat, gerbils and turtles. His pets included a dog, a cat, gerbils and turtles, to name a few.* The only effective use of *etc.* I can think of is this sort: *Tom showered Jane with apologies, whimpering, "I'm sorry, forgive me, I'll change, I was wrong, etc., etc.,"* but she held fast.

explicit/implicit

Explicit means clearly stated, with nothing implied; distinctly expressed; definite: *On Ralph's desk was an explicit memo from the boss: "Clean off your desk. You're fired."* *Implicit* means understood without being plainly stated: *Implicit in my mother's memo to me—"Your room is filthy"—was the message that I'd better clean it up or else.* *Implicit* also means without reservation, absolute: *I have implicit faith in my surgeon's skill.*

farther and further

Farther should be used only for physical distance, *further* in the sense of additional or continued. *Farther* has *far* in it, and that helps remind one of the physical-distance idea.

fewer/less

Use *fewer* when talking about countable things: people, animals, trees, houses, wishes, phone calls. Use *less* in reference to quantity or bulk: noise, hostility, sand, oxygen, money. Note: *less* water, but *fewer* gallons of water; *less* time, but *fewer* hours; *less* sugar, but *fewer* lumps of sugar; *less* anger, but *fewer* angry words. Use *less* when the number is only one: *Today I received one less card than yesterday.* Use *less* for quantities of time, distance, weight and money: *less than five minutes ago; less than five miles to go; three less ounces in this box; less than $40 a day; $40 less than I earned last week.* Use *number* where you would use *fewer;* use *amount* where you would use *less (the number of hours; the amount of time).*

flaunt/flout

To *flaunt* is to show off or to display in a defiant way: *The football team flaunted their victory by wearing their uniforms in school the next day. The police flaunted their search warrants as they invaded the bookie joint.* To *flout* is to show contempt for or scornfully disregard: *Simpson flouted every training rule and still played better than anyone else. Thousands of New Yorkers are flouting the traffic laws by going through red lights, double parking and ignoring "Stop" signs.*

flutist/flautist

Either is correct, but in the U.S. at least, *flutist* has it over *flautist* (FLOUT ist). Julius Baker, principal flutist of the New York Philharmonic Orchestra, says that's the word he and his colleagues use, but that English musicians say "flautist." *Flutist* has been a word since 1603; *flautist* since 1860.

forbidding/foreboding

Forbidding, an adjective, means looking dangerous, threatening or disagreeable: *Children kept far away from the forbidding shack. Income-tax forms have always looked too forbidding for me to try to compute my own. Foreboding* (note the *fore,* meaning ahead), a noun, means a portent or presentiment, especially of something bad or harmful: *With a sense of foreboding, Norman opened his report card. An unexplainable foreboding kept Ann from boarding the plane that night.*

foreword/forward

A *foreword* is an introduction or preface, as in a book, as distinguished from *forward,* meaning in front or ahead.

forgo/forego

Forgo (sometimes spelled *forego*) means to do without, give up: *I think I'll forgo dessert tonight. Mike and Ike spoke civilly to one another, forgoing their usual sarcastic jabs. Forego,* meaning to go before, precede, is rarely used and archaic: *The soup course will forego the fish.* But its gerund *foregoing,* meaning just past, previously said or written, is common: *The foregoing was a paid political announcement.* Thus, it's *forgo* and *forgoing* when you mean doing without, and *foregoing* when you mean previous.

graduate from

You can *graduate from high school* or *be graduated from high school,* but you can't *graduate high school. To graduate* means to raise a step. Therefore, you can't graduate your high school; it has to graduate *you.* The *from* is always needed, unless the school also is left out, as here: *We graduated in 1981. We were graduated in 1981.*

hanged/hung

People are *hanged,* pictures are *hung.*

healthful/healthy

Healthful means helping to produce good health: *Florida's healthful climate has attracted millions of Northerners. You're not eating enough healthful foods like fruits and vegetables. Healthy* means in good health: *The President has been feeling healthy since his recuperation.*

imply/infer

To *imply* is to state indirectly; to hint or suggest: *By checking my figures, are you implying that I can't add? Addie implied that she wanted to be invited by saying she had nothing planned for tonight.* To *infer* is to draw a conclusion from facts or evidence: *From her smile, I inferred that she was pleased with me. Her rumpled clothing led me to infer she had slept on the couch all night.*

in/into

In indicates location or motion inside something: *I swam in the pool. There's something in my eye. There's a mouse in the kitchen.* *Into* indicates movement from one place to a point within another place: *I dived into the pool. I got into bed, but lay awake for hours.*

irregardless/regardless

Always use *regardless*. *Irregardless* is a meaningless word and never correct.

its/it's

Use *it's* only as the contraction for *it is: It's hot.* Use *its* (no apostrophe) for everything else. Many people habitually place an apostrophe in the possessive pronoun *its*, but it has no more business being there than it does in *hers*, *his* or *theirs*, which are also possessives.

lie/lay

No words are more often misused than *lie* and *lay*. *Lie* is used when a person or thing sets *itself* down. *Lay* is used when a person or thing sets *something else* down. *I will lie down. I will lay the book down.* *Lie* has no object. *Lay* does—book. Some more examples: *If you're tired, lie down. If you're tired, lay down the cartons.* For the past tense of *lay*, always use *laid: Jim laid down the cartons. Jim has laid down the cartons.* For the past tense of *lie* you have two choices. The first—and this is the most confusing part of the whole lie/lay mixup—is *lay: Yesterday, I lay in bed all day. The lion lay in wait for the zebra.* The second choice is *lain*, which is used with *have*, *has* and *had: I have lain around for hours. The house had lain in ruins for a century.* *Lying* is a form of *lie: I am lying down. We were lying in the sun.* *Laying* is a form of *lay: Stop laying your tools on the furniture. I'm laying the linoleum tonight.*

loan/lend

Although *loan* used as a verb (*I loaned him my pen*) is acceptable to many writers and language authorities, others prefer to use only *lend* as a verb, and reserve *loan* for noun use (*a $500 loan*). Others use *loan* as a verb only in financial contexts. (*The bank loaned Apex $3 million.*) Whatever your choice, though, keep the tenses parallel: the past tense of *loan* is *loaned;* the past tense of *lend* is *lent.*

loud/loudly

Although *loudly* is the true adverb of the pair, *loud* (which is ordinarily an adjective) is optional after such verbs as laugh, sing, scream, say, talk, roar and sneeze. (See also *slow/slowly.*)

masterly/masterful

Masterly means skillful or expert. It connotes talent, being a master at something. *Masterful* (not as kind-sounding a word) means domineering, imperious, overpowering. It connotes force, one person's will over another's. Arturo Toscanini was a *masterly* conductor, but he often treated his musicians in a *masterful* way. A chef may be *masterful* toward his kitchen crew, but turn out *masterly* creations. And the San Quentin warden may run his prison with a *masterful* hand, while in Cell Block D someone is picking his cell lock with a *masterly* hand.

may/can

May and *can* are commonly used interchangeably for permission, but *may* is still considered the correct choice in formal speaking or writing: *May I leave the room? May I have a cup of tea, please? You may call me tomorrow if you wish. Can* should be limited to statements of power or ability: *Can I use the chair, or is it still broken? Can I see you a minute, or are you on your way out? You can use the stairs now; the paint is dry.*

oral/verbal

Verbal applies to all language, written and spoken, so it is somewhat ambiguous to refer to a nonwritten contract as *verbal*, when you should be talking about an *oral* contract: *Our oral agreement was sealed with a handshake. Verbal,* however, is used in relation to spoken language in these instances: *First they fought verbally* (the idea being that they fought with words), *then they took swings at each other. Hannah is quite verbal* (proficient with words) *for a two year old.*

practicable/practical

Practicable means capable of being done or put into practice; feasible; possible. *Practical* means capable of being done usefully or valuably. It might be *practicable* (possible) to construct a mile-high building, but would such a skyscraper be *practical* (useful or worth building)?

presently/at present

Presently means soon or before long: *The train will arrive presently. Presently, it began to rain.* At present means now or at this time: *At present, no tickets are available. He's living alone at present.*

preventative/preventive

Preventive and *preventative* both mean the same thing. *Preventive* is preferred.

slow/slowly

Slow usually serves as an adjective (a slow train), but may also be used as an adverb in place of *slowly* (go slow). Used as an adverb, *slowly* will never sound wrong, although *slow* may: *I'm catching on slow.* Your best guide, then, in using *slow* in place of *slowly,* is your own sense of what sounds right. (See also *loud/loudly.*)

stationary/stationery

Stationary means standing still. *Stationery* is writing paper. The best way to remember which one has the *ery* ending is to remember that a person who sells *stationery* is a stationer. Another way is to remember that the *e* in *stationery* stands for envelope.

teeter/totter

Although *teeter* and *totter* both refer to unsteady movement resulting from insecure balance, *totter* implies an impending fall that will be no farther than the base on which something stands *(he tottered homeward),* while *teeter* implies an impending fall from a height to a lower position than one on which the object is standing. *(The car teetered on the edge of the bridge.)*

tortuous/torturous

Tortuous means winding or crooked: *The tortuous mountain road led to the monastery*. In its figurative sense, *tortuous* means devious, deceitful or not straightforward: *The senator accused the Russians of tortuous reasoning in their Afghanistan policy*. *Torturous* means full of, or causing, torture: *She ran the last three torturous miles on blistered feet. Speaking in front of a group was always a torturous experience for Harry*. (Note that *torturous* includes all but the *e* in *torture*.)

Sources

Several reference works were invaluable sources of material for the definitions and language notes in this book. In some cases, sources were used only once or twice. These are mentioned in the text where their contribution was made. The most frequently consulted were the general purpose dictionaries: *Webster's New World Dictionary* (Collins + World); the *Random House Dictionary* (Random House); the *American Heritage Dictionary* (Houghton Mifflin); and *Webster's Third New International Dictionary* (G. & C. Merriam Co.).

The Barnhart Dictionary of New English Since 1963 and its companion, *The Second Barnhart Dictionary of New English* (both Harper & Row), provided valuable information about words and expressions that entered the language during the 1960's and 1970's.

A Dictionary of Foreign Words & Phrases by A. J. Bliss (E. P. Dutton) was useful for its definitions and background information about English borrowings from all languages, and Leo Rosten's *The Joys of Yiddish* (McGraw-Hill) was a particularly helpful source of Hebrew and Yiddish loan-word definitions and pronunciations.

The *Dictionary of American Slang* by Wentworth and Flexner (Crowell) is a fascinating and hilarious testament to the fertility, inventiveness and vitality of the American mind, and it was my most valuable source for the origins and definitions of American slang terms.

For information about words and phrases originating in literature, religion, mythology and history, I found *Brewer's Dictionary of Phrase & Fable* (Harper & Row) a treasurehouse.

I am indebted to all of these sources for much that the readers of this book will find interesting and helpful. Finally, the more than 350 names that follow attest to the great debt I owe the men and women whose contributions to *The New York Times* provided the material for the 1,500 entries in this book. It is my privilege to share the pages of this book with them.

Sidney Aberman	Neil Amdur
Harold E. Adams	Paul Anastasi
Ron Alexander	Dave Anderson
Lawrence K. Altman	Jack Anderson

Susan Heller Anderson
R.W. Apple Jr.
Karen W. Arenson
Associated Press
Anthony Austin
Charles Austin
B. Drummond Ayres Jr.
Richard M. Bacon
Russell Baker
Josh Barbanel
Isadore Barmash
James Barron
Ann Barry
Peter Bart
Leslie Bennetts
Ira Berkow
Robert Berkvist
David Bird
William J. Blair
Mary Kay Blakely
Eleanor Blau
Ralph Blumenthal
Raymond Bonner
William Borders
Stanley A. Bowker
Michael Brenson
Philip Brewer
Kenneth A. Briggs
Jane E. Brody
Malcolm W. Browne
Anatole Broyard
Nadine Broznan
Nelson Bryant
Tom Buckley
Leonard Buder
Edward C. Burks
John F. Burns
Marian Burros
Fox Butterfield
Robert Byrne
Colin Campbell
Vincent Canby
Dierdre Carmody

Maurice Carroll
Lawson A. Carter
Angel Castillo
Chris Chase
Murray Chass
Lydia Chavez
Craig Claiborne
James F. Clarity
Dudley Clendinen
Francis X. Clines
Debra Rae Cohen
K.C. Cole
Robert J. Cole
William Cole
Glenn Collins
Marianne Constantinou
Avery Corman
John Corry
George G. Cotter
Edward Cowan
Alan Cowell
John M. Crewdson
Steven Crist
Ann Crittenden
Barbara Crossette
Judith Cummings
Trish Curran
Suzanne Daley
Lee A. Daniels
John Darnton
Peter G. Davis
Paula Deitz
R.V. Denenberg
Frederick E. Dennard
Alma Denny
E.J. Dionne Jr.
Philip H. Dougherty
Lois Draegin
Leonard Drohan
John Duka
Georgia Dullea
David W. Dunlap
Jennifer Dunning

Joseph Durso
Richard Eder
Fred Ehrman
Thomas W. Ennis
Helen Epstein
Harold Faber
Florence Fabricant
Hans Fantel
M.A. Farber
Stephen Farber
William E. Farrell
Joan Lee Faust
Barnaby J. Feder
James Feron
Fred Ferretti
Arlene Fischer
Lisbeth Fisher
Elizabeth M. Fowler
Pierre Franey
Ben A. Franklin
Lucinda Franks
C. Gerald Fraser
Alix M. Freedman
Milt Freudenheim
Jonathan Friendly
Dorothy J. Gaiter
Barbara Gamarekian
Edward A. Gargan
William E. Geist
Leslie H. Gelb
Henry Giniger
Grace Glueck
Paul Goldberger
Sam Goldpaper
George Goodman Jr.
Michael Goodwin
Alexis Green
Linda Greenhouse
Paul Grimes
Jane Gross
Pranay B. Gupte
Mel Gussow
Bernard Gwertzman

Clyde Haberman
Richard Haitch
Richard Halloran
Robert Hanley
Chuck Hardwick
Aljean Harmetz
Fred M. Hechinger
Deborah C. Hecht
Carolyn G. Heilbrun
Neil Heims
Donal Henahan
Diane Henry
Robin Herman
Caroline Rand Herron
Martin Hershenson
Arthur Hertzberg
Gladwyn Hill
Michael deCourcy Hinds
Moira Hodgson
Eva Hoffman
Paul Hofman
Warren Hoge
Stephen Holden
Bernard Holland
Pamela G. Hollie
Arthur Holmberg
Kathy J. Holub
John Holusha
John S. Hoppock
Carter B. Horsely
Marvine Howe
Allen Hughes
Marjorie Hunter
Ada Louise Huxtable
Youssef M. Ibrahim
Richard R. Iverson
Molly Ivins
Carolyn Jabs
Janet Janjigian
Donald Janson
Gregory Jaynes
Tom Johnson
Laurie Johnston

Nadine Joseph
Michiko Kakutani
Henry Kamm
Jonathan Kandell
Michael Katz
Michael T. Kaufman
Fahd Kawasmeh
Shawn G. Kennedy
Walter Kerr
John Kifner
Peter Kihss
Seth S. King
Wayne King
Donald M. Kirschenbaum
Anna Kisselgoff
Jerry L. Klein
N.R. Kleinfield
Judy Klemesrud
Hilton Kramer
Albin Krebs
Paul Kresh
David B. Kriser
Carol Lawson
Frances Lear
Joseph Lelyveld
John Leonard
Anthony Lewis
Flora Lewis
Paul Lewis
Robert Lindsey
Frank Litsky
Steve Lohr
Elaine Louie
Arnold H. Lubasch
Frank Lynn
Richard D. Lyons
Marilyn Machlowitz
Richard L. Madden
Gene I. Maeroff
Andrew H. Malcolm
Raul S. Manglapus
James M. Markham

Janet Maslin
Elin McCoy
Edwin McDowell
Robert D. McFadden
Nancy R. McKenzie
Diane McWhorter
Richard J. Meislin
Drew Middleton
Mohammed Milhem
Bryan Miller
Judith Miller
Carolyn Mitchell
Herbert Mitgang
Anne Simon Moffat
Paul L. Montgomery
Ina S. Moore
Bernadine Morris
Alfonso A. Narvaez
Enid Nemy
Susan Newlander
Bernard D. Nossiter
Paul J. Nyden
John B. Oakes
Walter T. Oakley
John J. O'Conner
Eric Pace
Robert Palmer
Peter Passell
Robert Pear
Iver Peterson
Frank J. Prial
Leonard Probst
Anna Quindlen
Selwyn Raab
Howell Raines
Kasturi Rangan
Deborah Rankin
Steven Rattner
Wendell Rawls Jr.
Vivien Raynor
Rita Reif
Robert Reinhold

Ed Reiter
Reuters
Frank Rich
Carol Eisen Rinzler
Terry Robards
William Robbins
Steven V. Roberts
Nan Robertson
Ruth Robinson
John Rockwell
Thomas Rogers
Lynn Rosellini
Jack Rosenthal
Sheila Rule
John Russell
William Safire
Sandra Salmons
Agis Salpukas
Wolfgang Saxon
Sydney H. Schanberg
Ann-Marie Schiro
Harold M. Schmeck Jr.
Serge Schmemann
William E. Schmidt
Harold C. Schonberg
Edward Schumacher
Tony Schwartz
William Serrin
Richard Severo
Philip Shabecoff
Richard F. Shepard
William G. Shepherd Jr.
Nathaniel Sheppard Jr.
Mimi Sheraton
Mike Sheridan
David K. Shipler
E.R. Shipp
Leonard Silk
Cathy Silver
Milan B. Skacel
Norma Skurka
Margot Slade

Barbara Slavin
Suzanne Slesin
Hedrick Smith
Red Smith
Terence Smith
Michael Specter
James P. Sterba
Damon Stetson
William K. Stevens
Paul K. Stewart
Henry Scott Stokes
Reginald Stuart
Ronald Sullivan
Walter Sullivan
Leonard Sussman
David Tabacoff
Max M. Tamir
Henry Tanner
Philip Taubman
Angela Taylor
Stuart Taylor Jr.
Kathleen Teltsch
Jo Thomas
Robert McGowran Thomas Jr.
Audrey Topping
Samuel A. Tower
Joseph B. Treaster
Alan Truscott
James Tuite
Wallace Turner
Ralph S. Tyler
United Press International
Vartanig G. Vartan
George Vecsey
John Vinocur
Matthew L. Wald
William N. Wallace
Ray Walters
Marina Warner
Bayard Webster
Bernard Weinrub
Steven R. Weisman